I FEEL SO GOOD

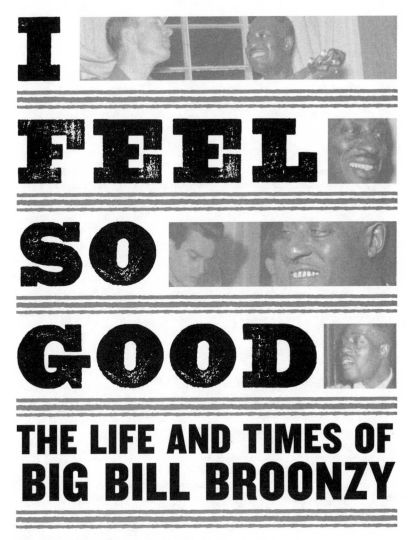

I FEEL SO GOOD

THE LIFE AND TIMES OF BIG BILL BROONZY

Bob Riesman

FOREWORD BY *Peter Guralnick*
APPRECIATION BY *Pete Townshend*

THE UNIVERSITY OF CHICAGO PRESS ≡ CHICAGO AND LONDON

BOB RIESMAN is coeditor of *Chicago Folk: Images of the Sixties Music Scene: The Photographs of Raeburn Flerlage*. He produced and cowrote the television documentary *American Roots Music: Chicago* and was a contributor to Routledge's *Encyclopedia of the Blues*.

The University of Chicago Press, Chicago 60637
The University of Chicago Press, Ltd., London
© 2011 by The University of Chicago
Foreword © 2011 by Peter Guralnick
All rights reserved. Published 2011.
Printed in the United States of America

20 19 18 17 16 15 14 13 12 11   1 2 3 4 5

ISBN-13: 978-0-226-71745-6   (cloth)
ISBN-10: 0-226-71745-3   (cloth)

Library of Congress Cataloging-in-Publication Data

Riesman, Bob, author.
   I feel so good: the life and times of Big Bill Broonzy / Bob Riesman; foreword by Peter Guralnick; appreciation by Pete Townshend.
      pages cm.
   Includes bibliographical references and index.
ISBN-13: 978-0-226-71745-6 (cloth: alk. paper)
ISBN-10: 0-226-71745-3 (cloth: alk. paper) 1. Broonzy, Big Bill, 1893–1958. 2. African American Musicians—Biography. 3. Blues musicians—United States—Biography. I. Title.
   ML420.B78R54 2011
   782.421643092—dc22
   [B]   2010047868

♾ This paper meets the minimum requirements of ANSI/NISO Z39.48-1992 (Permanence of Paper).

For Abraham, Clare, and Julia
and for Rachel

A biography is always constructed from ruins but, as
any archaeologist will tell you, there is never the means
to unearth all the rooms, or follow the buried roads, or
dig into every cistern for treasure. You try to see what
the ruin meant to whoever inhabited it and, if you
are lucky, you see a little way backward into time.

Loren Eiseley, *All the Strange Hours: The Excavation of a Life*

CONTENTS

FOREWORD
by Peter Guralnick

Sometimes it seems as if Big Bill Broonzy must have supplied the ur-text for each new generation that has come to the blues for the last sixty years.

There are, of course, many good reasons for this. The clarity of that soaring voice. The solid foundation of more than three hundred original compositions. The unfeigned warmth and easy accessibility of both the work and the man. These were the very qualities that put Big Bill Broonzy on top of the "race" charts in the 1930s and '40s, and they served him equally well with the white audiences who first discovered him from the early 1950s on, both here and abroad.

He wrote classic numbers like "Key to the Highway" (probably most familiar to contemporary listeners in Eric Clapton's gently swinging version). He established his ironic vision of a better world in the continually updated "Just a Dream" ("I dreamed I was in the White House / Sitting in the President's chair / I dreamed he was shaking my hand / Said, 'Bill, I'm so glad you're here'"). He even voiced genuine (and enduring) social protest with "Black, Brown, and White Blues," no less pertinent when it was alluded to by Reverend Joseph Lowery at President Obama's inauguration.

But what he possessed above all, what sustained him in a far longer and more diverse career than most popular singers are ever able to enjoy, was the ability to adapt to changing times, changing tastes, and changing circumstances. His wit and urbanity certainly served him well in this regard. But so did his forthrightness. In fact, the 1947 round-table discussion in which he participated with Memphis Slim and Sonny Boy Williamson, with Alan Lomax serving as moderator, was sufficiently forthright to keep it from being issued in this country for many years. And when it finally did come out in truncated form in 1959, as *Blues in the*

Mississippi Night, the identities of the speakers were masked by pseudonyms.

Perhaps his greatest feat of adaptation, however, came with his embrace of a new, white audience, which first took wing with the concerts
that Win Stracke and Studs Terkel put on in Chicago as part of the na-
scent Chicago Folk Music movement, then with the European tours that
started in 1951 (he was in effect America's first ambassador of the blues),
and finally with those memorably heavy (both the cardboard covers and
the vinyl pressings) Folkways recordings by which a national folk audience came to know him. In those recordings, both in his own presen-
tations or prodded by Studs Terkel's interview questions, he revealed
himself as a keen observer and sly raconteur, discoursing on everything
from the origins of the blues to the identity of the "real" See See Rider.
At the center of it all were his Scott, Mississippi, roots and the extended
family and community from which he came, most vividly represented by
his centenarian Uncle Jerry, an old-time banjo and string-band player,
who had inducted his nephew at an early age into the world of spirituals
and reels.

It was an accessible, immaculately presented image and history, both
intimate and far-reaching—convincing not just for its vivid detail but in
its quietly insistent emotional tone. This was the world of the blues as
many of us first came to know it. And it would have been hard to imagine
a more trustworthy or reliable guide. Big Bill, Muddy Waters said, was
the one established blues singer to take him under his wing when Muddy
first arrived in Chicago in the early 1940s. And he offered the same un-
equivocal welcome, the same generosity of spirit, to all of us who came to
the blues from a much more distant place. He even went so far as to write
an autobiography, *Big Bill Blues*, full of arresting anecdotes and affectionate reminiscences, which was first published in 1955, three years before
he died. He was, in short, the most patient and understanding of guides,
presenting his story in a variety of forms and settings, employing metaphor and humor to illustrate his points, but always drawing upon a solid
bedrock of personal experience.

Except none of it turned out to be literally true.

By that I don't mean he was any less generous a guide. I don't mean
to suggest that the world of Big Bill Broonzy was any less true. But the
facts of his life as he presented them, the *creation* of Big Bill Broonzy
himself—as this book, warmly, affectionately, but conclusively proves—

represented no less a creative act than any of the hundreds of songs that he wrote or interpreted. The name, the dates, the birthplace, the detailed personal history, even Uncle Jerry—all were not so much fabrications as composite creations, all might better be seen not as the story of "Big Bill Broonzy" alone but as the story of the blues as he conceived it, in a way the story of the race.

I'm not going to spoil all the manifold surprises that this wonderful book holds in store. Suffice it to say that Bob Riesman has dug hard and deep into a world and a community to which few outsiders have been granted entrance. What is perhaps most remarkable about *I Feel So Good* is that for all of its revelations, for all of its insistence on unearthing the plain, unvarnished truth, you come away . . . feeling so good.

This is, quite simply, because of the warmth and affection that Riesman shows for his subject—and because of the clean, classic lines with which he has constructed his story. Thoughtful, admiring, clear-eyed, lucid, and well-organized, *I Feel So Good* gives us wonderful cameos—of record man Lester Melrose, early blues singers Georgia Tom and Papa Charlie Jackson, folklorist Alan Lomax, and Old Town School of Music co-founder Win Stracke—laid out on a sometimes skeletal frame. In a manner of which I am certain Big Bill would approve, Bob Riesman presents the story as a kind of journey, sinking his teeth into details when they present themselves but capable of teasing out the story in brief strokes when they don't. The musical and social context, the songs themselves are considered with sensitivity and sophistication. But the book never falters under the weight of its impressive research, as a new picture gradually emerges. This sharply etched portrait gives us a Big Bill Broonzy not so much larger-than-life as full of life, no less imposing, no less self-delighted, no less reliable than his own self-portrait, but freed for the first time from the encumbrance of myth and presented in all of his glorious, serendipitous, self-aware, and self-created multiplicity of masks and motivations.

Check out the "Envoi" (no, wait till you get to the end of the book, I don't want to spoil that surprise either)—I think it should be enough to say that this is the kind of book so engaging it simply leaves you wanting more.

APPRECIATION

by Pete Townshend

A record by Big Bill Broonzy was the first blues record I purchased. I got it in the spring of 1960 at my local music store in Ealing in West London, where I grew up. Bill's record was in the folk music section, alongside Pete Seeger, Sonny Terry and Brownie McGhee, Leadbelly and possibly Joan Baez. I listened to these other artists a year later. Bill had toured in Europe quite a bit and was a well-known name to me. I loved his voice, his guitar playing, and his handsome face. I was fifteen years old and had been playing guitar for four years. It wasn't until two years later that I discovered that in Ealing we were lucky enough to have the Ealing Club, a crypt-like basement where Alexis Korner and Cyril Davies regularly performed (as did the fledgling Rolling Stones a little later)—they had met and worked with Big Bill a few times and played some of his songs. I always felt close to Big Bill. He was my first blues crush. I felt I had sat at his feet. If I were to allow my heart to tell the tale, I would say that I had actually sat at his feet and had heard the pain and joy of his life firsthand through his wonderful songs.

Bob Riesman's book makes quite a bit of the way Big Bill reinvented himself and possibly invented much of his past in a creative manner. I'm not known for my love of facts either. If a blues, R&B, or rock 'n' roll career life story is worth telling, it's worth dressing up. I'm not an academic biographer. Riesman is that, and he gets close to the real truth about Big Bill's life, but he does so in a generous and nonjudgmental way that actually deepens the impact and power of everything Bill did as a creative artist and musician who reserved the right to gild the lily. In particular, Bill's family life, his years doing rough work, and his ability to reflect the stories and experiences of his contemporaries, all combine in this book to bring the terrible racial events and atrocities of those times back into relevance as historical facts rather than blues hearsay.

We've heard the songs; we've seen the face; we may even have listened to Big Bill himself telling interviewers like Alan Lomax how it really was, in his own inimitable and creative way. This book sets Bill's extraordinary life and career in meticulously researched perspective. This giant of a man—Big Bill Broonzy—deserves such a book, and Riesman is clearly the right man for the job. His affection for his subject is as evident as his respect. This is a compelling historical biography of an artist who sang right at the beginning of a musical era that later included rock 'n' roll. If rock 'n' roll and all its recent spawn can in any sense be regarded as art, or carries any social meaning, or transmits reflective or historical relevance to those who love it, this book will help to explain why.

Back before it all caught fire, we heard Big Bill, and we knew that music could tell the truth as well as entertain. Riesman makes it clear that such music might not relate the facts, but he never for a second doubts that Big Bill Broonzy knew the truth, even if he couldn't resist dressing it up sometimes.

I toast the research. I toast the show business. I mourn the big African American man who taught me that when you are a minstrel, your main job is to entertain. The truth will follow.

PREFACE

When I started work on this book almost a decade ago, I knew next to nothing about Big Bill Broonzy. I was looking for a project in blues or folk music, and, as I read histories and biographies in those fields, I was struck by how often Bill's name appeared. I learned that he had been one of the leaders of the Chicago blues world of the 1930s and '40s, well before the rise of Chess Records and the figures who made that label deservedly famous. During his trailblazing European tours of the 1950s, he had been an early and powerful inspiration to British musicians such as Eric Clapton and Ray Davies. American artists from Elvis Presley to Johnny Cash identified Bill as an influence, and he had helped to launch folk music revivals in both the United States and Great Britain.

As I began to look more closely at Bill's life and work, it soon became clear that Bill's legacy included at least two significant areas in addition to his recordings. He had demonstrated through his handwritten autobiography, *Big Bill Blues*, that his skill with words extended beyond songwriting. From his descriptions of his upbringing in the rural South to his observations on racial injustice, he expressed himself with clarity, insight, and wit. Bill had also served as a mentor to many younger blues musicians, to whom he offered guidance and encouragement. Muddy Waters, in particular, identified him as a role model, saying of Bill: "Mostly I try to be like him."

Over the course of researching and writing the book, I've learned that Bill was exemplary in many respects, flawed in others, and capable of exquisitely contradictory behavior. He left invaluable material for future historians by writing dozens of letters to correspondents in Europe, Great Britain, and the United States, many of which were preserved. During the same period, he provided substantial amounts of misleading or just plain wrong information about himself, his family, and his colleagues to interviewers, readers, and audiences on three continents that would take decades to untangle.

Because of Bill's success at what magicians call misdirection—directing the audience's attention away from where the crucial action is being performed—the challenges facing a would-be biographer have not been simple or straightforward. He specified incorrect marriage dates to wives whose names he changed in the telling, heaped praise on a favorite uncle who is absent from all family records and memories, relocated his own birth to a different state and set it in a different decade, and gave himself different first and last names. It turned out that it was necessary to retrace his steps in Europe to find out who he was and where he came from.

In 2003 I traveled to Amsterdam to interview Pim van Isveldt, the Dutch woman with whom he had fathered a son, Michael, in 1956. Near the end of our conversation, Pim handed me a shoe box in which she had kept the many letters Bill had written her. He had written one of them while visiting his sister Lannie Bradley Wesley in North Little Rock, Arkansas. Her home address, which Bill had given as the return address, was a vital clue.

Several months later, I attended the Wednesday-night Bible study at the church in North Little Rock where Lannie Wesley used to worship. A member of the congregation offered to make a phone call of introduction on my behalf, and so the next evening I met and interviewed Jo Ann Jackson and Rosie Tolbert, who are Lannie Wesley's granddaughters and Bill's grandnieces. They were willing to provide information about their uncle Bill that had been previously unknown outside their family. Although they had not known about Michael van Isveldt, their Dutch first cousin once removed, they were pleased to be put in touch with him. For his part, Michael was gratified to hear from them, as he had tried unsuccessfully to locate his father's family in the United States.

Bill's imaginative powers enabled him to obscure his origins and many portions of his journeys, while illuminating the worlds he grew up in and passed through. In my view, Bill's life and work can best be understood and appreciated by considering both the facts and the truth—as Studs Terkel put it, "Bill is speaking the truth—*his* truth." Here is my version of Big Bill Broonzy's story.

ACKNOWLEDGMENTS

I could not have produced this book without the assistance of many people. Even though I won't be able to mention everyone by name, I hope that each person who contributed knows how grateful I am for his or her help.

Beginning with our first meeting, Jo Ann Jackson and Rosie Tolbert have generously provided information about their family, into which Big Bill Broonzy was born in 1903 as Lee Bradley. They have welcomed me into their homes, graciously responded to every question I have asked, and unhesitatingly shared with me their family records, photos, and stories. Their introductions to their uncle Frank Wesley and their mother's childhood friend Hermese White gave me an additional set of firsthand perspectives on the world of the Bradleys of Lake Dick and North Little Rock, Arkansas. To Jo Ann and Rosie: thank you for all you have done to make it possible to tell the story of your uncle Bill and his family.

I was very lucky to spend several hours talking with Pim van Isveldt in her home in Amsterdam in 2003, along with the Dutch blues scholars Erik Mossel and Guido van Rijn. With candor and grace, Pim described her life and her relationship with Bill, opened her scrapbook to us, and even led us in a sing-along of her favorite Lead Belly song. Although it was not possible for her son Michael to be present that day, he has been a thoughtful and informative correspondent by e-mail. I am grateful for all the ways in which Pim and Michael have supported the research for this book, and I hope the day will soon come when Michael will be able to realize his dream of visiting his father's country.

No one has done more than Yannick and Margo Bruynoghe to ensure that Bill's legacy would be preserved in numerous ways. From an award-winning documentary film to recordings, photos, letters, and his autobiography, the Bruynoghes have either produced or protected some of Bill's most significant creations. I am grateful for Margo's willingness to provide me with access to her collection and also for having had the chance to experience at close range her shrewd observations and her inspiring joie de vivre.

I am grateful to two people in particular for their steadfast support and wise counsel at many junctures. Peter Guralnick has helped me navigate the unfamiliar waters of research, writing, and publishing, and has done this consistently with insight, illustrative anecdotes, and good humor. His unspoken but palpable confidence that I would reach my goal has been a source of strength along the way. I met Ron Cohen just as the idea for the book was taking shape, and his initial and continuing encouragement played an important role in my decision to proceed. His introductions to key people for interviews and his suggestions for archives to visit have greatly enhanced my research efforts, and his careful reading and comments have strengthened my manuscript.

From the early days of my research, Chris Smith has been an unfailing source of both knowledge and wisdom about Bill, as well as his musical colleagues and the worlds in which they traveled. His recommendations as to people I should contact, materials I should locate, and revisions I should consider have all been consistently on target. Beyond that, his willingness—gently but firmly—to question my assumptions or assessments when they were veering off track have improved my thinking and my writing. I encourage you to read his many articles and liner notes, and especially his superb essay "A Guide to Big Bill Broonzy on Record" in his discography of Bill's recordings, *Hit the Right Lick*.

Guido van Rijn made substantial contributions to this project while playing two different roles. As an eminent Dutch blues scholar, his initiative in locating letters and other materials associated with Bill's tours of Holland provided important additions to my research. In addition, Guido made the arrangements for my interview with Pim van Isveldt, and his presence, along with Erik Mossel, ensured that the discussion could alternate between English and Dutch, which helped to put Pim at ease (although her English was, in fact, excellent).

Thanks to Val Wilmer for her willingness to share with me her extensive knowledge of the British blues and jazz scene of the 1950s and '60s, as well as her contacts with many of the key figures. By putting me in touch with Walter Hanlon, Nick Jones, and Dave Bennett, she is also responsible for the inclusion of a number of the photos.

Long before he graciously responded to my initial fax, André Vasset had published his memoir of Bill, *Black Brother*. The book combined his firsthand recollections of Bill with a meticulously researched discography and timeline of Bill's life. André also opened his files to me, and the letters, articles, and photos relating to Bill that he shared all represented valuable contributions. To André—*merci beaucoup*.

When blues researcher Alan Balfour posted a note to an online blues discussion group in early 2001 asking whether someone would ever write a biography of Big Bill Broonzy, I screwed up my courage and sent him a note saying I was thinking of doing just that. Alan's help in identifying materials and archives, as well as his referrals to several key contacts—especially John Pilgrim—were vital in launching and sustaining my research for this book.

Jane Stracke Bradbury mailed me a set of items in early 2002 that included copies of nearly a dozen letters that Bill had sent from Europe in the early 1950s to her father, Win Stracke. These were truly a gold mine in making me aware of the significant role that Win had played in the last decade of Bill's life. My thanks to Jane and her husband, Bill, for them, as well as for the additional materials they have provided.

I particularly want to thank Bob Eagle and Eric LeBlanc for their collaboration in pursuing the goal of determining the location and date of Bill's birth, as well as his name and those of his family members. Working on separate tracks but sharing information at different points along the way, we each independently identified Bill as the Lee Bradley of the Bradley family in Jefferson County, Arkansas.

Jim O'Neal provided contacts, recommended archives, shared the tapes of his interviews with Blind John Davis, and responded to numerous questions with patience and clarity. The trip that he and Amy van Singel made to visit the Bruynoghes in 1979 resulted in the later publication of the extraordinary collection of photos, letters, and other items relating to Bill and his colleagues in *Living Blues*. Jim and Scott Barretta were also responsible for the handsome and informative Mississippi Blues Trail marker honoring Bill that was unveiled in Scott, Mississippi, in April 2009.

I met and interviewed Bill Randle, the person responsible for Big Bill Broonzy's last recording sessions in July 1957, because of the help provided by his daughter, Pat Randle, and Jim Eng. With their cooperation, combined with that of radio journalist David C. Barnett, I was able to listen to the unedited tapes of those sessions and to review the contracts, royalty statements, and other items in the Bill Randle Collection, which had never been previously made available to a researcher. My thanks to Pat, Jim, and David, and also to Terry Stewart and Howard Kramer of the Rock and Roll Hall of Fame and Museum, who provided a crucial introduction.

Thanks to all who agreed to be interviewed: Billy Boy Arnold, Mildred Asbell, Dick Baer, Duck Baker, Long John Baldry, Chris Barber, Graeme Bell, Lore Boas, Jane Stracke Bradbury, Paul Breman, David Bromberg, Margo Bruynoghe, Martin Carthy, Ian Christie, Eric Clapton, Norman Cleary, Terry Cryer, Metta Davis, Nathan Davis, Jacques Demêtre, Diz Disley, David "Honeyboy" Edwards, Larry Ehrlich, Ramblin' Jack Elliott, Leonard Feinberg, Richard Flohil, Hardy Freeman, Lola Gordon, Frank Hamilton, Walter Hanlon, Sheila Hori, Jo Ann Jackson, Bert Jansch, Ella Jenkins, Wizz Jones, B.B. King, Leo King, Vera Morkovin King, Mark Knopfler, Bob Koester, Bobbie Korner, Jean-Pierre Leloir, Humphrey Lyttelton, Woody Mann, Jo Mapes, John Mayall, Chas McDevitt, Kurt Mohr, Mick Mulligan, Eric Noden, Paul Oliver, Valerie Oliver, Roxana Paulson, John Pilgrim, Bill Randle, John Renbourn, Peggy Seeger, Pete Seeger, Hudson Shower, Irwin Silber, Nevil Skrimshire, Willie "Big Eyes" Smith, Hanne Sonquist, David Stevens, Bob Stracke, Studs Terkel, Pete Townshend, Jack Tracy, Michael van Isveldt, Pim van Isveldt, Jav Walker, Norma Waterson, Frank Wesley, Hermese White, Bert Wilcox, Armilee Williams, Jody Williams, and Uncle Johnny Williams. My thanks also to Jennifer Armstrong, Oscar Brand, Raeburn Flerlage, Jacques Morgantini, Jimmie Lee Robinson, Ron Sweetman, Fred Vanbesien, and Garry Winkler, who provided memories of Bill in a variety of formats. I am particularly grateful to Dick Shurman for his introductions to several interviewees.

Most of the interviews would still be trapped in the cassettes if not for the superb transcribing work done by Judy Hergenreder and Sydney Lewis. Thanks also to Syd, Dan Terkell, and J. R. Millares for their assistance with arranging visits with Studs Terkel.

I am indebted to several people for sharing with me their raw and unpublished interviews, as well as other recorded material. Thanks to Mark Dvorak for the tapes of his interviews with Win Stracke; to Jim O'Neal for the tapes of his interviews with Blind John Davis, as well as the transcript of his interview with Memphis Slim; and to Paul Breman and Guido van Rijn, each of whom provided copies of the tape recording made at Michiel de Ruyter's home in Amsterdam in November 1955. Special thanks to Tom Holzfeind and the Holzfeind family for providing me with a copy of a recording of a performance by the "I Come for to Sing" group.

For their help with locating and translating articles in languages other than English, thanks to Marc Boxerman, Jorge Coronado, Ramón del Solo, Nicole Fabricant, Luciano Federighi, Klaus Kilian, Chantal Luehmann, Luigi Monge, Thomas Simpson, Chris Smith, Allan Stephensen, and Guido van Rijn. Special thanks to Emilie Potonet-Stec for her skillful work as a liaison with several French-speaking contacts, as well as for her excellent translations.

For their help with research on Bill's 1951 tour with Graeme Bell and His Australian Jazz Band, thanks to Graeme Bell, Pat Bentley, Bill Haesler, Tony Standish, and Mike Sutcliffe.

The following archives, cultural institutions, and individuals were of great help in my research, and I am most grateful to all of them:

ALAN LOMAX ARCHIVE: *Anna Lomax Wood, Matt Barton, Don Fleming, Ellen Harold, Bert Lyons, and Nathan Salsburg*

AMERICAN FEDERATION OF MUSICIANS, CHICAGO LOCAL 10-208: *Ann Gregor*

AMERICAN FOLKLIFE CENTER, LIBRARY OF CONGRESS: *Judith Gray, Joe Hickerson*

BIBLIOTHÈQUE NATIONALE DE FRANCE: *Anne Legrand*

BLUES ARCHIVE AT THE CHICAGO PUBLIC LIBRARY: *Richard Schwegel*

BRITISH LIBRARY NEWSPAPER COLLECTION (COLINDALE)

CENTER FOR CREATIVE PHOTOGRAPHY, UNIVERSITY OF ARIZONA: *Leslie Calmes, Tammy Carter, Denise Gosé*

CHICAGO HISTORY MUSEUM: *Russell Lewis, Phyllis Rabineau, John Alderson, Michael Cleavenger, Alison Eisendrath, Sharon Lancaster, Rob Medina, Elizabeth Reilly, and Lesley Martin and her colleagues in the Research Center*

CIRCLE PINES CENTER: *John Glass and Angel Leone*

CHICAGO JAZZ ARCHIVE, NOW LOCATED IN THE SPECIAL COLLECTIONS RESEARCH CENTER OF THE UNIVERSITY OF CHICAGO LIBRARY: *Deborah Gillaspie, as well as Julia Gardner in Special Collections, and the Interlibrary Loan staff*

CLAYTON LIBRARY CENTER FOR GENEALOGICAL RESEARCH, HOUSTON, TEXAS

COUNTRY MUSIC HALL OF FAME AND MUSEUM: *Kira Florita, and special thanks to Dawn Oberg for suggesting that I look at the microfilms of the RCA Victor session logs*

ENGLISH FOLK DANCE AND SONG SOCIETY: *Malcolm Taylor*

INDIANA HISTORICAL SOCIETY: *Betsy Caldwell*

INSTITUTE FOR JAZZ STUDIES AT RUTGERS UNIVERSITY: *Dan Morgenstern, Tad Herschorn, Joseph Patterson*

INTERNATIONAL ARCHIVE FOR JAZZ AND POPULAR MUSIC OF THE LIPPMANN+RAU FOUNDATION, EISENACH, GERMANY: *Reinhard Lorenz, Nico Thom*
IRVING S. GILMORE MUSIC LIBRARY, YALE UNIVERSITY LIBRARY: *Suzanne Eggleston Lovejoy, Emily Ferrigno*
MARIA AUSTRIA INSTITUUT, AMSTERDAM: *Adriaan Elligens, Iris Wijnoogst*
MÉDIATHÈQUE DE VILLEFRANCHE DE ROUERGUE, FRANCE: *Daniel Alogues, Patrick Brugel*
NATIONAL PORTRAIT GALLERY (UK): *Bernard Horrocks*
NEDERLANDS JAZZ ARCHIEF, AMSTERDAM
OAK PARK PUBLIC LIBRARY INTERLIBRARY LOANS: *Grace Lewis*
OLD TOWN SCHOOL OF FOLK MUSIC: *Bau Graves, David Roche, Colby Maddox, Colleen Miller, Dawn Patch, Dayna Calderon, Gary Snyderman, Jimmy Tomasello, Mark Dvorak and Chris Walz*
ROCK AND ROLL HALL OF FAME AND MUSEUM: *Howard Kramer*
SMITHSONIAN CENTER FOR FOLKLIFE AND CULTURAL HERITAGE: *Stephanie Smith*
SMITHSONIAN FOLKWAYS: *Margot Nassau and Jeff Place*
UNIVERSITY OF TEXAS AT SAN ANTONIO LIBRARY: *Jeff McAdams*
WALLA WALLA COLLEGE ARCHIVES: *Mark Copsey and Brooke Davey*

My sincere thanks to those who took the time to read the entire manuscript in draft form: Andy Cohen, Ron Cohen, Marcie Cummings, Rachel Kaplan, Alan Kaufmann, Chris Smith, and Guido van Rijn; and to Scott Barretta and Bucky Halker, who read portions. Special thanks to S. L. Wisenberg for her comments on the drafts of early chapters. Each reader offered informed and constructive suggestions, and their questions, observations, and recommendations spurred me to clarify my thinking and my writing.

All of the following people were helpful in tracing Bill's Arkansas origins, and I offer my thanks to each of them. At the Arkansas History Commission: Russell Baker, April Goff, Jane Hooker, Jeff Lewellen, and especially to Caroline Hervey for recommending that I go to the Wednesday-night Bible study class at the Warren Hill Baptist Church. At the University of Arkansas: Robert Cochran, Charles Robinson, Jeannie Whayne, and Patrick Williams. At the Pine Bluff Jefferson County Historical Museum: Sue Trulock and Lola Gordon. At the Pine Bluff/Jefferson County Public Library: Jana Blankenship. At the University of Arkansas School of Law: Ned Snow and especially to Judith Kilpatrick for all of her help. At the University of Arkansas Library, Special Collections: Tom Dillard and especially to Tim Nutt for his responsiveness to my many inquiries.

My thanks to the people who helped in piecing together the story of Bill's year in Ames, Iowa: Leonard Feinberg; his daughter, Elyn Aviva, and Elyn's husband, Gary White; Jauvanta "Jav" Walker; Jorgen Rasmussen; Norman Cleary; Tanya Zanish-Belcher and Becky Jordan at the Iowa State University Library; Jeslyn Jackson at Iowa State University; Kathy Svec at the Ames Historical Society; Daniel Stevenson at the American Federation of Musicians, Des Moines Local 75; Susan Kuecker at the African American Historical Museum and Cultural Center of Iowa in Cedar Rapids; and Karen Kellogg.

Thanks to all of the following individuals for their various contributions: Deborah Ardizzone, Leigh Armstrong, Paul Asbell, Scott Barretta, Dave Bennett, Leif Bjerborg, Colin Bray, Jim Brown, Ray Bush, Jean Bystedt, Val Camiletti, Richard Carlin, Larry Cohn, André Clergeat, Geoff Coates, Nadine Cohodas, Shirley Collins, Bob Copper, Bob Corritore, John Cowley, Paul Crockford, Sarah Cullen, Steve Cushing, André Dael, Bill Dahl, Barbara Dane, Scott Dirks, Constance Ditzel, Barry Dolins, Frank Driggs, Josh Dunson, Clay Eals, Bee Engler, David Evans, Joe Filisko, Michael Flug, Rob Ford, Gus Friedlander, Stefaan François, Paul Garon, John Giggie, John Glass, Lance Greening, Dave Gregory, Bill Haesler, David Hajdu, Ann Hay, Mary Hamilton, Jane Hanlon, Colin Harper, Dick Hawdon, Chris Heiser, Cal Herrmann, Drew Holzfeind, Matt Holzfeind, Tom Holzfeind, Chris James, Loren Jansch, Nick Jones, Nicola Joss, Ruth Finesinger Kellam, Jim Keller, Michael Kleff, Susan Koester, Harold Koh, Leif Kristiansen, Harold Leventhal, Susan Ley, Norman Litowitz, Sarah Lockwood, Paul Lovelace, John Macey, Keith Madderon, Geoff Muldaur, Jim Newcomb, Ray Nordstrand, Justin O'Brien, Christian O'Connell, Cecil Offley, Paul Pelletier, Jacques Périn, Meredith Plant, Claudia Portillo, Michael Prussian, Bob Pruter, Barry Radix, Millie Rahn, Iris Riesman, Carol Rosofsky, Meg Ross, Dr. Richard S. Ross, Mike Rowe, Howard Rye, Patrick Rynn, Robert Sacré, Sal Salvato, Sharon Salvato, Dave Samuelson, Tim Samuelson, Bob Santelli, Raymond Saublains, Anthony Seeger, Harry Shapiro, June Shelley, Ida Shoufler, Dick Shurman, Margaret Sieck, Betsy Siggins, Rick Simon, Rebecca Sive, Tony Standish, Bill Steber, Rob Stone, Dan Stout, Terry Straker, Mrs. Jos. Thevelin, Steve Tomashefsky, Brian Towers, Mel Townsend, Marc Van De Moortele, Alex van der Tuuk, André Van Meenen, Michel Vasset, Wim Verbei, Paul Vernon, Stephen Wade, Elijah Wald, Jeff Walden,

David Waldman, Gayle Dean Wardlow, Dick Waterhouse, Dick Waterman, Tom Weinberg, David Whiteis, Robert Wylie.

My thanks to my editor, John Tryneski, at the University of Chicago Press for his support in guiding a first-time author through the publishing process. His initial and ongoing enthusiasm for the book has provided much-needed encouragement, and his informed suggestions have strengthened it in a variety of significant ways. Rodney Powell's responses to my steady stream of questions have been consistently helpful, and I have particularly appreciated his willingness to research the answers to all of them thoroughly. I am indebted to my copy editor, Erin DeWitt, for her keen observations, perceptive questions, and good cheer all the way through a painstakingly detailed process. I am grateful to my two anonymous readers for their helpful recommendations and valuable comments on the manuscript. My agent, Erin Hosier, has been nothing short of stellar in every respect. She stuck with me when we had to back up and try again, and I am very grateful to have her on my side.

Many friends have provided vast levels of support, and in a multitude of ways. My thanks especially to Michael and Debra Gordon, André and Lil Hobus, Bruce Iglauer and Jo Kolanda, Chris Jacobs and Hank Webber, Alan Kaufmann, Mari Philipsborn and Eric Terman, Bill Pollak, and Marlene Richman.

My family has been a vital source of encouragement. I am grateful to my mother, Marcia Riesman, for her unflagging interest in the book's progress, and also for calling one afternoon to tell me that Eric Clapton was talking about Big Bill Broonzy on National Public Radio. My sister, Jean Riesman, has set a dauntingly high standard for siblings by asking regularly about the book and then actually listening to the answers. My three children—Abe, Clare, and Julia—have been utterly reliable sources of support, inspiration, and laughter. Each of them has made this journey with me cheerfully, and I cherish them in ways that I cannot put into words. I am especially grateful to Abe and Clare for their incisive comments on portions of the manuscript.

Thanks to my wife Rachel Kaplan's parents, Marge and Harvey Kaplan, and to her siblings and their spouses, for their consistent and vocal support and for welcoming me into their family with such warmth. Special thanks to Helen Kaplan for her insights about ways to resolve the writing challenges posed by the early chapters; and to Jon Smollen for his faith, which was ultimately rewarded, that a long-anticipated interview would eventually take place. I appreciate all the encouragement from my Riesman, Finkelstein, and Stone aunts, uncles, and cousins, especially from my uncle Gene Riesman and from Helen and Ed Kaden, my ninety-two-year-old cousin with three Red Sox World Series wins under his belt. And I wish that my father, Robert Riesman, my uncle Micky Riesman, and my dear friend Harold Richman had lived to see the publication of this book.

To Rachel: your faith in my ability to write this book has been un-wavering. I could not have asked for more focused, clear-sighted, and loving help and encouragement to accomplish this task. Thank you, with all my love.

Swing Low, Sweet Chariot

In the end, it was Win Stracke who made the arrangements. In the weeks before he died, Big Bill Broonzy had pleaded with his wife Rose to let him stay home instead of returning to the hospital. But when Win arrived at the apartment after getting the phone call at 3 a.m. that Bill was failing, he decided that it would be too difficult for the family members gathered at the bedside to witness the final painful moments, and he called the ambulance. He also made sure that a room was waiting at Billings Hospital on the University of Chicago campus, only two miles away. But by the time Bill arrived there in the early hours of Friday, August 15, 1958, he had already passed.[1]

There was, of course, a lot more to do once Bill was dead: coordinating the memorial service, selecting the location of the grave at the cemetery, and raising the money so these events could take place. The life insurance payout from the Local 208 black musicians' union wouldn't be enough by itself to cover the funeral, although the $500 that Win collected from friends and admirers over the weekend would help close the gap.[2]

Win had known Bill for a dozen years, since 1946. Win's broad face and deep, warm, bass voice were familiar to Chicago television audiences from his appearances as a working-class singer of operatic arias and folk ballads on Studs Terkel's popular show *Studs' Place* and as the genial host of the children's program *Animal Playtime*. Bill and Win had traveled together through the Midwest in a folk song revue called "I Come for to Sing," playing Big Ten college campuses and Chicago nightclubs. It was Win who had launched Bill on the European tours that made him an internationally known name. When Win fulfilled his longtime dream by opening a folk music school in Chicago in December 1957, Bill performed at the opening-night concert, strumming as the school's first teacher diagrammed his technique on the blackboard for the first class. Bill had trusted Win enough to name him as the executor of his estate.[3]

Win wanted to make sure that Bill would be honored in ways that underscored his importance to his various constituencies. He started by arranging for several musicians to perform at the funeral at the Metropolitan Funeral Parlors, located at Forty-fifth and South Parkway, two blocks from Bill and Rose's apartment. There was no shortage of talent at the service, with offerings from gospel star Mahalia Jackson, who had performed overseas with Bill in 1952; her informally adopted son, Brother John Sellers, who had appeared with Bill during his last tour of England in 1957; and Studs Terkel, whose connection with Bill went back to the earliest "I Come for to Sing" shows in the late 1940s. Win himself picked up his guitar and sang for the several hundred mourners as well, choosing the recently written but seemingly ageless folk song "Passing Through," whose chorus stressed that "We're all brothers and we're only passing through."

But the leads in the next day's newspapers told of something unusual and probably unprecedented: "Big Bill Broonzy sang at his own funeral," wrote the reporters for the *Chicago Daily News* and the *Chicago Sun-Times*.[4]

It was indeed Bill, recorded barely a year earlier during his final recording session, before a doctor's scalpel had nicked his vocal cords during surgery on what turned out to be the lung cancer that killed him. He sang "Swing Low, Sweet Chariot" in a slow tempo, stretching out the words, strumming almost to himself, as if the guitar were an organic part of him and the playing was like inhaling as he gathered his strength for the next phrase. The effect, not surprisingly, was powerful, bringing many of those in attendance to tears. As they cried, they could see Bill in an open casket surrounded by an impressive array of flowers that featured a huge arrangement in the shape of a guitar.[5]

After the service, at the cemetery, two more of Win's ideas combined to leave a lasting imprint. He had written to a friend that "the pallbearers will be four white and four colored singers," and that he had hired a professional photographer. So Mickey Pallas, whose photos had appeared in *Ebony* and *Sepia*, was there to document Bill's final journey. One of Pallas's images of Bill's casket, borne by the pallbearers, succeeded in capturing the image that Win had worked hard to create.[6]

At the head of the procession, white handkerchief in breast pocket, eyes downcast, his face a somber mask, walked Muddy Waters. Not long after Muddy had arrived in Chicago in the mid-1940s, Bill had reached out to him, and Muddy always spoke of Bill with admiration, affection, and respect. To Muddy's left was Brother John Sellers, and in sequence behind him was a trio of Chicago blues musicians: Tampa Red, who, along with Bill, ruled the Chicago blues world of the 1930s and '40s; Otis Spann, Muddy's gifted piano player, his eyes fixed on the ground; and pianist Sunnyland Slim, whose most visible feature was the balding top of his bowed head as he brought up the rear. "Little Walter" Jacobs would have been included among the pallbearers if the harmonica star had not been shot in the leg earlier that year.[7]

On the opposite side of the casket were Win, Studs, bassist Ransom Knowling, and Chet Roble, a cabaret piano player who had joined the "I Come for to Sing" revue in the early 1950s.[8] Roble was glancing to one side, Studs was staring down even harder than Spann, and Win—a big man, tall and broad-shouldered—looked ahead to the approaching grave site. Bill might have wasted away to less than a hundred pounds by the time he died, but these were men bearing a load that weighed on them, no matter how light the casket.

What the picture showed was what Win had likely intended, and then some. Certainly there was the image of blacks and whites united in common cause—as Win had sung earlier, we're all brothers. It was not a trivial public statement less than a year after Arkansas governor Orval Faubus confronted federal troops sent to Little Rock by President Eisenhower to enforce school integration. In fact, eight years after Bill's funeral, white crowds cursed the Rev. Martin Luther King Jr. as he marched in the streets of Chicago for an end to unfair housing practices. The pallbearers were also brought together by their shared professional commitment to music with a link to Bill. Each made his living in some part by performing and recording blues and folk music. In addition, it was a picture of Chicago in 1958, a vibrant and dynamic center of music made largely by people who had been born someplace else. Waters, Sellers, Sunnyland, Knowling, and Spann all came originally from Mississippi, Tampa Red from Georgia, Terkel from New York, and Stracke from Kansas.[9]

The photo showed Muddy assuming the role of a leader of the Chicago blues community, even though both Tampa and Sunnyland were older. While other blues musicians had a more direct musical influence on Muddy, he always talked about Bill as someone who demonstrated how to act when you've had some success, how to carry yourself—how to be a man. By 1958 Muddy's band had been among the most dominant in a fiercely competitive city for nearly a decade. Although the personnel had changed over time, Muddy's vision, talent, and determination had driven its success. If there was a rite of passage, a ceremony where Muddy claimed the status he had earned, it was this event. The passing of a giant like Bill, and its effect on Muddy, was visible in his solemn expression and dignified posture.

There were other people who had played meaningful roles in Bill's life who were not in Chicago on that hot August day to hear Bill's voice and to watch as his friends laid his body down. Broadcaster and musician Alexis Korner, whose radio commentaries and liner notes brought his passion for Bill's music to a growing audience of British blues fans, was in London, where he had helped organize a benefit concert for Bill five months earlier. Yannick and Margo Bruynoghe were in Brussels, where they had welcomed Bill into their home and had arranged for Bill to star in an award-winning short film. Jazz writer Hugues Panassié was in France, where he had introduced Bill to European audiences in 1951. And Pete Seeger, who had played with Bill at college concerts and hootenannies since the 1940s, was somewhere on the road.

These individuals were among the numerous friends Bill had made since he started playing for white audiences, mostly after World War II, in New York and Chicago and Europe. They and others had helped him present to the world the stories in which he entwined his own life with the history of the blues and the black experience in America. They had arranged for Bill's concerts on stages in Copenhagen, Barcelona, and Milan; recorded his songs in Paris and Amsterdam; and edited his autobiography, which had been published in four countries and two languages. And then there were his missing colleagues from the early days of the blues world who had died, whose names he had called out in the final recording session a year before: Leroy Carr, Big Maceo Merriweather, Jim Jackson—men who had played for whiskey at rent parties and recorded their songs on 78 rpm discs sold as "race records."

Win's plans had truly honored him, and the Big Bill Broonzy buried in the hot sun on August 19, 1958, at Lincoln Cemetery in Blue Island, Illinois, was a significant and internationally acclaimed figure: author, singer, guitarist, songwriter, a black man who spoke and sang about racism, a man of admirable character. Only the family members who were gathered there knew that the man they buried that day was not born with that name, and that his story was different from the one he had told his friends and fans. Big Bill Broonzy was a tremendous storyteller, and his greatest invention may have been himself.

My Name Is
William Lee Conley Broonzy

There are several pieces of paper that Big Bill Broonzy's grandniece Rosie Tolbert keeps among her prized family possessions. They are a set of printed forms dating from the end of the nineteenth or the beginning of the twentieth century. Each has an elaborately drawn crimson-and-gold border enclosing the preprinted text appropriate to its purpose: to record births, marriages, and deaths. Each has an engraved image related to the event, ranging from an infant sitting in a half-shell on a beach surrounded by flowers to an angel kneeling at a grave site. On these pages, brown with age but carefully preserved, are the names and dates of these events for the members of Bill's family. Along with census records and other documents, they contain the vital statistics of the story of Big Bill Broonzy's origins.

His father, Frank Bradley, was likely born in South Carolina during the early to mid-1860s, as the Civil War was under way. The family records list a birth date for him of November 22, 1861.[1] By 1882 he had made his way to Jefferson County, in east-central Arkansas, and in August of that year he married Anna Lou Sparks, age eighteen. The date of Frank's birth year varies by several years among different census records, as well as on his 1882 marriage license.[2]

On December 29, 1889, Frank married a second time, to Mittie Belcher in New Gascony, Arkansas, a rural community several miles outside of Pine Bluff. Mittie was probably born in Arkansas sometime in the range of 1869 to 1873, with various birth dates indicated on census records, her marriage license, and her death certificate.[3] The family records show that she was born on March 1, 1869, in Arkansas. Whether Frank had become available because the first Mrs. Bradley had died or because they had split up is not known, but the union with Mittie Belcher was to last forty years.

By the time the census-taker stopped by the Bradley household in

Vaugine Township in rural Jefferson County in June 1900, the family included seven children. Andrew, the oldest of the three boys, was born in 1882, followed two years later by Mattie. Rachel, born in 1887, was likely the first child born to Mittie Belcher Bradley. Their numbers had swelled in the 1890s with the births of James in 1890, Sallie in 1892, Frank Jr. in 1897, and Gustavia in 1899.[4]

On June 26, 1903, Frank and Mittie welcomed Lee Bradley, the fourth and last boy. The entry in the family birth record appears as "Lee Conly Bradley," but in all other official documents in which he is listed as a Bradley, it is just as Lee Bradley. "My name," he told a Danish jazz club audience in 1956, "is William Lee Conley Broonzy," and he was half right. His full given name was most likely Lee Conley Bradley.[5]

Lannie Bradley, the sister Bill was closest to, was born on August 4, 1906.[6] The youngest child, Mary, was born in 1909, when Mittie was either thirty-six or forty years old, depending on her actual birth date. She had been bearing children for at least two decades, and Frank had been a father to small children for over twenty-five years.

Here is Bill's account of his family history in his autobiography, *Big Bill Blues*:

> My father told me how he met my mother in slave time. He said they had to pick so much cotton a day and she didn't get her task done and he'd seen her get a lashing, and after that he said he would pick cotton fast to get his task done and crawl through the grass and weed and help her, and he did that every day.
>
> So when they was freed and sent back to their home they found out that both lived in Baton-Rouge [*sic*], Louisiana, and they got married.
>
> Often I have heard my mother say:
>
> "Any time a man takes a chance on his life to help me, he's good enough for me to marry and have a baby for."[7]

If this is Bill's creation myth, it is a good place to start in looking at the ways in which he chose to present his family and himself. There are elements here that run through much of his creative output in songs, commentaries, articles, interviews, and autobiography. In fact, they include some of his most characteristic themes and devices.

First, he linked his family's personal events to the larger African American experience. In Bill's telling, his parents were slaves, forced to work under coercive and abusive conditions. In this way, he claimed the status of the son of a survivor, who had heard the stories of his parents' suffering from the intimate perspective of a child. This gave his words a powerful authenticity that established his authority as a commentator.

Beyond that, he had a deep understanding of what made for a gripping tale. In a few short sentences, he told a story with dramatic tension—the reader can easily picture his mother straining to maintain her dignity under the blows of the overseer while his father scuttles along the rows of green plants, quickly peeking above the tops as he scans for white faces. With the economy that writing good blues lyrics demands, he presented characters, engaged the audience, and resolved the tension.

He also ended with a statement of philosophy. In noting that he "often" heard his mother conclude that his father had met her conditions for marriage, he offered a vision of a world where it was possible to make sense of things. Evil existed, as his mother's beating demonstrated, but out of that pain some wisdom could be found. The world as Bill saw it contained much injustice, but there were alternatives to hopeless despair and blind rage.

The Bradley family lived in the rural areas of Jefferson County outside Pine Bluff from the 1880s into the 1920s. The Arkansas River dominates the landscape of the region as it flows southeast from Little Rock and cuts the county into two sections. The smaller section that lies between Little Rock and Pine Bluff is higher and drier, and was home to plentiful stands of pine that supported a thriving timber industry in the early twentieth century. The larger portion mainly consists of land that is reliably fertile because it is constantly damp or wet. These are lowlands or bottoms, where farmland is often bounded by what one observer described as "a profusion of bayous, lakes, creeks and sloughs of no regular size."[8] From the eighteenth century onward, man-made levees guarded the farms and homes against flooding.

During the period in which the Bradley family lived in Jefferson County, the majority of the county's residents were African American. The censuses of 1890 through 1920 counted two black residents for each white resident, and a New Deal–era analysis of the county noted that the black population comprised "one of the largest groups of negroes in the State."[9] Cotton was the region's dominant cash crop, growing abundantly in the rich soil of the lowlands. As in the better-chronicled Mississippi Delta, the systems under which the cotton was cultivated, harvested, and sold were sharecropping and tenant farming. Nearly 90 percent of the black farmers in Jefferson County in 1930 did not own the land they worked, and Frank Bradley was one of them.[10]

Under sharecropping, the owner of the land rented access to it to the sharecropper. If, as was generally the case, the sharecropper lacked the materials needed to do his job—such as hoes, plows, seed, or mules—the owner would provide those as well. This was known as "the furnish," because the owner furnished them to the renter. Many sharecroppers and their families also lived in shacks they rented from the owner on or near the land they farmed. At harvesttime the two sides would settle up, with the sharecropper turning over a hefty percentage—commonly one-half—of the year's crop to the owner. In addition, the owner would charge the farmer for the cost of his home and the furnish. Beyond that, if the owner had extended credit at the plantation store—for which few competing options existed—that came out of the remainder as well. Tenant farmers had relatively more bargaining power in this negotiation, as they owned the crop and could in theory keep more of the profits in a good year.

It was a system ripe for exploitation, and stories abound of often-illiterate black sharecroppers manipulated and intimidated by unscrupulous white owners. Owners could and did maintain the indebted status of the sharecroppers by maximizing the value of the credit they extended and understating the worth of the crop. Once the debt was established, the options for black farmers were poor: they often weren't equipped to challenge the calculations, and if they tried to move or flee, they would be at the mercy of the police and the justice system. It was a rigged game with no good exit strategy, and as a Mississippi planter told a sharecropper who accused him of unfair calculations, "This plantation is a place for *me* to make the profit, not you."[11]

At the turn of the twentieth century, Frank Bradley did not have much to his name—in fact, he had less than some of his black farmer neighbors. The tax rolls for Vaugine Township for 1900 show that he owned no horses, sheep, cattle, hogs, or mules. Because he also didn't own any gold or silver watches, or "Pianofortes," or carriages, bicycles, "or Wagons of whatsoever kind," the taxing authority determined that his total taxable property amounted to $10. This was the standard minimum in Vaugine Township for black sharecroppers, as those who owned a horse, a mule or two, and a watch were assessed as if they were worth $90 or even $120. On March 25, 1901, Frank paid a total of 17 cents to the township. The distance between his world and that of Leo Andrews, a prominent local landowner, was only suggested by the gap between Frank's pennies and the $69.24 that Andrews paid that year.[12]

Big Bill Broonzy maintained from at least the late 1930s onward that he was born in Scott, Mississippi, on June 26, 1893. He used that birthplace and date on his 1939 applications for Social Security and to the Chicago black musicians' union, and in all succeeding writings and interviews. He told Alan Lomax in an oral history Lomax recorded shortly after World War II that he had moved with his family to Arkansas from Mississippi around 1900. First, he said, they came to Scott's Crossing, and about four or five years later they moved to Langdale.[13]

Yet the documentary evidence is clear that the facts are otherwise. Lannie Bradley Wesley's granddaughter Rosie Tolbert keeps the family records. She and her older sister Jo Ann Jackson remember their uncle Bill and his sister (their grandmother Lannie), their great-grandmother Mittie, their great-uncle Frank Bradley Jr., and their great-aunts Gustavia and Mary. The censuses of 1900, 1910, and 1920 all show Frank and Mittie Bradley and their children living at home in Jefferson County. Tax records, marriage licenses, Social Security applications, and death certificates all confirm and reinforce the fact that Big Bill Broonzy was Lee Bradley of the Bradley clan.[14]

Why Lee Bradley chose to assemble a revised past for himself and his family may never be known for sure. Stories have been passed down in the Bradley family that when he left Arkansas in the 1920s, he left in a hurry. He may have done something that, even if it was not technically illegal, left someone in Arkansas feeling wronged in some significant way. As his grandniece Jo Ann Jackson put it, before the 1950s "he didn't come home that often. They were afraid for him to come home, like he was going to get caught, or whatever the situation was that went down."[15] In searching for an explanation, it is tempting to consider whether the lyrics to his song "Willie Mae" might contain a clue about his involvement with another man's wife: "All my life, Willie Mae, you know I've had to roam / Lord, just on account of me breakin' up one poor man's home."[16] But there is no evidence, or even hearsay, to support this hypothesis. If he was convicted of a crime, he left no obvious traces in the records of the Arkansas prison system.[17]

His reasons for selecting the name "Broonzy" are also unclear. The family death records show entries for two people with a name not unlike Broonzy. Although "W. B. Bromzie" and "Mittie Bromzie" were each listed as dying in 1926, Jo Ann Jackson and Rosie Tolbert had no more information about the individuals or the name.[18] The Bromzie name, which he might have known through some connection with his family, could have been a starting point, and with only a slight adjustment he could have upgraded it to the smoother sounding "Broonzy." With the addition of "William," his 6-foot-1½-inch size would be a natural for "Big Bill," and he could be on his way, at a safe distance from whatever he was intent on leaving behind.

But Bill did more than change some of the facts about himself and his family's name. He crafted a set of stories about his relatives that made them characters in a larger story. He described an African American family in the American South at the turn of the twentieth century with two parents married to each other, twenty-one children, plus aunts, uncles, and grandparents. His parents worked hard, his father as a farmer and his mother managing the household, and they stayed married and together until his father died at an advanced age. At least one of his brothers learned to read and write, and the church was a central part of the lives of both parents. His father taught him the farming skills he would need to make his way in the world they lived in. There were conflicts within the family, and the conditions they grew up in were often difficult and painful because of racism and poverty. It is a powerful and compelling portrait, and even if Bill altered some factual details, it is a rich source of keen and wise observations about the world he grew up in.

In his autobiography Bill wrote:

> [My mother] had twenty-one babies. I believe it because I've seen sixteen of them and they all's still alive. She said the others were born dead, three of them, and two lived to get two years old. She said it was because she had to help my father haul wood and cut down trees and plough the crops.[19]

The vivid images that leap out of those four sentences convey just how risky it was to bring a child into the world on an Arkansas farm a hundred years ago. While precise infant mortality numbers weren't kept in a region where birth certificates for children of black tenant farmers were virtually unknown, it was not a sure bet that children would survive their first years. And even though there were other children to help, the tasks that Bill identified that his mother had to perform were essential and required the strength of an adult—even a pregnant one. Whether it was in fact his mother, or another relative, or a friend's mother, or just someone he heard someone talk about, or even a composite of some or all of these, Bill brought the reality of the life he knew to people who hadn't been there or anywhere like it.

In 1946 Bill wrote Alan Lomax about the circumstances under which he and his sister Lannie were born.

My mother and father told me this story. They said in 1892 it come a big flood and they lost every thing they had and had to move to the hills, and in 1893 they started another crop and he said he had just borrowed enough money on his crop to last until the 24 of June.

They had 12 children already and he left to go get some more food. He left on the 23 of June and didn't get back until the 28 of June. He brought back food enough for him and my mother and 12 children. But when he got back my mother had twins and that was me and my sister Lanie. He was looking for one but it was two. It was an old lady by the name Lizer Thompson. She was the midwife for all the women down there. They did not use a doctor at that time. When my father came home and Lizer met him at the door and told him, "Say, Frank, you done a good job that time." He said, "What do you mean?" She said, "I mean you shot both barrels that time. You have got twins: a boy and a girl." My daddie stood still for a while and then he said, "I just got enough food enough [sic] for 12 and now I have got 14." Then he caught his breath and said, "OK, lead me to them."

So she did and my mother kissed my dad and said, "Ain't you lucky?" And my dad said, "Like hell I am lucky. I brought food enough for 12 and now it's 14." He said, "What can I do now? This [is] all the food they would let me have on this year's crop." My mother told my dad, "Don't worry, it will be a long time before they eat meat and bread. They will live on milk and corn meal gruel."[20]

Here Bill brought the reader into his parents' home, where it's possible to imagine the conversations taking place by the flickering light of an oil lamp or a candle. Overshadowing this domestic scene were the hard financial realities of a sharecropper's life: Frank had to leave Mittie as she was about to give birth because of the unmovable schedule of securing credit for the year's crop so that he could get additional provisions for his family. Whatever negotiating he had been able to do he did with an eye to the number of mouths to feed. Even allowing for some slippage in his math—if he was expecting another child he should have figured thirteen mouths—it still meant less for all when Frank learned he had been doubly blessed.

With the midwife, Bill introduced a figure who underscored the radical differences between the world he came from and that of his audience. The notion of births without doctors added historical credibility to the scene. Lizer Thompson also provided something that Bill brought into stories and songs throughout his career: humor, often of the sly, ironic kind. When she told Frank that he "shot both barrels that time," it fit her earthy, straight-talking character and provided a light moment in an oddly ambivalent episode about Bill's birth.

In trying to disentangle or reconcile the connection between facts and truth in Bill's stories, this one offers a case where one might reasonably decide that it doesn't much matter. Bill focuses the story on the birth of twins, but the family records and Lannie's documents confirm that they were born three years apart. The emotional truth was that, of all his siblings, Bill was closest to Lannie. When he visited Arkansas in the 1940s and '50s, he would stay with Lannie at her home in North Little Rock. Lannie's son Frank Wesley and her granddaughters Rosie Tolbert and Jo Ann Jackson all spoke of the bond between Lannie and Bill. When Bill described to Alan Lomax their forced separation following Lannie's first menstrual period (which occurred while the two thirteen-year-olds were swimming in a favorite swimming hole), he heightened the poignancy of the transition from childhood by employing the image of twins suddenly split into inevitably separate identities.

The choices Bill made in establishing and maneuvering the characters in his stories consistently enhanced the tale. As a reader or listener, it meant that you would be well advised to be skeptical of any particular fact he stated—a date, a location, and whether a specific person was at a given place or time. One of Bill's most astute European observers noted that the giveaway that he was going to say something highly unlikely to be true was when he started a comment by asserting "I know for a *fact* that—"[21]

But it also meant that although the specifics he invoked might be unreliable, Bill could provide something else: an indelible sense of what it was like to be in a particular place at a particular time. This was both his gift and his artistry. It is impossible to determine how much of this skill he inherited and how much he learned. In his later years, he worked with a number of people with formidable storytelling abilities, especially Alan Lomax and Studs Terkel. But the skillful way he introduced characters, wrote dialogue, and narrated the action strongly suggests that he had been doing so for many years before he got up on stages, or sat in front of an interviewer's microphone, or picked up a pencil to start writing. And when he took the lead in the conversation recorded in *Blues in the Mississippi Night*, and later with Brownie McGhee and Sonny Terry in his last recording session, he sounded like a man who as a child had sat and listened carefully to his older relatives and their buddies, and who as an adult took his full place in the banter and ragging and tale spinning among his peers in countless gatherings in Arkansas, Chicago, New York, and many points in between.

One way, then, to understand Bill's history of his childhood is to conclude that while he may have changed the words, the music they made was right on target. One noteworthy example in his account of growing up is his description of his parents overseeing his education as a farmer.

> I was eight years old . . . when my mother and father found out that I was big enough to walk good and without falling down all the time. So they put me behind a plow. I wasn't big enough at that time to handle the big plows, but the small ones, such as double shovels, single plows . . . that's when I was a little fellow. . . . After I got to be about twelve years old, then I could handle all the plows. Four years later I could handle all the plows. Which is what we call down there middle busters. That was a man's job. When you get big enough to handle one of them, that's what you call a man's job. And I got so I could handle them plows. . . .[22]

The world Bill described was one where a boy could become a man in clear and tangible ways. It was also one, in his account, in which both parents took the initiative to identify him as ready to begin the training. The first step was familiar to him, because he had watched others—including his father, his older brothers, and other older boys and men—at work using the same tools. It is easy to imagine him anticipating the time he would be selected for duty as the first concrete step in becoming a man.

What he depicts is a society in which it was possible for a boy to become recognized as a man and to recognize himself as a man. If he mastered each step in the sequence, he could achieve the status he desired. It required some guiding intelligence by adults—in this case, his parents—and hard work on his part, but it was possible.

Bill took the lesson of mentoring with him and many years later passed it on to the young bluesmen who arrived in Chicago after he had become a star. When Muddy Waters, Little Walter, Jimmy Rogers, and J. B. Lenoir were unknown to club owners and record producers, Bill was one of the established musicians who helped each of them. Like sharecropping, the music business was a tough and often profoundly unfair one, but a more experienced man could offer younger ones some assistance and guidance, and with that, perhaps, they could develop their skills and succeed.

How much farming Frank Bradley actually did during Bill's childhood is not clear. The 1900 census lists his occupation as "Farmer," but by the 1910 census he had moved both geographically and occupationally. The Bradleys, while still in Jefferson County, had moved a few miles over to Plum Bayou township, settling in a community named after a small body of water, Lake Dick. The census-taker listed Frank's job as "porter" in the "General Store." This was an unusual status, as it was very likely that his workplace was the plantation store that sold on credit to the tenant farmers and sharecroppers. There is no family lore about Frank's job change, and Bill never described his father as anything other than a farmer. One possible explanation is that Frank was no longer able to work in the fields because he had been injured or that his health had been compromised by an illness.

By the 1920 census Frank had become a "Salesman" of "General Merchandise." This may have reflected a promotion, or possibly a different interpretation of his duties by a different census-taker. The worker in a plantation store was far more likely to spend his time bringing items from the back of the store to the front or logging in the transactions than persuading a customer to "buy" more goods.

Over the course of his reminiscing, Bill told differing stories about his formal education. He told Alan Lomax that he had learned to read and write in the U.S. Army during World War I;[23] other times he claimed that it was not until he lived and worked at Iowa State University in the early 1950s that he became literate when the college students there tutored him.[24]

When the census-taker arrived at the Bradley home on April 15, 1910, he entered a "yes" in the column asking whether Lee, age six, had "attended school any time since Sept. 1, 1909." In 1920, despite some crossing-out and rewriting by an indecisive census-taker, the census appears to confirm that Lee, Lannie, and Mary, the three school-aged Bradley children, had each attended school since the previous fall, and that each could read and write.

How much Bill and his siblings learned in the schools they attended is called into question by an analysis done in 1938 by a writer for the Federal Writers' Project of the Works Progress Administration. In September of that year, Bernice Bowden prepared an overview of the "Educational Facilities" of Jefferson County as part of a history of the county.[25]

The disparities between educational opportunities for white and black children nearly two decades after Bill finished his formal education are striking. Schools were segregated and information was gathered separately for white and black schools. The length of the school term—that is, how many days school was in session—was 168 days for white students and 110 for black students. Bowden states that "one and two teacher schools do not meet the requirements for modern educational training," and then notes that over half of black students (54.9 percent) attend such schools, compared with less than 12 percent of white students. Nearly three-quarters (73.4 percent) of black students were "too old for the grade they are in." Although a program of free textbooks had been instituted for black schools, she observes that previously "many were handicapped by the lack of funds for books."

Bill may have spent some time in a school building near his home during his childhood and teenage years, but it is hard to imagine that he learned much beyond the basics. It is likely that he did learn those, because he could sign his name to contracts in the 1920s, and he handwrote a nine-page description of his life for Alan Lomax in 1946.

The same Federal Writers' Project history contains a description of race relations in Jefferson County that presents a view of the mind-set of at least one observer of the social institutions and social relations of the world from which Bill emerged.

The Negro race, is in larger numbers than the Whites, but in no part of the South, do the races get along any more amiably than they do here. There is no degree of social equality, the whites would not tolerate it, and the negroes do not wish it. The racial lines are sharply drawn, there is no inter marrying. The whites are kind and considerate, the Negroes kind and grateful for the friendship of the white people.[26]

It goes on to address jobs and schools:

The Negro race, has precluded the need of large numbers of foreign born workers. From them has come [sic] all domestic servants, and laborers employed in industry, agriculture, and manufacture. Jefferson Co. has provided splendid educational facilities for its Negro population. They have their own teachers, ministers, doctors, lawyers, dentists, nurses, undertakers, operators of beauty parlors, barber shops, etc. Good schools for the grades and a first class A&M College, with a $100,000 library.[27]

The entry, written in the late 1930s, is a stunningly revealing glimpse of a white observer's assessment of race and race relations in the area in which Bill grew up. That they felt a sense of gratitude for the "friendship" of whites and the "splendid" quality of their schools, combined with a lack of a desire for social equality, would surely have come as a revelation to the black citizens of Jefferson County.

What is not visible in this account is an element of racial prejudice within the African American community that Bill did not shy away from commenting on. "On my father's side," he wrote in *Big Bill Blues*, "he had four brothers and one sister. His mother was a mulatto coloured woman. Her family throwed her out when she married my grandfather, because he was real black."[28] The version Bill gave to Alan Lomax was that

[Frank's] mother was half white, sired by a white slave owner upon one of his slave girls. Frank's mother raised him in the house to "flunky work," chopping wood and milking the cows and doing around for the white folks, hoping he would escape the harsh labor of a field hand. But Frank married a dark-skinned girl, slim and beautiful. His mother called her "black Nettie" until the couple moved away out of reach of her bitter tongue.[29]

Bill described how this legacy of discrimination affected his childhood:

I remember when I was big enough I had to walk my grandmother to church and sit outside the gate and wait until the church meeting was over and take her home. The reason I had to sit outside was because they didn't allow black Negroes in their churches and schools.[30]

Surviving pictures and family memories both portray Bill's mother, Mittie, as a dark-skinned woman. There are, however, no pictures or family memories of Bill's father or of his father's mother. What has survived is Bill's forthright presentation of the experience of being discriminated against by light-skinned African Americans because of the color of his skin. He didn't spare his own family in his image of a child excluded from full participation in the life of his community. In Bill's worldview, heroes and villains could come from unexpected places, and a person's character and actions might surprise observers who think it possible to predict a person's outlook or behavior by his race or social status. It was the philosophy of a skeptical idealist, of someone who was not too surprised by disappointments, yet who stopped short of despair, and in fact was still capable of being surprised by how well or badly people treated each other.

Bill's extended family, in his various descriptions, was a large one. He wrote in his autobiography that his father had "four brothers and one sister,"[31] which he revised several years later in talking with interviewer Bill Randle to "seven boys and one girl."[32] Similarly, his mother in *Big Bill Blues* had "ten sisters and one brother," but he added another sister when he spoke with Randle.[33] He told his Copenhagen jazz fans in 1956 that his name, William Lee Conley Broonzy, was assembled from various relatives: William came from one of his father's brothers, Lee from the husband of his father's sister, and Conley from the husband of one of his mother's sisters. As for Broonzy—"I was *that* [meaning his last name was Broonzy] when I arrived that day."[34] The naming story is particularly powerful because it illustrates Bill's strong sense of the connections among generations and branches of his family.

One relative towers above all the rest in Bill's remembrances of his youth. In his view, his uncle Jerry Belcher, his mother's brother, was "the greatest man in the world in music at that time."[35] When Bill described his early interest in music, he highlighted Uncle Jerry's contributions. Many of the songs he said he learned as a kid—"See See Rider," "Mindin' My Own Business," "Alberta"—he claimed that he first heard played by Uncle Jerry and his buddy Stonewall Jackson. Uncle Jerry was a blacksmith, and in one extended description in *Big Bill Blues*, Bill relates how Uncle Jerry enlisted Stonewall and another colleague to invent instruments from plow points, tubs, and brooms.[36] For Bill, Uncle Jerry was a link to the time before the blues: "They didn't exactly call what they was playin' then blues but it was . . . they called it reels, Negro reels, that's what it was."[37]

No one matching a description of Uncle Jerry Belcher appears in official records, so whether he actually existed is a mystery. There is a photo that Bill gave to the Bruynoghes of what could be a light-skinned black man with a shock of frizzy white hair, dressed in a white suit and standing on a street in front of some stores, dating from roughly the 1940s. It has an inscription on the back: "Uncle Jerry?" but no family members recognize the man, and none recall an Uncle Jerry from their youths of the 1930s, '40s, or '50s. Although Mittie's father is listed on her 1956 death certificate as "Jerry Belchaire," he is absent from family documents and recollections.

Whether there was an Uncle Jerry or whether Bill assembled him from an older man or group of men who took a liking to the musically inclined Lee Bradley, he is a prominent figure in Bill's commentaries, wise but a bit of a rascal, not unlike how Bill presented himself. "Here's a song that I remember my uncle used to sing a lot of times. And he'd get in a lot of trouble with my mother because the words kind of sound spiritual-like. . . . She wouldn't know what he was going to sing until he mentioned gambling. See, and that's in the third verse, and then she'd run him out of the house."[38] Unlike Bill's mother and father, Uncle Jerry wasn't a churchgoer, and he could reliably get a rise out of his religious sister with the right selection of material.

Music, in Bill's telling, can praise, as in spirituals; it can express a vast spectrum of emotions, as in the blues; or it can be a way to reinforce the bonds of family or community if the performer chooses the right selection to tease or provoke. A song is more than just a story about its characters—when and how you sing it can have significance, too. Uncle Jerry demonstrated for Bill how a musician could wield power and use it as he chose. It was a lesson he would find irresistible.

When Will I Get to Be Called a Man?

In the world that Bill described, music was a vital element of an eco-nomically poor but culturally rich community. He talked of "two-way picnics," where black performers played on stages with whites dancing on one side and blacks on the other. In the juke joints, "the people didn't dance, they just jumped up and down and stomped the floor, and we guitar pickers we learned to play the guitar that way."[1] His mother may have objected to sinful songs, but at the church services she attended, the air was filled with the well-remembered verses of spirituals. His older relatives laboring away from home swung hammers and lifted railroad ties to the rhythm of work songs, and as he was mastering the use of the various plows, Bill likely heard some individual or group chants echoing through the Arkansas fields.

In the 1940s and '50s Bill related various versions of his musical ori-gins. Although he became internationally recognized as a guitarist, his first instrument was the fiddle. There are some consistent themes and some colorful variations in his descriptions of learning to play the fiddle. He told Alan Lomax that his first instrument was a "cornstalk fiddle," which he made from cornstalks he had brought back from the fields in which he was chopping cotton. "I rubbed it hard when I wanted a loud tone," Bill recalled, "and I rubbed it easy when I wanted to play soft."[2] Lo-max even sketched a rendering of a cornstalk fiddle in his notes, showing two tube-like sections set at a forty-five-degree angle, each with the ends trimmed. Pulling one across the other enabled Bill to produce the melo-dies to songs like "Turkey in the Straw" and "Uncle Bud," and Lomax included two of the least risqué verses of "Uncle Bud" in his chapter on Bill in the 1993 book *The Land Where the Blues Began*:

Uncle Bud, Uncle Bud, he's a man in full,
He walks all around like a Jersey bull.

Uncle Bud's got corn that never been shucked,
Uncle Bud's got gals that never been touched.[3]

It was his first experience of the power to move other people with his music: "Every night I would come home and bring me some corn stalks and I would go in the back room and rub them together and make music and the other children would dance while I would play the corn stalk fiddle and sing."[4]

In his various versions of his musical origins, Bill attributed his interest in the fiddle to "a blues singer we knew as See See Rider. . . ."[5] Bill was insistent even when questioned by interviewers that this blues singer was a real person, although no other historical account of him has ever been confirmed. "I never saw anyone else play a home-made fiddle except See See Rider," Bill declared. One explanation may be that the singer's nickname corresponded to a song that was prominent in his repertoire—in this case, it was his version of "See See Rider." Inspired by the musician, Bill told of how "me and a boy named Louis made a fiddle and guitar from wooden boxes we got from the commissary. The neck was a broomstick and we'd get broken strings from See See Rider and patch them up. I made me a bow out of hickory wood by bending it and leaving it to dry. We'd cut a tree with an axe and go back the next day for rosin."[6]

In Louis he had found a playing partner, and with a fiddle to play the melody and a guitar to chop out the rhythm, they were ready to start performing. Bill's imaginative reconstruction of how he was discovered is also a description of one of his first encounters with the world of white Southerners.

A white man heard us playing and come in the chicken house and asked us what was that we was playing. We both was scared to death because we both had got a beating from our mother[s] about playing. They wanted us to be preachers. We would go to church [and] as soon as we got back home we kept them [their instruments] hid under the house and we would go and get them and [take] them out in the woods and the other children would follow us. But that day the old folks had gone to town and all the kids was in the chicken house. We had killed 3 of my mother's chickens and the girls was cooking them and when we got things going good and the kids was dancing and I and Louis was playing the chicken reel, and the white men walked in. We all started to run but he said, "Don't run, just tell me what [it] is that you all is playing."

So I told them what I had heard See See Rider call it, a homemade fiddle.

So he laughed and said, "Well, what's that on the fire?"

I didn't want to tell him so he said, "Don't be scared . . . no one's going to bother you."

So I told him. He said, "Let me hear you all play some more."

So we played one piece, and he said, "Play some more," and we played. We didn't know but 3 pieces and when we played the last one, he said, "Bill, you and Louis come and go with me," and we did.

He taken us to his house and carried us out on the sun porch and called his wife and kids and some friends [who] was visiting his wife from town. And me and Louis were scared to death almost, and he said, "All right boys, start playing just like you did in the hen house!" And we started playing and I sang and all the white people and the negro cook and the handyman all come and started dancing and patting their hands. By that time it was dinner time, and he told the cook to fix us some dinner. We sat down to eat. He asked the cook, "What have you got for dinner?" She told him, "Baked ham." He said, "These boys like chicken," and she cooked us chicken and plenty of it. So when we got through he carried us home and told our mother[s] and fathers he had us cleaning up the commissary and paid us 2 dollars apiece, and my mother said, "That's all right, you can work there any time," and he laughed and said to us, "I will come and get you all again." He helped us to hide the fiddle and guitar before we got home.

It was 3 or 4 weeks before we see him again, but we would play every day and night we got a chance. So one day he came and got us and told us he had something for us, and he did. He had sent to Sears and Rowback [sic] in Chicago and got us a brand new fiddle and guitar. We opened the box and got them out and we could not play them. So he just laughed and said, "Come here every day and play," and we did, so we learnt to play them.[7]

It is a tale in which a white man helps Bill, a theme that appeared regularly both in Bill's life and in his artistic creations. In his later years, he would play the extended story-song "Joe Turner Blues," in which he told of the anonymous generosity that a wealthy white landowner showed to a poor black community. Bill made a point of saying that he had learned "Joe Turner Blues" from his uncle Jerry, and that it had been based on an actual person. Whether there was a real person who identified Bill's talent—and Bill gave him a name, Mister Mack, in other accounts of this tale—the story portrays a white benefactor who advances the careers of Bill and his friend by providing improved technology in the form of new instruments.

Yet it is also worth noting that the white benefactor uses the threat of exposure to secure the cooperation of Bill and his friend. In fact, he does it as smoothly as any courteous but vaguely menacing character in a Raymond Chandler novel, as he laughs when asking what the kids are cooking and then reassures them that no harm will come to them. He has all the cards and he'll play them as he wishes. The two young musicians get new instruments and a shot at earning some money and recognition, but Bill has no illusions about who is in the driver's seat. In a deft touch, when the benefactor instructs the black cook to prepare dinner, he underscores that "these boys like chicken," just in case they need a reminder that he could reveal their crime of stealing and cooking the chickens. It is possible that something like this actually happened to Bill, and it is also possible that after several decades in the music business, he decided to present his initial entry into it as a distilled compilation of countless actual experiences. Like many of his songs and stories, one could miss the savvy and disturbing undercurrents by focusing on the surface of the tale.

One element of historical authenticity is that the source of the new instruments was Sears and Roebuck. The emergence of mail-order stores with national customer bases was one of the most powerful social trends of the late nineteenth and early twentieth centuries. For the first time, people of modest means living in rural areas could purchase a wide array of household items at a variety of price levels. Choices were no longer limited by what the local general store stocked, and the size of the catalogues published by Montgomery Ward and Sears grew rapidly as the expectations of buyers and sellers exploded. Mail order was a way for mass-produced items to reach masses of consumers, and musical instruments were no exception.[8] Bill may have needed a sponsor to get his fiddle, but he was growing up in a society where musical instruments were increasingly accessible to both amateur and would-be professional musicians.

A setting in which Bill often described performing was the picnic: "Well, I played for big picnics in the South, from the time I was around 14 years old, in Arkansas, I was in Arkansas then."[9] In particular he noted that he played "two-way picnics . . . something that they have a big stage, two stages: one on one side of the band and one on the back of the band. The white on one stage and Negroes on the other stage. That's the way we called it. And I played for those things a lot of times in the South." Specifically, "there would be one band and it would be white dancing on this side and colored on the other side. . . . The band would be in between the two stages."[10]

The reality of southern entertainment venues divided into two areas that were segregated by race persisted well beyond Bill's early years as a musician. R&B star Ruth Brown, who toured the South regularly in the 1940s and '50s, remembered playing in settings where "there'd be a clothesline down the center, with a piece of cardboard or paper folded over it, and somebody would take a pencil and write 'white' on one side of it and 'colored' on the other, hang it over the rope, and staple it." She added to her interviewer, "Believe it, my darling, it was real. I tell you."[11]

Being a musician was a way, if not to escape the family farm, then at least to supplement the often-meager earnings. He told Alan Lomax that "we played around, dances for white people, and all over the country, all down through Arkansas and Mississippi, and some parts of Texas, we played around through there, too, and different places, fish-fries, picnics and things like that, all kinds of big gatherings."[12]

When Lomax asked, "Did you live pretty good?" Bill replied, "Well, I did, after I started to playing the fiddle I lived pretty good because I played for white people practically all the time and the white people liked us and they would take us from place to place."[13] The picnics were often three-day gigs, where Bill and his partner would play Thursday, Friday, and Saturday nights. The two musicians could make $50 each for the three nights, plus an equal amount in tips.

Other black musicians whose careers stretched back into the early twentieth century have provided comparable accounts of playing for white audiences. Harmonica player Hammie Nixon, born five years after Bill, recalled that "we have played a lot for white peoples," in his case in southwestern Tennessee. Nixon described playing "set dances," which was another name for square dances, and noted that he and his colleagues were well received: "We'd want to leave but they'd keep us there all night."[14] Guitarist Houston Stackhouse, born in 1910, remembered that with his band, the Mississippi Sheiks Number 2, "Sometimes we'd play for white people every night of the week . . . that was where we were makin' our money!" When Stackhouse played with several members of the original Mississippi Sheiks, whose records sold thousands of copies in the early 1930s, they were "playin' for the white people down there . . . they did a lot of two-step stuff, and then they played 'em square dances, too."[15] Sam Chatmon, born in the last years of the nineteenth century, was a member of the Chatmon family that made up the nucleus of all the various Mississippi Sheiks groupings. He recalled that "when we moved to the Delta in Hollandale here, in '28, we got to playin' up at Leroy Percy Park for the white folks all the week. 'Eyes of Blue,' that's what we played for white folks. 'Dinah,' that's another for white folks."[16] According to blues scholar David Evans, the much-recorded Mississippi guitarist and singer Charley Patton "played frequently for white house parties, picnics, dances, and wedding parties."[17]

The fiddle and guitar that Bill and his friend played were the core instruments in the string bands that performed all through the southeastern states from the late 1800s well into the first half of the twentieth century. Add a bass fiddle and a mandolin, as Bill did in other accounts, and the musical unit was complete. It was such a group that composer and bandleader W. C. Handy described stealing the show from his nine-piece orchestra one night shortly after the turn of the century. His ensemble played "an old-time Southern melody, a melody more sophisticated than native," but when "a local colored band . . . of just three pieces, a battered guitar, a mandolin, and a worn-out bass," played during an intermission, the audience went wild, showering the players with "a rain of silver dollars . . . around the outlandish, stomping feet." Handy was astonished to see that the way "those country black boys" played "had the stuff the people wanted. It touched the spot. Their music wanted polishing but it contained the essence."[18]

Bill's descriptions of what he played offer insights into the musical fare of the time and the region. The list of songs he recalled for Alan Lomax that were in his repertoire included "Over the Waves," "Missouri Waltz," and "Sally Goodin." He later told Moses Asch of Folkways Records and jazz historian Charles Edward Smith that "we played things, waltzes and two-steps and one-steps, and glides and polkas," and in the same interview mentioned "what we called reels, what we called them chicken reels in those times."[19] He went on to mention schottisches, as well as blues.

The songs give a flavor of what the dances might have been like. Both "Over the Waves" and "Missouri Waltz" would have been played slowly, as befitting waltzes. "Over the Waves," interestingly, was also noted by Son Simms, another black fiddle player who spoke with Lomax, as one of the songs he performed around the Mississippi Delta. "Sally Goodin" was and is a hot fiddle number, one that would have given Bill a chance to rev up the crowd and feel the excitement as he kept the momentum going with energetic bowing and fingering.

Bill's menu of dance music options underscores several points about musical styles, as well as the people who played and were entertained by them. Bill was likely describing a period that started around the beginning of World War I, before records and the equipment on which to play them were available for large social gatherings. Musicians needed to be able to hold an audience's interest for the duration of the day or evening to get paid or invited back. To do that, they had to vary their numbers by tempo, mixing fast and slow, and they had to make sure they knew what people wanted to dance to. The one-step, for example, became popular around 1910, and the sheet music for the song "Chicken Reel" was published the same year.

For Bill, this was wonderful professional training. He would become one of the most versatile musicians in American popular music, changing styles numerous times over a thirty-year recording career. To accomplish this, he had to be able to adapt and adjust to shifting trends and tastes, and have both the vision to recognize that change was necessary and the talent to alter his playing and singing successfully. His experience playing a variety of dance tunes to both black and white audiences allowed him the chance to refine whatever natural gifts he had. In addition, to succeed in performing in groupings of different instruments, he had to acquire a sense of ensemble playing. For the group to work, each member needed to be aware of how to support the others. It was in the anonymity of his early playing days that Bill developed his talent for making his fellow performers sound good, a skill that would keep him in demand as a studio musician in the decades to come.

There was a line that divided Bill's musical world in two, one that is suggested in his story about the white benefactor. The white man helped Bill and his friends hide their guitar and fiddle because, in the minds of

Bill's parents, the instruments and the music Bill and his friends played on them were sinful. This was not a casual distinction, or one without consequences. As Bill described Frank and Mittie, "My mother was a great churchwoman. Same as my dad. My dad was a great churchman."[20] They would not tolerate the kind of music that gave Bill pleasure and status. While the precise dates in which this conflict played out remain elusive, the church, as well as the music of the church, made an enduring impression on Bill.

Even if his parents had not held religion in high regard, the church would have had an impact of some kind on Bill. It was the dominant institution of the rural black communities of the South. The building was a center of Sunday gatherings that were opportunities for both religious observance and social networking. From the preacher, the worshippers learned biblical stories and how they applied to their lives, while from their fellow congregants, they picked up the latest news on all kinds of secular matters. It was also a place where, for one day a week, black people were free to spend time in public without white supervision and all the carefully managed social acting which that required. As Bill's description of waiting outside the church because of his dark skin illuminates, it was hardly free of prejudice. Still, it was a place where a black preacher stood as the visible leader of an exclusively black community that "could be free and relax from the toil and oppression of the week."[21]

In many versions of his life, Bill speaks of becoming a preacher for a while. He wrote in *Big Bill Blues*, "So I started to preaching and I preached for four years."[22] He told Alan Lomax, "I was around 12, 13 years old then. And so I joined the church there [in Scott's Crossing, Arkansas], was baptized up there. And I came to be a good member of the church and I was a pretty good singer in church and people likeded [*sic*] it . . . and finally I started to be a preacher, be a preacher for about four years."[23]

It is easy to imagine Bill doing this job. His singing voice had a clarity and expressiveness that likely set him apart from his peers. The same qualities would have equipped him to stand out when reading Scripture and speaking with the authority expected of a preacher, especially when augmented by the confidence and forcefulness that so often characterized his comments. In interview after interview during the 1950s, he was nimble and resourceful in his responses to questions, skillfully turning the discussion to the points he wished to make in the way he wished to make them. His persuasive abilities would have served him well in using a biblical passage to express a viewpoint or to exhort his congregation to behave in particular ways.

The world of the church made impressions on Bill that stuck. His lyrics, his choice of songs at various stages of his career, and his commentaries all reflect the language and issues of the black church. Beyond that, if part of the job of a preacher was simply to sound like a preacher, Bill would have excelled. In an informal conversation with Memphis Slim and Sonny Boy Williamson recorded by Alan Lomax, Bill tells a dirty joke in which he expertly mimics the rolling cadences, sonorous tones, and over-correct pronunciation of the stereotypical preacher.[24]

When he wasn't playing music or in church in the period around World War I, Bill was either in school or working. Work on the family farm would have continued as long as cotton prices and favorable crop-growing conditions permitted. But Bill also spoke of work experiences beyond the homestead that required him to labor in dangerous environments. "I've worked in levee camps, extra gangs, road camps and rock camps and rock quarries and every place."[25] These were settings whose existence was a direct result of some of the most powerful forces driving the southern economy and society, and whose realities must have been painful awakenings for Bill. Levee camps, fortunately for future generations if not their contemporary occupants, have been documented in some detail.

The Mississippi River is the central geographical fact of the South. Its influence on the southern economy over several centuries has been determined by its proximity and prominence as a waterway for shipping, and by its power as a source of irrigation or destruction for farmland. After the colonial French discovered that building levees, or artificial embankments, could keep their settlements from being flooded, planters recognized that they also could be used to protect fertile croplands along the Mississippi and other major rivers. Through the Civil War, plantation owners used slaves to build and maintain levees, as well as to drain nearby swamplands. With the advent of Reconstruction and the onset of the Jim Crow legal system, which switched the responsibility for punishment for offenses from owners to judges, black convicts became a prime source of laborers for the difficult work on the levees. In the early years of the twentieth century, the convict-lease system was replaced in name but effectively replicated by "an equally iniquitous arrangement that had developed alongside it—that of peonage."[26] Employers served as subcontractors for the Army Corps of Engineers, who managed the overall set of embankments that made up the levee system. The employers, known as levee contractors, operated with minimal if any oversight by legal authorities, and at times brought in prisoners as workers during periods of flood.

The conditions in levee camps of the kind where Bill lived and worked were appalling. In 1929 the U.S. Public Health Service, at the request of the public health officials of seven states, sent an investigator to review the sanitary conditions of fifty-six camps, including ones in Arkansas and Mississippi. The investigator found that nearly two-thirds of the camps' population was black, and that "at many of the negro tent camps no excreta disposal facilities were provided with the result that probably needs no elaboration on the part of the writer."[27] Four years later, journalist Roy Wilkins—who would go on to lead the NAACP—published a scathing indictment of camps he visited in northwestern Mississippi. Characterizing both working conditions and financial practices as "virtual slavery," Wilkins tells of laborers working shifts of twelve, fourteen, and eighteen hours. In particular, he describes how the contractors benefited from manipulating the finances: "The longer the pay days are withheld, the more food and clothes the men buy at the camp commissary at the high prices in vogue there. Then, too, there is the money lending business which all foremen carry on at twenty-five cents interest on the dollar. If pay days are dragged out two and three months apart, with commissary prices at the pleasure of the contractor, a workman has only a dollar or two cash money coming in at the end of three months." That residual amount did not include deductions for essentials such as tent rent and drinking water.[28]

Contractors used more than shabby financial treatment of workers to maintain control over the camps. Another study, using information collected in 1934, specifically mentioned the employer's "organization of extensive facilities for gambling and prostitution." In addition, the report noted that "the use of physical violence by white contractors and foremen in 'driving' colored levee workers was frequently reported by workers. One foreman made a practice of beating each new colored worker."[29] Bill and his fellow musicians Memphis Slim and Sonny Boy Williamson discussed the conditions in levee camps with candor and wit during a conversation recorded by Alan Lomax in 1947. Their comments brought the details of levee camp life to record buyers in the United States and beyond when Lomax released the *Blues in the Mississippi Night* LP in the mid-1950s.

When the United States entered World War I in 1917, draft boards across the country got busy with the task of registering civilians for their military duties. Bill gave several accounts of how he met this responsibility. In one, the same white man who had launched his career as a fiddler found him in his field "plowing along" and brought him and a dozen other "plowhands . . . to town to be examined." After their subsequent selection, induction, and training, he "stayed in the army for 2 years."[30] In a more detailed version, he described the white man telling the field hands, "I'm going to try to keep you from going because you're good workers. I don't want you to go to the army."[31] Once again Bill was clear-sighted in recognizing that the help he would get from a white landlord would be driven as much by economic self-interest as by altruism.

His memories of basic training at Camp Pike—located just northwest of Little Rock and now called Camp Robinson—are characteristically wry. To cleanse their systems, the draftees were issued "Camp Pike lemonade," which Alan Lomax noted was "a very strong purgative." As Bill recalled, "We drink that and jump over the fence, and come back in and go to camp." When he was asked to choose his preference for an area within the army he replied, "Engineer—I knew how to handle engines in the [cotton] gin or a rice pump, so I was interested. The only engine I see [at Camp Pike] was some of them big mules we had."[32]

A month later Bill and his fellow recruits were sent to Newport News, the jumping-off point for thousands of doughboys headed to Europe. Conveyed on one of the huge transport ships chugging across the vast Atlantic, Bill remembered later that he had no more idea where he was going "than a goat . . . the thing was out in the middle of the ocean there. . . . I didn't know whether it was the ocean or the sea or whatsoenever [*sic*] it was . . . the biggest water I had seen was the Mississippi River, and . . . we was out too devilish far to even see any land anywhere."[33]

They landed in Brest, France, and from there Bill's supply company marched to various locations around the country, including Bordeaux and a place he remembered phonetically as "Ishiterre." Along the way, they were busy doing "all the dirty work," which Bill itemized as "digging up stumps and building barrack houses and cutting down trees and building roads, putting roads through where there was never a road before . . . so you could get supplies through." For the laborers in the labor battalion, there was no novelty in performing these tasks in a foreign war. For "practically all of us that was there, the kind of work we were used to doing *was* the dirty work."[34]

What was even more disturbingly familiar was the racial discrimination that permeated the army. Black draftees were called up at a higher rate than whites, who were often able to evade service. Although blacks made up less than 3 percent of the army when the war began in 1914, by 1917 black soldiers comprised over one-third of the American forces serving in Europe.[35] Bill overheard white officers explaining that the reason they assigned menial tasks to black enlisted men was because of their perceived limitations—that "we didn't know anything else to do." He noted that some of his fellow soldiers "had nerve enough to ask for different jobs . . . and some of them got good jobs. Some of 'em was cooks, and some was what we called 'em, flunkies. . . . The rest of us had the same old hard work we had at home." But he also deplored "the way they treated the Negro there. . . . Some of 'em, they'd just punish 'em for just little or nothing. Anyone who'd speak up for his rights, why he generally got punished too."[36]

The segregation extended beyond the assignment of jobs. As Bill told Alan Lomax, they had "more crap games over there than anything else. Guys sure shoot craps in the army, don't they?" But there were different rules for the two races in determining where they could mix to play. "Our camp was on one side of the highway and the whites' was on the other. The whites could come over to our camp but we couldn't go over to their camp and shoot craps . . . because they said that they were trying to break up the germs. The didn't want the germs to get over 'mongst the white soldiers. That's what they said."[37]

The armistice in November 1918 brought little change to Bill's grueling routine. "We did some cleanin' up after the war. I didn't know the war was over. We was fillin' up holes in highways and sawin' up trees [that] had blowed across the roads. Lotta times a little man would get up on a box and call us up to listen, but I was so salty [mad] that I didn't pay no attention. [I] thought we might be movin' again and man, I hated that movin'—walkin' 25, 30 miles without stoppin' in mud up to our knees sometime."[38] Finally, sometime in 1919, Bill sailed from France to New York City and traveled from there to Camp Pike to be discharged.

Bill's account of his World War I service was insightful, eloquent, and compelling, with a real "You Are There" quality. But was he there? If he was born in June 1903, could he have convinced a draft board in 1917 (the date he gave Lomax for his induction) to accept him as a fourteen-year-old? There is no draft registration card in Jefferson County for Lee Bradley. There is a card for his older brother, James Bradley, who was twenty-seven at the time, married with two children, and working as a tenant farmer "near Lake Dick," although there is no discharge form for James among the hundreds of those who returned to Jefferson County in 1919.[39] If Bill had in fact been drafted, he would have had to enter the system under someone else's name. Given that in 1920 he was listed as Lee Bradley on his marriage license, which he obtained in Jefferson County, it seems unlikely that he would have had the need to create a new identity for himself in 1917. It is also difficult to determine why he would have gone to any lengths to join the army with the risk of dying on a battlefield, as there is no indication that there was anything he was fleeing at age fourteen. Finally, there is the murky notation in the 1920 census for Lee, age sixteen, that he had attended school since September 1, 1919. It seems highly unlikely that he would return from the army and resume his high school education full-time rather than going back to work.

The most credible explanation is that Bill did not enter the U.S. Army in 1917, did not travel to France to serve in World War I, and did not personally experience the humiliations of the black veterans returning from Europe. Instead, it is much more likely that he spent a lot of time soaking up stories of Camp Pike lemonade, racist officers, and mind-numbing labor from those who did serve overseas. In particular, his older brother James would surely have been a source for information.

What is truly noteworthy about Bill's accounts of the details of racial politics played out over crap games and the vastness of the Atlantic is his skill at applying his first-rate imagination to the firsthand reports he had heard. In crafting his World War I memoirs from what he learned from others, he was an attentive listener, for his account reflects numerous realities. There were instances of black workers whose induction was delayed in 1917 so they could complete the cotton harvest.[40] Also, southern whites were reluctant to encourage black recruitment because they were afraid of the consequences of black trainees being issued arms. Black draftees were trained at Camp Pike, and thousands were transported to Newport News, which was their port of debarkation for Europe.[41] About 350,000 black soldiers served in the U.S. armed forces during World

War I, and almost 90 percent of them served in labor battalions performing the type of duties Bill described.[42]

In describing his imagined return to Arkansas, Bill distilled the experiences of thousands of black soldiers who did serve in the U.S. Army during World War I and found the transition to civilian life to be jarring.

All the guys that was in Arkansas, we went back to Camp Pike and got our discharge. Well, then, my people was livin' down in, way down in Arkansas and so I had to go down there to my family. . . . I had a nice uniform and everything. . . . And I got . . . off the train. I met a white fellow that was knowin' me before I went into the army. So he told me, said, "Listen, boy," says, "Now you been to the Army." I told him, "Yeah." He says, "How'd you like it?" I said, "It's OK." He says, "Well," says, "You ain't in the army now." Says, "And those clothes you got there," says, "you can take 'em home an' get out of 'em an' get you some overhalls." Said, "Because there's no nigger gonna walk around here with no Uncle Sam's uniform on up and down the streets here, see?" Says, "Because you gotta get back to work." "Alright," I told him, I said, ". . . I haven't *got* any clothes. That's all the clothes I had when I left here. I been gone two years." I said, "I haven't got any money to *buy* any." So he said . . . "We'll let you have some overhalls to work in." Says, "Far as your suit of clothes, anything like that," says, "you don't need that no way until you make up for the time you been gone, that is, go to work and pay for some of them things that you wore before you left here." So I told him, I said, "Well, the things that I wore before I left from here," I said, "they're all worn out now and they're all gone." I said, "Fact of the business, I *paid* for those things once." He says . . . "You still got a bill up here though." So he give me overhalls to wear to go to work and that's all. . . . They wouldn't let me have anything, no clothes, no suits of clothes and shirts and things like that, nothing but work shirts and work clothes.[43]

Bill presented a white employer zeroing in on the military uniform as a threat to the established social order. In fact, Bill paints a portrait of what his boss fears and loathes: a black man using the uniform not simply to express his dignity but to assert a sense of power. The image he uses is of a black man who should be at work—working for the white employer—instead of parading "up and down the streets here," as if by wearing the uniform he could try to make himself exempt from the strict requirements of menial labor and racial deference.

In the vignette, Bill understated the severity of the tension in many communities that greeted the returning black servicemen. The NAACP reported 83 lynchings nationally in 1919 (compared with 62 in 1918), and 77 of the victims were African American. Ten of those were veterans. Mobs often burned their victims alive in addition to hanging and other forms of torture. In one case in Georgia, the victim was reported to have "told a white that he had fought in France and did not intend to take mistreatment from white people"; while serving a thirty-day jail sentence, apparently for making this statement, a mob seized and killed him "still in his uniform." Bill did not have to travel far to find the violence. That same year in Pine Bluff, a black male veteran who refused the order of a white woman to "get off the sidewalk" met his death at the hands of a mob who "lashed him to a tree with tire chains and shot him forty or fifty times."[44]

Bill's story also contains explicit reminders of who controlled the finances in his community. When Bill replies that he has neither clothes nor the money to buy them, his boss cannily offers to provide them, without specifying who will pay for them. He also is direct with Bill in stating flatly that he will have no need for any clothes other than work clothes, because he is still in debt for the work clothes he bought prior to leaving for the war. Bill's arguments that he had paid for the old clothes and that they had worn out long ago are both dismissed. In a neat capsule of the rigged game between white employer and black worker, he reminds Bill that he has an outstanding debt: "You still got a bill up here though." Whether in sharecropping, levee camps, or, later, the music business, the house had an insurmountable advantage.

In a separate commentary, Bill noted one way in which the army experience made the return to working conditions back home even more intolerable. "In the army you had to keep yourself clean and when I went in the army I got used to that, keepin' clean. And then when I went back they would still want to put me back in one of those places [levee camps] and I couldn't stand it anymore, see? . . . I wanted to be clean, I wanted to be presentable."[45] Bill identified that the army established a minimal baseline for its soldiers. A key piece of this story is the observation that for him the army would have been the first white-dominated social institution in which blacks could expect some basic level of attention. Even with its flaws, the army needed its soldiers to stay healthy enough to fight a war and therefore would provide them with necessities and insist that they use them. There would have likely been an esprit de corps among the soldiers that would have enforced a standard of cleanliness as a mark of pride in their unit even (or especially) under wartime conditions. Again, as with his white benefactor buying him the fiddle, Bill would have had no illusions about the motive, but as a pragmatist he recognized that black soldiers would have seen an opportunity to assert their dignity and pride, and that being clean would have presented to the world a visible level of self-respect.

In "When Will I Get to Be Called a Man?"—a song Bill recorded several times late in his career—he presented his anger from the viewpoint of a returning World War I vet:

> *When Uncle Sam called me, I knew I would be called the real McCoy*
> *But when I got in the army, they called me soldier boy . . .*

He even included the welcome he received from his employer:

> *When I got back from overseas, that night we had a ball*
> *I met the boss the next day, and he told me, "Boy, get you some overalls!"*

> *I wonder when,*
> *Yes, I wonder when,*
> *I wonder when will I get to be called a man,*
> *Or do I have to wait till I get 93?*[46]

In *Big Bill Blues*, he added a commentary on the song that provided an additional portrait of a figure trapped by the facts and the language of the social order.

> There was a man that I knew, when I was ten years old, that the white people called a boy. He was about thirty then.
>   When I went into the army and came back in 1919, well he was an old man then and the white people was calling him Uncle Mackray. So he never got to be called a man, from "boy" to "Uncle Mackray."[47]

Bill's description reads like a stinging editorial cartoon, conveying in clearly drawn images what many had experienced. It put into words the intense frustration that soldiers felt who had worked and fought for their country under demanding conditions and then returned to wonder what it was they had risked their lives for. Even veterans' organizations such as the American Legion had rules that made it easy for segregated posts to keep out black members. One black newspaper wrote that "for valor displayed in the recent war, it seems that the negro's particular decoration is to be the 'double-cross.'"[48]

But there was another event that took place during the spring of 1919 that brought home the realities of life in Arkansas to Bill in cruel and indelible ways. On April 10, his older brother James was working as a laborer on a project to shore up the revetments that protected the city of Pine Bluff from floods on the Arkansas River. As one newspaper reported, "A barge on which he was standing suddenly swung into the river, causing him to lose his balance and fall in."[49] His body was later recovered, and he was buried near the family home in Lake Dick.[50]

Although the custom of the time dictated that the death of a black laborer did not merit a death notice in either local newspaper, his drowning at a work site was considered newsworthy. Stories appeared in both of the Pine Bluff newspapers several days after the incident. The coverage of the tragedy must have infuriated James Bradley's family, especially his fifteen-year-old younger brother.

The news story in the *Pine Bluff Commercial* presented this account: "A white man, whose name could not be learned, fell into the river at the same time Bradley was drowned, but he was rescued. Workmen who saw the drowning, declared that Bradley was badly frightened and that this prevented his rescue. Apparently he was virtually paralyzed with fear and even when a rope was flung to him he could not avail himself of the help offered to him."[51] A similar version appeared a day later in the *Pine Bluff Daily Graphic*, and the identical phrases used in sections of each indicate that they drew from the same account given by the unnamed authorities.[52] Both stories identified the victim as "Will Bradley."

Each paper subsequently reported that the body of "Jim Bradley" had been recovered from the water. The *Commercial* noted that the county coroner "did not think it necessary to hold an inquest."[53] The *Graphic* described how workers pulled his body from the river after it rose to the surface "several blocks down stream" from the accident. It went on to state that Bradley lived in Pine Bluff and that a "pocketbook containing five cents was found in one of his pockets."[54]

Bill never mentioned to any interviewer or correspondent how his older brother perished. Yet it could not have escaped Bill's keen mind that James died under a set of circumstances that presented clear warning signals to his surviving friends and family. By working for a levee contractor, James was employed by businessmen whose indifference to the working conditions of their employees was legendary. Even if by working in Pine Bluff they were much closer to public view than was often the case, it is highly unlikely that much attention was paid to safety precautions. If James could not swim, as the account suggests, the risks he took in working on a barge were even higher, and it is hard to imagine that any supervisor would have asked in advance if he could swim or made any adjustments if he had answered that he could not.

More disturbing than the facts, if they were as reported, was the message that the reporting conveyed. The *Commercial* story described an anonymous white coworker who succeeded in being rescued where James failed. The eyewitness accounts highlighted James's fear and paralysis under duress, so severe that, despite the efforts made to save him, he could not do his part and so drowned.

When Bill read these accounts or listened as other family members read them, he would have heard that James had been responsible for his own demise because, unlike his white colleague, he had not kept his composure. That was what the world would know about his death, with very little added to account for his life. It is not difficult to imagine Bill standing with his parents and some of his brothers and sisters by James's graveside on an early spring day, glancing down at the simple coffin and then out beyond that to the fields he already knew well, starting to plan how, as he would title a song years later, he would make his getaway.

Let's Go Away from Here!

On December 17, 1920, Bill obtained a license to marry Gertrude Emery of Lake Dick, and two days later they were married. He had persuaded the Jefferson County Clerk that he was twenty-one, and Ms. Emery was listed as age eighteen. In all likelihood her real name was Gertrude Embrey, and she had been logged in at age fifteen in June 1920 by the same census-taker in Plum Bayou Township who had enumerated Bill and his family.[1]

Bill's description of receiving his father's blessing to marry Gertrude is an unusual coming-of-age story. The tale appears in a section of *Big Bill Blues* where he describes mastering various types of plows, each requiring more strength to operate than the last. The standard for impressing the local young ladies was the ability to handle "a middle buster, the hardest plough on the farm." It took him several years, but by age fifteen he succeeded, which won him the affections of three different girls. At age twenty he went to his father to ask for permission to marry the one he liked best, a light-skinned woman named Mary Crow. His father refused and asked Bill whether he knew that she was a prostitute. When Bill replied that he did because he had paid for her services more than once, his father flew into a rage, shouting, "Shut up before I smack you down. As hard as I tried to make a man out of you I would rather see you dead than to see you married to a red-light district woman."[2] He told Bill that he could marry Gertrude, a fourth local girl, the following year when he turned twenty-one.

Some time later, Bill violated his father's orders and paid another visit to Mary. He had just finished his session with her when he heard his father in conversation with the madam of the house. She was telling him that he couldn't go in because Mary was with "'one of the best plough-hands on your farm.' So my father knew that it was his son Big Bill the plough-hand who sang the blues."[3]

When Bill told Alan Lomax on different occasions about his marriage, he placed the date as either 1911 or 1914 and said that he and Gertrude knew each other because they attended the same church. He underscored that he was "a good Christian then. I didn't run around at all . . . [and] hadn't never slept with a woman in my life."[4] The contrast between this characterization and the one in the brothel story is substantial and reflects Bill's preference for presenting himself in different ways at different times. He likely told the story to Lomax sometime in the late 1940s, which predates the version in *Big Bill Blues* by six or seven years. The difference may be explained in some part by Bill's wish to present himself as an upright citizen to Lomax, whom he did not know very well at that point. By the time he wrote the brothel story over half a decade later, he had traveled to Europe at least three times and was comfortably established in his role as the traveling representative of the blues. The consistent theme connecting the conflicting versions is Bill's view of his life history as a collection of fluid possibilities instead of fixed events—and his talent for carrying off each reinvention.

Gertrude and the church both played central roles in Bill's story of a choice he made during this period, recounted in *Big Bill Blues*. It took place when he had spent, by his reckoning, four years as a preacher, while he and his guitar-playing buddy Louis Carter were also playing for white dances. In contrast to what he had earlier told Lomax, he said that he and Louis didn't receive cash but were paid in food and clothes. The duo was, in Bill's evaluation, "the best two Negro musicians around there."[5]

While sitting on a fence one day, he was approached by his uncle Jerry, who brought Bill up short with an assessment of his life: "That's the way you's living: straddle the fence. Get on one side or other of the fence."[6] Bill immediately understood that his uncle had cut to the essence of his dual career yearnings. He was trying to reconcile two separate and perhaps irreconcilable realms: the sacred of the church with the secular, or profane, of the dance party and juke joint. This choice has been a perpetual dilemma for many southern musicians from a religious background, tormenting performers from Son House to Johnny Cash and Jerry Lee Lewis. It has not often been presented as succinctly as Uncle Jerry did.

Bill described going home and struggling over his fitness to lead a congregation: "I said to myself, 'I can't read or write, and I'm trying to lead people and tell them the right way and don't know how and what is right myself.'" This dark night of the soul was followed the next day by an opportunity. His boss came to Bill when he was taking a break from his work in the field and offered him $50 to play a four-day picnic. To sweeten the deal, the man threw in a new fiddle for Bill and a new guitar for his colleague.

Gertrude was present for the transaction because she had brought some water out to the fields for Bill to drink. As Bill tells it, she

> took the fifty dollars and put it in her stocking and said to me: "This is more money than we've ever had and you'd better play that fiddle and play like you never did before because out of all your preachin' you haven't never brought no money home." So she said: "I'm going to town tomorrow and spend this, so Mister Mack [the boss] can't take it back and you know what that means, don't you, Bill . . . ?" "Yeah, that means I'd better play, or run away and leave you and my baby." "Yes, or lose your wife," she said. So I played those four days and nights.[7]

Gertrude's forthright approach may have impelled Bill to make a difficult professional decision, but over time their partnership began to fray. Bill explained their difficulties to Alan Lomax as his unwillingness to accept her direction once he returned from the army: "I couldn't stand that bossin' around by nobody."[8] He may have been speaking for many of his fellow African American servicemen who found the society to which they returned intolerable, but it seems likely that he was describing a more personal domestic situation, for on another occasion he stated plainly, "Things were different between me and Gertrude. It look like she didn't sympathize with me no more."[9]

Bill ascribed the final breakup with Gertrude to an argument over money. Gertrude wanted Bill to give up farming and find a job working for the railroad, where several of his friends had gotten jobs that paid well. He refused, because "I didn't know anything about workin' on the railroad at that time." He told her, " 'That's all right,' I says, 'Now, you been tellin' me what to do around here about long enough. I'm gonna show you what I'm gonna do.' " With that parting shot, he caught a freight train, "hoboed from there into St. Louis," and headed north.[10]

In the late spring of 1923, Gertrude hired a lawyer in Pine Bluff and filed for divorce in the Jefferson County Chancery Court. Her attorney, Stuart Pryce, had been born a slave, and when he took her case, he was one of fewer than twenty African American lawyers in the state of

Arkansas.[11] Gertrude claimed in her complaint that Bill had deserted her in August 1921, the first summer after they had gotten married. She asserted that he was in Chicago and that he had been there for over a year. Her filing stated, in the standard legal language, that he "left her without cause or excuse and without fault on her part, as she was at all times loving kind and affectionate to him, and know [sic] of no reason for his deserting her as he did."[12]

Bill responded by signing a document denying Gertrude's allegations but waiving his twenty-day period to file a formal answer. He was not represented by an attorney and found a notary to certify his response.[13] The case was heard shortly thereafter, with Gertrude and her attorney present, and Bill absent. Following "testimony of witnesses," the judge found in Gertrude's favor. After two and a half years of marriage, Bill and Gertrude were "restored to all the rights and privileges of single and unmarried persons."[14]

The language of the legal documents offers an insight into the state of Arkansas race relations at that time. The final judgment echoed a phrase from Gertrude's initial filing when it stated: "The Court further finds that the parties hereto are Negroes."[15] The most likely explanation for the inclusion of this statement is that interracial marriages were illegal under the state's anti-miscegenation law. As a result, in order for the divorce to be necessary, let alone lawful, it was crucial to establish that husband and wife were of the same race.[16]

The three-paragraph decree confirming the end of their marriage makes no mention of children. In many of his accounts of his life with Gertrude, Bill referred to having a child with her. When he and Gertrude debated whether he should accept Mr. Mack's money, Bill specifically said that he was running the risk of losing "you and my baby." He told Alan Lomax that in the early days, Gertrude and he "got along alright, and I liked her and she liked me. Fact of the business, she proved it, because she started a family."[17] In one exchange with Lomax, he even said that after he got out of the army he returned "home . . . to where my wife was and my kids."[18] It is possible that he had a child or children by a woman other than Gertrude, although there is no mention of infidelity in her complaint launching the suit. The testimony of witnesses at the hearing might have shed some light on this, but all that survives is the court's judgment. It is also possible that they had a child who died young, but there is no record in the Bradley family history of Gertrude or a child who died during Bill's marriage to her, and Bill never alluded to the death of a child in any of his stories.

Bill's ultimate destination in his journey north was Chicago. He was one of hundreds of thousands of southern blacks in one of the largest internal migrations in American history. In 1910 the population of Chicago was just over 2.2 million, of whom 44,103, or 2 percent, were black. By 1930 the black population had risen to 233,903, or just under 7 percent of the total.

A combination of forces motivated those, like Bill, who left the South in the years shortly before and after World War I to come to Chicago. The demand for armaments and other military supplies generated by the war meant that job opportunities were increasing significantly in Chicago's steel mills, stockyards, and factories. At the same time, current or potential white workers were heading to Europe to fight the war, and immigration from Europe had halted due to conscription. As a result, black workers newly arrived from the South became attractive candidates for jobs in the booming wartime industrial economy. An equally potent motivating factor was the desire to escape the world of Jim Crow restrictions, lynchings, and sharecropping. In addition to injustice at settlement time, farmers were at the mercy of destructive pests like the boll weevil that destroyed millions of dollars' worth of crops in 1915 and 1916, as well as natural disasters such as droughts and floods. Because black migration to Chicago had been steadily on the rise in the last half of the nineteenth century, many southerners considering a move north already had family members or friends established in the city. Their letters home to relatives below the Mason-Dixon Line had a powerful effect, especially when reinforced by stories and editorials in the weekly black newspaper, the *Chicago Defender*.

The *Defender* played a significant role in promoting Chicago as a destination for blacks in numerous southern states, where it was widely read. Copies were "virtually smuggled into the region, often by Pullman porters working the North–South lines."[19] News stories and features highlighted the successes of Chicago's black community, and classified ads specifically targeted blacks living in the South in an effort to recruit them for jobs. At the same time, the editor, Robert S. Abbott, ran editorials asking southern readers point-blank: "If you can freeze to death in the North and be free, why freeze to death in the South and be a slave, where your mother, sister and daughter are raped and burned at the stake, where your father, brother and son are treated with contempt and hung to a pole, riddled with bullets[?]"[20] In the South, a black person risked a beating or worse if caught reading the *Defender*. During the *Blues in the Mississippi Night* session, Memphis Slim described once finding a group of men in Mississippi reading the *Defender* in the back room of a small restaurant—with a lookout posted at the door. "And if a white man or something come into the restaurant, they'd stick the *Defender* into the stove, burn it up, and start playing checkers."[21]

The most common way to get to Chicago from the South in the early 1920s was the Illinois Central Railroad. Traveling north from New Orleans, the line brought thousands of people to the city from Louisiana, Mississippi, Arkansas, and Tennessee. The last stop on the ride north was the station at Michigan Avenue and Twelfth Street. Richard Wright, who was only five years younger than Bill, put some of his feelings into words in his autobiography, *Black Boy*, when he describes the end of his trip from Memphis in the 1920s:

> The train rolled into the depot. Aunt Maggie and I got off and walked slowly through the crowds into the station. I looked about to see if there were signs saying: FOR WHITE—FOR COLORED. I saw none. Black people and white people moved about, each seemingly intent upon his private mission. There was no racial fear. Indeed, each person acted as though no one existed but himself. It was strange to pause before a crowded newstand and buy a newspaper without having to wait until a white man was served. And yet, because everything was so new, I began to grow tense again, although it was a different sort of tension than I had known before. I knew that this machine-city was governed by strange laws and I wondered if I would ever learn them.[22]

Bill arrived at the Twelfth Street Station in the early 1920s secure in the knowledge that he would have a guide to this unfamiliar world: "When I got to Chicago I had a brother here." He told Lomax that he found work at the Pullman Company through a friend of his brother. Bill landed an entry-level position, where he was "cleanin' cars, and . . . cleanin' up the yards, stuff like that," but after a few years he rose to the coveted status of Pullman porter. "I made 5 or 6 runs," he reported, "then I quit. Starting to playin' music then, see? . . . I played around and I got to makin' money and so I quit."[23]

In fact, his oldest brother, Andrew Bradley, was in Chicago, and in 1930 was working for Pullman as a sleeping-car porter. To make the jump from the dirty, badly paid, and monotonous work of a railroad yard laborer to become a porter was a significant move up the economic and social ladder. Black manual laborers in this era, according to one study, were doing "a disproportionately large share of the poorly paid and less desirable work" in the city.[24] By contrast, Pullman porters—like postal workers, and maids and butlers in wealthy white households—were seen by the African American community as integral members of the "solid middle class."[25] About 64,000 black workers came to Chicago from the South in the 1920s, and by 1930 there were 4,000 Pullman porters based there, so climbing up the ranks was an uncommon accomplishment.[26]

For Bill to have attained that level of economic security and then chosen to abandon it would have been a huge gamble, and other accounts he gave of continuing to work for Pullman while pursuing a musical career seem much more likely. But he did make a purchasing decision at this time that opened new doors of opportunity for him. "I never started playing the guitar until 19 and 25. . . . Well, I bought me a guitar, paid a dollar and a half for it on Maxwell Street in Chicago. And I played that thing for about a year."[27]

For several generations of aspiring musicians newly arrived from the South, Maxwell Street was a place they could not afford to pass up. It was a stretch of several blocks on the eastern end of the city's West Side, about a mile southwest of the center of the Loop, and it offered shoppers a staggering variety of items for sale in a crowded and tumultuous marketplace. It was known to generations of musicians as "Jewtown," a name that memorialized the thousands of Jewish immigrant families whose first and often subsequent Chicago residences were in the area's densely packed tenements. In addition, they often set up their stores there, which made for a steady flow of customers—a potential audience for enterprising performers who would play and pass the hat for tips.

Bill's move to Chicago had thrust him squarely in the midst of one of the country's most dynamic centers of African American music. Cabarets featuring jazz artists like Jelly Roll Morton had flourished on the South Side since before World War I. Through the 1920s, bands that featured some of the most prominent and creative of the transplanted New Orleans jazz players—Joe "King" Oliver, Sidney Bechet, the young Louis Armstrong—performed in venues such as the Royal Gardens (later

Lincoln Gardens), the Plantation Café, and the Dreamland Café. Vaudeville performers such as Butterbeans and Susie appeared at the Grand Theater at Thirty-first and State, which also was the site of sold-out shows for singer Bessie Smith when her touring schedule brought her to Chicago.

At the same time, advances in technology created new opportunities for artistic expression and financial enrichment, though seldom for the same people. The recording industry boomed during the 1920s, and record companies were eager to find musicians whose performances would appeal to the emerging markets for their product. One set of performers whose records sold very well through the first half of the decade were African American female singers, usually accompanied by jazz or near-jazz musicians. Beginning with Mamie Smith's 1920 recording of "Crazy Blues"—generally considered to be the first blues record by a black vocalist, and one that very quickly became a hit—the popularity of 78 rpm records made artists such as Bessie Smith, Ma Rainey, Clara Smith, Lucille Hegamin, Ida Cox, and Trixie Smith nationally recognized names.[28] They later came to be known to jazz critics and fans as the "Classic Blues" singers, and their recordings and tours reinforced their popularity in cities extending from the South to New York and Chicago.

It wasn't until the middle of the decade that male blues singers began to be recorded in substantial numbers, and these men, by contrast, were largely solo performers. One of the earliest of these musicians to record was a veteran of the traveling minstrel shows, William Henry Jackson, whose stage and recording name was Papa Charlie Jackson. One side of his second record was a song called "Salty Dog Blues," and his jaunty singing and danceable plucking on the six-string banjo-guitar, along with the catchy and sexually suggestive lyrics ("God made a woman and he made her mighty funny / Lips round her mouth as sweet as any honey"), made the record a hit. As a result, Jackson became "the first solo, self-accompanied male blues singer to be a record star."[29] Over the next several years, gifted artists such as Blind Lemon Jefferson and Blind Blake would follow and overtake Jackson as popular successes.

It was in the midst of this influx of male singer/players that Bill re-entered the music business, and he chose his mentor well. "I didn't play any for a few years until I met Charlie Jackson in 1924. He found out I could play a fiddle and had me come around," Bill later recalled. "Charlie first got me started on guitar at that time and showed me how to make chords." With Bill's musical background as a solid foundation, Papa Charlie's instrumental guidance bore fruit quickly. The difference that Papa Charlie really made in Bill's career was to use his clout to get Bill access to a man who could make things happen for him. "Charlie was a well-known recording artist at that time and he got me to go to Mayo Williams, who was working for Paramount then."[30]

Since its earliest days as a frontier outpost, Chicago has been a place where if you want to get something done, you have to know the right people. If you were an aspiring blues artist in the mid-1920s and you wanted to make your first record, J. Mayo Williams was the guy to see.

Williams had grown up in a middle-class African American family in Monmouth, in rural western Illinois, and he graduated from Brown University in 1921, where he played football and studied philosophy. After moving to Chicago, he played in the predecessor league to the National Football League, where the tiny number of black players also included actor and political activist Paul Robeson. (Williams later commented that he "had the pleasure of playing with Robeson and the displeasure of playing against him."[31])

A fraternity brother from Brown who was the treasurer for Black Swan Records recruited Williams to collect the receivables for the company, which was notable for being "the first successful record label entirely owned and staffed by African Americans."[32] When Black Swan ran into financial difficulties, the owner attempted to raise funds by selling their masters (the copies of the artists' original recordings preserved in a form from which acoustically accurate copies can be manufactured) to Paramount Records. Williams guessed that Paramount might offer some job prospects and took the train up to Paramount's headquarters in Port Washington, about twenty-five miles north of Milwaukee. Reflecting years later, he described his ambitions in this way: "I wanted to go into something where I could be the organizer; show people how to do it." He succeeded in landing a position by using a time-honored interviewing technique for Ivy League college graduates: "I just jived my way into the whole situation."[33]

When Mayo Williams walked into the Paramount offices in the spring of 1923, he found a set of furniture company executives, all white men, who were in the record business primarily as a way to stimulate sales of phonographs in the wooden cabinets they manufactured. Paramount Records was a subsidiary of the Wisconsin Chair Company, which was expanding its music-related operations in response to the growth and competitiveness of the music industry.[34] Paramount's executives had recently decided to create their own music publishing company, the Chicago Music Company, which later became the Chicago Music Publishing Company. Now when Paramount Records released a newly recorded pair of songs on a 78, the affiliated music publishing company could also make money by collecting the royalties due to the publisher. It was a new business model for Paramount, and when Mayo Williams was hired to manage the Chicago Music Company's copyrights, it gave him the foot in the door to the record business that he was looking for.

A gifted entrepreneur with an ear for talent, Williams set up shop at Thirty-sixth and State Street on Chicago's South Side and quickly went far beyond his clerical duties to establish himself as Paramount's man in Chicago. By frequenting the vaudeville shows at the Monogram Theatre and enlisting the help of Cora Calhoun—professionally known as Lovie Austin, who observed performers from her vantage point as piano player at the more prestigious Grand Theatre—Williams identified and recorded some of the biggest-selling classic blues singers. Ma Rainey, Ida Cox, and Trixie Smith all recorded for Paramount because Williams signed them. He later explained his gamble that Papa Charlie Jackson would succeed even though he was a solo male singer accompanied by one instrument instead of a band: "I could just see myself dancing to Papa Charlie. . . . If you follow Papa Charlie, you find that he had good rhythm—you could dance by nearly every song Papa Charlie made. He was a one man band."[35]

The standing rule in Chicago politics for decades has been that "we don't want nobody nobody sent," and the music business in the 1920s operated along similar lines.[36] When Papa Charlie sent Bill to Mayo Williams, his introduction got Bill through the door, but it was not enough to get him onto a record the first time out. Bill went with "a boy called John Thomas" to audition for Mayo Williams. He found "a gang of guys sittin' round so I played a couple of pieces for him. So he told me to go back home and rehearse some more because I wasn't good enough to make a record."[37] They auditioned two songs: "House Rent Stomp" and "Big Bill Blues." Bill may have been disappointed, but he didn't dispute the judgment: "I guess it wasn't very good because I was just starting on guitar. I had my job for the Pullman Company and only played once in a while at house parties."[38]

Bill rehearsed with Thomas for either two weeks (in one account) or eight months (in another) and then contacted Williams again. They got another chance to play for the man known as "Ink" in recognition of the number of acts he had signed. Bill described the scene years later to Lomax: "'All right,'" [Williams] said, 'You play all right now. I'll let you make a record.' So we did. We made a record."[39]

While the exact dates of either of Bill's visits to Williams are hard to confirm—he generally placed them in 1925 and 1926, although in his autobiography he claimed the first one was as early as 1923—his first record was available for sale in the summer of 1928. The advertisement in the *Chicago Defender* of August 25, 1928, listed "House Rent Stomp" and "Big Bill Blues," as performed by "Big Bill and Thomps." Paramount, like the other race record companies, had been running eye-catching ads for its records in the *Defender* since the mid-1920s, usually with dramatic scenes that related in some way to a featured song title or lyrics. Bill's debut was one of the smaller items appearing under a vivid image of a terrified woman in a party dress standing in a jungle clearing and re-coiling in horror from a menacing snake coiled around a tree trunk and limb. The featured record was "Rumblin' and Ramblin' Boa Constrictor Blues," by Blind Blake, whose portrait appeared in an inset above the tear-out coupon that a reader could use to order any record for 75 cents. Bill was in good company in his debut, as other blues artists listed in the ad included Ma Rainey and Blind Lemon Jefferson, both of whom were among Paramount's biggest stars. The range of musical styles covered by race records was illustrated by the inclusion of titles such as "Jimmy Rodgers Blue Yodel," performed by Louis Warfield and Guitar (a pseud-onym for the white artist Frank Marvin), as well as "Inspiring Sacred Selections" such as "When the Saints Go Marching In," by Blind Willie Davis and Guitar, and "I Wouldn't Mind Dying If Dying Was All," by the Norfolk Jubilee Quartet.

A man's voice—perhaps that of Ink Williams—springs "House Rent Stomp" into action, crying, "Let's go away from here!" as Big Bill and Thomps launch into their guitar interplay. It's a song without words, one that will get the dancers up and on their feet, and the speaker's occa-sional comments pump up the party atmosphere: "Man, a one-legged man just gotta dance! Get up out of that corner, brother! Do something!" Like Papa Charlie, the two guitarists have "good rhythm," and they drive the melody forward, Thomps firmly holding down the bass line while Bill picks out the riffs on the high end that give the tune some flair. "Play it till the sergeant comes!" the speaker tells them. "Bring on that law!" And then, "The house rent's all paid!"

The imagined setting for "House Rent Stomp" was one of the house rent parties that were the most common venue for performances by blues musicians in 1920s Chicago. The hundreds of thousands of African Americans who had come to Chicago since the beginning of the century had few options in choosing where to live. Thanks to the widespread use of restrictive covenants by Chicago landlords, they were overwhelmingly concentrated in the South Side of the city, with a few enclaves in the West Side. The restrictive covenant section of a real estate contract specifically stated that a residential property "could not be rented or sold to Negroes." By 1930 "three-quarters of all the residential property in the city was bound by restrictive covenants."[40] The effect of this entirely legal segregation—which was not outlawed until 1948—was to maintain a steady level of demand for rental apartments in buildings in Chicago's African American communities that operated without the covenants. In many cases, the landlords of these buildings charged exorbitant rents for units that were structurally unsound, inadequately maintained, and barely fit for human habitation.

In the late 1920s, the house rent party was a logical response to the circumstances in which Chicago's black residents found themselves. People looking to raise money to pay their rent would throw their apartments open and supply the food and illegal alcohol (Prohibition was still the law of the land) for guests to buy. The other vital ingredient was music. There would be a piano player if there was a piano, and one or more guitar players to keep the house rocking, often well into the early morning hours. The quality of the performers and the music could be first rate. Thomas Dorsey recalled how, when he was known as "Georgia Tom," he would play his hits at rent parties before he recorded them: "Oh yeah, we sang 'em at the parties, dance parties. I used to have a circuit of Saturday night parties, house rent parties, and so forth for to raise the money for the house rent."[41]

Blues historian Paul Oliver has described how the cramped space at a rent party spurred the creativity of the dancers: "In the confined space of a tenement parlor there was as little room for freedom of movement as there was on the congested, sand-strewn floor of the juke, and the dancers evolved their 'shimmies,' their 'shakes,' their bumps and grinds that recalled the *danse du ventre* of the Oul'd-Nail, in which the dancers shrugged their shoulder [*sic*], fluttered their fingers, traced and retraced the seams of their trouser legs, twitched and rippled and did the belly-rub, 'dancing on a dime.' "[42]

Bill and other blues musicians looking for places to play in Chicago had limited options beyond the house rent parties. Clubs featuring jazz bands were flourishing, but they were generally large ballrooms accommodating hundreds of patrons, and they targeted a wealthier clientele. Despite the occasional inconvenience of a police raid to close them down for serving liquor, the nightclubs where performers such as King Oliver and Louis Armstrong played drew a steady stream of mostly white audiences, as well as their cash. The taverns where a blues musician like Bill could go to play for working-class black audiences would only emerge in significant numbers later in the 1930s, after Prohibition ended and the Great Depression waned.

The song on the other side of the Big Bill and Thomps record was "Big Bill Blues," which they likely recorded in February 1928. It was different in significant ways from "House Rent Stomp": it was slow, almost dirge-like in its cadences, and this time Bill sang. He plays an introductory figure on the guitar, and after exhorting Thomps to "Play it, boy," he commits the high end of his baritone register to wax for the first time. The first two verses are mournful, even frightening, and they use a number of images that even in 1928 were familiar blues phrases:

Mean, my hair's a-rising, my flesh begin to crawl [x2]
I had a dream last night, there's another mule in my doggone stall.

Lord, well, some people say these Big Bill blues ain't bad [x2]
Mean, it must not have been them Big Bill blues they had.

The phrase "mule kicking in the stall" as a metaphor for his woman taking another lover is a compelling image but hardly original, and other musicians had used the "[insert your name] blues" formula. But the next verse introduced one of Bill's most enduring qualities—his ironic take on life:

Lord, I wonder what's the matter, Papa Bill can't get no mail [x2]
Mean, the post office must be on fire, mailman must undoubtedly be in jail.[43]

As he lamented the failure of the woman whom he imagined had been unfaithful to him, he delivered the quietly sarcastic clinching line to her, to himself, and to the listener. By extending the sentence with "undoubtedly," he underscored his exasperation without raising his voice. In his first recorded effort at songwriting, Bill was able to establish himself as a lyricist who could say something familiar in an original way.

Bill's first recording session also introduced him to the business side of being a musician. He learned the hard way that he would need to keep his wits about him if he wanted to protect himself. For openers, Bill was paid half as much as John Thomas for the recording session:

> John Thomas told a lie and got a hundred dollars. He told them his father had just died and that it would take a hundred dollars to bury him. But I know that Thomas's father had died when he was twelve years old. I didn't tell no lie and I got fifty dollars, and that's all I got because they told me that I had broken one of the recording machines which cost five hundred dollars by patting my feet on it. . . . And when he told the lie and got a hundred dollars I couldn't say anything but: "Yes, Mister Williams, Thomas's daddy did die last night at about ten o'clock."[44]

In addition, Bill believed that he had been tricked into relinquishing his rights to receive the future royalties to which he was entitled as the composer of the two songs they had recorded:

> Me and [John] Thomas was sitting down, talking about what we had to do to make a record. They had my head in a horn of some kind and I had to pull my head out of the horn to read the words and back in it to sing. And they had Thomas put on a pillar about two feet high and they kept on telling us to play like we would if we was at home or at a party, and they kept on telling us to relax and giving us moonshine whiskey to drink—and I got drunk.
>
> I went to sleep after the recording and when I woke up, on the way home, John Thomas told me that I had signed some paper. I told him I hadn't.
>
> "Look in your jumper pocket," he said.
>
> And sure enough there the paper was, signed with ink.
>
> "You've let them make you drunk," Thomas said, "and you've signed our rights away."

And that's what I had done. All I could do was cry and tell him how sorry I was.

As Bill recalled bitterly, "I got nothing out of those two songs." He found that particularly galling because he had observed that the records "sold good." In fact, he and John Thomas had even contributed to the brisk sales when they bought up fifty copies from two Maxwell Street shops.[45] He put the lesson he drew from this experience in plain terms: "What is a blues singer, a good one or a bad one? I say he's just a meal ticket for the man or woman who wears dollar-signs for eyes."[46]

By the time he set down these memories on paper in the 1950s, Bill had certainly witnessed and experienced many instances in which unscrupulous individuals in the music industry had taken advantage of musicians. The evidence he presented regarding his first recording session, however, does not support all of the conclusions he drew. The total amount of $150 that Paramount paid to him and John Thomas very likely represented the recording fees for the session. Fees of $50 per recorded side were fairly common, which would have meant a payment of $100 for the two sides they cut, and it is possible that Paramount added $50 to that amount because they were a duo.

As for having "signed our rights away" and getting "nothing out of those two songs," those concerns have to do with Bill's rights to receive the royalties that, by law, a record company is supposed to pay a song's composer. It was a standard practice for a songwriter to assign his or her rights to a publishing company, and artists recording for Paramount generally used the Chicago Music Publishing Company. Bill was not specific as to whether the paper he signed related to the recording session fees or the publishing arrangement for royalties. In addition, "William Lee Broomsley [sic]" is listed as the composer of words and music for both songs, and it is unknown whether he ever received any publishing royalties for them, as well as how many copies of the record were actually sold.

The lesson he clearly drew from the experience was that he had to look out for his own interests in a field where the opportunities for exploitation were common. Many years later, he would go out of his way to counsel younger blues musicians about ways to protect themselves and their rights as composers.

It was while making his first records that Bill received the nickname he would carry for the rest of his life. Bill described arriving at the studio and meeting Aletha Dickerson, Mayo Williams's secretary, who asked him his name. When he responded that he was "William Lee Conley Broonzy," she replied, "'For Christ's sake, we can't get all that on the label.' She said she'd think of a name for me and later on when she wanted me for something, she said, 'Come here, Big Boy.' That gave her the idea to call me Big Bill and that's the way I've been known ever since."[47]

On his first two sides Bill had demonstrated his versatility, as he played, wrote, and sang in musical styles that differed significantly from each other. The versatility was an attribute that was a defining characteristic throughout his recording career. He consistently adapted to the changes that he observed going on around him or that he anticipated were on the way. Embedded in this were two distinct skills. One was a talent for identifying the need to change, and the potential benefits of altering his approach. Another was having the ability to master different playing techniques, instruments, and singing styles.

Bill had come to Chicago in the early 1920s with his musical résumé consisting of experience as a fiddler in a black string band playing for rural dances. By late 1928 he had found a mentor, mastered a new instrument, located a musical partner, cut two records for a record company with national distribution, and acquired a memorable performing name. He had learned that as a musician and songwriter he would need to be informed and vigilant to get the compensation he was due. All in all, it was a pretty good start.

And then the next big thing in the music business hit. It changed the sound of the blues, and it provided the next step in Bill's career.

"I'm Gonna Play This Guitar Tonight from A to Z!"

The two musicians set the stage with a short instrumental introduction, the piano paving the way for the fluid but punchy notes from the slide guitar, and then the pair jumped right into it:

Listen here, folks, I want to sing a little song,
Don't get mad, we don't mean no harm,

You know it's tight like that, beedle um bum,
Boy, it's tight like that, beedle um bum,
Don't you hear me talkin' to you?
I mean it's tight like that.

By the time Georgia Tom and Tampa Red were through, just over three minutes later, they had sung eleven verses of mostly risqué lyrics to a tune that dancers found hard to resist. The listeners had heard how

Mama had a little dog, his name was Ball
If you gave him a little taste he'd want it all.

and

Uncle Bill came home 'bout half past ten
Put the key in the hole but he couldn't get in.[1]

"It's Tight Like That" became a huge hit in late 1928, and it made Georgia Tom and Tampa Red the leading figures in a musical style known as hokum.

Georgia Tom was the best known of the many pseudonyms that Thomas A. Dorsey used on the records he made during the 1920s and early 1930s. Born in Villa Rica, Georgia, in 1899, he left school as a teenager and began playing piano professionally at house parties and bordellos in Atlanta in the years before World War I. Moving to Chicago in 1919, Dorsey recognized that learning to read music would expand the range of jobs available to a high school dropout, and he enrolled in classes at the Chicago School of Arranging and Composition. His shrewd assessment proved to be on target when Ink Williams tapped him to work as an arranger for the Chicago Music Publishing Company. It was a day job well above average in compensation and working conditions for a musician, which Dorsey continued to be at night, playing piano in Ma Rainey's band—a position for which Williams had recruited him.

At the same time that Dorsey was pursuing opportunities as a blues musician, he was straddling the fence that Bill's uncle Jerry had described. He had had a transforming experience in 1921 while listening to a charismatic performer sing at the National Baptist Convention, during which, he later noted, "I was converted to this gospel song business."[2] Dorsey could see himself reflected in the preacher, especially his religious quest, his passion for music, and his keen business sense:

> I heard a man sing "I Do, Don't You?" Named Nix: Great, big, healthy, stout fellow, handsome fellow. I said, "That's what I'd like to do." It looked like he's havin' such a good time with it, and when they passed the collection plate, they took up hundreds of dollars, I said, "That's where I ought to be!" And here from that, it never got off my mind. And I went on through the years, on through with Ma Rainey and all of those, until about 1927 or '28, and I was writing some gospel songs all along the time.[3]

Tampa Red, who was born in Georgia like Dorsey, was raised by his grandmother in Florida and made his way to Chicago by the mid-1920s. He was born Hudson Woodbridge and later adopted his grandmother's last name, Whittaker, but he was known by his nickname, which highlighted "his point of departure and light complexion."[4] Tampa's older brother had been his first guitar teacher, but along the way he had picked up the technique of playing bottleneck guitar, using the broken-off neck of a bottle, worn on a finger of his left hand, to slide and press the strings against the neck of his guitar. Tampa had a talent for coaxing warm tones from the glass-on-metal contact, which became his calling card once his career took off.

By 1928 Thomas A. Dorsey had started a gospel music publishing company in Chicago, a business decision that, as his biographer has observed, was "premature, not unwise."[5] The sacred songs he was writing lacked the emotional depth of the ones he would start to produce in response to a personal tragedy four years later. In addition, the sheet music failed to convey to preachers the need to do what Dorsey described Ma Rainey doing: "She possessed her listeners." He found himself walking "through the snow from church to church . . . very thankful to God for a good day when I had a dollar and a half in my pockets to take home to [my wife] Nettie."[6]

Dorsey told two different versions of how he and Tampa Red came to record their biggest hit. In one account, Tampa stopped by his home on the South Side with the words to a song already written and persuaded him to write the music, despite Dorsey's prolonged objections that he "did not do that kind of music anymore." Tampa closed the deal when he observed to Dorsey, whose sheet music sales were few and far between, that "there is big money in it if it clicks." Dorsey assessed his "poor furnishings and our limited wearing apparel," and when Tampa added, "Come on, once more won't matter," he agreed to reenter the blues world.[7] In the other version, Dorsey said that he and Tampa picked up "a phrase they used around town, you know, folks started saying, 'Ah, it's tight like that! Tight like that!' So we said, 'Well, that oughta work.' So, we picked out a song."[8]

However they came to write it, Ink Williams used his new position at Vocalion Records to bring their song to the record-buying public. Tampa and Dorsey recorded it at two separate sessions in the fall of 1928 before they nailed a version on October 24 that was worthy of release. A month later Vocalion's ad in the *Defender* highlighted "It's Tight Like That" as the week's featured record, catching readers' eyes with a drawing of a slender woman with a flapper haircut and a low-cut dress whose raised hem echoed one of the verses: "I wear my britches up above my knees, strut my jelly with who I please."[9]

As that phrase suggests, Tampa didn't exercise much restraint in writing frisky lyrics, and when Dorsey added a melody based on Papa Charlie

Jackson's hit "Shake That Thing" from three years before, they had a winner. Dorsey's piano provided the steady beat that the dancers craved, and Tampa's guitar filled the breaks with licks that sounded effortless. Their voices blended smoothly, and the record sold hundreds of thousands of copies. The phrase "tight like that" was popular in various African American circles at the time. Blind Lemon Jefferson had dropped it in at the beginning of "Maltese Cat Blues," recorded about two months before, and Louis Armstrong used it in his spoken introduction to his song "Tight Like This," which he recorded at the end of 1928.[10] Tampa's prediction came true: Dorsey's first royalty check totaled $2,400.19, and he bought his wife new clothes and began what his biographer called his "relapse into secular blues."[11] Among its other effects, that relapse would provide a steady stream of recording work for Bill.

While Georgia Tom and Tampa Red became the hottest act around, Big Bill and Thomps enjoyed some sustained visibility into the fall of 1928. Paramount's *Defender* ads mentioned "House Rent Stomp" and "Big Bill Blues" twice more before the end of September. During this time they recorded two more sides, which Paramount released in January 1929: "Down in the Basement" and "Starvation Blues."[12]

Both songs were in the manner of "Big Bill Blues": slow-paced, melancholy laments, with Bill taking the lead in the singing and guitar playing. "Down in the Basement" was the first of Bill's many songs in which trains played a key role. He introduced phrases and elements that would reappear in his future songwriting, including having the singer head "down to the depot," where he asks the ticket agent, "How long the southbound train been gone," and then has to persuade the conductor to let him on board so he can find the woman he's looking for. In "Starvation Blues," he set the scene in hard times, with "starvation in my kitchen, rent sign's on my door," adding, "I ain't got no job, I ain't got no place to stay." When he sang, "I walked in a store / I ain't got a dime," his voice cracked, and he "asked for a dime neckbone / But the clerk don't pay me no mind." Even under these conditions, the final verse is hopeful, as he notes, "I've got me a brand new sweetie / Don't you know I need me a brand new bed." In each song, as he had in "Big Bill Blues," Bill closed with a brief guitar phrase that wrapped up the piece with a small flourish.[13]

Around this time, Bill met Lester Melrose, a white man working in the jazz and blues recording business in Chicago, and someone with whom Bill would be closely connected for the next several decades. Melrose was born in 1891 on a farm outside of Olney, in southeastern Illinois, and worked in his father's livery stables as a teenager when the family moved a few miles down the road to the town of Sumner. He moved to Chicago to manage a grocery store there with his older brother Walter before going overseas to serve in France in 1918–19. In 1922 he joined forces with Walter to start an enterprise in a new field for them, the music business—which at the time, Melrose noted years later, "was very slow."[14]

In their store at Sixty-third and Cottage Grove on the South Side, the Melrose brothers stocked "pop sheet music, piano rolls, small musical instruments and records." They were at a disadvantage trying to sell records because large record companies like Victor and OKeh sold their records through agents who had designated territories. Record buyers in search of hits merely had to check the ads in the *Defender* to find the stores that carried them. The Melrose brothers were only able to offer less popular records from smaller companies such as Gennett. They caught a break when the lavishly decorated Tivoli Theatre opened just down the block, advertised as "A Sensational Spectacle—A Blend of Stage and Screen Novelties" and featuring seating for 4,500.[15] This generated more passing trade, and when buyers began streaming in to buy sheet music and records, the brothers moved to larger quarters across the street and persuaded OKeh and Paramount to add their store to the list of Chicago dealers.

Once they became an established presence on the music scene, Melrose recalled, they began to get "inquiries from various composers, including colored, about publishing their music or getting it recorded on phonograph records."[16] It was these two lines of business that Lester Melrose pursued for the rest of his professional life with considerable success. King Oliver's Creole Jazz Band had just started its residency thirty blocks north at the Lincoln Gardens with Louis Armstrong playing second cornet. The Melrose brothers made money for Gennett—and some for themselves—when they persuaded the Richmond, Indiana, firm to record the band. When Jelly Roll Morton stopped in at their store, they got him a recording session in New York with the house orchestra from the Tivoli Theatre, and it was no coincidence that they were the publishers of four of the songs Morton recorded.[17] Lester Melrose and his brother had become people who could make things happen in the music business, and their store "was headquarters for many musicians," who would come in to buy instruments or sheet music, or just to catch up on the latest news in the Chicago music world.[18] In 1926 Lester went off on his own, selling his portion of the business to his brother, and set out to make his way equipped with his savvy and his connections.

Bill wrote in *Big Bill Blues* that he had met Melrose in 1928 while he was working as a grocery boy. He described how Melrose brought Bill to a studio to record four songs, and then two months later he recorded four additional songs. It is unlikely that these sessions happened in this period, since none of the songs that Bill mentioned match up with recording dates before 1932.[19] Melrose remembered recording Bill for Paramount, however, and Bill's connection with Paramount was secured, at least temporarily, by a contract in the fall of 1929. Given Bill's limited track record as a recording artist, it is certainly possible that Melrose may have had a hand in getting Bill his new deal.

On October 15, 1929, Bill signed an agreement with the Wisconsin Chair Company in which the company agreed to pay him $50 for "each accepted and completed record, a record to be a phonograph record with two selections, one on each side thereof." He would get the money "immediately after the releasing of any such completed record for sale to the public." The deal was for "a minimum of four separate recordings or two completed phonographic records." Bill was listed as "Willie Lee Broomsley (and accompaniest [sic])," and he signed his name as "Willie Lee Broonzy."[20] Whoever negotiated the arrangement wasn't able to get as good a deal for Bill as some other African American musicians got in the same period: his compensation of $25 per side was half what Paramount reportedly paid several artists who recorded in late August 1930, including Charley Patton, Willie Brown, and Son House.[21] Still, for a performer yet to become established in the public eye—unlike Patton, he hadn't been featured in Paramount's eye-catching advertising artwork—the contract kept him in the recording business.

In late October and early November, shortly after Bill signed his Paramount contract, the U.S. stock market collapsed. The *New York Times* average of selected industrial stocks, which had been at 452 in early September, plunged to 224, less than half its value, by mid-November. In the months that followed, the American economy experienced a widespread and persistent decline, accompanied by unemployment that would rise to alarming levels. The record business was as hard-hit as other U.S. industries that depended on consumer spending. Columbia, a major jazz and blues label featuring artists like Bessie Smith, slashed the average pressing of each blues and gospel record from 11,000 in 1927 to 5,000 by the end of 1929, and Paramount ran its last *Defender* ad in April 1930. In August 1929 three small record companies merged to create the American Record Corporation (ARC). The labels that were now controlled by ARC—Banner, Cameo, Oriole, Perfect, and Romeo—were known as "dime-store labels," because their records were distributed through chain stores such as Kresge and W. T. Grant. The dime-store label records sold at a price significantly under the standard 75-cent level established by the larger companies. Black record buyers had fewer dollars to spend, but ARC's executives reasoned that if the company could offer them music by artists they knew and liked at 25 cents a record, there would be enough business to make the venture worthwhile.[22]

Many of Bill's recordings over the next several years were released on the dime-store labels, and it was Melrose's music industry contacts that led to the recording sessions. "In 1930," Melrose wrote in a brief memoir, "I received a request from the American Record Corp. to record some of my blues talent. . . . I got together a dozen musicians and vocal artists and went to New York City and recorded about thirty selections for them."[23] Melrose's roster of talent was led by Georgia Tom Dorsey and included Bill and guitarist Frank Brasswell.[24] Driving from Chicago in Dorsey's Ford—probably bought with the "Tight Like That" royalties— the three musicians recorded as the Famous Hokum Boys.[25]

It would be an understatement to say that hokum music featured double-entendre lyrics, as there was often very little attempt by the performers to disguise what they were singing about. It was good-time dance music, party music, with verses that were often raunchy, and it flourished as the optimism of the late 1920s gave way first to the uncertainty and then to the deepening gloom of the early 1930s. With titles like "Somebody's Been Using That Thing" and "Selling That Stuff," hokum offered sheer escapist entertainment.

Once the engineer turned on the machines in the studio by the East River on Monday, April 7, 1930, they stayed humming all week, as the group that Melrose had assembled turned out to have considerable musical chemistry. Dorsey and Bill opened the session with their first recorded duet, a slow number called "My Texas Blues." As Bill launched into his guitar solo after the second verse, Dorsey introduced him by name for the first time on record: "Oh, play that thing, Mister Big Bill. Ladies, that's Mister Big Bill from down east, making his way to the west."

Two songs later, Frank Brasswell joined the duo to sing his composition "The Western Blues" as Bill continued on guitar. Little is known about Brasswell, as his only recorded output came during this visit to New York City and another session less than a month later.[26] But before Brasswell began his nasal singing, Bill delivered a powerful tremolo attack on the strings that led into a strongly plucked set of phrases introducing the melody. He then set down his guitar and returned to his first instrument for "Mountain Girl Blues," with his country fiddle playing providing a down-home contrast with Dorsey's more urbane piano style.

The next day Bill came ready to play. He warmed up on "Somebody's Been Using That Thing," which, like several of the songs the group played over the course of the week, was a livelier, more raucous version of a song Dorsey had recorded the previous summer for Gennett. Once it was finished, it is possible to imagine Dorsey getting up from the piano bench as Melrose tells Bill that it's his turn to step forward. Bill might have played a few figures on the guitar as he gathered his thoughts and strength before nodding to Brasswell. What he did next was to fire off three consecutive instrumental numbers that made it clear that he was a guitar player to be reckoned with. On "Black Cat Rag," "Pig Meat Strut," and "Guitar Rag," Bill combined precision with power to bring a distinctive and vigorous sound to his performances. After what must have been hundreds of hours of practice, he bent strings and snapped notes as he delivered runs and flourishes with a new, bold level of assertiveness. Describing "Pigmeat Strut," master guitar teacher Woody Mann has noted Bill's "breakneck tempo," which makes the clarity of his playing even more impressive.[27] Brasswell's ability to anchor the bass line with his second guitar support, as well as to blend it with Bill's virtuoso lead, indicates that they had practiced and played together regularly back in Chicago.

On the following day, April 9, Bill and Brasswell combined for another energetic instrumental duet on "Saturday Night Rub"—described by Mann as "one of the most hard-driving rag tunes ever recorded"—and then Dorsey rejoined them for three songs.[28] One of them, "Eagle Riding Papa," stands out as a performance in which several key elements came together for a memorable recording. Dorsey's lyrics proclaimed:

We'll make you loose, we'll make you tight,
Make you shake it till broad daylight,
Eagle riding papas from Tennessee

The group bragged and boasted:

> Now we never do brag, never do boast,
> Played this tune from coast to coast,
> Eagle riding papas from Tennessee.

Dorsey's piano work provided both a rocking melody for the singers and a solid rhythm section for the dancers. Bill punched out his breaks on guitar with authority and dropped in fills between the sung lines that sustained and augmented the good-time feel. With Brasswell holding down the bass line and joining in on vocals, the trio proudly announced what they had to offer:

> Now, some want to know just what we got,
> Got good hokum and serve it hot.[29]

Bill had brought some new songs with him to New York, and with Brasswell backing him up, he then sang three of them. These recordings show Bill finding his way as a songwriter, trying different tempos for the melodies and a variety of images for the words. He used phrases, both musical and lyrical, that he had previously employed: the instrumental introduction to "I Can't Be Satisfied" had the same distinctive tremolo phrase he had used to open "The Western Blues" for Brasswell the day before, and—in an odd juxtaposition with the bouncy beat—he recycled the phrase "Starvation's in my kitchen, rent sign's on my door" from "Starvation Blues," which he had recorded for Paramount two years before.

In "Grandma's Farm," he reached back to the rural settings of Jefferson County to illustrate a relationship breaking down. In one verse he used dark humor:

> Now my girl caught the train and she left me a mule to ride [x2]
> When the train turned the corner, God knows my black mule died.

In the next two verses, he sang about his wish for his woman to embrace him like "the grapevine grows all around that stump" and his anger that her faithfulness was no better than "the rabbit, baby, [that] plays on your grandma's farm." He may have left behind the world of the sharecropper and tenant farmer, but when he wanted to describe an emotion for an urban black audience who had made the same journey, he could be sure that they would know what he meant when he sang about mules and stumps and rabbits.[30]

Over the course of the final two days, the three musicians, playing in various combinations, recorded ten more songs. When the week's output later appeared on ARC's dime-store labels like Oriole and Perfect, record buyers heard the voice previously attributed to "Big Bill" coming from a new name. Probably in deference to Bill's existing obligation to Paramount, his latest batch of songs was issued under the name Sammy Sampson.

Back in Chicago, Melrose wasted no time in getting down to business. On Monday, April 14, using an old Melrose Brothers Music Company form—which he changed with some strategic typing to "Melrose & Montgomery"—he secured the publishing rights to fifteen of Bill's songs, as well as three of Brasswell's songs. The list of Bill's songs included three instrumentals and the five issued under the Sammy Sampson name.[31]

While his 1930 contract offers some factual certainty about Bill's professional life, the 1930 census provides only more ambiguity about his personal life. On the same day Bill signed the agreement with Melrose, a Willie Lee Broonsey was enumerated living on the West Side at 1323 Washburne Street. He was twenty-eight and working as a laborer in a foundry. The person responding to the census-taker's questions reported that Mr. Broonsey had been born in Mississippi, and that his father had been born in Arkansas and his mother in Louisiana. His wife, Annie, age twenty-five, whom he married in 1921, and son Ellis, age six, were part of the household as well. It could well have been Bill, pushing his birth date back a couple of years and relocating his birthplace to Mississippi. If the son was born between April 1923 and March 1924, that lines up with a relationship or marriage dating from the period in 1923 when Bill's divorce became final. The occupation also is similar to the one Bill identified to Alan Lomax years later as his job in this period. In addition, "Willie Lee Broonzy" was how Bill had signed the Melrose agreement that day.

At least two of Bill's Bradley siblings were living in Chicago during the 1930 census. His oldest brother, Andrew, the Pullman porter, was counted at 4630 South Michigan Avenue. He reported that he had been born in Arkansas, that he and his wife, Mary, were married in 1918, and that—in the language of the census—he was not a veteran of "any war or expedition." Mary was from Georgia, and she brought in income as a dressmaker working from home. In addition, Bill's older sister Mattie had married Ben Burford in 1904, and while they were not counted in the 1920 census anywhere, by 1930 they were living in an apartment on Chicago's South Side at 660 East 42nd Street. Ben was working in a meat-packing house, and Mattie was earning a living as a maid. Both Andrew and Mattie reported that they could read and write.[32]

With two older siblings in town, it seems surprising that news of a son would not have traveled south to Arkansas, but Bill may have gone to some lengths to keep his Chicago life separate from his Arkansas rela-tives. Although no stories or memories of Annie and Ellis—not even their names—have survived in the family history, the probability that there was another Willie Lee Broonsey, born within a couple of years of Bill and living in the city of Chicago, seems low. It may well have been Bill, but the exact nature of his relationship to Annie and Ellis remains unclear.

In early May, Melrose brought Bill and Brasswell to the Gennett stu-dios in Richmond, Indiana, the first of two trips Bill would make there that year. As with the Wisconsin Chair Company and Paramount Rec-ords, Gennett Records had emerged from the Starr Piano Company's desire to stimulate sales for its Starr Phonograph subsidiary. The list of jazz musicians who had traveled there to record in the 1920s included King Oliver, Jelly Roll Morton, Louis Armstrong, Bix Beiderbecke, and Hoagy Carmichael. Carmichael later recalled the setting: "The studio was primitive, the room wasn't soundproof, and just outside was a railroad spur with switch engines puffing away noisily."[33]

Melrose made sure he got the most production he could out of a 250-mile round-trip for a one-day recording session. Bill and Brasswell re-corded thirteen songs on May 2, 1930—all songs that the pair had pre-viously recorded. As long as their names were not used, it was unlikely that Paramount would object or even be aware that Bill was recording elsewhere. Only seven sides were released, and four of them came out on the Champion label, which had been the dime-store label for Gennett since the mid-1920s. Champion was a rich source of pseudonyms for mu-sicians from bandleaders Guy Lombardo (whose sides were issued as the Hill Top Inn Orchestra) and Fletcher Henderson (whose band became Jack's Fast Steppin' Bell Hops) to Georgia Tom Dorsey (whose Cham-pion name was Smokehouse Charley). This was a result of Gennett's wish to keep the higher-priced Gennett label separate in the minds of record buyers from the lower-cost Champion.[34] Bill and Brasswell's Champion releases came out under Bill and Slim as well as the Western Kid (for two songs on which Brasswell sang lead), and one record was attributed to the Hokum Boys. The trail of aliases for Bill grew longer with the release of "I Can't Be Satisfied" on Gennett under the name Big Bill Johnson.

The May 2 session did not break new ground musically for Bill, but the marathon day (by comparison, on the most productive day of his April trip to New York he had played on eight songs) helped him feel more at home in the recording studio. He declared his intent as a guitar player during "Saturday Night Rub": "I'm gonna play this guitar tonight from A to Z!" The session was also the last time he recorded with Frank Brasswell, who slipped into obscurity after that. Brasswell's musical legacy was small but not insignificant: by playing second guitar behind Bill on the thirty-one sides they recorded together, he helped Bill get his musical footing in the early days of his career. Never competitive and consistently in the right place at the right time, Brasswell supported Bill's showcase performances while spurring him to push himself to the outer limits of his ability. In the years to come, Bill would find comparable musical partners among his piano players.

In September Melrose gave Bill another chance to hone his skills when he brought him back to New York City, along with Dorsey and two other musicians, for another multi-day set of sessions for ARC. The group recorded twenty-five songs in three days, and it was a good yield for Melrose, as all but two were released. Most of the numbers were hokum songs, and Dorsey had a field day with the lyrics. They were raunchy, as in "Pussy Cat, Pussy Cat":

You can play with my pussy, but please don't dog it around [x2]
If you're going to mistreat her, no pussy will be found.[35]

They celebrated still-illegal drinking, as in "What You Call That?":

Hannah May: *"Now, what you call that?"*
Georgia Tom: *"Oh, drinkin' my liquor."*
Hannah: *"Now, what you call that?"*
Tom: *"Gettin' drunk, gettin' drunk."*[36]

And they included comic dialogue, as on a side titled "Terrible Operation Blues," which was more of a vaudeville routine than a song. In it, Dorsey guided the "patient," a vocalist identified as Hannah May, through an experimental procedure, in which he assumed the role of a doctor about as convincingly as Groucho Marx did while playing Dr. Hugo Z. Quackenbush.[37] Once he succeeded in having May undress, there was the following exchange:

Hannah May: *"Oh, doctor, what you gonna do with that long knife?"*
Georgia Tom: *"Oh, don't worry about that, that's just the doctor's tool."*

When May asked, "Oh, doctor, what you gonna to do with that saw?" Dorsey replied, "Oh, we just take off legs with that." The operation proceeded to a successful conclusion, with the patient announcing that she's ready to start dancing, and Dorsey proclaiming, "Now, that's the way patients do that come to this hospital!"[38] Playing behind the repartee, Bill and Dorsey conducted what has been described as "a sublime musical dialogue."[39]

During these sessions, Bill recorded two songs that are his first compositions to be noteworthy as commentaries on racism. In "Police Station Blues," Bill describes getting arrested because he was "standin' on the corner, I was just sort of lookin' round." He goes on to note how he was "down in Maxwell Street station" where the policeman "left me there alone" with the instruction that "you've got to sleep with your head on a plank now, boy, put your head on your own right arm." In "They Can't Do That," he asked, "Have you ever been locked up in jail and you couldn't get booked? / Then you say, 'Oh well, I'm cooked.'" Later he observed sardonically, "I was tried by an upright judge / and he give me ten years to serve." Yet Bill could not remain exclusively grim-faced, as he introduced some ironic humor with an image right out of the only recently discontinued silent movie era: "They take me to the jail before they put me in the cell / Hit me so hard until both of us fell." He did not shy away from the realities of African American life in Chicago, and he made his observations memorable by seasoning them with wit.[40]

Bill concluded a busy year of recordings in November with a return trip to the Gennett studios in Richmond, Indiana. Along with Dorsey and Jane Lucas, he cut seventeen sides in two days, thirteen of them during a marathon session on the first day. Many of them were hokum pieces, either ones the trio had cut before ("What's That I Smell," "Terrible Operation Blues") or numbers whose melodies and rhythms were similar to previously recorded songs. But two striking up-tempo sides, "Hip Shakin' Strut" and "Hokum Stomp," gave Bill and Dorsey a chance to demonstrate their seamless musical compatibility, and Bill in particular set and sustained the driving pace with his single-string leads.

This trip was also memorable for Bill because it was the first time he recorded solo. He cut four sides, and two of them provided a glimpse of some things to come. In "The Banker's Blues," he introduced a melody using chord changes that he would rework over a decade later in his best-known song, "Key to the Highway." For "How You Want It Done?" he played with a flat pick to create an effect that has been described as providing "a harsher, more cutting edge" to his playing.[41] When he used the pick, Bill drove the melody forward, playing with a combination of clarity and urgency that marked him unmistakably as the guitarist. He would record the song again a year and a half later during his next solo recording session and would revive the flat-picking technique decades later when he returned to recording and performing as a solo artist.

By now, Bill was on his way toward developing several of the characteristic elements of his style of singing and playing. He had demonstrated his increasing confidence with the speed and accuracy of his showcase instrumentals in the ARC New York sessions in April, as well as the flat-picking of the November session at Gennett. Over time, he would play fewer songs that used the ragtime chord progression that had begun to fall out of fashion in the 1930s. Yet the influence of Blind Blake's fluid and precise playing stayed with him, and even his blues playing in the years to come would have a bounce to it that was reminiscent of the guitarist who was a star when Bill was just starting to record. Bill told Alan Lomax in the 1940s of the admiration he had for Blind Blake: "I've seed [sic] him sit down and take a guitar, just an ordinary straight guitar, and just, just play. And I've seen him make a guitar sound like every instrument in the band: saxophone, trombone, cornets, and clarinets, bass fiddles, pianos, drums, and all that whole thing."[42]

Bill may or may not have actually been present at a performance by Blind Blake, or, for that matter, at one by Blind Lemon Jefferson, whom he also claimed to have seen perform. What matters is that Bill was studying the two leading male blues stars of the era and finding ways to make use of some of their techniques. The powerful emotions that fueled Jefferson's playing and singing had a significant impact on the ambitious but still developing musician, then in his early to mid-twenties. Bill's earliest recordings present him in the process of finding his voice, and in "Big Bill Blues" and "Starvation Blues," he sounds anguished in a way that his later recordings do not. Yet perhaps it was only by starting out trying to model some of the torment of the popular Blind Lemon, as Samuel Charters suggested in *The Country Blues*, that Bill was able to discover how he could be convincing in a way that was unique to him.[43]

Serve It to Me Right

In the early 1930s, bleak economic conditions and corporate takeovers transformed the recording industry. Record purchases plummeted to 6 million in 1932, down from the total of over 100 million only five years before. The impact on recordings by and for African Americans was enormous, as the number of new race records fell dramatically as well. In the last quarter of 1932, no blues or gospel records were made at all.[1]

Bill's recorded output in this period reflected these changes. He had a prolific year in 1930, playing on over 80 sides. While that was fewer than the nearly 120 sides recorded by the ubiquitous Georgia Tom, it was more than twice as many as Tampa Red had appeared on. But in 1931 Bill recorded less than a tenth of the number of sides he had the year before.

Sometime in January 1931, he traveled for the first time to Paramount's studio in Grafton, Wisconsin.[2] When Paramount had built the studio two years before, prospects for a decent return on their investment in the recording business had looked significantly brighter. Recording for the last time with Georgia Tom and a vocalist listed as Jane Lucas, Bill demonstrated his mastery of sustaining driving dance rhythms on the guitar while at the same time fluidly picking the melody.[3] He played on five sides, including a version of the Mississippi Sheiks' hit record from the previous year, "Sittin' on Top of the World." On "Alabama Scratch (Parts One and Two)," Georgia Tom and Lucas spotlight Bill early in their party-time dialogue when they mention that "Big Bill" has come to play. Describing him as "the big man who plays the guitar," they underscored the connection for listeners between the catchy name and the clean, crisp licks he played.

Sometime in the spring, Bill returned to Grafton to record as a solo artist. He concluded his career as a Paramount artist by rerecording two of his own compositions, "How You Want It Done?" and "Station Blues."[4]

A year later, after several years of declining sales and output, Paramount issued its final record.

There were no more recording dates in 1931, and Bill had to rely on other sources of income. He reported to Alan Lomax that after he left work at Pullman in 1925, he earned $12 a week working as a "grocery boy."[5] From 1927 until 1934, he described working for $35 a week at a foundry owned by the Richigan Company, which he said was located in Melrose Park, a suburb about a dozen miles west of Chicago. This was not an uncommon work setting at that time for black men: *Black Metropolis*, the comprehensive multi-year study of African American employment in this period in Chicago, determined that 15 percent of black male workers in 1930, or four thousand men, were employed in steel mills, a category in which foundries would likely have been counted.[6]

The pay levels he reported provide a glimpse of the range of earning options for Chicago's African Americans in the 1920s and '30s. A 1919 study of black unskilled workers in Chicago found that they made an average of 50 cents an hour. At that rate, Bill would only have had to work twenty-four hours a week to earn his $12. Either it was a part-time job for him, or, more likely, he worked more hours at a lower rate. By contrast, the annual salary of just over $1,800 that he possibly earned from the foundry would have put him in the top third of black family incomes in Chicago by the mid-1930s.[7] Either way he was almost certainly better off economically than if he had stayed in Arkansas. As historian Allan Spear noted about the impact of a 50-cent-an-hour wage on southern black migrants in general, "For a man who had been earning 75 cents a day as a farm laborer in the South, this was an enormous salary."[8]

Bill also noted to Lomax that he didn't collect any royalties until 1939. But even if he had been paid his royalties in this period, he still would have had to keep his day job. The business-savvy Thomas Dorsey, who had figured out several years before that the money in the music business was in publishing, was struggling to keep himself solvent on royalty income. The Starr Piano Company—owners of Gennett Records and its two bargain labels, Superior and Champion—sent Dorsey a royalty statement on April 1, 1930, showing sales figures for the first quarter of the year. Since January 1, the three labels had sold a total of 5,303 recordings of 24 different songs for which Dorsey had registered the composer's copyright. Despite these sales, the statement showed that Dorsey actually owed the label 88 cents. The explanation was that although Dorsey was due royalties of $49.12, Starr had given him a $50 advance at a February recording session. As a result, after selling over 2,500 records with one of his compositions on each side, Dorsey still wound up owing the record company money.[9] The next quarterly statement, dated July 1, brought Dorsey back into the black, but he only netted $34.98 on sales of 3,823 records.[10] Even prompt payment by the record company could not make up for the impact of declining sales.

But people were still buying records in 1932, and on February 9 Bill made a final visit to Richmond to record for the Gennett/Superior/Champion labels. The sides present Bill sounding comfortable as both a singer and guitar player, and the experience of his four previous solo recording sessions brought an increased level of confidence to his studio performances. He had polished a set of guitar licks that he brought to songs like "Mistreatin' Mamma," where his assertive flat-picking first introduced and then became the driving force of the side. He also continued to find ways to express himself distinctively as a songwriter, such as the lament in the lyrics of "Too Too Train Blues" that "what I've got on my mind, no one in this world can know."

His musical partner on six of the twelve recordings made that day was a banjo player named Steele Smith, who cut his entire recorded output at this session.[11] Their collaborations included two ragtime-inspired instrumental numbers, and "Brown Skin Shuffle" was an especially fine showcase for Bill's propulsive and precise guitar playing. The final tune was "Mr. Conductor Man," for which Bill, playing by himself, made several changes in words and music from his initial recording of the song with Bill Williams a year and a half before in New York. In this song, he played the guitar with what has been described as "extraordinary suppleness and control," and he used musical effects to augment the lyrics: when he described the bell of the train on which his woman was leaving, Bill plucked a delicate and plaintive tone that reinforced the regret he expressed for lost love.[12]

The sides from the Richmond sessions came out under a bewildering array of names. For some of the issues he was Big Bill Johnson, while on others he was Slim Hunter. Record buyers could find his duets with Smith listed under Johnson and Smith, or Steele and Johnson, or the Hunter Brothers, or even—as Gennett tried to capitalize on the popularity of the Mississippi Sheiks—the Chicago Sheiks.

Fortunately for Bill, Lester Melrose was able to arrange another recording session, at the end of March in New York City. All the solo sides from these sessions were issued under the name Big Bill, and he performed as if he now believed that he truly was "Big Bill," singing with authority and using the guitar as a natural complement to his voice. He played several songs he had recorded before, slow numbers like "Too Too Train Blues" and the fast and powerful matched pair "Mistreatin' Mama Blues" and "How You Want It Done?" All the practice and prior recordings had equipped him to present them with the confidence of an experienced artist. He added three new songs: "Shelby County Blues," "Bull Cow Blues," and "Long Tall Mama"; some of the lyrics and musical phrases from the last two would become part of his repertoire for decades.

In particular, "Long Tall Mama" contained several key elements of Bill's distinctive style. In his careful analysis of Bill's playing, guitarist and teacher Woody Mann has drawn attention to how Bill used the thumb of his right hand—the one plucking or strumming the strings—to produce a "bounce in his playing" as he dragged it from string to string. The thumb barely finished the last note when it arrived at the next one, not hurried but in motion, which drove the song forward. Mann has also identified that when Bill plucked a single string, "instead of just hitting it with the fingers, he might alternate it with the thumb and the fingers." This generated the characteristic "pulse" to Bill's rhythm. At the same time that Bill was using these techniques to produce what Mann has called his "intricate fluid elegance," he sang in a relaxed, almost offhand way. Mann's advice to guitarists planning to tackle "Long Tall Mama" is that "in order to sing it smoothly you should learn to play the accompaniment off-handedly."[13]

During the three days of recording in New York, Bill picked up his violin again to play on a side that had an impact beyond the original jazz and early blues record buyers. A group of jazz musicians led by trombonist Roy Palmer and featuring clarinet player Darnell Howard and drummer/washboard player Jimmy Bertrand was recording at the same studio before and after Bill's sessions. On March 30, Bill sat in with them while the group, known alternately as the Memphis Nighthawks and the Alabama Rascals, warmed up with a slow, mournful number called "Biscuit Roller." On the next recording, "Rukus Juice Shuffle," Bill's violin seized the lead after a brief opening phrase from the piano, and the band responded with just over three minutes of tight and punchy playing.[14]

Music historian Marshall Wyatt has described the song as "red hot jazz at its finest." Among the people who listened intently to the recording was the Texas fiddler and bandleader Bob Wills. In 1936 he and his band, the Texas Playboys, released "Osage Stomp," which Wyatt describes as "an instrumental modeled directly on ['Rukus Juice Shuffle'], but given a Western Swing treatment."[15]

By 1934 three companies dominated the blues recording industry: ARC-BRC, through its Vocalion label; Decca, launched in August 1934 as a subsidiary of British Decca; and Victor, which had been bought by Radio Corporation of America (RCA) in 1929. Victor had started the Bluebird label in 1933 as its first low-priced venture, offering records at 35 cents (rather than the usual 75 cents) so that it could compete in a depressed market.[16] When Lester Melrose saw that the few companies still in the race record business might want to bring blues artists back into the studio to record, he seized the moment.

Melrose identified the convergence of two key shifts, one arriving with the end of Prohibition and the other in an emerging technology, as the right time to make his move. "In February of 1934," he recalled, "taverns were opening up and nearly all of them had juke-boxes for entertainment. I sent a letter, which was just a feeler, to both RCA Victor and Columbia Records, explaining that I had certain blues talent ready to record and that I could locate any amount of rhythm-and-blues talent to meet their demands." His timing was superb: "They responded at once with telegrams and long-distance phone calls."[17]

Thanks to Melrose's initiative, Bill returned to the recording studio on March 23, 1934. He had not recorded in Chicago since making the initial Paramount sides in 1927–28, and it had been nearly two years since he had last recorded. The set of eight songs he cut began his association with the Bluebird label, which lasted for nearly a decade. Even though Bluebird released only twenty sides with Bill as the lead performer, he appeared on dozens of other artists' Bluebird sessions as a sideman. The session included a piano player, which marked the beginning of a long period during which Bill always recorded with some kind of accompaniment. He would not record as a solo performer again until he entered a French recording studio during his first European tour in 1951.

The presence of the piano player complementing Bill's guitar and vocals reflected the impact of one of the most successful duos of the 1920s and '30s. Leroy Carr and Scrapper Blackwell had recorded the hit "How Long, How Long Blues" for Vocalion in June 1928, and their style and sound resonated deeply with the public and musicians alike. As music historian Tony Russell has noted, "Their way of integrating piano and pungent single-string guitar lines influenced virtually every piano-guitar partnership for the next 20 years."[18]

Carr was the pianist, and his training included several years traveling through the Midwest playing in settings such as house rent parties, where he could indulge his fondness for alcohol. Blackwell, the guitar player, had grown up in Indianapolis, as had Carr, and the two met there shortly before they made their first recordings. While Carr could play convincingly with assertiveness and vigor, he had a particular talent for establishing a reflective, melancholy mood in the slower pieces. His singing style was relaxed, and music historian Peter Guralnick has described his "warm insinuating voice [that] possessed a kind of mellow urbanity, a streetcorner authenticity that remains convincing today."[19] Blackwell's fluid fingerpicking provided a lively contrast to Carr's often understated piano, and there was an unmistakable authority to his playing.

The Carr-Blackwell collaboration also produced some of the most enduring songs in the entire blues repertoire. The popularity of "How Long, How Long Blues" led the duo to record numerous follow-up versions, including ones labeled "Part 2," "Part 3," "The New How Long, How Long Blues," and "The New How Long, How Long Blues—Part 2." The lyrics of songs such as "Mean Mistreater Mama," "Midnight Hour Blues," and "Blues Before Sunrise" ("I got the blues before sunrise / With tears standing in my eyes / It's the worst old feeling / A feeling I do despise") would become part of the vocabulary of the blues. As several writers have noted, Robert Johnson clearly drew on Carr and Blackwell's songs for his compositions. Muddy Waters told Alan Lomax that "How Long, How Long Blues" was the first song he had learned from a record, and he recorded several of Carr's numbers over the course of his career.

Bill was enthusiastic in expressing his admiration for Leroy Carr. "I think Leroy Carr was the greatest blues singer I heard in my life," he commented in a 1946 magazine article. "I knew him from seeing him around and listening to him and he was the best guy you ever met."[20] He also held Carr's songwriting in very high regard, noting during his final recording session in 1957 that Carr was "one of the greatest blues writers that I have ever known."[21]

Bill had already recorded a few times in a piano-guitar duo format with Georgia Tom Dorsey.[22] Each time it had been a matter of two or three songs squeezed into a multi-day set of recordings with a variety of participants. Bill's duo recordings with Georgia Tom reflect the comfortable and fruitful connection between the two men. It was a musical partnership that benefited both artists and that may well have predated their recording career. Dorsey later recalled that "we recorded together, worked together. Just around here [Chicago] in the suburbs. Somebody want to play, we'd get somethin' like Chicago Heights or Gary [Indiana], we'd go out and do that. That's as far as we got." This was during the same period that Dorsey was working with Tampa Red: "You'd work with anybody if you could get to where they gon' get paid. Tampa and I were a steady team, but if I wasn't working tomorrow night and Bill wanted me, I'd go on with Bill, see."[23]

Blues historians differ as to the identity of the pianist at Broonzy's March 1934 session.[24] But whoever he was, his reason for being there was to support Bill, and Bill responded with expressive vocals complemented by well-placed guitar fills. He was recording as the featured artist, playing exclusively songs he had composed, and accenting his singing with instrumental phrases that highlighted the words or reinforced the mood. Paul Oliver has linked the overall effect to two of Bill's influences: "He had the intonation of Leroy Carr with much of the effortless instrumental technique of Scrapper Blackwell."[25]

The songs reflected the suffering and desperation that Bill's audience had been enduring for the previous several years. In "Hungry Man Blues," he sang:

My wife is hungry, lord, and my baby, too [x2]
I've got the blues so bad, mama, I don't know what to do.

And:

Mama, my stomach's cryin' mercy, my pocket, I ain't got a dime [x2]
Neckbones is four cents a pound, baby, they keep me hungry all the time.[26]

In "Bull Cow Blues No. 2," he asked:

When you sell your cotton, please don't sell the seed [x2]
So when this winter get hard, baby, I won't have to eat grass and weeds.[27]

In "Milk Cow Blues," he used the same phrase of the cow in question having to "eat grass and weeds" when times get hard. He may have been living and recording in Chicago, but he knew that the images would resonate with his listeners, whether they were in the urban North or the rural South. He reprised 1928's "Starvation Blues," keeping the bleak first verse intact while adding an even darker concluding stanza:

When you see a little black wagon come rollin' to your door [x2]
Mama, you don't need no tellin' that I've found some place to go.[28]

But despite the stresses of Depression-era America, Bill's topics extended beyond social commentary to the relations between men and women. In "Serve It to Me Right," food was an easily recognized metaphor for affection and sex when he complained:

When I sit down to eat, you feed me peas and bread
When you cook chicken and cakes, you give it to Old Nasty Red.[29]

By casting people in animal forms, as in "Milk Cow Blues," he could turn a memorable phrase while lamenting a lost love:

Have you seen a big brown cow, she have no horns at all? [x2]
You don't need no chair to milk her, she will back right in your stall.[30]

He sang of the ache of separation in "Mississippi River Blues":

Mississippi River is so long, deep, and wide,
I can see my good girl standin' on that other side.

Then later:

I cried and I called, I could not make my baby hear . . .

And finally:

I went down to the landing to see if any boats were there
And the ferryman told me he could not find no boats nowhere.[31]

There is an almost dreamlike quality to his vision of a man whose beloved is in sight but with whom he cannot communicate, and when he tries to arrange for help, none can be found. He's describing a distance that is as much emotional as it is physical, and Bill's voice conveys the pain of being held apart from his woman by something so "long, deep, and wide." The eight-bar melody follows the chord progression of "The Banker's Blues" and anticipated that of "Key to the Highway."

With his June sessions for Bluebird, Bill began the next phase of his career. From that point through the late 1940s, Bill occupied two distinct positions in the blues recording world. As "Big Bill," he was one of the most productive and best-known artists in the business, with a name that was familiar to his audiences and reinforced by his easily recognized singing style. At the same time, he became the first-call studio guitarist for dozens of recording sessions that Lester Melrose organized for several record companies, particularly Bluebird. In that capacity, he was an integral part of the distinctive sound of numerous musicians, including some of the most prominent blues artists of the era.

Two artists whose careers were interwoven with Bill's were Washboard Sam and Jazz Gillum. Bill played guitar on almost every one of the more than 150 recordings that Sam made over a period of twenty years, as well as on many of the sides that Gillum recorded. From the mid-1930s into the late 1940s, the two musicians were among the most popular of the artists whose records were primarily bought by African American fans.

Washboard Sam's real name was Robert Brown. According to his 1937 application for a Social Security number, he was born on July 15, 1903, in Jackson, Tennessee, to Henry Brown and Mary Brown. He noted specifically on the form that his mother's maiden name was the same as his father's. Bill frequently referred to Washboard Sam as his half-brother, and he included an extended and gripping story in *Big Bill Blues* describing his mother's swift and furious response to the discovery that her husband had fathered Sam and several other children with another woman. Although the historical record doesn't back up his yarn, Bill's wish to draw Sam into his family circle may have reflected the affinity he felt for a musician with whom he could so consistently find a musical groove.[32]

At some point in his youth, Sam traveled the seventy-five miles southwest from Jackson to Memphis. Harmonica player and jug blower Hammie Nixon recalled seeing the young musician there: "He was a kid, always well dressed. He'd play his washboard with any musician on the streets. He followed [Nixon's musical partner, guitarist] Sleepy John [Estes] and me, and often played with us. He was called Bob Brown then. . . . I don't know why he called himself Sam."[33] By the mid-1930s, Sam had arrived in Chicago.

The washboard had emerged as a percussion instrument sometime in the late nineteenth or early twentieth century, as first amateur and then professional musicians found that the ancestor of the washing machine could provide a strong rhythmic complement to their vocals when they dragged a stick or thimble across the corrugated metal between the wooden frames. Groups with a washboard in the lineup, and sometimes even in the name of the band, had recorded since the early 1920s, and the celebrated New Orleans percussion wizard Baby Dodds was one of many drummers who incorporated a washboard into his array of instruments.

Sam became one of the most-recorded blues musicians of the 1930s and '40s because of the combination of his instrument, his singing, and his sidemen. The sound of his washboard gave him an identifiable niche in the increasingly crowded field of race record releases once the industry started back up again in 1934. His voice was powerful, sounding much less polished than Bill or Tampa Red, and often with a vibrato that accentuated the emotions he was describing. He was primarily backed up by Bill, whose jaunty fills gave a big-city flavor to Sam's rougher singing and often rural topics. In addition, Sam's piano players were among the best in the business, including Black Bob, Joshua Altheimer, Roosevelt Sykes, and Memphis Slim. Because all of the musicians, including Sam, were recording regularly with each other, the comfort they felt playing with each other was apparent.

William McKinley "Jazz" Gillum was probably born on September 11, 1904, in Indianola, Mississippi, where he was orphaned at an early age.[34] His first instrument was the harmonium, or pump organ, which was operated by foot pedals. It belonged to the uncle who raised him, and who would punish him if he used it to play blues instead of church music.

After learning to play the harmonica, he moved around Mississippi several times as a teenager and may have acquired his nickname because of his efforts at dressing sharply, or in a "jazzy" style. He supplemented his income as a drugstore clerk in Greenwood by playing and singing on the streets, and he was haunted by memories of being driven by whites to a remote dirt road and forced at gunpoint to dance for their amusement.[35]

Harmonicas had become popular in the United States during the latter part of the nineteenth century for a number of reasons. Manufacturers could produce them in mass quantities, so they were inexpensive and readily available. Even a novice player could use the instrument—which was also known as a mouth harp or French harp—to re-create the familiar sound of a train whistle or a steam engine, or to mimic a fox chase. A skilled performer could produce unusually evocative sounds that ranged from mournful to joyful, and both white and black musicians incorporated harmonicas into their performances and recordings of the 1920s and '30s.

Having arrived in Chicago some years previously, Gillum cut his first record for Bluebird in 1934, almost certainly because Bill had brought him to Melrose's attention. He became a mainstay of the Bluebird label in the 1930s and '40s, with over seventy recordings as a lead performer and many more as a sideman. His vocal style was relaxed, and his harmonica technique was easy and unforced. When he combined these attributes with lyrics that frequently referred to his southern rural background, Gillum offered listeners a reliable source of entertainment for listening and dancing. In the words of music writer Neil Slaven, "It's rare to hear Gillum straining for a note with either voice or instrument."[36]

In addition to being a talented vocalist and a skilled guitarist, Bill was a gifted songwriter, and a prolific one. From the very beginning of his career, he had recorded his own songs. When record companies began recording again in earnest in 1934, his connection with Lester Melrose brought him prominence and regular work as a musician. But for Bill, their business arrangement came at a price that cast an enduring shadow over their personal relationship.

The issue that put them in conflict involved royalty payments for the songs that Bill composed. The prevailing practice in the music industry was for publishing royalties to be split evenly between the composer (in this case, Bill) and the publisher (Melrose). When Bill signed music publishing contracts with Melrose, first in April 1930 and again in March 1934, he had to give up half of the 50 percent share to which he would normally have been entitled. As a result, Bill had to agree that Melrose as the publisher would receive 75 percent of the publishing royalties, and he would receive only 25 percent as the composer.[37]

Bill had little choice but to accept this arrangement if he wanted to continue to work with Melrose. He would almost certainly have seen it as a reduction in income that was legitimately his because the songs were his creations. Over time, Bill would characterize Melrose in harsh terms, accusing him of exploiting him and other blues artists in a variety of ways.

From Lester Melrose's perspective, however, securing the lion's share of the publishing royalties was an integral part of his business strategy, one that made it possible for him to sustain his role in the music industry. He was a freelance entrepreneur operating independently of both the musicians and the record companies. He was not a salaried employee of any record label. When he received or generated a request from a company for a recording session, he was expected to deliver material that could be pressed, shipped, and sold. The payment he received to supervise the session was all he would receive, no matter how well the record sold. He likely considered the half of the composer's royalties that went to him to be his insurance policy against slow periods for recording sessions.

In addition, few blues musicians in the 1920s and '30s were aware that if they wanted to secure their rights to composer's royalties, they needed to follow a designated procedure. Even if the musicians had known it, many would have needed another person to put their songs into standard musical notation, as not every artist who recorded a song could read and write music. The key to establishing the composer's copyright for any given song was to submit a copy of the song with musical notation and lyrics (known as a "lead sheet") to the Copyright Office of the Library of Congress. As a result, music publishers generally assumed this task; for example, this was the job that the young Thomas Dorsey had done for Ink Williams at the Chicago Music Publishing Company.

Bob Koester, owner of Chicago-based Delmark Records, has spoken of Lester Melrose with admiration for his accomplishments. As Koester has pointed out, Melrose was a businessman operating on thin margins in a difficult environment. In particular, the amount due to composers and publishers was relatively small in absolute dollars in the 1930s and '40s because Bluebird records only sold for 35 cents each. Even if a record sold 10,000 copies, which would have been a huge seller, the total dollar base off of which a percentage would have been calculated was only $3,500. So if the royalty was 1 cent per record—as reflected on royalty statements from the 1940s—it would have resulted in a total royalty payment to Melrose of $35. After giving Bill the 25 percent due him as composer under the contract, Melrose would have netted a total of $26.25, which, if he had received it in 1944, would have been the equivalent of $325 in 2010 dollars.[38] What made this arrangement work powerfully to Melrose's advantage was his ability to get the additional percentage from enough composers whose songs would generate a sufficient amount of royalties over time.

Finally, as Koester once wrote about Melrose, "Lester Melrose is remembered with unusual fondness by the artists he recorded. There are noticeably fewer complaints of sharp practices and frequent praise of his musical perceptions and social attitudes."[39] Koester knew and recorded a number of artists who had worked with Melrose, and his assessment of Melrose is that "I think he earned the extra points."[40]

While other musicians shared Bill's reservations about Melrose's business practices, they had few options if they wanted to record in Chicago in the mid- to late 1930s. The primary alternative was Ink Williams at Decca, and, like Melrose, he had recognized the value of the publishing rights a decade before. In any event, as musician and songwriter Willie Dixon recalled in his memoirs, "Very few black artists at that time had a contract with the company. They had to have their contract with the go-between man."[41] Bill may have had to sign contracts that were less than ideal for him, but he was signing them with a go-between man who had real clout. The record companies wanted to make race records again, and they needed Lester Melrose to find them some artists whose discs would sell. Both Melrose and Bill were well positioned as a new era of blues recording in Chicago began.

State Street Boys

By the mid-1930s, the musical tastes of African American record buyers were changing. Instead of solo performers accompanying themselves on guitar, records increasingly featured ensembles, usually with a piano. The style that guitar-piano pairings like Leroy Carr and Scrapper Blackwell had popularized became the musical foundation for hundreds of recordings.

Chicago was now the center for recording this popular style of blues. Many musicians had moved there, and others who lived in nearby cities, such as St. Louis, could get there on short notice. Like Bill, they mostly worked day jobs to pay the rent, but they could always manage to be in the studio when Lester Melrose and Ink Williams scheduled recording sessions.

Bill's recording career took off in this era, and his prodigious output was nearly unmatched among blues musicians. From 1934 until 1942, when the combination of a musicians' union ban and the diversion of shellac to the war effort halted virtually all recording for two years, Bill averaged better than thirteen double-sided 78 rpm records each year as a featured artist. In addition, he played on an average of forty-eight sides each year as a sideman. In other words, for nearly a decade, he averaged one new Big Bill record a month, and he appeared on two more as a studio guitarist. It was a pace that only Tampa Red could match as a lead performer, and one that no other blues guitarist could approach as a sideman.

Bill's output in this period was greatly aided by a shift in the model of record production. As record companies emerged from the bleak days of the early 1930s, they wanted to be sure that they could recoup their investment in making and selling records. It was a strikingly different approach from the methods that prevailed in the mid- to late 1920s, when record companies could afford to send teams to a dozen or more southern cities and towns to record local talent, anticipating that some of the unknown artists would come up with hits. Now, record buyers were indicating that they liked the sound of the urban blues with the guitar-piano combination at its core. The goal for recordings was now consistency, and individual performers identified themselves through distinctive vocal styles or recognizable instrumental work.

Both Lester Melrose and Ink Williams could recognize an opportunity as it was developing, and Melrose in particular moved to seize the moment. He quickly made himself indispensable to all of the players in the Chicago blues recording business. Blues historian Mike Rowe has described Melrose's strategy:

> Melrose had more than a large stable of blues artists under his control. Since only a few of them had regular accompanists most of them would play on each other's records and thus Melrose had a completely self-contained unit which made great sense economically, if less artistically. . . . Melrose had effected the greatest rationalisation in blues recording. Whereas the major companies had clumsily sought to record artists who sounded like each other, the Melrose machine provided them with artists who *were* each other![1]

As time went on, Melrose integrated a rehearsal space into his cost-conscious business model. A week or so before a session, Melrose would assemble the musicians in the house at 3432 South State Street, where Tampa Red and his wife lived. Pianist Blind John Davis, who began working for Melrose in the mid-1930s as an arranger, recalled that Tampa Red "had a house, it went all the way from the front to the alley. He had a big rehearsal room, and he had two rooms for the different artists who came in from out of town to record. They would stay there. Unless they know someone in Chicago, they stayed there. . . . Melrose would pay [Tampa] for the lodging, and Mrs. Tampa would cook." The musicians would spend days getting the repertoire ready for the recording session so that Melrose could be sure of delivering the product he had promised the record company. Fewer takes in the recording studio meant lower costs for the record companies, reinforcing the wisdom of using Melrose as their independent contractor.[2]

Bill was an integral part of Melrose's operation. By the mid-1930s, his records were reliable sellers, as record buyers knew what they were getting when they bought the latest 78 by "Big Bill." His steady presence on the guitar helped break in new performers like Washboard Sam and Jazz Gillum, and he also provided solid backing for better-known artists such as Bumble Bee Slim, Casey Bill Weldon, and Merline Johnson, the "Yas Yas Girl."

Bill also provided the Melrose music powerhouse with two other key dimensions. First, he was a prolific songwriter, which was a crucial element of the industrial-style production process. Bill's various estimates of the number of songs that he wrote throughout his career ranged from 250 to 360. In addition to the ones Bill himself sang, other Melrose artists recorded songs that Bill had written. The list included the Yas Yas Girl, Lil Green, and Washboard Sam, of whom Bill said with pride in his autobiography, "I wrote many blues for him."[3] Bill's ability to generate material was very useful to Melrose, as he delivered to RCA Victor and Columbia the product they were counting on.

In addition, Melrose was constantly on the lookout for new talent, both to generate records and to increase the stream of royalties flowing into his publishing companies. He relied on a small number of musicians to serve as his eyes and ears in identifying prospective artists. Along with pianist Roosevelt Sykes, Bill was at the top of his list. Melrose was shrewd in choosing Bill for this assignment, as it was a superb fit. Bill was a prominent figure among the musicians, and he was a gregarious, well-liked, and trusted person.

Melrose described searching for artists in "clubs, taverns, and booze joints in and around Chicago," as well as "all through the Southern states." The headstrong entrepreneur ran into some difficulties on at least one occasion when he chose to ignore Bill's advice.[4] In his autobiography, Bill told of the guidance he offered Melrose in advance of a trip to Mississippi to bring blues singer and guitarist Tommy McClennan to Chicago to record for the first time:

> When Mr. Melrose, who is a white man, went to get Tommy I told him what he should do to keep out of trouble in Mississippi, but he told me that he knew and that he was a white man, too.
>
> "It doesn't matter in Mississippi," I told him. "You's a Northern white man and they don't like you down there if they see you around Negroes, talking to them. Get some Negro out of town to go and talk to Tommy."
>
> But no, he wouldn't do like I told him and he did get in trouble—and

a lot of it too, because he had to run and leave his car and send back after it and leave money for Tommy to come to Chicago. When I saw him he laughed and said:

"Bill, you was damn right, they don't like me down there."

Tommy lived on a farm about fifteen miles out of Yazoo City and there ain't but one road, that means one way to go out there and one way to come back and you have to pass the bosses' house both times, so they know a stranger's there and they hate it.

"They don't call me a white man down there," Mr. Melrose told me. "They call me a Yankee. What does that mean, Bill?"

"I told you they don't like a white man from the North out on their farm or anywhere they have five or six hundred Negroes working. I told you that you might get hurt out on one of them farms or camps."

"Get hurt, get hurt, hell, they nearly killed me, and they would have done it if I hadn't run like hell. I'll certainly never go down there again."

So he used to send me all the time after artists. He never did go down South again.[5]

Through the end of 1934, Bill returned to the studio for sessions in June and October, cutting thirteen sides as a leader and two dozen more playing guitar behind other artists. The most unusual recordings Bill made in these months were the pair he cut in October when he turned again to the fiddle on two vigorous takes of "See See Rider." In addition to the memories he may have had from his childhood encounter with the mysterious traveling bluesman of the same name, Bill would likely have known the song from Ma Rainey's 1924 version, as well as from Blind Lemon Jefferson's 1926 recording of "Corrina Blues." Bill would return to the song decades later, when it became a staple of his 1950s repertoire.

The fiddle was soon back in Bill's hands for one of the most distinctive Chicago recording sessions of the era. On January 10, 1935, he was a member of a group that gathered in a recording studio for the first and only time to record as the State Street Boys. The eight sides they cut that day reveal musicians caught between the South, where they had grown up, and the North, where they now earned their living. As music historian Tony Russell has described several of the songs, they were "the sort of music a country stringband might make after it had spent a few years in the city." Bill's fiddling was a key element in creating this atmosphere, with his unhurried playing on songs such as "She Caught the Train" combining with Jazz Gillum's back-porch harp to reinforce the story of lost love. Bill took the lead vocal on a number of songs, including the lively rendition of "The Dozen," which Russell notes was "an old New Orleans song, also known as 'Don't Ease Me In.'"[6]

The sessions also included a version of "Midnight Special," a song that would over time become closely associated with the African American songster and icon Lead Belly. John and Alan Lomax had recorded Lead Belly singing it the previous summer at the Louisiana State Penitentiary in Angola, and his numerous recordings and performances of the song made lasting impressions on many white folk music fans from the 1930s onward. According to jazz historian Eric Townley, the reason for the repetition in the chorus of the phrase "Let the Midnight Special / Shine a light on me" was the convicts' belief that the one who was lucky enough to be spotlighted by the beam of the "Midnight Special" locomotive would be the next to be released. But to listen to Bill sing over Black Bob's percussive piano, Zeb Wright's straight-ahead fiddling, and the slaps of the anonymous gut-bucket bass player is to hear it not just as social protest but also as raucous, good-time dance music. For Bill and his colleagues, the two were not mutually exclusive.[7]

Bill's regular piano player for the next several years was a man who played on hundreds of sides but whose identity blues historians have debated for decades. Known professionally as "Black Bob," he recorded with many of the most popular artists of the 1930s, including Tampa Red, Memphis Minnie, Washboard Sam, and Casey Bill Weldon. His steady rhythms and tasteful fills provided consistently solid support for Bill and his colleagues, and he was another contributor to Lester Melrose's success.

Over the next six months, Bill played behind an intriguing variety of musicians at different points in their careers. In March he cut two sides with the man who had started him off on the guitar, Papa Charlie Jackson. Jackson's career had slowed down considerably since the late 1920s, when his records were hits and he was recording duets for Paramount with some of the biggest names in the blues, such as Ma Rainey and Blind Blake. Now, even though Bill's career was on the rise, ARC decided the sessions between student and teacher didn't have enough commercial potential, and the sides were never issued. Jackson died several years later, probably in 1938, and an enduring part of his legacy in the blues world, beyond his trail-blazing success as a solo male blues singer, was the recognition Bill gave him as his mentor.

A month later, Bill recorded several songs with boogie-woogie pianist Cripple Clarence Lofton. Although Lofton was a few years younger than Jackson and had been playing in the South Side clubs and at rent parties in Chicago for some time, the April sessions with Bill were his first recordings. Lofton's colorful act included dancing (despite his eponymous lame leg), whistling, and joke telling. Their first side, "Strut That Thing," was an early version of a tune that Lofton would later rework as "I Don't Know," which would become an R&B hit in 1953 for singer/pianist Willie Mabon.[8] Bill's steady treble string work nicely complemented Lofton's playing, singing, and whistling, and a later session in July produced a rocking collaboration between the two on "Brown Skin Girls."

Around this time, a new generation of blues stars was emerging, made up of younger players who, like Bill, had been born in the first decade of the twentieth century. One was a smooth singer named Amos Easton, who recorded under the name of Bumble Bee Slim, and Bill backed him on a dozen sides, beginning in late 1934. Like Bill, Slim had greatly admired Leroy Carr, whose death the following year he mourned with a song titled "The Death of Leroy Carr (Dedicated to the Memory of Leroy Carr)." Slim added dozens of his own compositions to his Carr tributes and covers, and for several years, before he left Chicago for California in 1937, he was one of the busiest of the blues recording artists.

Washboard Sam made his debut in June 1935 under the tasty but short-lived name of Ham Gravy. Sam plunged early into the easily recognizable style he sustained for nearly two decades, as he sang the verses to "Mama Don't Allow No. 1" over the frisky up-tempo beat telling how he and his pals would do "wigglin', wobblin'" and "booglin', wooglin'," despite Mama's objections.[9] He added that "we gonna do rough stuff anyhow," and it's easy to believe his swaggering boast. In his autobiography, Bill described Sam working as a Chicago cop twenty years later and noted that "he should make a good policeman and know how to arrest people because he's been arrested so many times, and I always had to go and get him out of jail. He was always into something in them old times."[10]

Bill had recorded two sides just prior to the Ham Gravy session, and for one of the last times in his career, he was joined by a second guitarist. Louis Lasky played with Bill on a total of only six cuts, but his ability to interweave his punchy and precise guitar lines with Bill's seems effortless. As Frank Brasswell had done several years before, Lasky let Bill's playing dominate, but he pushed him hard to stay right up against the beat, and the resulting artistry in "C and A Blues" was one of Bill's finest performances of this period. In some ways, Lasky can be seen as the kind of sideman to Bill that Bill was to so many other performers.

Lasky joined Bill, Black Bob, and unknown male and female singers in recording two sides in early July that were unique among Bill's recordings prior to the 1950s. The name given to the group on the record label was the Chicago Sanctified Singers, clearly directing it to a religious audience. The songs were spirituals, with unmistakably sacred content, while the arrangements, instruments, and performances bore many resemblances to the blues that Bill and his colleagues were recording regularly. The first song, "Tell Me What Kind of Man Jesus Is," describes various miracles Jesus performed in calming the seas, healing the sick, and raising the dead. There is a brief section in the middle where an unknown man invokes Jesus' help, using some of the language of the Lord's Prayer. The second song, "I Ain't No Stranger Now," is similar in tempo, with someone contributing another "preaching" portion halfway through. As "Cryin' Holy to the Lord," the song has been a staple of white country and bluegrass music for decades, performed by the Carter Family, Bill Monroe, and Flatt and Scruggs. Bill's voice can be heard in each cut, and his experience in the church had clearly prepared him to throw himself into the words of praise. It is not apparent whose decision it was to record these songs, with these musicians, for this audience, as Melrose's overwhelming focus was on secular music. What is evident is that Bill was comfortable enough with sacred music to give a performance worthy of the content.

In 1936 a new group emerged that had an impact on Bill's recordings over the next several years. Ink Williams assembled a group of Chicago-based musicians that included the McCoy brothers (Charlie on mandolin and Joe on guitar), as well as several artists from the New Orleans jazz world. Williams brought them into Decca's Chicago studio, and, under the name the Harlem Hamfats, the group issued a string of successful records through the late 1930s.

By including clarinet and trumpet players as integral members of the band, the Harlem Hamfats blended jazz instruments into the blues coming out of the Chicago recording studios. Their sound was frequently up-tempo, with the experienced session players laying down a driving dance beat as the jazzmen took crisp solos. Their songs were often written for audiences looking to celebrate the party life, and they didn't shy away from singing about reefer, prostitutes, and pimps, sometimes in unvarnished terms. Two songs in particular, "Root Hog or Die" and "Weed Smoker's Dream," are harsh directives from a pimp to his employees to turn more tricks so he can make more money.

Prior to the Hamfats, Bill had played on a few sides with musicians who primarily played jazz. While the success of the group didn't radically alter Bill's approach, about half of the sides he played on between 1937 and 1939 included horns or clarinets.[11] Playing with artists whose primary training and focus was jazz meant that Bill had to make adjustments in his playing style, learning the chord progressions and turnarounds required of a jazz guitarist. These skills not only brought a new swing to his own records, but prepared him to make the most of an opportunity that would come a few years later to record and tour with singer Lil Green's group. In fact, Bill would be playing guitar behind Green when she sang composer Joe McCoy's revised version of the Hamfats' song "Weed Smoker's Dream" called "Why Don't You Do Right?" The song would help to launch Green on tours that took her far from Chicago, and then later, when performed by singer Peggy Lee, would become a hit for the Benny Goodman band.

Just a Dream

In the fall of 1938, John Hammond was searching for what he described as a "primitive blues singer." Hammond, a white jazz writer and a producer for Columbia Records, had a vision of a blockbuster concert in New York City that would unite his two great passions: music performed by African Americans and progressive politics. He was well on his way to realizing his dream of an event that "would bring together, for the first time, before a musically sophisticated audience, Negro music from its raw beginnings to the latest jazz."[1] He had secured financial backing, rented Carnegie Hall, and signed an impressive array of musicians from the jazz and gospel worlds.

But the artist he really wanted, the one he called "the best there was," was Robert Johnson.[2] Unfortunately, Johnson had died in Mississippi in August 1938, under circumstances that would later attain mythic status. Hammond turned to executives at the American Record Company (ARC) for suggestions because he thought that several artists on ARC's Vocalion label might be acceptable substitutes. When he mentioned Durham-based guitarist Blind Boy Fuller as a potential candidate, his ARC contacts put him in touch with J. B. Long, the North Carolina talent scout who had arranged for Fuller's recordings. Hammond headed south at the wheel of a Terraplane convertible, the same model that Robert Johnson had paid tribute to in his "Terraplane Blues," to meet with Long. But he found Fuller in jail, he later recalled, "charged with shooting at his wife . . . [which he] had managed by standing in the center of a room, rotating slowly, and firing intermittently—fortunately missing."[3] Although during his stay in North Carolina Hammond did sign up other artists from Long's roster of talent—blues harmonica virtuoso Sonny Terry and the gospel quartet Mitchell's Christian Singers—he still had not accomplished his original purpose.

At this point, Hammond recounted in his memoirs, "instead, we signed Big Bill Broonzy, another primitive blues singer whose records I loved."[4] Not long after, Bill traveled to New York to participate in what turned out to be a memorable evening in American music. On December 23, 1938, the sellout crowd that flooded Carnegie Hall for "An Evening of American Negro Music" was so overwhelming that temporary seating for three hundred people had to be set up onstage. After Hammond played a set of field recordings from Africa to link jazz to what he identified as its origins, the parade of musicians began and didn't let up for the next four hours.[5]

The performers reflected Hammond's keen interest in presenting a wide and dynamic variety of types of African American music. Boogie-woogie pianists Albert Ammons, Pete Johnson, and Meade Lux Lewis gave an energetic boost to the musical style that was soon to sweep popular music. The vitality of the Kansas City jazz scene became immediately apparent when vocalist Big Joe Turner joined his regular pianist Pete Johnson for two compelling numbers. In one of her first appearances outside the circuit of black churches in which she was a rising star, Sister Rosetta Tharpe sang two gospel tunes, with her driving guitar amplifying her evocative vocals. Mitchell's Christian Singers gave the New York City audience one of its first experiences of the power of a cappella gospel quartet singing, a performance in which one reviewer found "the elements of jazz inherent in the most isolated Negro music, no matter what its subject matter."[6] Sonny Terry's whoops and yelps in his rendition of "Fox Chase" combined with his harmonica artistry to draw the crowd into a vivid rural scene as the hounds pursued the elusive fox. Soprano saxophonist Sidney Bechet led a group that Hammond had assembled for the concert, which honored the New Orleans origins of jazz with rousing versions of several songs.

When it was Bill's turn to step up to the microphone, he had a new song ready. He picked out a short introductory phrase on his guitar, and then began with the chorus:

It was a dream, just a dream I had on my mind [x2]
And when I woke up, not a thing could I find.

I dreamed I went out with an angel, and had a good time.
I dreamed I was satisfied, and nothing to worry my mind

But that was a dream, just a dream I had on my mind
And when I woke up, not an angel could I find.

I dreamed I played policy, and played the horses, too
I dreamed I winned so much money, I didn't know what to do
But that was a dream, just a dream I had on my mind
And when I woke up, not a penny could I find.

I dreamed I was in the White House, sitting in the President's chair
I dreamed he shaked my hand, said "Bill, I'm glad you're here."
But that was a dream, Lord, a dream I had on my mind.
And when I woke up, not a chair could I find.

I dreamed I got married and started a little family.
I dreamed I had ten children, and they all looked just like me.
But that was just a dream, Lord, a dream I had on my mind
And when I woke up, not a child could I find.[7]

The audience's first wave of chuckles came when Bill described his abrupt realization that it was "just a dream" that he had so much money that he didn't know what to do. But this reaction paled next to their enthusiastic response to the prospect of Bill sitting in Franklin Roosevelt's chair—the closest thing to a throne America could offer—and the president gripping Bill's hand as he expressed his gratitude for Bill's presence. It was an audacious image, one that required both a vivid poetic imagination and the songwriting craftsmanship to carry it off. Bill had opened with the idea of a dream, the ingenious device in which he could show something to the audience and then take it away. As he moved in successive verses through lust, greed, ambition, and betrayal, the audience could not help but identify with him, first in his hopes and then, each time, in his disappointments.

The surge of laughter that burst out of the crowd when Bill revealed that his visit to the Oval Office was "just a dream" marked a crucial point in Bill's career. He had come to Carnegie Hall to perform in front of the largest crowd he had ever played before, one that was predominantly comprised of white concertgoers. He had played for white audiences years before, when he was in Arkansas, but they were dancing and carousing, not sitting and listening intently, and back then he was a member of an ensemble. As he stood in front of the New Yorkers, even with Albert Ammons's piano accompaniment in the background, he was relying on his voice, his guitar, his songs, and his ability to blend all three together to win over the crowd. When Bill heard and felt the audience's approval and delight, he saw that he could stand up in front of hundreds or even thousands of people whose worlds were quite different from those he was familiar with, and find a way to connect with them. This knowledge about his capabilities would become very useful in the years to come.

The final segment of the evening consisted of performances by the Count Basie Band, which played in various configurations with vocalists Jimmy Rushing and Helen Humes, as well as reuniting with a former band member, trumpeter Oran "Hot Lips" Page. As the *New Masses* reviewer noted, "These orchestras capped the evening with just the right amount of well-punctuated verve, leaving the audience gasping at the spectacle of powerful talent let loose."[8]

The success of the 1938 concert encouraged Hammond to organize another "From Spirituals to Swing" concert a year later, on December 24, 1939, also at Carnegie Hall. He set it up with a similar theme, so that performers would offer different styles of African American music. This time the emcee was the African American academic and poet Sterling Brown, whose introduction offered, as he said, a "capsule" history of "the music of the American Negro." The roster included the Golden Gate Quartet, representing gospel quartet singing; Ida Cox, who had recorded hits for Paramount Records in the 1920s; and the Benny Goodman Band, featuring electric guitar virtuoso Charlie Christian. Bill returned, as did the Count Basie Band, Sonny Terry, and stride piano player James P. Johnson.

The evening produced numerous examples of first-rate music, but, in Hammond's words, it "was not the success the previous one had been. . . . [It was] in some ways better performed, but it lacked the audience-performer rapport of the earlier concert."[9] Bill, accompanied again by Albert Ammons, played two songs he had recorded previously, "Done Got Wise" and "Louise, Louise." He got a laugh from a clever line in "Done Got Wise," and the audience applauded heartily in both cases. But as with the concert overall, it was difficult for him to compete with the intense, walking-a-high-wire-without-a-net atmosphere of the previous year.[10]

The concertgoers who came to Carnegie Hall both years reflected several emerging audiences for the music Bill played on those nights. One group could be identified by the sponsor of the 1938 concert, the left-wing literary publication *New Masses*. The magazine's publisher, Eric Bernay, had provided Hammond with financial backing for the concert after the National Association for the Advancement of Colored People and the International Ladies' Garment Workers' Union had turned him down. The orientation of *New Masses* was Marxist, and it published articles by politically engaged writers like Richard Wright, Langston Hughes, John Dos Passos, and Theodore Dreiser. Readers did not have to be Communists to turn to its pages for informed and passionate perspectives on unjust social conditions, including outrage against racism.

It was an era in which popular-interest magazines such as *Fortune* and the recently launched *Life* used disturbing photos and evocative writing to document the devastating effects of the Great Depression on Americans. Hammond himself exemplified the non-Communist anti-racist perspective: as a reporter for the *Nation*, he had covered the perversions of justice that had occurred during the series of trials of the Scottsboro Boys several years before. While he was pleased to obtain the support of *New Masses*, he insisted as a condition of the deal that Bernay refrain from explicitly advancing a Marxist viewpoint in promoting the event. Hammond correctly guessed that some of the readers who had concerns over racial injustice would turn out in numbers to hear an array of talented African American musicians.

Another group in attendance both nights was jazz fans, some of whom were developing a keen curiosity about its musical and cultural sources. Hammond wanted to feature styles that had flourished in different eras, so he presented musicians such as Sidney Bechet and Tommy Ladnier, who had started their careers in New Orleans in the early decades of the 1900s; vaudeville blues stars of the 1920s such as Ida Cox; and rising talents like the Count Basie Band. His clear intent, in the words of one observer, was to assemble "a powerful genealogy of black American music."[11] The 1938 concert caught the rising crest of a wave that accelerated over the next decade in jazz, as researchers and fans searched for the roots of jazz. The next year two white jazz historians, Frederic Ramsey Jr. and Charles Edward Smith, published *Jazzmen: The Story of Hot Jazz Told in the Lives of the Men Who Created It*. In it, they identified New Orleans in the late nineteenth and early twentieth centuries as the crucible in which the various elements that formed jazz all came together. The writers' quest to understand the origins of jazz led to discussions of the importance of the music that, as they understood it, predated jazz in the African American communities of the South. In the words of the author of the chapter simply titled "Blues":

> What are the blues and into what category of music do they fit? They are not spirituals and they are not work songs nor do they fit into the pattern proscribed by many music critics as folk music in a lighter vein.
>
> To me, they are filled with the deepest emotions of a race. They are songs of sorrow charged with satire, with that potent quality of ironic verse clothed in the raiment of the buffoon. They were more than releases, temporary releases, from servitude. The blues were the gateway to freedom for all American Negroes.[12]

In performing "Just a Dream," Bill recognized what those in the audience who shared the author's admiration for the blues might have been looking for, and he gave it to them. His song was one of "sorrow charged with satire," and it certainly qualified as "ironic verse."

Bill had previously demonstrated his ability to identify an emerging trend and adapt to it. When he had switched from rural fiddle to urban guitar, from slow and mournful blues guitar duets to the fast-paced hokum stomps, and then again to the multi-instrument ensembles of the mid-1930s, each time it was because he had discerned what his audience wanted and then delivered it. Perhaps Bill had observed black and white intellectuals working on Chicago's South Side for the New Deal–era Federal Writers' Project or had heard from jazz musicians of the sparks of interest by white researchers in the roots of black music. No matter how he gathered and interpreted his information, he marshaled his protean musical talents, and at Carnegie Hall he quickly learned from the audience's enthusiastic response that his guess was correct.

One audience member at Carnegie Hall for the 1938 show who was delighted by what he saw and heard that night was Alan Lomax, the twenty-three-year-old head of the Archive of American Folk-Song at the Library of Congress. Over the previous five years, Lomax had helped to record Lead Belly, as well as hundreds of less famous musicians, on field trips throughout the American South and elsewhere. He was so impressed by the caliber of the performers that he immediately contacted Hammond, who helped him set up recording sessions by several of them for the Library of Congress's collection. Bill was not included in that group, most likely because he was under contract at the time to ARC/Brunswick.[13] But his performance clearly made an impression on Lomax; eight years later, when he was looking for an artist to personify the blues tradition to New York audiences, he would remember the power of Bill's delivery.

In the 1950s Bill sent Yannick Bruynoghe a handwritten reminiscence that acknowledged how important John Hammond and the "From Spirituals to Swing" concerts had been to his career:

> In 1938, '39, and '40, three years straight [*sic*], I was called to sing them ["Just a Dream" and "Done Got Wise"] in Carnegie Hall by one of the best men to a lot of musicians and blues singers. I do believe that I never would have been heard in a big hall like that and nobody would have ever heard of Big Bill and a lot more if it hadn't been for that man, Mr. John Hammond. He told me to just sing the blues—never mind my clothes and my hair, just sing the blues. "Trucking Little Woman" and "Just a Dream" was his favorite songs by me. . . . I will always love that man, John Hammond, and never will forget him for what he has done for me. He is the cause of me seeing and meeting a lot of people who wouldn't have ever heard of Big Bill Broonzy.[14]

Big Bill and Josh Are Here to
Play the Blues for You

In the early spring of 1939, Bill went to the offices of Local 208, the black musicians' union in Chicago. The union's headquarters had been located for twenty years in the three-story building at Thirty-ninth and State, in the heart of the South Side's vibrant Bronzeville district. In fact, Local 208 had done well enough that it had owned the building outright for most of that time. By coming to join the union, Bill was making an expensive choice. The initiation fee was $50, which would be the equivalent in 2010 of nearly $800. He put down $12 as an initial payment, and received his union card, which he carried for the rest of his life.[1]

Bill's decision to become a member of Local 208 reflected the significance of the union for the musicians who made their living playing blues and jazz in Chicago in this era. Chicago had been a center of union activity in America since the mid-nineteenth century, and by the 1930s unions represented workers in many industries with a strong presence in Chicago, such as meatpacking and steelmaking. But the long-standing racial tensions between Chicago's various white ethnic groups and its African American community extended to the labor movement. In a number of areas of employment, such as building trades, blacks were not welcome as union brethren.

In the music business, the lines of segregation had been drawn since musicians began to organize in the late nineteenth century. The national musicians' union, the American Federation of Musicians, confirmed at the turn of the century its official preference for "separate locals for black and white musicians." In Chicago the predecessor to Local 10, the white musicians' local, had explicitly restricted membership not only by race but gender, limiting the pool of applicants to "every white male of good character and repute." After Local 10 voted to "refuse black membership in the local," a group of African American musicians founded

Local 208 and so, on July 4, 1902, "became the first black local in the country."² The union grew and prospered as the South Side jazz night-clubs and ballrooms thrived in the 1920s, and then after the downturn of the Depression brought lean years, new leadership began to stabilize and rebuild the organization.

By 1939 Local 208 membership had swelled to nine hundred members, the highest count in its history. Bill was probably motivated to join the union by several factors. First, the new set of leaders had begun to assert the power of the union, both to the club owners who were hiring musicians and to the musicians themselves. To the club owners, the union insisted on a uniform pay scale for all clubs, replacing the previous arrangement that allowed different pay for different clubs. At the same time, Bill was prevented from playing guitar in a number of 1938 recording sessions because, as a non-union musician, he was not eligible to be paid for performing on that instrument.³

Union membership also provided access to significant financial benefits. The newly elected officers established an unemployment fund, which would have been especially attractive in the wake of the economic downturn of 1937–38. In addition, the death benefits were substantial, especially during an era when most musicians were unlikely to have bought a life insurance policy. When Joshua Altheimer, Bill's pianist from 1937 to 1940, died in late 1940, his mother and his wife each received a death benefit of $101.25 from Local 208, which was the equivalent in 2010 of just under $1,600 apiece. For musicians whose employment both in day jobs and recording studios was often intermittent, a union card ensured that their families could have some measure of security if anything happened to them.⁴

Even during the 1930s, Bill was generally able to find work outside the music business. He told Alan Lomax that he worked on the WPA (Works Progress Administration) from 1934 until 1936 and was later employed at Chicago's Merchandise Mart for what he described as the "US state Gov 1938. To. 1943."⁵ The WPA was, in the words of one historian, "the biggest employment project in the history of the United States." Employing nearly nine million people from 1935 until 1943, it became one of the best known of the many job-creation efforts that President Franklin Roosevelt's administration introduced as part of the New Deal. WPA workers built or upgraded thousands of schools, playgrounds, and hospitals around the country. The program provided jobs for workers who would otherwise have been unemployed, but it also paid fairly low wages, as it was designed not to draw workers away from the private sector.[6]

In his autobiography, Bill wrote that "the WPA had been going on for about a year before I got broke enough to get in there."[7] His comments on his experiences convey a vivid sense of what it was like to be on one of the work crews. Fairly or not, one image of the WPA in the popular imagination was a laborer resting on a shovel, referred to by contemporary observers from political cartoonists to Louis Armstrong and the Mills Brothers.

Bill made reference to this perception in a spoken aside during an instrumental break during his 1938 recording of "W.P.A. Rag," when he commented, "Jump off that shovel, boy." In his autobiography, he told of how he came to write the song and indicated one way the phrase was used on the WPA job site:

> We had a boss that we called "Big George" and when he would see one of the men standing, leaning on his shovel he would holler:
> "Get up off that shovel, boy, if you's tired go to the office and check out, and come back tomorrow and try it again."
> So we all started to tease each other about leaning on our shovel and I got to like working on the WPA.[8]

While Bill was not specific about his next stint as a government employee at the Merchandise Mart, he was most likely working in some unskilled position, such as a janitor, for one of the many federal agencies whose offices were located in the mammoth complex. He never described working at any white-collar job, and he mentioned on several occasions having been a janitor. His tenure at the Mart fit the general description he gave of his decades-long need to find a day job in order to support himself:

> I had a job all the time I was playing music and making records. I worked every day and played music at night, because I didn't make enough money, just playing music and recording, to take care of my family.[9]

Exactly whom he would have meant by "family" in this period, to the extent of feeling responsible for providing for them financially, is unclear. Over the course of his adult life, he stayed in touch regularly with his mother and several of his siblings, as well as a number of their children and grandchildren. He might have had in mind his older sister Mattie, who had moved to Chicago and was married to meatpacker Ben Burford. His union membership record card, dated April 3, 1940, lists his beneficiary as "Mattie Buaford [sic]," although her name was scratched out in early 1958 and replaced by the name of Bill's last wife.[10] There is no mention in the union records of the wife or child of the "Willie Lee Broonsey" listed in the 1930 census.[11]

About a year after he listed his sister's name on the union records, Bill once again became a married man. As he later wrote to Yannick Bruynoghe, "I got married to a creole woman in 1941 in Houston, Texas."[12] The woman's name was Rose Allen, and the marriage license was dated June 7, 1941.[13] In an article published in a jazz magazine in 1946, Bill described a whirlwind romance: "I met my wife and married her sixteen days later."[14] All that Bill ever revealed about the early days of the marriage was that "I left her in Texas for two weeks and then I sent for her to come to Chicago and we lived there until 1947."[15]

By contrast, Bill was very clear about the reason he had traveled to Houston in the spring of 1941: "I was on the road then with Lil Green, playing guitar for her."[16] Bill played an important role in Lil Green's meteoric rise from obscurity to national headliner in the early 1940s, and he maintained a personal connection with her even after her star faded. Her story sheds light on the opportunities and pitfalls for a singer in Chicago in this period in search of success in the music business.

According to Lil Green, after she had been orphaned at age ten in Clarksdale, Mississippi, she had moved in 1929 to Chicago, where she dropped out of high school.[17] R. H. Harris, the gifted lead singer of the gospel group the Soul Stirrers, reported that she had killed a man in a brawl and been sent to prison for her crime. He remembered visiting the prison so that he could hear her sing in the Sunday services. Her professional career was launched around 1940, when the manager of a Chicago club hired her on the spot after a group of her friends had arranged for a bandleader to call her up from the audience to sing.[18]

By May 1940 Green had come to the attention of Lester Melrose, who brought her into the studio to record on the Bluebird label. He assigned a trio of musicians to back her, including Bill, Simeon Henry on piano, and New Orleans veteran Ransom Knowling on bass. That session produced her first hit, "Romance in the Dark," for which writing credit was split between Lil and Bill. The song, often abbreviated to "In the Dark," went on to become a standard and over time entered the repertoire of artists such as Dinah Washington and Nina Simone. Jazz historian Leonard Feather notes that the song "was remarkable in its day for the relatively frank sexuality of its lyrics," in which the singer proudly proclaims that "In the dark I get such a thrill / when he presses his fingertips upon my lips." The song showcased Green's voice, which Feather described as "salt-and-vinegar," to which it might be added that she was able to sound vulnerable, sexy, and brassy, all in the same three-minute song.[19]

Based on the song's success, Melrose recorded Green several times over the next year. Soon she was the subject of articles in the entertainment section of the *Chicago Defender*, which indicated that she had become identified as more than a blues singer. It meant that she was getting booked into clubs that catered to black audiences looking for an evening of music that they might identify as jazz or pop music. Clubs that presented blues artists were at two disadvantages when it came to coverage in the *Defender*: first, because they usually didn't make enough money to be able to afford the larger ads in the paper, they didn't receive the perk of a "feature" piece, which generally amounted to a press release for the venue. In addition, the guiding philosophy of the *Defender* was to present African Americans—often referred to in its pages as "the Race"—in a way that underscored the achievements and industry of the middle and upper classes. While jazz and popular musicians, and those who could afford to attend their shows, fit that profile, the blues musicians who usually played in less respectable settings were generally absent from the newspaper of record of Chicago's black community.

The other song with which Green's name continues to be associated was Joe McCoy's composition "Why Don't You Do Right?," which she recorded in April 1941. After the song brought some success to Green, mostly with black record buyers, Peggy Lee's later recording became a national hit for the Benny Goodman band, and, in the words of one music historian, "essentially established Lee as a name vocalist."[20]

While Lil Green's prominence ultimately fell short of Lee's, the two hits launched her into star status, and in 1941 she began a two-year period of touring the United States. Appearing with the Tiny Bradshaw Orchestra, Green performed on some of the most prestigious stages in the country, including the Apollo and the Savoy in New York City.

During her return visits to Chicago, she played the Regal Theater, where stars like Louis Armstrong and Count Basie appeared when they came to town.

Bill played guitar on all of the sides Green recorded before the 1942 recording ban. Near the end of the 1930s, he had begun to record with an amplified guitar, which guitarists playing in jazz and swing bands were using with increasing frequency. Bill's first exposure to the new technology in a recording studio had come in 1938, when a white teenaged guitarist from the Chicago suburbs named George Barnes had played at several sessions backing him, Jazz Gillum, and Washboard Sam.[21]

Bill's work behind Lil Green demonstrated his ability to adapt to a new playing style, as well as to become comfortable with the different capabilities of an amplified guitar. He was now supporting a vocalist who was performing songs that were as much pop or jazz as they were blues, so he needed to learn chords and strumming techniques that jazz guitarists used. At the same time, Bill was learning to use an instrument that presented him with additional possibilities and pitfalls for volume, tone, and phrasing. These were recordings made without the drums, horns, washboards, and harmonicas that characterized many of the sessions for which he had been a sideman. Because the goal was to showcase the vocalist, Bill's guitar solos, alternating with Simeon Henry's piano breaks, were key elements in reinforcing the atmosphere Green created with her singing. Bill's multi-year tenure as Green's guitarist through her recordings and tours of the early 1940s reflected his success at mastering these challenges.[22]

Lil Green also benefited from Bill's talents as a songwriter. He was modest in the description in his autobiography of the process he followed:

> I played for Lil Green for two years as her guitar player. I wrote some songs for her, like "My Mellow Man" and "Country Boy," "Give Your Mama One More Smile" and some more that I fixed up for her. I wasn't really writing them songs—I just hummed the tune until Henry, the piano player, and the bass player Ransom Knowling, could find the right chords to fit the tune. I hummed to them then she would sing the words that I'd wrote down for her.[23]

As Bill described it, he, Henry, and Knowling accompanied Green on her first two tours, and then she gradually dropped the three musicians, eventually replacing the small combo with a big band. Bill told of going to performances she gave at the Apollo Theater in the mid-1940s and receiving a warm greeting from her each time: "It made me feel good to know that she hadn't forgotten the ones she had started out with." Green even went so far, in Bill's account, to invite the trio over for dinner in Chicago, although he noted that "she would eat most of it herself and then tell us to help ourselves."[24]

In the years after World War II, Green would still record and tour, but there would be no follow-up hits on the scale of her early successes. She performed occasionally in Chicago clubs in the early 1950s, and her final recording session was in 1951. When she died in 1954, the *Defender* made no mention of her passing. Bill sustained her memory by including her in his autobiography, which was first published the year after she died. When Bill was in the final months of his life, Yannick and Margo Bruynoghe visited him in Chicago and photographed him at home with his wife and several friends. A careful look at the background of one of the photographs they took reveals a framed photo of Lil Green on his mantelpiece.

Around the time Bill was starting to record and tour with Green, his mother was settling in to a new neighborhood. According to family records, Bill's father had died in 1930.[25] "I was the kind of boy that I was crazy about my mother," he told Alan Lomax. "So I didn't want my mother to live on this plantation, I wanted her to live in town, because . . . I figured the little money I make, I could always send her $5 a week, or $2 a week, $1 a week, whatsonever I could stretch out from me and my woman living on, I'd send it home to my mother to live on, see."[26]

Acting on his desire to provide for his mother's well-being, Bill continued, "I bought my mother a home in 1939." It was located in North Little Rock, Arkansas, about sixty miles northwest of Lake Dick. When Mittie Bradley came to North Little Rock, where she lived for the rest of her life, the city became the center of family life for the Bradleys. With Mittie and three of Bill's siblings based there, North Little Rock had a powerful gravitational pull on Bill, and he was a frequent visitor for the next two decades. He was by now a longtime resident of Chicago, but because of some distinctive characteristics of North Little Rock, visiting there must have felt to him more than a little like coming home to Jefferson County.

The Bradleys were not alone in their move to the city from Arkansas's rural regions. In addition to those who headed to Chicago and other northern cities in the Great Migration, many black families had been relocating for some time to southern cities in search of better prospects than places like Lake Dick could offer.[27] Located across the Arkansas River from the state capital of Little Rock, North Little Rock had a population in 1940 of just over twenty thousand, about one-third of whom were African Americans. Bill's younger sister, Lannie, was the first of the Bradleys to settle there. She had married railroad worker Mack Wesley in 1924, and they and their children had lived in the general area at least since 1930, when they were counted in the census.[28]

By 1940 Mittie was sharing a house with Frank Jr. and Gustavia, who was by then a widow, like her mother. Most of the Bradley family and their friends and neighbors were able to find blue-collar employment. Mack Wesley supported his family on the laborer's wages he earned from the Missouri Pacific Railroad, a major employer in the area, while Gustavia worked as a laundress and a maid.[29]

While North Little Rock was the fifth largest city in Arkansas at the time,[30] living conditions were in some ways as rural as they were urban. Rosie Tolbert, who is Lannie Wesley's granddaughter and Bill's grand-niece, recalled that growing up there in the 1940s and '50s, "we didn't have a hot-water tank. We used an outdoor toilet until we moved . . . [in] 1960." In the house that Bill's mother lived in from the mid-1940s on, "the kitchen floor was just dirt; it was a dirt floor." In fact, "they used kerosene lamps . . . they didn't have electricity and didn't have running water there either," and had to make do with a hand-operated pump.[31]

Rosie also remembered that her relatives brought other elements of farm life to the city. "All of them had gardens," she said, and she recalled there were "some chickens, [and] some ducks." Even the mailboxes were rural: while some streets had mailboxes on their front porches, her family had to go "down the street and around the corner . . . they had to walk down there to get the mail." Hermese White, a neighbor and contemporary of Rosie's mother, said that not all the roads were paved: "You know, we had red dirt. That red mud. You'd go to someone's house and you better pull them shoes off before you walk in there." She also told of going "up in the woods [in her neighborhood] and get[ting] hickory nuts and blackberries."[32]

While a trip to North Little Rock would have had elements of Bill's Arkansas youth, there were also reminders of Chicago. One would have been the active music scene in North Little Rock: Hermese White remembered on "Twenty-second Street [there were] four dance halls, taverns, and one nightclub. . . . We'd stay at the places until they closed. [And] Robinson Auditorium, that was a big auditorium. They had all of them big dances there, oh yeah . . . Lionel Hampton and all the different bands would come through."

A good example of where the country and the city overlapped in North Little Rock was the presence of juke joints. Rosie recalled, "I think there was a juke joint on every street. They had the one on Thirtieth Street, and we used to sit . . . and just watch the commotion over that juke joint. Until there was shootin' and stuff, and then our grandma would run us in the house." With a local nightspot featuring a jukebox and a menu of "barbeque and fried-fish sandwiches and beer," the neighborhood would have felt familiar both to the Lake Dick Bradleys as they adjusted to an urban environment, and to Bill on his regular visits from the North, where he had lived for nearly two decades.[33]

Bill identified one key event as the reason he was able to buy his mother a house in North Little Rock. "All the records I made, up until . . . 1939, I never got no royalty on mine, up until 1939, the first time I drawn a royalty," he told Alan Lomax. "That's when I made 'Just a Dream' and 'Done Got Wise' and things like that."[34]

A set of ten royalty statements from Lester Melrose to Bill has survived, and they begin in August 1940 and continue through August 1948. While there is currently no way to determine whether Melrose had prepared earlier royalty statements for Bill, these statements confirm that Bill did receive some royalties from Melrose roughly when he said he did.[35]

The two statements for records sold in 1940 provide a rare snapshot of the number of records sold by an artist of Bill's stature, as well as the amount of money he actually received as the composer of the songs. The August statement is for "the Quarter ending June 30, 1940," while the March 1, 1941, accounting is "for the period up to December 31, 1940," so it is not clear whether the later statement is for a period beginning in July or October. Because the total sales figures are within a percent of each other (June 30 at 33,338 sides and December 30 at 31,702), it is hard to know whether April–June was an unusually good quarter or July–December an uncharacteristically bad six months.

Yet even without full information about the accounting, what is clear is that some of Bill's records were selling thousands of copies per month. Between April 1 and June 30, four sides (making up two 78 rpm records) sold over 4,000 copies: "Leap Year Blues"/"Make My Get Away" (4,445 copies) and "Plow Hand Blues"/"Lookin' for My Baby" (4,232 copies). Four other sides sold over 2,500 copies, and Melrose paid royalties on a total of 58 sides.

During the period ending on December 31, 1940, only two sides sold over 4,000 copies: the pairing of "Hit the Right Lick"/"Merry Go Round Blues," which sold 4,016 records. Twelve other sides, making up six records, sold over 1,000 copies, and the statement showed sales on a total of 62 sides. Interestingly, the songs Bill later recalled being associated with the start of the royalty payments, "Baby, I Done Got Wise" and "Just a Dream," were not big sellers, amounting to just over 1,500 sides over both statement periods.

For all of the record sales, totaling just over 65,000 sides, Bill received the following royalty payments: $83.42 for the first statement, and $57.95 for the second one. Melrose calculated 1 percent of the sides sold, and then, under the terms of their contract, he sent Bill 25 percent of that amount. In the later statement, Melrose deducted $20 for an advance on royalties he had given Bill previously.

Bill told Alan Lomax in the mid-1940s that "the only money I made off of records, I couldn't have even bought a car, much less own a house." The figures in the statements back up his assessment. He added that "I've made more . . . money playing my guitar for around in taverns and nightclubs than I've made off of records." That may have been true in some stretches of his life, but in the early 1940s, as Bill acknowledged, "there wasn't no jobs . . . working around then. In '41 the only job that I had, excusin' the little recording I did, was going out on the road with Lil Green."[36]

For over two and half years in the 1940s, from July 1942 until March 1945, Bill did not play at a single recording session. It was the longest stretch of his entire career with no new recordings, and it was the direct result of the recording ban set by James C. Petrillo, the head of the American Federation of Musicians. Petrillo was battling several forces in the music industry, ranging from record companies to jukebox operators and broadcasters, to ensure that musicians received royalties from their recorded performances. To exert pressure on his adversaries, Petrillo called for what amounted to a strike beginning on August 1, 1942, which lasted until the union reached settlements with the Victor and Columbia record companies in late 1944.

The records Bill had made previously continued to sell in this period, as the record companies had made sure to accumulate recordings in anticipation of a labor action that would interrupt production. During a six-month period in 1944, one of Bill's records sold over 52,000 copies ("I'm Gonna Move to the Outskirts of Town"/"Hard Hearted Woman"), and another sold over 15,000 copies ("Bad Acting Woman"/"I'm Woke Up Now").[37] These successes were spotty, though, as other records of his only sold 100 or 200 copies over the same time frame.

Overall, the challenge for Bill during the World War II years was to try to make ends meet financially. The latest date he gave to Alan Lomax for working at his day job at Chicago's Merchandise Mart was 1943.[38] He was playing gigs on the South Side in mid-1944, but they would have been far from lucrative. It is possible that his wife was employed in a job that brought in some income, but if she was, he never made any mention of it.

What the royalty statements show is that his publishing royalties provided, at best, a small supplement to his income. For the periods ending June 30 and December 31, 1941, he netted his biggest royalty payments, with a combined total of $354.58. After that, the only surviving statement he received from Lester Melrose before the end of the war was for royalties earned through December 1944, and it showed that, instead of getting a check, Bill owed money to Melrose. According to Melrose's calculations, although Bill was due over $200 in royalties, Melrose had given Bill a series of advances that left Bill with a debt of over $140.[39]

Melrose's position may seem to be clear: that by paying Bill cash advances against anticipated publishing royalties, he was justified in holding Bill accountable when he had advanced him more up front than Bill wound up earning. A few years later, however, Bill gave his version of how the process worked with Melrose:

I remember I was working for Mr. Melrose, and a lot of Negroes were working for him at the same time. So one day he told me:

"I'll go make out a check in your name for twenty-five dollars, Bill. You go and get it cashed, buy a fifth of whiskey and some beer. Bring the change back."

The whiskey and beer costed five dollars. So I went, cashed the check, [and] brought the whiskey and beer and the twenty dollars back to Mr. Melrose.

Three weeks later he called and told me to meet him at some place. There he gave me another check to cash, for the same amount. I went, got some beer and whiskey, and brought the change back. After I had drunk about enough to be drunk, he said:

"Bill, I'll pay your royalties now."

So he started figuring:

"Do you remember me giving you two checks for twenty-five dollars each?"

"Yes," I said.

"Your royalties come to one hundred dollars and you owe me fifty dollars."

So you see what I mean: he just paid me fifty dollars and I bought the whiskey and beer out of my royalties. And that's disgusting.

That kind of things [sic] happened many times to Big Bill Broonzy. Mr. Lester Melrose received all Big Bill's money from the Columbia Recording Co., RCA, Victor, OKeh, Vocalion, and many other record companies that Mr. Melrose had him to record for.[40]

Musically, this was a time during which, when he did get a gig in a club, it was usually with a piano player. The death of one whose talent Bill greatly admired, Joshua Altheimer, created an opportunity for another, Memphis Slim, whose career he would shape.

Bill described Joshua Altheimer as "my favorite piano player" and said of him, "He seemed just right for me. I think he was the best blues piano player I ever heard."[41] From 1938 until his untimely death in November 1940, Altheimer played on over fifty sides with Bill. He was born in 1910 in Altheimer, Arkansas, which was located only a few miles from Bill's birthplace of Lake Dick. The village took its name from the family plantation of the largest landowner, who had emigrated there from Germany. According to Bill, Josh (as he called him) was the son of a Jewish father and a mixed-race mother, although Bill appears to have been describing Josh's grandparents instead. On a collecting trip to Pine Bluff in 1953, a professor of folklore encountered educator Reverend Silas Altheimer, who was Josh's father. The professor described Silas as a "sharp-featured, soft-spoken, lightskinned old man," who spoke about his father, a German immigrant and plantation owner, and his mother, an "ex-slave woman." Silas added wryly, "They didn't stop their old habits after slavery time, you know." The only known picture of Joshua Altheimer shows him standing with Bill and two other African American musicians; he is noticeably lighter-skinned than Bill and the others.[42]

Joshua Altheimer was a gifted pianist, and from Bill's enthusiastic praise, it is clear that their musical partnership was one of the most gratifying of the many Bill enjoyed over his career. In their 1940 recording of "Midnight Steppers," Bill announced that "Big Bill and Josh are here to play the blues for you."[43] Altheimer was equally at home with fast and slow tempos, and he supported Bill on piano the way that Bill backed the featured performers when he was a sideman, his notes and chords accenting without competing. French blues historian Jacques Demêtre has speculated that Altheimer may have received some formal musical education. In Demêtre's view, some familiarity with "scales and exercises" might help to explain Josh's "technique on the piano and his perfect tempo."[44] Although Altheimer never recorded as a featured performer, the French jazz historians Hugues Panassié and Madeleine Gautier described him in their 1956 *Guide to Jazz* as "the greatest blues pianist on records."[45]

It was as a member of the team of Big Bill and Josh that Bill's name appeared for the first time in an advertisement in the *Chicago Defender* for a live performance. The notice ran in the September 14, 1940, issue, and it announced their appearance at Ruby's Tavern on the city's West Side, at Lake and Artesian Streets. The ad listed John Gatewood as the proprietor, but according to jazz and blues guitarist Lonnie Johnson, Gatewood's wife, Ruby, the club's namesake, was in charge, and she "was a hard person to work for. That's right. You work all right—but try and get your money! Memphis Slim was the only one could get it, he'd go behind the bar and get it. Go to the cash register and just take it. He was the only one would do that. The union got behind her—and still didn't make no difference. She still wouldn't pay, that's all."[46]

If Bill or others were reluctant to force the issue with the Gatewoods of actually getting paid for a gig, they very likely had good reason. John Gatewood was one of the defendants in a 1942 case in which twenty-six individuals were accused of operating policy wheels.[47] These were illegal gambling operations, also known as the "numbers," based in the African

American neighborhoods on the South and West Sides, and run primarily by African Americans. Since their origins in the late nineteenth century, the policy wheels had been "a major source of jobs and investment capital in African American neighborhoods."[48] If Gatewood had been involved with running policy wheels, he would have been operating as part of an illegal industry that generated millions of dollars each year in Chicago and that was eventually taken over by the successor to Al Capone's organized crime syndicate. Although the judge dismissed the case after numerous witnesses who had given testimony to the grand jury declined to testify, Bill and his colleagues were being prudent in deciding to steer clear of confrontations with the Gatewoods.

Just two months after playing with Bill at Ruby's Tavern, Josh Altheimer died of a variety of causes, including pneumonia. While Bill surely grieved for his friend—observing later that "he couldn't have been very strong because he died when he was only 30"—he needed a piano player right away for gigs and recording sessions. "So," he recalled, "I asked Memphis Slim to play with me and so he did." For Slim, then in his mid-twenties and with only a handful of recordings to his credit, it was an important turning point in his career, and it gave Bill the chance to provide a promising talent with some sage advice.[49]

Born John L. Chatman in Memphis in 1915, Slim had spent his childhood absorbing blues and boogie-woogie piano from his father, a musician who also operated juke joints.[50] In the vibrant Memphis club scene of the 1920s and '30s, he heard pianists of the caliber of Roosevelt Sykes and Speckled Red, as well as talented local musicians. He settled in Chicago in the late 1930s after spending much of the decade working as a piano player on a circuit of honky-tonks, dance halls, and gambling joints around the South. Lester Melrose arranged for his first recording sessions and gave him the name "Memphis Slim" on his second record, probably to avoid contract problems resulting from having signed him with a different company to record as "Peter Chatman" on the first one.[51]

In addition to his musical aspirations, Slim's entrepreneurial skills enabled him to start and run a successful business in a seven-room South Side apartment he had rented. He later told an interviewer: "Because I had my union card, I went to the union, and got permission to put a sign in my window: 'Rehearsal Room, Local 208,' which meant that the police left me alone and never interfered with the music. . . . So I started selling whiskey, bootleg whiskey, and renting my rooms to Lester Melrose, who used to bring his musicians there when he came from the South, Sonny Boy Williamson, Curtis Jones, Tommy McClennan. . . . I charged them seven or eight dollars a week for a room, which wasn't much for a single person, but it ended up being a lot of money. Between the rent, the rehearsals and the whiskey, which I sometimes cut with a little water, I was making a lot more than by working in the clubs. So I wasn't playing any more when Big Bill's pianist, Joshua Altheimer, fell ill. Because I liked Big Bill a lot, and since at that time I was really the only one who could play with him, because he sang very much in his own way, I teamed up with him."[52]

Bill began cutting records with Slim in December 1940, and, until the recording ban began in mid-1942, Slim accompanied Bill on sixteen sides. He may well have joined Bill on a series of club performances at the Cozy Corner at 1323 South Morgan Street during the spring and summer of 1941, during which Bill was advertised as the "World's Greatest Blues Singer." By December Slim's visibility had increased substantially, as the pair was billed for another West Side gig as "Big Bill and Memphis Slim, Two of the World Known Famous Blues Singers."[53]

From pianist Eddie Boyd's description, the Cozy Corner needed to do all the marketing it could to draw customers, because even by blues club standards, it was not for the faint of heart. Boyd, who made his Chicago debut around this time, spoke of how "[guitarist Johnny Shines] and I played over at Jerry's Cozy Corner on Maxwell and Morgan Street: The Bucket of Blood. That was a *rough* joint. I was always afraid over there because I could see the police paddy wagon bringing people in there shot half to death and cut. Many of 'em just walked up and down the street where they'd get in an argument with each other, drunk and stabbing and just pistols shooting all the time over there. It used to be something else."[54]

After the recording ban hit in the summer of 1942, Bill and Slim continued to perform together around Chicago. They had a contract with John Gatewood for a four-month run of weekend shows at Ruby's Tavern, starting that August.[55] For working until 2 or 3 a.m. for three nights, the pair would get a total of $30 for the two of them. As Slim described it, the gig "paid weekly—very weakly."[56]

The pair also was featured several times over the next year at the renowned "Midnight Ramble," held at the Indiana Theater. As Saturday night turned into Sunday morning, the managers of the South Side movie house switched off the projector and put on a variety show that became a popular drawing card both for general audiences and other entertainers. Chicago jazz historian Dempsey Travis recalled how "comedians, singers, and dancers put on their 'bluest' jokes, their 'special material' songs, and their most revealing dance routines. . . . Occasionally the dancing would get so wild that the police would stop the show and warn the performers to turn down the burner."[57] While performers gained some status by participating—the longtime manager of the nationally known Regal Theater stated that "whenever he really wanted to see show business at its best, he went to the Indiana Theater"—the pay was paltry: Bill and Slim made just $7.75 apiece for the gigs they played there.[58]

Not long after that, Bill pulled Slim aside and gave him some advice. When Bill had first met Slim, Bill later recalled, "He was playing and singing exactly like Roosevelt Sykes. That was in 1939. I told him about playing like Roosevelt, which he denied, but I knew better that he was certainly playing like Roosevelt." Now, Bill had decided, it was time for Slim to set up and claim his place in the spotlight. "So one day I finally told to Memphis Slim, 'You's good enough now to go out on your own. You don't need Big Bill or no other blues singer with you. Just get you some good musicians to play with you and you'll be Memphis Slim just like I'm Big Bill.'"[59]

Then, as Bill described this interaction in his 1955 autobiography, "And so he did. . . . Memphis Slim is going big in the USA. He made some hit songs with his band. . . . Now [he] has a good six-piece band and every man he has is a good musician." The pride Bill took in his protégé's success was evident, as he applauded Slim's ability to rise from sideman and then collaborator with Bill, all the way to establishing himself as a bandleader and a power in his own right in the blues world.

It is hard to know who Bill's role model was for acting as a mentor to younger musicians. Whether it came from his father or from the older man or group of men whom Bill shaped into the figure of Uncle Jerry, Bill clearly relished guiding and encouraging artists on their way up in the music business. In the years to come, some of the most talented musicians in the Chicago blues scene would benefit from Bill's coaching. Over time, his willingness to help the next generation of Chicago blues artists became a standard that musicians used to measure themselves.

Years later Slim confirmed the importance of Bill's advice. He told a British interviewer, "You see, Bill said, 'Now you sound like yourself—

you got your own original style, so you go for yourself from now on.'"
Coming from Bill, it had a particularly powerful impact, because as Slim
noted, "Big Bill was the greatest that I have known. There may have been
some better, but I didn't know them. He was a wonderful person and a
lovely artist."[60]

 Preachin' the Blues

Through his output of over two hundred songs from the mid-1930s to the mid-1940s, Bill offered his views on numerous topics, and often from a variety of perspectives. Sometimes he emphatically endorsed lust, while other times he bemoaned the risks of romance. In considering the pleasures and pitfalls of alcohol, he boasted in one song that he would "keep on drinkin', till good liquor carry me down," while later recording a side with a markedly different tone: "Now, I don't fly high, 'cause it hurts when you hit the ground."[1] In his songs that reflected on his rural southern roots, he alternated between nostalgia for a simpler life and relief at escaping from a world that offered little hope of change for the better.

Many of Bill's compositions were intended to be music that people could dance to or to serve as background music to conversations in taverns or around the record player at home. Their titles reflect the straightforward nature of the topics: "Tell Me What You Been Doing," "Hard Headed Woman," "My Woman Mistreats Me," "My Gal Is Gone," "Let's Have a Little Fun." Even Bill's fertile imagination was hard-pressed to turn out fresh images and clever turns of phrase dozens of times a year for nearly a decade, under the deadline pressure of delivering batches of recordable three-minute tunes to the Melrose machine.

But few other blues songwriters of his era produced as much material of as consistently high a level of quality as Bill did. If there had been the blues equivalent of a Tin Pan Alley in Chicago in the 1930s and '40s, Bill would have been recognized as one of its most prominent figures. When he wrote about love, it was often in a wry voice:

I've been married three times, I was drunk as I could be,
I only had one wife, and the other two women had me.[2]

He could apply the same tone when describing the poor state of his finances and his prospects:

> Gal, poor me's so low down, baby, hoo, Lord, gal,
> Big Bill is looking up at down.[3]

Studs Terkel once remarked on Bill's "razor-whet lovely sense of irony," which was a perspective that permeated his songwriting.[4]

As a songwriter, Bill would sometimes cast himself in roles in which he could swagger and boast with any blues singer. In "Bull Cow Blues No. 3," he was the "bull with the long horn" and "the bull that bellows," who can "call milk cows from everywhere." He proclaimed in "Down in the Alley":

> I'm a tough man, I don't want nothin' nice
> I'm goin' down the alley where the women shootin' dice.[5]

And in "The Mill Man Blues," he announced:

> Gal, it's grindin' time in Dixie, and they call me Grindin' Bill [x2]
> Gal, just tell me your trouble, baby, ooh gal, 'cause I've got the mill.[6]

When it came to describing passion, Bill could employ a fresh image, as in "Nancy Jane":

> I went out walkin' with Nancy Jane, sat down in the dirt.
> My heart started pumpin' and it got so hot, I burned a hole in my
> undershirt.[7]

In "Truckin' Little Woman," as he described a willing partner, he managed to be both deftly and frankly sexual when he sang, "She can look up long as you can look down."[8] He could also shift into a more amorous tone, with some exaggeration for effect, as he did in "Rockin' Chair Blues" when he asked his partner to be gentle with him:

> Take me home with you, baby, and put me in your big armchair,
> You know I'm young and tender, gal, and you've got to handle Big Bill with
> care.[9]

In a few of his songs, Bill took on the part of a man who could threaten a woman with violence. In "Low Down Woman Blues," he declared:

I'm gonna buy me a pistol, a shotgun, and some shells
I'm gonna stop these lowdown women, because now I'm gonna start to
    raisin' hell.[10]

He imagined using weapons to establish his control over his partner in "Looking for My Baby":

Now when I find that woman, Lord, I'm gonna show her my forty-four,
Now, when I get her back home, Lord, I'll bet she don't leave me no more.[11]

And again in "Oh Yes":

Gal, you been out truckin' all night long,
You know I'm gonna whip you when I get home.[12]

He could envision making what he hoped would be a credible threat to a guy who had been "hangin' around my home," as in "Somebody Got to Go":

So look-a-here, buddy, now don't get hard
Because somebody may go to the graveyard
It may be three, it may be two
It may be me, and it may be you.[13]

In perhaps his most extreme expression of a figure whose self-loathing could trigger murderous rage, he confessed in "Evil Hearted Me" that "I'm so evil, don't even love myself," and added:

I don't care if the sun don't shine
I feel like killin' you, baby, and goin' on down the line.[14]

In contrast to these portrayals of amoral, violence-prone figures, Bill at other times wrote in the voice of a man haunted by the words of the Bible. In two different songs he used a specific phrase that would have been familiar to any listener who had spent some time in church. The first time he connected the lesson with the story of a young man who failed to heed his mother's guidance:

> *I remember my mother told me, it's been a long, long time ago*
> *Son, as you sow, boy, you gonna reap it, don't care where you go.*[15]

In the second song, the singer was alone in a desolate landscape:

> *Look down, look down, down that old lonesome road,*
> *Now, just sittin' here wondrin' how I gotta reap everything I've sowed.*[16]

In "Preachin' the Blues," Bill brought together several strands of his thinking about religion. Opening with the clear statement that "Now, brothers and sisters, I'm preachin' to you," he warned his listeners against assuming that it may be others who needed to change their ways:

> *If your friends is wrong, I'll tell you what to do*
> *You look over your hand and look it through and through*
> *And take your time, 'cause it may be you.*

Once he established that he was addressing every member of his "congregation," he was unflinching in his message:

> *Boy, you better get down on your knees, boy, and pray both night and day*
> *You may be havin' a good time with other women, and you may go to hell*
>   *that way.*

· Having staked out unfamiliar territory for blues songs by advising listeners that they were at risk of eternal damnation, Bill allowed himself a pointed comment about what drew people to religious institutions:

> *Men go to church just to hide their dirt*
> *And women go to church just to show their skirts.*

Then he swiftly turned the focus right back on the fallen:

> *But there's a day comin', it may be for you*
> *When Gabriel blow his trumpet, now what you gonna do?*

In his conclusion, Bill made it clear that, in his self-appointed role as a secular preacher, his own track record may be less than exemplary:

Now I have preached the blues, I have sung them too
Now don't you do as I do, just do as I tell you to.[17]

Bill was clearly skeptical that those who regularly stood before congregations would be able to withstand scrutiny of their own actions, even as they judged the actions of others.

In addition to expressing his concerns about reaping what he had sown, Bill invoked his mother in portions of several of his songs. Put another way, he introduced a mother figure to which the singer directed his comments. While his heartfelt lyrics may not have reflected his precise feelings for his own mother, Bill's connection to her was, in fact, strong enough to merit some mention of these lines.

In "Mean Old World," he lamented, "Sometimes I get so blue till I don't know what to do." Bill concluded by wishing: "Yes, if my mother's praying, I hope she prays for me some, too."[18] Based on his descriptions of his mother's strong religious beliefs, her prayers would likely have been a resource he could count on. He struck a regretful note in "When I Had Money" with a couplet that was evocative, if not original:

Lord, if I'd a-listened to my mother, Lord, what she said,
Lord, I would not have been here now, baby, layin' in this old hospital
    bed.[19]

When he imagined receiving a letter with the news of his mother's death in "Sad Letter Blues," he was nearly overcome with regret:

I left home, I thought my mother was mean to me . . .
Now today I wished I was what my mother tried to make me be.

Adding that "deep down in my heart there lies an achin' place," Bill offered his perspective to those who had not yet experienced a loss that he, in real life, had also not yet endured:

You may have plenty money and a whoppin' good place to stay,
Boy, but a dear old mother mean more, I don't care what you say.[20]

In reality, Bill's mother, Mittie Belcher Bradley, lived until late 1956, and he visited her regularly on his trips to see the Bradley clan in North Little Rock. Bill told Studs Terkel in 1957 that he never brought his guitar into his parents' home, out of respect for her wish that there be "no sinful things done around the house."[21] According to Bill, the first time she ever saw him play was in 1940, when he played in Little Rock while touring with Lil Green. "Somebody told her that I was playing up there," Bill related, "... and she came up there. And ... well, everybody knowed her around there, they wouldn't even charge her for to come in. And she came in and stood in the door and actually looked at me playing. That's the first time she ever seen me play anything."[22]

Bill spoke with pride about his mother's attendance at his performance, and he took pains to respect her rules for her home. Even though he chose a path that led away from institutional religion, his lyrics conveyed some ambivalence about the choice he had made. In "Lone Wolf Blues," he wrote about the thoughts that crept into his head when he was by himself. He chose not to be specific, which left listeners free to speculate about the maternal guidance he was pondering:

> Now, the hills is my pillow, green grass is my bed,
> Lord, every time I get alone, I think about what my mother said.[23]

Bill also used his lyrics to address the status distinctions among lighter- and darker-skinned blacks. In his 1935 recording of "I'm Just a Bum," he sang:

> Sometimes I wonder why my dad give poor me away
> Lord, because I was dark in complexion, [I] mean, and Lord, they all throwed me away.[24]

Twenty years later, he would describe in his autobiography his feelings of rejection at having to wait outside the church for his lighter-skinned paternal grandmother. In "Dreamy Eyed Baby," he used the flip side of prejudice based on skin color to sweet-talk the young lady described in the song title:

> I bet you was a beautiful baby, lord had them big black curls in your hair,
> Gal, if you was over in England, I believe you would pass over there.[25]

While comments on this topic were not unknown in race records, they were uncommon, and Bill's decision to use them reflected his expectation that his audience would be comfortable with his candor.

Among the hundreds of songs Bill wrote and recorded, there is one with which he has become most strongly associated over time. Yet while the music and words of "Key to the Highway" remain compelling, its origins are murky.

The first recording of the song was made by a piano player from Florida named Charlie Segar.[26] Segar, who was billed on some records as the "Key Board Wizard Supreme," recorded his version for Vocalion in Chicago on February 23, 1940. Most of the lyrics were similar or in some cases identical to the versions that Bill and Jazz Gillum recorded over the following fifteen months. The biggest difference was that Segar played the song as a twelve-bar blues, while both Bill and Gillum's versions were in the form of an eight-bar blues.[27]

On May 9, 1940, Jazz Gillum, during his only recording session of that year, recorded his version of "Key to the Highway" as the last song in a four-song session for Bluebird in Chicago. The accompanists were Bill on guitar and a bass player, probably Ransom Knowling. Almost exactly a year later, on May 2, 1941, Bill recorded his version of the song for Vocalion in Chicago, with Gillum on harmonica, Washboard Sam on washboard, and an unknown bass player.

While the facts of recording dates and most personnel are clear, harmonica player Jazz Gillum later argued that he was the song's composer. In Gillum's view, Lester Melrose was at fault for crediting Bill with the song. In a 1961 interview, Gillum described how he had composed the song in response to a request from Melrose for a "highway" song. Delmark Records owner Bob Koester remembers a contrasting perspective from his discussions with Gillum and Washboard Sam in the early to mid-1960s: "I was told by both guys that Big Bill wrote all their tunes, and Gillum specified Broonzy as the real author of 'Key to the Highway.'"[28]

According to Bill, he had learned the melody as a child from his uncle Jerry Belcher, who would play it on his five-string banjo. He recalled that "the melody, they've been playin' it for about, ever since I was a boy, I guess." As for Charlie Segar, Bill said, "I got connected with him here in Chicago and he was a good piano player.... [H]e wrote some lyrics ... well, he played it a little different from me. And, fact of the business, the melody that I'm singing it in was originally my melody. And some of the verses he was singing it as in the south, the same as I sung it in the south."[29]

Despite the uncertainty surrounding the authorship of the lyrics, Bill's 1941 version contains several of the most indelible images in blues songwriting. Few phrases have the emotional urgency of the singer's announcement that "I'm gonna leave here runnin' / 'Cause walkin' is most too slow." The words can apply either to a flight from a personal situation or to an exit from a set of larger social or political forces. The description of the nighttime escape, crystallized by the moment "when the moon peeps over the mountain," heightens the tension further. As the singer looks to the path ahead, declaring, "I'm gonna walk this old highway until the break of day," listeners can imagine their own ongoing or anticipated journeys.[30]

It is not clear how much of an impact any of the first three versions of "Key to the Highway" made on the audiences of the 1940s. The only listing for the song in Bill's surviving royalty statements shows sales in 1947 of about 1,500 sides of the Jazz Gillum version, for which Bill received just over $5.[31] A relatively small number of artists recorded it in the 1940s and '50s, with the list including John Lee Hooker as well as the duo of Sonny Terry and Brownie McGhee. Sonny and Brownie's recordings of the song, coupled with their regular touring schedule through the 1960s, helped to establish and sustain its popularity among fans of both blues and folk music. In addition, singers of the stature and range of Dinah Washington and Jimmy Witherspoon included versions on their LPs in the early 1960s.

The version that harmonica master Little Walter recorded in August 1958 for Chess Records would play a significant role in bringing "Key to the Highway" to a even broader white audience. The authors of the Little Walter biography speculate that Walter may well have chosen to record the song to honor Bill, who had died earlier that month. His version— with Chess heavyweights Muddy Waters, Willie Dixon, and Otis Spann, as well as session players Luther Tucker and Francis Clay—rose to number six on the *Billboard* charts and became Walter's last top-ten hit.[32]

It was the combined impact of Little Walter's version and Bill's original on a British guitar player that led to "Key to the Highway" achieving international recognition among rock fans. Eric Clapton heard both versions when he was a young guitarist intently pursuing a self-directed musical education. He has praised the two versions as "untouchable," adding, "Because I'm a guitar player, Bill's version is the one I always hark back to." When Clapton and his musical colleagues in the band Derek and the Dominos decided in 1970 to include "Key to the Highway" on their hugely successful 2-LP set *Layla and Other Assorted Love Songs*, they made the song a staple of blues-rock band repertoires around the world.[33]

An overview of Bill's songwriting would be incomplete if it failed to mention a perspective that Bill inserted into some of his songs. The viewpoint was one that was not often found in blues lyrics. The tone Bill used in a song like "I Feel So Good" could be described as cheerful and optimistic, as he spoke in the voice of a man anticipating that he stood a good chance of succeeding in love. In the song, the singer on his way to the train station to meet his "baby" proclaims, "Now, I feel so good, baby, I feel like ballin' the jack." In case there was any doubt about what he was looking forward to, he adds, "I feel just like a Jack out with a Jenny, way out behind the hill." He concludes by describing how "I love my tea, crazy about my Gordon gin," so the scene is clearly set for a reunion accompanied or enhanced by marijuana and alcohol.

What is noteworthy here is how different the singer is from the protagonists of many blues songs as they gear up for love or sex. There is no boasting or bragging, no need to raise himself up by demonstrating his prowess in comparison to others. The character Bill created is not arrogant—after all, he feels so good and he *hopes* he always will, but there are no guarantees. But he feels comfortable enough with himself, and secure enough with his audience, to make a joyful proclamation. The precise sources of Bill's belief that things just might work out for him are hard to trace, although the element of hope runs powerfully through the spirituals he heard in his Arkansas youth and later sang to white audiences in the 1950s. He even imported a line from a hymn composed at the turn of the twentieth century by the Reverend Charles Albert Tindley, an African American Methodist minister, when he sang, "I say, that's all right, mama, I will overcome it someday." Whether it was a religious, political, or romantic outcome, Bill's outlook embraced the possibility that things could improve.[34]

Blues at Midnight

In 1946 Bill performed for more white audiences than he ever had before. He still made records that were marketed primarily to African American buyers, and he continued to appear in Chicago clubs where it would have been unusual to see a white face. But a new organization had been formed in New York City that played an important role in providing Bill with bookings as he began to set his new course. Its name was People's Songs, and it brought together several people with whom Bill's career would be interwoven in various ways over the next decade.

The impetus for People's Songs came from a number of politically engaged musicians who had returned from serving in World War II, and who were eager to devote their talents to fighting for causes that had taken a backseat during the war effort. During the war, the labor unions had adopted a no-strike strategy in support of the massive industrial effort needed to defeat the Axis forces. With the end of the war, and the pent-up demand for labor to address working conditions and compensation issues in many industries, numerous strikes broke out across the United States. In addition, the quest for racial justice was on the minds of many who came home from the still-segregated armed services to a country where laws maintained the legality of segregation in the South, and in which widespread discrimination continued in the North.

People's Songs emerged from a gathering on New Year's Eve of 1945, at the Greenwich Village apartment of the in-laws of Pete Seeger. Then twenty-six years old and back from a tour of duty in the Pacific, Seeger had been a member of the Almanac Singers, whose recordings and performances before the war had established a precedent for urban-based folk musicians dedicated to fighting for unions and other causes. With Seeger taking a leadership role, the fledgling organization soon published its first newsletter, which proclaimed, "The people are on the march and must have songs to sing. Now, in 1946, the truth must reassert itself in many singing voices."[1]

A vital building block in People's Songs' strategy for attracting crowds of "many singing voices" was the informal, small-scale concert they called a hootenanny. The group borrowed the idea from the Almanac Singers, who had held these gatherings as a way to raise rent money. People's Songs took the "hoots" seriously enough to prepare and distribute a manual, *How to Plan a Hootenanny*. This user's guide laid out the essential factors for a successful hoot, from setting low admission fees for maximum attendance to making sure to include a range of song styles.[2]

Along with support for labor activism, the primarily white members and supporters of People's Songs identified the struggle for civil rights for all Americans as a key issue for the organization. In the assessment of one historian, "A significant portion of People's Songs' work was devoted to black music, black artists, and the theme of freedom." As the hoots got under way, the organizers began to feature a set of African American performers who had been performing for white New York audiences over the past several years, and who had incorporated into their repertoires some of the "field hollers, work songs, hymns, and spirituals [that] were presented as black contributions to American culture."[3] The list included Lead Belly, Josh White, and the harmonica-guitar team of Sonny Terry and Brownie McGhee.

The first announcement of an appearance by Bill at a People's Songs event was for a New York hootenanny in July 1946, in which he joined Woody Guthrie, Lead Belly, and Seeger on the bill. It was apparently a successful debut, because in the fall, when the group opened an office in Chicago, Bill immediately became a regular at the hoots for the Midwest branch. The office's first executive secretary was Raeburn "Ray" Flerlage, a white midwesterner in his early thirties with strong views about the importance of African American music and the injustices of racism. Flerlage immediately began to organize hoots, and he arranged for Bill to perform with Pete Seeger in late September. A week later he presented Bill and another black performer, Dock Reese, at the Parkway Community House, a bustling multi-service center in the heart of the South Side black community, a few blocks from where Bill was then living. Flerlage, in an effort to attract a racially integrated audience to a People's Songs event, even arranged to place a small notice about the hootenanny in the *Chicago Defender*.[4]

A month after Bill helped to launch People's Songs in Chicago, he returned to New York. Alan Lomax, under the auspices of People's Songs, was organizing what was billed as "The Midnight Special: A Series of American Folk-Music Concerts" at Town Hall. As John Hammond had done eight years before at Carnegie Hall, Lomax had selected a setting that would attract white audiences interested in hearing black artists playing in a variety of styles. For his inaugural presentation on Saturday evening, November 9, titled "Blues at Midnight" and scheduled for 11:30 pm, he assembled several veterans of the "From Spirituals to Swing" concert, including jazz master Sidney Bechet, pianist Pete Johnson, and Sonny Terry. Although Bill's name appeared on the poster as "'Big Bill' Broomzy," his 1938 performance had clearly made enough of an impression on Lomax to merit an invitation along with featured billing.

Bill's performance attracted the immediate attention of the New York music press. Composer and music critic Virgil Thomson, in his review in the *New York Herald Tribune*, singled out Bill and the trio of Bechet, Johnson, and bassist Billy Taylor as "the most masterful" of the performers. While Thomson focused most of his comments on the "elevating musical experience" provided by the trio, comparing it to "chamber music," he reiterated that Bill (whose name he rendered as "Bromzy") was one of "the stars of the evening." The *New York Times* reviewer, while less enthusiastic than Thomson about the show overall, spotlighted Bill as receiving the second-largest hand of the night, after Bechet. The writer also noted that "the audience of 1,500 had a good time, and didn't want to leave at 1:15 am."[5]

The "Blues at Midnight" concert was a noteworthy event in Bill's career for three reasons. First, the crowd's positive response to the show would have demonstrated to Bill the wisdom of the business decision he was making to appeal to a white, politically liberal-to-left audience. As he had at the "From Spirituals to Swing" concerts, he had performed for over a thousand people in a formal and acoustically stunning New York City concert hall and had been greeted with cheers and applause.[6]

Second, the song for which he had received the second-biggest round of applause was one of the first he had written in this new stage of his career. Different reviewers gave it different titles, but the chorus made it instantly identifiable:

Now if you's white, you's all right
If you's brown, stick around,
But if you's black, oh brother, get back, get back, get back.

Over time, "Black, Brown, and White Blues" would become as much of
an anthem as anything Bill ever wrote, an unmistakable indictment of
discrimination on the basis of the color of one's skin. Bill told various
versions of when he had composed it, but the reviews of this concert
are the earliest surviving mentions of his performing it, as well as of
a crowd's reaction to it. The song's verses, in later years augmented by
Bill's spoken introduction, documented a series of scenarios in which he
was treated unfairly in a variety of settings solely because he was black.
The Town Hall audience's response would have confirmed for him that
he was on the right track. As a reviewer for a jazz publication put it, the
song was "a really potent thing."[7]

The third element of the evening that served as a guidepost for Bill's
future was the onstage role Alan Lomax had assumed. As Virgil Thomson
described him, Lomax was the "guiding spirit and master of ceremonies
(the program called him, in radio style, 'narrator')."[8] Another reviewer
commented on how "throughout the evening, between the sets, Mr. Lomax interviewed, as it were, each of the artists. These discussions were serious, humorous, and interesting."[9] Bill would have seen that a performer
could have a significant impact on his listeners if he gave some context or
background to a song. In other words, if a performer could bring the audience along with him to a setting in which the song might have taken place,
or could have been written, it could amplify the song's impact. As Bill observed Lomax using commentary to enhance a musical presentation, he
was starting to craft a new way of presenting himself to an audience.

On his return to Chicago, Bill began a stretch in his career that would
last for several years in which he straddled his two audiences, one black
and one white. He cut records for predominately African American buyers as both a featured performer and a sideman, releasing sides under
band names such as Big Bill and His Rhythm Band, and Big Bill Broonzy
& His Fat Four. He continued to appear at the clubs where he was an
established name, such as Ruby's Tavern on the West Side and the Hollywood Rendezvous on the South Side. At the same time, he was becoming
a familiar figure to the politically engaged folk-music fans who attended
the People's Songs hootenannies in Chicago.

Bill recorded eight sides in two separate sessions for Columbia in December and January, the latter marking one of the last times he cut a commercial recording with Memphis Slim, now a rising star. After a February 1947 session backing Washboard Sam, which featured pianist Roosevelt Sykes and bass player Willie Dixon, Bill traveled back to New York's Town Hall for another of Alan Lomax's "Midnight Special" concerts.

Lomax and People's Songs had continued the late-night series they had launched in November, presenting concerts that focused on calypso, spirituals, and "strings," which had paired Pete Seeger with classical guitarist Carlos Montoya. The March 1, 1947, show, "Honky Tonk Blues at Midnight," brought back several artists from the earlier "Blues at Midnight" event, including Sidney Bechet and New Orleans bassist Pops Foster, as well as the pianist (and "From Spirituals to Swing" veteran) James P. Johnson. Bill and his colleagues Memphis Slim and harmonica star Sonny Boy Williamson were billed as "Coming from Chicago."

While Lomax later reported that "the trio tore down the house," it was an informal session held the next day that eventually had a more enduring impact. As Lomax recalled, Bill, Slim, and Williamson had stayed at his Greenwich Village home, where "they entertained my daughter Anna and sampled our Southern cooking." On the heels of the successful concert and congenial dinner, he decided to bring the group into the recording studio the next day. Lomax, who was working at the time for Decca Records, recalled later: "I took them to Decca, where we could have a whole studio to ourselves that Sunday. We had a couple of drinks, I put my little one-celled Presto disc recorders on the floor, and I sat at their feet, flipping the discs as they reminisced. There was only one microphone."[10]

After a brief musical warm-up, Lomax got the discussion started by asking them to define what the blues were. The three Chicago-based musicians spent the next two hours responding to his opening question with comments, snatches of songs, tall tales, and verbal exchanges about the often-brutal southern world they had each left behind. They described a tumultuous landscape of levee camps and chain gangs, honky-tonks and barrelhouses, and frequent beatings, murders, and lynchings. As they related what they had seen, heard, or remembered, the tone of the discussion ranged from matter-of-fact to impassioned to lighthearted, and their verbal interplay occasionally veered into back-and-forth banter, often at Williamson's expense.

The animated dialogue produced a wealth of compelling observations and anecdotes. Bill and Slim traded examples of black workers who redirected into songs the rage at their bosses that they felt but could not express, which Slim eloquently summarized as "signifying, and getting your revenge through song."[11] The portrait of life in the levee camps was bleak, with Slim commenting at one point that "if you were a good worker, you could kill anyone there, so long as he's colored. . . . You could kill any Negro, if you could work better than him. Don't kill a good worker."[12] Bill reinforced that by quoting the owner of one of the most notorious camps as saying, "If you boys keep yourselves out the grave, I'll keep you out the jails. . . . If you kill a nigger, I'll hire another."[13]

Bill told two horrifying stories about the violence that resulted from black men choosing to resist directions from whites. In one case, his uncle was lynched for refusing to force his pregnant wife, who was also caring for a young son, to return to field work on the plantation where they were sharecropping. In another, a white man not only killed a black man who married the black woman that he wanted for himself, but then proceeded to murder the man's parents, pregnant widow, and other family members.

Interspersed among these chilling accounts were some tales that owed as much to Mark Twain as they did to Richard Wright. Bill described how when a man was shot in a barrelhouse located in a levee camp, "some little short guy be standing around the craps table, and that table is high, he can't get up there, and I've seen them pull him, pull that dead man up there and stand on him, and still keep shooting dice."[14] The biggest whopper of the session came near the end, when Bill told of "a man at my home, they called him Mr. White," who insisted that everything on his farm be white, from all the farm animals to the fences, and even the trees ("he painted them white up as far as he could get").[15]

Once the session was over, Lomax faced a challenge: what to do with the material he had collected from the trio? The issue was not merely a question of editing the conversation into a more compact format. The stories the three men had told, if published or released on a commercial recording, could have put themselves or their families at risk of the kind of violent retribution they had described. In addition, each was recording at the time for a label other than Decca, which could have produced sticky contractual problems.

Lomax's solution emerged over time, and in several stages. The first step was to publish an article in 1948 in *Common Ground*, a journal dedicated to cultural diversity whose contributors included poets Langston Hughes and Archibald MacLeish and playwright William Saroyan.[16] The piece incorporated a vital part of Lomax's strategy, which was to reproduce much of what the men had said while disguising their specific identities. He had written Bill in early April 1947 to tell him about the proposed article and promised to send a copy for the three men "to read so you can make sure yourselves that it doesn't endanger you or your families."[17]

In the article, titled "I Got the Blues," each musician was given a new name, so Bill became Natchez, Slim was Leroy, and Williamson was introduced as Sib, and the location for the conversation was moved to "a little country tonk, somewhere out in the Arkansas blackland across the river from Memphis."[18] Lomax brought himself into the tale as the narrator, and he offered his own observations on the setting, the conversation, and the three individuals.

When Lomax traveled across the Atlantic in 1950 to begin what would become an eight-year European residency, he brought the tapes with him. He played segments on his BBC Third Programme show in November 1951, two months after Bill had performed for the first time in England.[19] Although Bill's "character," unlike Slim and Williamson, was identified by name as "Bill the grave guitar player," Lomax must have believed that it was highly unlikely that anyone listening would have been able to recognize and expose him.

It was not until 1957, a decade after the original recording session, that Lomax released portions of the conversation on a commercial record. Issued on the British label Pye Nixa under the title *Blues in the Mississippi Night*, the LP contained nearly an hour of the discussion, interspersed with sections of music the trio had played or sung, as well as several segments of other singers whom Lomax had recorded elsewhere. In his ongoing effort to conceal the identities of the participants, Lomax's liner notes dated the original session as taking place nearly five years before the actual date, at "a country dance, where I was recording rural folksongs."[20] Included with the record was a transcript of all of the spoken and sung material, which took up three of the four LP-size pages in three newspaper-style columns of small print type. The album was popular enough in England to spend several weeks on the list of "Top Jazz Discs" published by *Melody Maker*, which was the rough equivalent at the time of the *Billboard* magazine charts in the United States.[21]

Two years later, Lomax released virtually the same record in the United States, on the United Artists label. In this version of *Blues in the Mississippi Night*, the liner notes were almost identical to the British release, and although there was no transcript, the back of the LP announced that the content was "The Real Story of the Blues, Sung and told by three MISSISSIPPI DELTA BLUES MEN."[22] Over the succeeding decades, it was reissued several times, including a two-LP set also containing another collection of Lomax's field recordings, *Murderer's Home*, as well as several reissues on CD.[23]

While *Blues in the Mississippi Night* was never a commercial success, it had a significant impact on the musicians and writers who listened to it. Greil Marcus, in his influential 1975 book *Mystery Train*, described the record as "a brutal and poetic prehistory of the civil rights movement."[24] Johnny Cash picked up a copy in the Home of the Blues record store in Memphis and praised it in his autobiography as "still one of my favorite records." Cash skillfully incorporated elements of several of the stories that the trio had told into his song "Going to Memphis" on his 1960 LP *Ride This Train* and later acknowledged that "I borrowed a good song title there, too."[25]

In all the commercially released versions of the sessions, several elements of Bill's personality and worldview emerged. He was the one among the trio who took the lead in directing the discussion, and his style likely had some similarities with how he handled himself as a bandleader. While there is no doubt that he was in charge, he made sure to draw the others into the conversation, especially Sonny Boy Williamson, who was less fluid and polished in his comments than the other two. Memphis Slim's stories and comments were often keenly observed and well expressed, and Bill was secure enough not to be threatened by the younger man's abilities, as he gave Slim all the time he needed to make his points. Some of the most energetic parts of the discussion featured exchanges between Bill and Slim, where they would each contribute phrases in what was as much a joint narrative as two separate speakers. The many hours they had spent playing and recording together had clearly produced a creative bond between the two men that extended beyond the format of twelve-bar blues.

One tale in particular followed a theme that Bill would pick up again in the years to come. Slim took the lead in telling about a white man named Charlie Houlin, whom he and Bill described as the "mercy man" who would employ black workers and protect them from attacks by other whites. As Bill told it, "Even if it come to a fight, he'd fight this bad man for the, for the Negroes."[26] According to Slim, Houlin's reputation for using force against those who would threaten his workers was enough to ensure that a white driver would offer a drink to a hitchhiking black man who identified himself as under Houlin's protection.

In the mid-1950s, Bill wove the notion of a white southern landowner who provided meaningful assistance to the local African American community into a song-story he called "Joe Turner Blues." He made some significant adjustments from Charlie Houlin in the portrait he drew of Joe Turner, with one of the most striking being to emphasize that Turner's generosity was anonymous and was revealed only after his death. By the time he recorded "Joe Turner Blues," Bill had been playing for white audiences for over a decade and had a clear sense of the warm reception they would give such a story. One of the early indicators of this direction for Bill would likely have been the keen interest Lomax expressed in the Houlin story during the *Blues in the Mississippi Night* sessions. In a comment that was not included in the commercially released versions of the sessions, Lomax attempted to steer the discussion back to Houlin after Bill started to ask Williamson about a different topic: "Let's not change the subject. Let's keep all that in. I want to hear more about the mercy man, Charlie."[27] Bill's musical and cultural antennae, consistently attuned to emerging trends, would certainly have picked up that message.[28]

After the sessions at Decca, Bill returned to Chicago. He was becoming accustomed to straddling the two different worlds in which he was making his living as a musician. As a blues artist, Bill would go into the recording studio for Columbia Records, backed by a six-piece band with a trumpet and two saxophones, to record songs like "I Can Fix It" and "Saturday Evening Blues." His guitar would be a crucial ingredient in backing Washboard Sam and His Washboard Band on "You Can't Have None of That," or behind the Yas Yas Girl as she lamented about the "Bad Whiskey Blues," or Sonny Boy Williamson as he located a previously undiscovered groove in the nursery rhyme "Polly Put Your Kettle On."

Bill had also become a regular performer for People's Songs in Chicago. He was now being billed at the hoots as "The Greatest of the Blues Singers," and when the national *People's Songs Bulletin* printed the words and music to "Black, Brown, and White Blues," Bill was featured with a photo and a short write-up. The text proclaimed, "Here is a great new blues song, right out of the Jim Crow bitterness of 1946 America. Big Bill Broonzy, who composed it, should know what it's all about." Bill shared the billing at two of the Chicago hoots with a thirty-eight-year-old singer whose range ran from opera to Schubert lieder to folk songs, and who had recently joined the national board of People's Songs. His name was Win Stracke, and his personal friendship and professional collaborations with Bill would link the two for the rest of Bill's life.[29]

Winfred John Stracke (pronounced "STRAH-kee") was born in Lorraine, Kansas, on February 20, 1908, and arrived in Chicago two years later when his father, a Baptist minister, moved the family there to accept a position at a church in the North Side neighborhood of Old Town. His early exposure to music came from his parents, who had met in the United States after each had emigrated from Germany, and who sang "mostly religious" folk songs to him in German. From singing in church choirs and his high school chorus, he learned that his powerful bass-baritone voice might offer the possibility of a career in music.

Instead of pursuing that option upon his graduation from Senn High School in 1926, Stracke headed west in a Model-T Ford in search of "employment and adventure."[30] While working as a roustabout on an oil well in Thermopolis, Wyoming, he encountered a picaresque figure who made a lasting impression on him. Flat Wheel Harry was a miner with a gimpy leg who was a member of the Industrial Workers of the World, often called the Wobblies.[31] The IWW, a union known for its unflinching stances on behalf of its members, had a tradition of spreading its message of worker solidarity through song. According to Stracke, Flat Wheel Harry "was the first person who really gave me the feeling of the oral tradition of American folklore. After working at the well, he'd tell me amusing stories about Babe and the Blue Ox, and he taught me to sing 'The Big Rock Candy Mountain.'"[32] The introduction to American folk music, coming from a man whom the eighteen-year-old adventurer saw as the embodiment of the workers' struggle for justice and dignity, would influence Stracke for years to come.

Returning to Chicago, Stracke pursued a career as a singer, working in settings that ranged from commercial theatrical productions to traveling opera companies. In 1931 he was hired for $40 a week by Chicago radio station WLS to join the Melody Men quartet as their bass singer. The Melody Men were regulars on WLS's enormously popular Saturday-night program the *National Barn Dance*, which the station's powerful 50,000-watt signal carried across a wide swath of the midwestern United States. The success of the *Barn Dance* had helped to inspire the founders of the Grand Ole Opry in Nashville, and Stracke took notice of the talented performers who appeared on the program with him, as well the songs they played. He became a familiar figure on Chicago radio in the 1930s through his regular appearance on programs such as *Hymns of All Churches* and *Chicago Theater of the Air.*[33]

In the late 1930s, Stracke found a way to apply his musical talents to the social causes he believed in. The Chicago Repertory Group had begun earlier that decade as the Chicago Workers Theater, which had been founded by six amateur performers who were eager, as they said in their statement of goals, "To crystallize in drama the informed but pressing problems of our times."[34] With a commitment to cooperative decision making, shared professional responsibilities, and affordable ticket prices, the Rep Group (as its members called it) became, in the words of longtime *Chicago Tribune* theater critic Richard Christiansen, "acknowledged as a significant force in theater."[35] The group put itself on the Chicago theater map in 1935 with its production of Clifford Odets's *Waiting for Lefty*, which the *Chicago Daily News* called "stirring, exciting, and vivid." Its 1938 staging of Marc Blitzstein's *The Cradle Will Rock* brought the composer out from New York for the opening.[36]

The Rep Group's production of *Waiting for Lefty* was particularly noteworthy because it marked the acting debut of a twenty-three-year-old transplanted New Yorker who had graduated the year before from the University of Chicago Law School. Louis Terkel had moved to Chicago from New York City in 1921, at age nine, and prior to his legal education at the Hyde Park campus, he had learned much about the ways of the city and the world from the sporadically employed residents of the rooming hotel his parents ran. Having sampled several post-graduation possibilities, including a brief stint at the FBI, Terkel was in the midst of what he called "my aimless search for a career" when he learned about the Rep Group from one of its members, the actor and director Charles DeSheim. After DeSheim persuaded him to watch how the group operated, Terkel was drawn in, and he soon appeared regularly in its productions. As he later described it, a significant element of the Rep Group was their politically charged work: "We'd perform street theater at picket lines and soup kitchens; we regularly appeared before unions, performing *Waiting for Lefty* as various strikes were being organized—performing in Union halls. . . . This was the world I was engaged with and it was exciting."[37]

It was the prospect of being a politically engaged artist that drew Win Stracke to the Rep Group. In addition to his various singing jobs on the radio, Stracke had begun, in the words of his daughter, Jane Stracke Bradbury, to get "involved in politics, in helping with unions and supporting union activity."[38] In joining the Rep Group, Stracke also began a decades-long friendship with Terkel, who had adopted the nickname "Studs" in tribute to author James T. Farrell's streetwise Chicago character Studs Lonigan.[39]

In the Rep Group, as actor and group member Nathan Davis recalled, "There were people who were interested certainly in the theater, but then there were those who were very political, which included a whole spectrum of political. And that was the crux and the strength of the Repertory Group. Because there were Communists and Socialists and whatnot." There was no doubt in Davis's mind about the dramatic impact that the Rep Group experience had on Stracke, who was his friend for five decades. In Davis's words, "It radicalized him, there's no question."[40]

The onset of World War II drew many members of the Rep Group away from Chicago to serve in various ways with the war effort. Stracke enlisted in the army and served as an anti-aircraft gunner in the U.S. Army, where he traveled through North Africa, France, and Italy. Terkel was drafted and spent a year in the U.S. Air Force, but a perforated eardrum prevented him from going overseas. The Rep Group effectively disbanded before the end of the war, but once the veterans returned to Chicago, the bond that had formed between Stracke and Terkel produced the revue that would launch the postwar era of Chicago folk music.

When Pete Seeger and his New York colleagues announced the formation of People's Songs in early 1946, Stracke and Terkel recognized that the key goals of the new organization were nearly identical to those of the Rep Group. People's Songs opened a Chicago office in the fall of 1946, and the two friends lost no time getting involved. Terkel served on the Chicago Steering Committee and wrote a review of a jazz concert at Orchestra Hall for the *People's Songs Bulletin*, while Stracke sang at a number of events and was named to the national board. Stracke had also performed in early 1947 at a People's Songs hoot on the campus of the University of Chicago, which merited an article in the school newspaper, the *Maroon*. Terkel was known to students on the South Side campus as the host of a Chicago radio show, *The Wax Museum*, in which he played records from a wide range of musical styles, offering comments in a voice whose tone the *Maroon* described as "molasses-and-gravel."[41]

When a University of Chicago student named June Myers contacted Terkel in the fall of 1947 about presenting a concert of folk music, he seized the opportunity.[42] Terkel later described the organizing principle for "I Come for to Sing" as "songs of a similar vein sung through three different epochs of humankind." He would serve as a narrator whose commentary would connect the performances of three singers, each of whom would present music of a particular genre. The themes would be subjects such as fickle love, traveling, or work. The cast included Stracke for songs from the American frontier, while a tenor named Larry Lane, whom Myers knew, provided what Terkel described as songs from "Elizabethan England."[43]

The third genre was the blues, and when Big Bill Broonzy stepped onto the Mandel Hall stage on November 7, 1947, for the first performance of "I Come for to Sing," it was his University of Chicago debut. Of his three fellow group members, Bill likely was most familiar with Stracke, having performed with him at several People's Songs events over the previous year. A longtime fan of jazz and blues, Terkel certainly knew Bill's music from his records, as he had started shopping for 78s in Bronzeville during his law-student days. Terkel had probably seen Bill and Stracke perform as recently as the previous month, when they appeared separately at a concert with Woody Guthrie and others at Chicago's Orchestra Hall, as part of People's Songs' first and only national convention.

Although "I Come for to Sing" drew on veterans of People's Songs hoots like Bill and Stracke as performers, the content of the songs was not explicitly political. This was not accidental, as People's Songs had begun to attract the attention of newspapers and congressional committees caught up in the rising tide of Cold War anti-Communism. In the summer of 1947, the organization had been the subject of testimony before the House Committee on Un-American Activities, the body soon to become notorious for its attempts to force artists and others to "name names" of people with alleged Communist connections. In September People's Songs had appeared on a list of "Party-line organizations" published by a newsletter dedicated to exposing "subversive" entities.[44]

"I Come for to Sing" represented a timely opportunity for the quartet to perform apolitical folk songs for audiences who could enjoy them for a variety of reasons. Those with an interest in American history would have appreciated Stracke's version of the lament of Irish railroad workers, "Drill, Ye Tarriers, Drill," and Lane's performance of "Greensleeves" would have appealed to British folklore fans. When Bill sang of the battle between man and machine described in "John Henry" or of the call of the lonesome road in "Key to the Highway," the sounds and images could resonate for listeners as compelling and evocative stories simply on their own merits. By launching the revue at an internationally renowned research university, the group could stress the academic nature of the event in its publicity.[45]

The response from the opening night crowd for "I Come for to Sing" was enthusiastic; as Terkel later described it, "Something electrifying happened."[46] The campus that had been responsive to the People's Songs' hoots showed that it would embrace a concert of folk music. Although the national commercial success of the Weavers was still several years away, the "I Come for to Sing" group had demonstrated that there was an audience in Chicago for songs from several ethnic and cultural traditions. The quartet would remain intact for the first few years, as they traveled first to colleges and universities in the Midwest, usually during the summer, and later headed farther west to campuses as distant as New Mexico and Washington State. On the road trips, Bill generally drove, because, as Stracke pointed out, he "had a car, and the rest of us didn't have one."[47]

For Stracke, the "I Come for to Sing" revue provided a bridge from People's Songs to a broader folk-music audience. For Terkel, who played no instrument and whose vocal skills were limited to narration, the group gave him a vehicle in which he could take a more active role in folk-music performances than simply serving as a master of ceremonies. For the two of them, the revue would become a significant professional lifeline during the 1950s, when they would each suffer the consequences of being blacklisted. When the revue later established a residency at a prestigious jazz club in the Loop, it would raise the profile of folk music in Chicago substantially. For audiences in Chicago, a city where racial covenants in 1947 still permitted white landlords to refuse to rent to African Americans, "I Come for to Sing" offered something unfamiliar: a racially integrated group singing folk songs.

During these years in the late 1940s, Bill's career was in transition, in the midst of a shift that was unprecedented for a blues musician who had enjoyed the level of success that he had. After a sustained run of nearly twenty years as one of the most prolific artists in the blues recording world, he was creating a new professional identity. He was increasingly immersed in a world of folk songs that he played on an acoustic guitar, requiring him to assemble and master a very different repertoire than the one he had been performing and recording for decades. His professional colleagues were white, and while he enjoyed their respect and camaraderie, it was different from the comfort level and the set of common reference points he shared with musicians like Memphis Slim and Sonny Boy Williamson. He would continue to play for African American audiences, but he was increasingly orienting his professional focus to the tastes and preferences of whites.

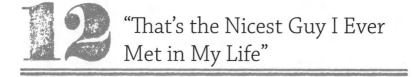

"That's the Nicest Guy I Ever Met in My Life"

In the years that followed the end of World War II, the Chicago blues world underwent a dramatic transformation. It began slowly, but by the mid-1950s, the best-known musicians, the most influential record companies, and the most powerful decision makers were different from those who had occupied those positions previously. Some of the forces driving these changes were at work on a national scale. Popular tastes were changing, as artists such as Louis Jordan, Big Joe Turner, and Wynonie Harris brought rocking arrangements with powerful saxophones to up-tempo tunes, while singers such as Charles Brown and Cecil Gant crooned ballads for slow dancing. In 1949 the U.S. music industry's premier magazine, *Billboard*, dropped "race records" as the title of the category for African American record buyers and replaced it with "Rhythm and Blues," which was quickly shortened to "R&B."[1] The end of the wartime rationing of shellac, the raw material for records, made it easier for independent labels run by entrepreneurs to compete against the established companies like Columbia and RCA Victor.

But there were other trends under way that were either specific to Chicago or that had a particularly strong impact there. While Lester Melrose still controlled much of the access to blues recording sessions, the owners of a few record stores and clubs were starting to make and release records featuring local musicians. These recordings often featured bands with horns and pianos, which reflected the dance numbers in their repertoires. In some cases, though, the performers were bluesmen who were playing in the smaller taverns or in the tumultuous outdoor market on Maxwell Street. These recordings had a less polished sound, and the instruments were likely to be harmonicas and guitars.

Many of the men who played those portable instruments arrived in Chicago between 1940 and 1950 in the large wave of African American immigrants from the South. The black population of Chicago increased during that decade by nearly 215,000, reaching a total of almost half a million. By 1950 African Americans comprised over 13 percent of the city's population, and over half of them had been born somewhere else. The recent arrivals—such as Muddy Waters, harmonica player Little Walter, and guitarist Jimmy Rogers—included some of the artists who would go on to define what blues fans around the world would identify decades later as "Chicago blues." But in their early days in the city, they struggled to break into the world of the taverns, clubs, and recording sessions.

One of the most influential roles that Bill played in this transition period for the Chicago blues scene was to provide guidance and encouragement to the newer arrivals. Bill was older than they were, as most of them had been born between 1910 and 1930, and few of his contemporaries were as well established and well connected as he was. Of those Bill helped, Muddy Waters not only reached the highest levels of recognition, but spoke at the greatest length and with the most emotion about his goodwill. "Big Bill," he once said in an interview, "that's the nicest guy I ever met in my life."[2]

Muddy Waters was born McKinley Morganfield in 1913 in Mississippi, where he had honed his guitar playing and singing skills at the parties he called "Saturday night fish fries" in the local juke joints. His first recorded sides were made on the Stovall plantation outside Clarksdale, in Coahoma County, in 1941 by Alan Lomax and John Wesley Work III. The recordings were part of a joint research project by the Library of Congress and Fisk University, with the goal of studying the role that music played in a predominantly African American county. As Muddy described it, hearing Lomax play back the recordings he had done on the folklorist's portable recording machine was "the great thing of my life—never heard my voice on records, man, and to hear that . . . that was great."[3] Buoyed by this confidence, Waters had come to Chicago in 1943 in the hope of establishing himself as a musician.

While working a series of day jobs, Waters began to play in the evenings at house parties and taverns. He met Bill not long after he arrived, and the younger musician was well aware that "at that time Bill was the top man."[4] Among the ways that Bill, as Muddy later recalled, "helped me to get my start" was to provide an introduction to Silvio, the owner of Silvio's Tavern, a club on the West Side where Bill often played.[5] Just as the older Chicago musicians had opened doors for Bill two decades before, he used his stature to give the next generation a chance to suc-ceed. Waters contrasted how Bill responded to him with the treatment he received from other musicians. "It [wa]s hard to get on record then. And [if] you in, you done made hits, and you got a big name—the little fellow ain't nothin'. But Big Bill, he don't care where you from; he didn't look over you 'cause he been on records a long time."[6] The consideration and respect Bill showed to Muddy had a powerful impact on Waters, both in his view of Bill and in his awareness of his responsibilities to others on the way up if he ever became successful himself.

It was not a matter of Bill singling out Muddy for special treatment. Numerous musicians spoke with warmth and appreciation for the way Bill welcomed and advised them. Jimmy Rogers was a member of Mud-dy's band for nearly a decade, and his guitar work was an integral com-ponent of the sound that carried Waters to success at Chess Records. Rogers, whose real name was James A. Lane, was born in Mississippi in 1924 and came to Chicago to stay in the mid-1940s. He once told an interviewer that "Big Bill taken a liking to me. When Muddy came to Chi-cago, he taken a liking to Muddy, too. I didn't play with Big Bill, but he had time for me. He told me a lot of points about life and about the blues scene."[7] On another occasion, Rogers expressed his regard for Bill in this way: "I really admired him, hair stand on my head to see that man. Big Bill gave me a lot of points on what was going down in this blues field."[8]

Not everyone in the younger generation of blues musicians held Bill in high regard. Robert Junior Lockwood—the guitarist and bandleader who was born in Turkey Scratch, Arkansas, in 1915 and who recorded for Melrose in Chicago in 1941—once described his unsuccessful efforts to improve Bill's guitar playing. "I used to try and teach Bill things on the guitar; he didn't even try to learn it. He said, 'Aw, you can't teach an old dog new tricks.' He'd look at me and say, 'Hell, I'd never be able to do that.'" Lockwood, who was well-known for his candor, may have been a dozen years younger than Bill, but his guitar teacher had been Robert Johnson, who was his mother's boyfriend, and, as he pointed out in the same interview, "Robert was the boss. Robert was a mystery." Lockwood also told of an unsuccessful attempt by Bill and Memphis Slim during his 1941 visit to Chicago to get him to pay the $25 tab for a "set-up" (a pint of whiskey with glasses and ice) that the two men had ordered while taking him to a nightclub. After failing to stick the rookie out-of-towner with the bill, Lockwood remembered, "one of them paid for it."[9]

By contrast, Little Walter Jacobs, generally acknowledged to be the harmonica player who set the standard for postwar Chicago blues, went out of his way to praise Bill in a 1964 interview with the British music journalist Max Jones. Walter was generally reserved in acknowledging the talents of other musicians, so his choice of words for Bill was unusual and significant: "There's one man I can give credit to—a friend and a good musician: Big Bill Broonzy, he could play, and not just blues."[10] Pianist Eddie Boyd, whose song "Five Long Years" was a number one R&B hit, also spoke highly of Bill. Boyd, born in 1914, had come to Chicago in 1941 and recalled, "I had to learn my way about this city, you know, what's going on. I spent a lot of time with Big Bill Broonzy, and he helped me a lot, too. I mean in information. He was sure never a selfish guy."[11]

While Bill's stature in the Chicago blues community was secure in the years following World War II, he was starting to record less often. From 1945 to 1950, he played on significantly fewer sessions as both a featured performer and a sideman than he had before the war.[12] The decline in sideman sessions for Bill was the most telling, as it was an indicator that both he and the cohort of artists who had been connected with Lester Melrose since the 1930s were starting to lose favor among the African American record-buying public. Other forces that worked to diminish Melrose's influence were the 1948 strike by the American Federation of Musicians and the decision by the major record labels to eliminate their series of race records. By the early 1950s, artists such as Lil Green, Washboard Sam, Jazz Gillum, and the Yas Yas Girl, each of whom Bill had backed regularly in prewar sessions, were not able to sustain the levels of success they had enjoyed in the years before the war.

For two of Bill's friends and colleagues, Major "Big Maceo" Merriweather and John Lee "Sonny Boy" Williamson, factors beyond shifting musical tastes brought their careers to an end in the late 1940s. Big Maceo had recorded several sides for Melrose in 1941, including "Worried Life Blues," which was a hit that became a blues standard. His muscular playing influenced the next generation of Chicago blues pianists, including Otis Spann, and has been described by blues historian Mike Rowe as sounding "as though the whole 245 pounds of his frame was transmitted directly through his finger-tips."[13] Just after returning from a national tour in May 1946, he suffered a stroke, which left his right side paralyzed.[14] Although he continued to perform for a brief time with another pianist playing the right-hand part, he suffered two more strokes in succeeding years, which limited his opportunities to record.

Bill's connection with Big Maceo was both personal and professional, with an element of mostly friendly rivalry. In his autobiography, Bill described him as "a good friend of mine but we would always argue about playing."[15] Big Maceo had backed Bill on a dozen sides for Columbia in February 1945, and Bill noted with pride that a combo they had put together "got a lot of good jobs playing together at theaters, night clubs, and for cocktail parties."[16] The piano player was close to Bill's age, as he had been born in 1905, and at times they lived in the same apartment building at 4706 South Parkway.[17]

In his portrait of Big Maceo in the book, Bill described their efforts to direct their competitive feelings into collaboration: "We used to argue and fall out with each other, but no licks were ever passed. He knew more about real music than I did but I knew more about the real blues and the arguments was because he would tell me to make the right chord." According to Bill, it was Big Maceo who summarized the resolution of their differing views: "'OK, Bill,' he'd say, 'we will play your way when you's singing and you play my way when I'm singing, please.'"

Bill emphasized in *Big Bill Blues*, published several years after the pianist's death in 1953, that "Big Maceo was a favourite of the blues world and he was liked and known by all singers in the USA." Bill closed his section on Big Maceo by eulogizing him, stating, "We can all say that one of the greatest blues singers is dead and gone."

Bill's other friend and colleague whose career was cut short in the late 1940s was Sonny Boy Williamson. Bill played on over forty sides by the younger harmonica star from 1939 until 1947. Sonny Boy, who was born John Lee Williamson in Jackson, Tennessee, in 1914, had been one of Melrose's biggest stars, winning over audiences with his compelling combination of talents. As a singer, he had a warm, engaging delivery that, because of his slight speech impediment, drew in listeners, as it often seemed that he was speaking directly to them. As one of his contemporaries said, "I never heard a man couldn't speak well, but he could sing!"[18] His songwriting reinforced the personal connection a listener might feel with him, as he would often describe his hometown of Jackson in terms that could, as has been observed, make it feel like "everybody's hometown."[19] In other songs, he was unusually candid about his affection for drinking and for women he should not have been involved with—particularly the student he addressed in perhaps his best-known song, "Good Morning, School Girl." In Mike Rowe's words, "Happy or sad, Sonny Boy reached out from the grooves to his listeners and his pleasures or his sorrows became theirs."[20]

Williamson's most enduring impact was to establish the harmonica firmly as a lead instrument of a Chicago blues band. When he came to Chicago to record for the first time in 1937, the harmonica had been present on some recordings made there, particularly those of Jazz Gillum, but in more of a supporting role than a starring one. Gillum's harmonica playing came almost exclusively in the intros and the choruses of his songs. By contrast, Williamson brought the instrument to the forefront by using it to highlight or underscore his lyrics, augmenting the story he was telling or the mood he was trying to establish. With his expressive singing and playing, and the backing of a guitar, piano, and drums, Williamson found himself fronting what became the basic template for the Chicago blues bands of the 1950s.

As with Big Maceo, Bill's relationship with Sonny Boy was friendly but not without conflict. In his section on Sonny Boy in *Big Bill Blues*, Bill portrayed him as "good-hearted," generous, and well-liked, noting that "he would give the shirt off his back to his friend, and he had a lot of them, too." In describing how he, Memphis Slim, and Sonny Boy "played together for a long time," Bill added that when "Sonny Boy would get drunk he would jump on me or Slim for a fight."[21] Harmonica player Billy Boy Arnold, who as a twelve-year-old took lessons from Sonny Boy, heard that Bill once broke a guitar over Sonny Boy's head in an argument outside a West Side bar. Guitarist Hudson Shower, who performed and recorded as Little Hudson, knew both men and confirmed that Sonny Boy "and Big Bill used to get hung up together. . . . But then after the fight, that was all over with . . . they were big buddies."[22]

Williamson was violently attacked after performing at a South Side club on June 1, 1948, and died after making his way home to his wife, Lacey Belle. Various hypotheses about the circumstances of the murder have been advanced, but the crime has never been solved. Williamson's memorial service was held at the Metropolitan Funeral Parlors, where almost exactly ten years later Bill would be mourned, and thirty-five years later throngs would gather to bid farewell to Muddy Waters.

Not long after Sonny Boy Williamson died, Bill was finally able to sever his ties with Lester Melrose for his recording and publishing arrangements. Bill had already established a business relationship for his out-of-town bookings with Joe Glaser, one of the most powerful agents in the world of jazz and popular music. Melrose had never acted as a booking agent for Bill, because he had never needed one for his Chicago-area gigs or his tours with Lil Green. For a period of time that likely began in 1945, Bill was represented by Glaser, who had emerged from the rough-and-tumble world of Prohibition-era Chicago to become Louis Armstrong's manager. By the time he was representing Bill, Glaser had founded Associated Booking Company, later described as "the country's biggest black talent booking agency."[23] Oscar Cohen, who succeeded Glaser as the agency's head, recalled, "Big Bill was one of Joe's big favorites."[24]

Glaser was likely responsible for booking Bill for his one appearance at the Apollo Theater in New York. In June 1945 Bill had played for a week at the famed Harlem venue, a showcase for African American performers for decades. His appearance had been advertised in New York's leading black newspaper, the *Amsterdam News*, as "America's Most Popular Blues Singer," and he had received second billing to a band led by jazz saxophonist and arranger Teddy McRae.[25]

Glaser may also have had a hand in arranging for the first commercial recording session Bill had played on without Melrose's involvement. In March 1945 Bill had recorded four sides in New York with a quartet of jazz musicians led by saxophonist Don Byas. The sides were issued on Hub Records, an East Coast label run by Ben Bart, whose talent agency, Universal Attractions, was later bought by Glaser. Because Bill was still under contract to Columbia, he was listed as "Little Sam," although most listeners would have recognized him from his distinctive voice and choice of songs, including "Just a Dream."

By December 1948 Bill had not recorded for an entire year. Although recording had ceased for most of that period because of another musicians' strike called by James Petrillo, Bill could see that Melrose's influence was waning. Bill was mindful of which way the winds of popular music were blowing, and he had been able to establish relationships with influential people in the music industry beyond Melrose.

On December 15 he turned to Alan Lomax for assistance. He wrote a letter to Lomax informing him that he had received a contract from Mercury Records. After noting that his relationship with Melrose had begun twenty years earlier, Bill stated simply, "He said he would release me."[26]

Mercury had started in Chicago only three years before and was quickly transforming itself from an emerging independent to a major label. A central component of Mercury's business model was to record African American artists whose styles covered a range of categories that embraced jazz, blues, pop, and R&B. The key person at Mercury from Bill's perspective was John Hammond, who had recently taken a position there as vice president.

Having secured permission from Melrose to go his own way, Bill asked Lomax to contact Hammond on his behalf and to find out whether Hammond would advise him to sign the Mercury contract. Among Bill's concerns was that, as he understood it, the contract restricted him to recording eight songs a year, which was less than half the number specified in some of his ARC contracts from the 1930s. While a copy of the contract has not survived, it is possible that the language, as was true in the earlier ARC ones, confirmed a minimum number of songs rather than a maximum. Over the following two months, Bill recorded a total of nine sides for Mercury, so it appears that any response Bill might have received reassured him that the contract was worth signing.[27]

Extricating himself from the business relationship he had with Melrose would certainly have given Bill satisfaction and relief. The anger he felt toward the man who had directed the terms of every recording contract he had signed for two decades remained a potent force within Bill. Bill expressed his frustrations about his treatment by Melrose in letters he wrote in the 1950s to Yannick Bruynoghe and others, as he was sharply critical of what he identified as Melrose's consistent abuse of the power he held over Bill and other musicians who wished to record in Chicago. The initiative that Bill took in providing guidance to younger musicians, especially about protecting the publishing rights to their songs, reflected his efforts to help others learn from his experience.

At the same time, now that he would be representing himself in negotiations over recording and publishing contracts, he had to learn how to protect his own interests. By turning to Hammond and by using Lomax as an intermediary, Bill was responding to his new challenges with pragmatism, using his best judgment to identify the most reliable and trustworthy people who were available to him. As his travels took him farther from Chicago, and from the community of musicians and friends in which he was a respected figure, he would need to take more of these leaps of faith.

 Stranger in a Strange Land

Like Bill, Len Feinberg knew something about living as a stranger in a strange land under a new name. He began life as Lev Aleshker, born in 1914 in Vitebsk, a city in Eastern Europe that alternated for generations between Polish and Russian control. His father was a prosperous businessman who died in a Bolshevik prison after the Russian Revolution, while he and his mother fled to Chicago, where she had a relative. Because his mother made ends meet by working full-time as a private nurse, Len lived at the Marks Nathan Jewish Orphan Home, which in his case served more as a boarding school. There he learned to speak English without an accent, and he won a scholarship to the University of Illinois, where he earned his bachelor's and master's degrees, and, after serving in World War II, his PhD in American literature. He married Lillian Okner before the war, and with one child and another on the way, they arrived in Ames, Iowa, in 1946 after Len received an offer to teach at what was then called Iowa State College.

When the "I Come for to Sing" revue came to sing at Iowa State at the end of June 1950, Studs Terkel knew where he could get a home-cooked meal for the four members of the troupe. Len Feinberg's sister-in-law had done some interior design work for Studs and his wife, and Len had also attended elementary school, high school, and college with Nathan Davis, whom Terkel had worked alongside as a member of the Chicago Repertory Group.[1] The Feinbergs were delighted to have the four musicians over for dinner before the concert, and the gathering was so congenial that they came back for a party at the Feinbergs' house after the show.

"Several weeks later," Feinberg recalled, "I got a letter addressed to 'Mr. Finburg [sic], Ames, Iowa.' Ames was a smaller place at that time, so the letter was delivered to me." It was from Bill, who had written that his doctor told him he was getting sick from the smoke from the nightclubs where he was performing, and unless he got out of them he would die.

According to Feinberg, "Bill had been brought up on a farm, and in his letter he asked, 'Can you find me a job in Iowa on a farm?'"[2]

Feinberg immediately got in touch with the man who ran the college's dormitories and food services, a tall southerner named Julian Schilletter. Schilletter was a second-generation college administrator—his father had had the same responsibilities at Clemson University in South Carolina—and, in an ironic nod to his height, Julian was known by his father's nickname of "Shorty." Shorty Schilletter told Feinberg that although he was not able to provide a farming job for Bill, he could offer him a position as a janitor at Friley Hall, then the men's dorm on the campus. In addition, he could offer Bill a place to live: a corrugated metal Quonset hut. The success of the financial aid package offered by the GI Bill had created a tremendous demand for cheap housing for the huge influx of students and faculty, and Iowa State had responded by installing dozens of the semicircular, prefabricated structures right on the main campus.

"Broonzy at that time was making $400 a week in Chicago," Feinberg remembered, "and all Shorty could offer him was $150 a month, so I didn't think Broonzy would take it. But Big Bill phoned me at midnight one night, which was ordinary time for him I suppose, and said 'Thank you. I'm coming.' A week later an old black Cadillac pulled up in front of our house."[3]

If Bill told Len Feinberg that he was earning $400 a week at that time, he was exaggerating. During 1949 and 1950, Bill frequently played at Silvio's Tavern, the West Side club where he had helped Muddy get started, as well as at a number of other venues.[4] It may have amounted to fairly steady work, but even when he held down the more lucrative weekend performing slots, Bill would likely have made closer to half that amount, or less. Given the lower cost of living in Ames compared with Chicago, the Iowa State arrangement was a financially attractive one for Bill.[5]

Bill began his stay in Iowa by lying down on Feinberg's son's bed and sleeping around the clock, a sign to the family that he was not exaggerating about the state of his health. He soon moved into his Quonset hut at 188 Pammel Court and started work at Friley Hall not long after that.[6]

Bill's street address on Pammel Court linked him to the most famous African American ever to have been associated with the overwhelmingly white college and town. Almost exactly sixty years earlier, in 1891, George Washington Carver had come to Iowa State to study horticulture, and so became the school's first black student. Banned from staying in the dorms, Carver lived in the office of his mentor, a botanist named Louis Pammel. When Carver graduated in 1894, the only job he could find was with a local florist, so Pammel offered him a position as a graduate assistant. This position established Carver as the college's first black graduate student and faculty member. In 1896 Booker T. Washington succeeded in recruiting Carver for the faculty at the Tuskegee Institute in Alabama, where Carver's groundbreaking research on peanut farming and practical uses for other crops established his international reputation.[7]

Bill was a frequent visitor at the Feinberg home, and the Feinbergs often included him in the informal gatherings they hosted for other faculty members and their families. A colleague from the English department, Albert Walker, had studied classical piano and had played in a jazz band in college, and he and his wife, Jauvanta, or "Jav," became friendly with Bill. The Walkers lived close to Bill, in one of the hundreds of one- and two-bedroom barracks built around the same time as the Quonset huts. They began to invite Bill over, and he and Albert would spend evenings playing music and talking. "The two of them had a good time," Jav Walker recalled. "He'd come over, and gradually it got so that there was less playing and more talking. They discovered sort of common things in their backgrounds." Walker had put himself through college by working in a meatpacking factory in Kansas City, and during visits to Chicago he had stayed on the South Side near where Bill lived. "They just had a good time. And Bill told more and more about his life."[8]

As the connection between the professor and the bluesman deepened, it extended beyond jamming and conversation. "[Bill] was writing things down," Jav remembered. "He had not done much reading or writing in the past, but he was really wanting to get the story about the blues as he knew it down. And so sometimes he would bring things over and show Albert." With the encouragement of Walker, whose class on Shakespeare was popular among Iowa State students for four decades, Bill worked on his material, both on paper and as an imaginative raconteur. Among his other stories, he told the Walkers about a French girl he was dancing with during his World War I tour of duty who kept reaching around behind him. When Bill asked her what she was doing, she replied that she was looking for his tail, certain that he had the feature associated with monkeys.[9]

There had been African Americans living in Iowa at least since the 1830s, when work at the lead mines outside Dubuque, on the Mississippi

River, drew the first documented group. White abolitionists, especially in some Quaker communities, and free African Americans assisted escaped slaves into and through Iowa, both before and during the Civil War. Black communities grew in a number of cities as workers found jobs in industries such as railroads and meatpacking. By World War I, Des Moines emerged as "the center of black life in Iowa."[10] The state passed a law establishing civil rights for all citizens in 1884, but it was rarely enforced, which left schools and communities segregated, and limited career opportunities for black professionals such as doctors and lawyers. The 1950 census counted just under twenty thousand black residents of the state, which was less than 1 percent of the total population. It also identified eighty-eight black residents of Story County, of which Ames is the largest city. Given the racial makeup of the other towns in the county, virtually all of the black residents of the county were likely living in Ames.

African Americans were not very visible in the Ames community, as estimates by whites who lived in Ames at the time ranged from two to ten black families. One family, the Smiths, included a coworker of Bill's at Friley Hall, and Jav Walker accompanied Bill when he paid a visit to the Smith household on Easter Sunday of 1951. Bill clearly felt connected to the Smiths, and he played his guitar and sang for the family's adult children who were visiting from out of town. While Bill may have enjoyed his friendship with his Friley Hall colleague, Bill had a different status in Ames. As Len Feinberg observed, "I think he was regarded in a special sense as a musician who was temporarily a janitor, rather than as a janitor who played music. I think that the feeling of the community was that this is a unique individual rather than this is a black individual."[11]

As Bill started to look for opportunities to play, Lillian Feinberg mobilized her formidable persuasive powers and considerable determination to work on his behalf. "My wife did a lot to promote him," Len noted. "She would get him gigs and would introduce him to people."[12] By winter, her efforts were bearing fruit. The *Ames Daily Tribune* reported that at a January 1951 meeting of the Parent-Teacher Association, Bill "delighted the audience by inviting their participation in the chorus of 'The Blue Tail Fly.'"[13] Two weeks later he was on the list of local performers appearing on the campus radio station, WOI-FM, during a March of Dimes pledge request show, and the following month he appeared at the Ames Lions Club's "Ladies Night."[14]

His presence in Ames did not go unnoticed by the students. In an article in the campus daily newspaper titled "Blues Singer Shelves Guitar to 'Just Relax' at Iowa State," Bill was quoted describing Iowa State students as "'the most appreciative audience' he has ever known." Accompanied by a large photo of him singing and playing the guitar—suggesting that it may not have been shelved too far—the piece conveyed Bill's assessment that "of all the places I've been in 25 years of show business, I like it here best. The people sure do treat me nice." The writer added that Bill had "traded a microphone for a broom."[15]

As a musician, Bill was still connected to music scenes beyond Ames. He traveled back to Chicago several times for gigs at blues clubs, once in September 1950 at the Zanzibar, and again in May 1951 at the Dew Drop Inn, appearing there with Muddy Waters. He continued to straddle the black and white audiences in Chicago, performing with "I Come for to Sing" at a benefit concert in April and appearing solo at Temple Sinai, a Reform Jewish synagogue in Hyde Park, on the same day as the Dew Drop Inn gig. In addition, Des Moines was only thirty-five miles from Ames, and a number of jazz clubs there featured performers of national stature, as well as local favorites. It is possible, as both Len Feinberg and Jav Walker remembered, that Bill traveled there from time to time to perform.[16]

Whatever the state of his health had been when he arrived, the time Bill spent in Ames allowed him to live at a less stressful pace than he had been maintaining while based in Chicago. He had a small but regular paycheck in return for doing work that was not physically demanding. He didn't have to make the long-distance drives from campus to campus with "I Come for to Sing," and he discontinued his trips to New York. Yet there was a different challenge for him that came with these advantages: it was the first time he had ever lived for an extended period of time in a predominately white community.

The year Bill spent in Ames laid much of the foundation for his professional success in the years that followed. He was an African American man staying in a white community, and every time he entered a home or a store, he stood out from almost everybody else. In the small town of Ames, whose population was only twenty-three thousand, plenty of people knew who he was. He would walk to work from the Quonset hut, leaving its corrugated semicircle behind as he passed the horse barns on his way to Friley Hall, and people who walked or drove by would recognize him instantly as Big Bill.

It is difficult to assess how Bill really felt about working and living in Ames. If he experienced stress or discomfort about being there, he did not indicate it to the white individuals and families he interacted with. Overall, it appears that he could tolerate his very visible status as an outsider, and that he was able to find ways to make the best of it. He had been fortunate to have the Feinbergs as his initial hosts, because they enjoyed entertaining, and they liked to bring together faculty colleagues from a variety of departments. Jav Walker recalled that "they both, both Len and Lil, had eclectic tastes, and they were catalysts," so that professors and their spouses with an interest in music, such as the Walkers, had the chance to meet Bill in a social setting. In addition, the comments and encouragement Bill received on his writing from Albert Walker, a Shakespearean scholar and jazz pianist, would have reinforced Bill's determination, as Jav Walker described it, "to get the story about the blues as he knew it down." Several years after Bill had given Alan Lomax his first set of handwritten pages, and several years before Yannick and Margo Bruynoghe initiated a formal and sustained effort to capture Bill's stories, Bill was documenting them for a small but appreciative literary audience.

A particular quality that endeared Bill to his Ames neighbors was the way he got along with children. Norman Cleary, then a graduate student in sociology, lived with his wife and two small children on the other side of Bill's Quonset hut, with a wall separating the two living spaces. Cleary remembers Bill volunteering to sing lullabies to the youngsters, which were well received despite—or perhaps because—they "were hardly very soft. They . . . usually contained a lot of shouting, and loud chords."[17] Bill cemented the affections of the Cleary family when he helped to locate the two toddlers when they escaped from their playpen, an event that merited an article in the campus newspaper.[18] Len Feinberg recalled that "he got along beautifully with my kids," and years later he kept on his desk a photo of Bill bending over the two Feinberg children as they beam at the camera with delight. Bill's comfort in being around children would help him in several settings over the next few years.

When Bill went home at night in Ames, accounts differ regarding whom, if anyone, he went home to. Len Feinberg remembered that his wife came out to join him not long after he arrived in Ames, and that she "never permanently lived in the Quonset hut, but she came from time to time."[19] The January feature article on Bill in the campus newspaper stated that he was living with his wife in the Quonset hut.[20] Norman Cleary, who noted that, as his neighbor, he generally had some interaction with Bill every day, stated categorically that he never saw his wife and added, "If she did [visit], I certainly never met her. Never even heard of her."[21] Jav Walker recalled meeting two different women who visited Bill in Ames, referring to one as his wife and to the other, "a very pretty light skinned woman," as "the sixth Mrs. Broonzy, and I think that was a euphemism." Uncertainty among Bill's white friends and acquaintances in America and Europe as to the identities and numbers of Bill's wives would continue for the rest of his life, and beyond.

What is certain is that in the spring of 1951 Bill took action in his domestic life in a way that he never had before: he filed for divorce from Texas Rose. Win Stracke had put Bill in touch with a lawyer in Chicago, Joseph K. Hellmuth, who entered the complaint on April 13 in Cook County Superior Court. In noting that Bill and Rose (named "Rosia" in the court papers) had lived separately for the past three years, the complaint stated that the couple had not had any children together, nor had they adopted any.

Rose represented herself, and, in her response, she disputed that that she was the one who had "deserted and absented herself," as Bill's complaint had alleged. In advance of a hearing before the judge, the two sides agreed to what amounted to a no-fault divorce, in which neither would seek any support from the other. During the June 11 hearing, two witnesses testified on Bill's behalf. The first was Memphis Slim, who stated his name as Peter Chatman and, in his brief testimony, told the judge that Bill had treated his wife "swell," while she had been "cruel." Win Stracke, who followed Slim, gave a similar assessment, and both men confirmed, in response to the judge's direct question, that "she left him." There is nothing in the transcript to indicate that Rose appeared, or, if she was there, that she said anything in her own defense.

A week later the verdict was filed, and Judge Joseph Sabath granted Bill the divorce he had sought.[22] Stracke may have provided a referral to a knowledgeable attorney and testified on Bill's behalf, but he did it with a clear-sighted view of him. Nearly a decade later, he wrote to Yannick Bruynoghe about Texas Rose: "I knew her. She was a large handsome woman, full of life and I suspect she just got fed up with Bill's shenanigans and moved out."[23] Bill was careful to keep materials such as contracts and royalty statements, and he held on to the divorce decree.

This practice would work to his advantage in the future, as a legal document attesting to his 1951 divorce in Chicago from a woman named Rose Broonzy would eventually come in handy.

Just as he had expedited Bill's divorce, Win Stracke played a significant role in Bill's departure from Ames. In the course of collecting jazz and blues records, Win had begun a correspondence with the president of the largest and most active group of French jazz enthusiasts, the Hot Club of France. A writer, concert promoter, record producer, and collector himself, Hugues Panassié was one of the most powerful figures in the French jazz world. As Win later wrote to an author compiling a history of folk music and musicians, "If you want to say something good about me in your book[,] say that around 1950 while in correspondence with Hugues Panassié about some of Big Bill's records I suggested to Panassié that Big Bill would do very well with European audiences."[24] Win could make that recommendation to Panassié with confidence because he had seen Bill perform for the past three years in front of almost exclusively white audiences on college campuses for the "I Come for to Sing" revue.

As Len Feinberg described it, Bill was very reluctant to accept the invitation Panassié extended to him to travel to France, throwing into the trash the telegrams with the initial offer and a follow-up sweetener that "doubled or tripled" his fee. Lillian Feinberg was finally able to elicit from Bill his concern that if he were to leave Ames on a concert tour, he would be giving up his steady job at the college. It was only after she secured confirmation from Shorty Schilletter that Bill could get his Friley Hall job back when he returned that he agreed to make the trip.[25]

Bill's departure from Ames at the end of June 1951 was front-page news in the *Ames Daily Tribune*. The headline read "Paris-Bound Big Bill," and it ran over a two-column photo of Bill looking pensive while wearing a white open-necked shirt with a collar and strumming a guitar. The story described the combination birthday party and send-off for Bill that the Feinbergs threw, and, in true small-town newspaper fashion, it mentioned the names of all seventeen people who attended, down to the Feinberg children. A chemistry professor backed him up on second guitar, and his version of Leroy Carr's poignant song of farewell, "When the Sun Goes Down," was so well received that he sang it twice. Bill left them laughing when he bowed out at midnight. "There's two guys I want to find," he told his fans. "One that keeps me broke and the guy who invented work."[26]

A few days later, Bill packed some things into his Cadillac, stored the rest in the Feinbergs' basement, and headed back to Chicago. He was leaving a place that he had come to as a stranger a year before, knowing no one. As he drove south to Des Moines, he might have reflected on the newspaper's observation that "a good many people in Ames have got acquainted with Big Bill Broonzy since last August when he moved to town."[27] Bill would soon find out what kind of reception he would receive when he finally crossed the Atlantic Ocean for the first time.

14 Nourish Yourself on Big Bill

When Bill's plane touched down at Melsbroek Airport outside Brussels on July 18, 1951, he landed on a continent with a well-established base of passionate and knowledgeable jazz fans. American jazz musicians had been performing in Europe since before World War I. James Reese Europe's "Hellfighters" Band, composed of members of the U.S. Army's 369th Infantry Regiment, played in France during the war for American doughboys and French civilians. In 1919 Swiss conductor Ernest Ansermet wrote a review of a London concert by the U.S.-based Southern Syncopated Orchestra in which he praised Sidney Bechet's clarinet playing, adding pointedly that "many European musicians should envy" Bechet's skill.[1]

By the 1930s, many of the leading American jazz stars were touring continental Europe and Great Britain. Louis Armstrong visited twice, as did Duke Ellington, and each received large and enthusiastic receptions from the Mediterranean to the North Sea. In the vocabulary of the day, European jazz aficionados vigorously debated the respective merits of the "sweet jazz" of the dance bands or the "hot jazz" more associated with African American artists like Ellington and Armstrong. In 1932 a group of college-age fans in France formed the Hot Club of France, dedicating themselves to promoting an understanding of and appreciation for hot jazz. Within a short time, two men, Hugues Panassié and Charles Delaunay, emerged as the most influential forces in the organization.

Over the next fifteen years, both Panassié and Delaunay would make significant contributions to the jazz world as writers, record producers, and advocates for individual musicians and the music in general. Both had been drawn to jazz as a teenager in the 1920s while convalescing from illness, during which each had listened extensively to records. Panassié wrote several books, including *Le Jazz Hot*, one of the first attempts to present a rigorous and analytic study of jazz, and *The Real Jazz*, which underscored and amplified his perspective that "the real spirit of jazz" was "the musical inspiration of the Negroes."[2] In 1936 Delaunay published *Hot Discography*, the first jazz discography, for which visiting American musicians had provided otherwise unavailable information by identifying the soloists on the records he played for them. The two jazz enthusiasts also started a record company, Swing, for which they arranged original recording sessions with black American and white French musicians and also reissued U.S. recordings.

The combined talents and energy of Panassié and Delaunay as evangelists of jazz in France produced a network of Hot Club of France (HCF) branches throughout the country and beyond. With Panassié and others traveling on frequent lecture tours, and the two men and their colleagues generating a steady stream of articles for the club's publications, they were "creating a subculture of fans . . . a community of listeners who could gather at concerts or around record players."[3] These efforts were reinforced by their radio broadcasts, as well as HCF concerts, jam sessions, and informal gatherings where records were played and discussed. An American visitor to an HCF listening session described Panassié's passion for the music, as he "went into a frenzy of movement, jerking his whole body in time to the records, playing every solo in pantomime, smiling a particularly delighted and charming smile."[4]

After the war, the creative partnership between Panassié and Delaunay ended with a bitter split between the two men. It was called "*le Schisme*" in French, or the Schism, which did not overstate the religious intensity of the divide. It left little middle ground for anyone in the French jazz world.[5] The explicit disagreement was whether bebop represented a positive or a negative trend in jazz, with Delaunay arguing in favor of the emerging style and Panassié against it. A host of other issues reinforced and polarized the conflict, with accusations and denunciations appearing regularly in French jazz publications, and the two men at the center of the controversy never reconciled.

Despite *le Schisme*, the work that Panassié and Delaunay had done over the previous two decades was crucial in laying the groundwork for Bill's success when he arrived in Europe in the summer of 1951. The Hot Club of France had created a network on the Continent, so that there were official branches and affiliated organizations not only across France, but also in Belgium, Switzerland, Holland, and Germany. When Panassié sent his invitation to Bill in Iowa, he already had the infrastructure in place for a concert tour. Beyond the venues and promotional machinery, Panassié and Delaunay had been successful in stimulating and shaping the growth of an informed and enthusiastic audience for jazz.

The opportunity to bring Bill as a blues musician to France held a particular meaning for Panassié. In a 1949 magazine profile that introduced Bill to a French jazz audience, Panassié identified the blues as the roots of jazz, asserting that "the blues is not merely the origin of jazz; it is also one of its most fascinating aspects." Panassié also traced the integral presence of blues in jazz from the turn-of-the-twentieth-century New Orleans bands to those currently led by Duke Ellington, Count Basie, and Louis Jordan. After criticizing the "boppers" for their failure to recognize the "authenticity" of blues, he declared that it was vital for listeners to understand blues if they wanted to fully appreciate jazz. He presented Bill as "one of the greatest blues singers," emphasizing that he was a "natural" singer, who learned to sing "in the South, on street corners or riverbanks." Because of this, Panassié argued, if someone wanted to experience what the blues was all about, he or she could do no better than to "nourish yourself on Big Bill."[6]

European jazz fans had already seen two American musicians whose repertoires featured blues that they sang while accompanying themselves on an acoustic guitar. The first, Huddie Ledbetter, better known as Lead Belly, had traveled to Paris in May 1949, appearing at a concert that Panassié organized in conjunction with a jazz festival sponsored by the Hot Club of France. Although attendance was sparse, news of the appearance by the "King of the 12 String Guitar" traveled widely, particularly to Great Britain, where a few jazz critics had already been writing enthusiastically for some time about Lead Belly records. Shortly afterward, he was diagnosed with amyotrophic lateral sclerosis (ALS, or Lou Gehrig's disease), and he died that December.

The second American blues singer and guitarist to appear in Europe was Josh White. In the summer of 1950, White traveled through Norway, Sweden, Denmark, France, and Great Britain. Born in South Carolina, White had moved in the early 1930s to New York City, where he had recorded blues and gospel records on ARC. He used his engaging singing style and charismatic stage presence to establish himself as a successful performer for New York audiences, both at cabarets and at concerts for politically oriented organizations such as People's Songs. Having performed at the Roosevelt White House, White visited Scandinavia as part of a goodwill tour with former First Lady Eleanor Roosevelt, and he drew large crowds in several cities. White gave no public concerts in France, but he did record several sides for Vogue Records, backed by a small group of French musicians. He received a warm welcome in the United Kingdom, which included concerts, recording sessions with a British rhythm section, taped interviews for later broadcast over BBC Radio, and considerable coverage in the British music press.

Panassié made sure that British jazz fans knew about Bill's arrival in the summer of 1951. A front-page item in the *Melody Maker*, the weekly British newspaper covering popular music and jazz, announced on July 7 that Bill, the "famed Chicago blues shouter," would soon be touring the "main summer resorts" of France.[7] Panassié had arranged for Bill to be met at the airport on July 18 by a member of the Hot Club of France named Yannick Bruynoghe (pronounced BROO-noge, with a hard *g*). Bruynoghe picked Bill up in the late morning, brought him into Brussels for lunch, and then put him on an afternoon train to France to ensure that he would get to Vichy in time for his first European concert on July 20. In addition to hosting a jazz radio show, Bruynoghe had an interest in photography, and he snapped a few photos of Bill on a Brussels street during his brief stay. With his broad-brimmed white straw hat, a wide collar white shirt, a flower in the lapel of his double-breasted suit, two-tone shoes, and a big smile for the camera, Bill looked ready to play the circuit of French summer resorts.

Bill's tour took him to twenty-six cities and towns in thirty-nine days. Panassié assembled a group of five musicians to accompany Bill, and he traveled with them for some of the journey. The group included three French jazz musicians (Guy Lafitte on saxophone, André Persiany on piano, and Georges Hadjo on bass), as well as two African Americans (trumpeter Merrill Stepter and drummer Wally Bishop). It took some time for them to adjust to backing Bill, especially the French players, who were perplexed at first when Bill added extra verses to his songs.

With musicians and equipment stuffed into a bus, the group criss-crossed Normandy and Brittany before heading south, following France's Atlantic coast to the beaches on the Spanish border. The band drew only modest crowds in most places, because, as Panassié acknowledged, "Big Bill was unknown to most people."[8] The setting for at least one concert bordered on the surreal, as the band had been scheduled at the last minute to play at a gala dinner. The crowd, "dressed in black tie and evening gowns," ignored the performance, which amounted to background music for the cocktail hour.[9] The journey covered over thirty-five hundred miles and included an accident in which the vehicle rolled over and left two passengers with minor injuries, as well as destroying Hadjo's bass. Madeleine Gautier, Panassié's companion and co-author, reported that Bill kept his cool under these frightening circumstances: once he had confirmed that his guitar was intact, he retrieved his hat and sat patiently by the side of the road for the replacement car to take the band to the evening's concert in La Rochelle.[10] On August 19, after a two-day traverse of southern France, the group arrived in Hyères, a resort town on the Mediterranean coast, and for the rest of the tour they performed in venues on the French Riviera. Following the final concert on August 25, Bill took a few days off for a visit to Panassié's home in Montauban.

An unexpected bonus for Bill at the end of the tour was an invitation for a two-week residency at the Vieux-Colombier in Juan-les-Pins, located between Cannes and Nice on the French Riviera. The main attraction there was Sidney Bechet, who was backed by the French clarinetist Claude Luter and his band. The club was a replica of the owner's popular Parisian jazz venue, and it had been the site of the reception for Bechet's lavish wedding the previous month, which had made international headlines. One young jazz fan who saw one of their joint appearances at the club recalled that Bill played during an intermission after being introduced by Bechet, while another remembered Bill performing as a headliner for a few days when Bechet was on vacation.[11]

Wrapping up his engagement at the Vieux-Colombier, Bill headed for Germany for four dates with the Graeme Bell Australian Jazz Band, which had been touring in Europe for nearly a year. The first show was in Düsseldorf on September 15, and it was one of the first concerts by non-German jazz musicians to be held in Germany after the war. A nearly complete recording of the show captured the Bell Band, in bandleader Graeme Bell's assessment, "in the peak of its form."[12] For his part, Bill sounds remarkably at ease with musicians whom he had met earlier that afternoon. His full-throated vocals on "John Henry" and especially "I Feel So Good" are delivered with gusto, and when there is a pause before the band sets up behind him on one song, he jokes that he thought they had left. The audience, who had been advised at the beginning by the emcee that clapping was acceptable but that whistling was not welcome, roared their delight when the evening ended with a New Orleans–style parade of the musicians playing "When the Saints Go Marching In."

The live recording of the Düsseldorf show is the only one that has survived from Bill's first European tour. The songs he chose to play as a solo performer that night included several that would become standards for him over the next few years, such as "In the Evening," "Trouble in Mind," and "John Henry." His performance with the band of one song—"Who's Sorry Now?"—provides a compelling demonstration of Bill's musical versatility. The song was published and recorded in 1923 and might be described as a pop song that uses straightforward jazz progressions. He sings it with authority and panache, and his clean and crisp guitar work is a driving force in the band's up-tempo rendition. As music historian Elijah Wald has noted about this performance, "Broonzy's early work includes nothing that shows his ability to do this kind of straight-ahead rhythm chording and pop singing, but he was clearly a past master of the style."[13] Whether Bill had honed his jazz guitar skills playing with Lil Green or in jam sessions in Chicago or New York, it was only when he played with an Australian jazz band in postwar Germany that a rare three-minute example of the range of his talents was preserved.

The Düsseldorf concert had been arranged through the combined efforts of two entities that blended the present and the future of jazz and blues concerts in Germany. The event reflected Hugues Panassié's influence, as it had been organized by the Hot Club of Düsseldorf. The eight-page concert program drew heavily on materials that Panassié had prepared for Bill's appearances in France, including a biographical essay and a list of songs he was likely to play. The future of European blues tours was represented in the person of Horst Lippmann, one of the members of the German Jazz Federation, under whose auspices the concert took place. A photo taken by a band member's wife shows Lippmann, then in his mid-twenties, chatting with Bill and others in the Bell Band touring group on the way to one of the gigs. A decade later, Lippmann would work with his colleague Fritz Rau and blues musician Willie Dixon to bring dozens of blues artists to Europe for a series of American Folk Blues Festivals.

Bill and the Bell Band played four gigs in four days to packed concert halls, traveling by bus from Düsseldorf to Stuttgart, Frankfurt, and Hannover. Graeme Bell noted in a newspaper article shortly after the tour that Bill "was received with such warmth and enthusiasm that one would never have believed that his race and his music were condemned by Hitler."[14] It was impossible for the group to miss the physical impact of the war on the country as they traveled through it. Norman "Bud" Baker, the band's banjo player and guitarist, kept a diary of the group's European tour, in which he noted that "the bomb damage all over Germany is tremendous, there is not a building in any town that wasn't touched."[15] For the Hannover concert, Bill and the band stayed in an air-raid shelter that had been converted into an underground hotel. Although he did not mention it to his traveling companions, Bill took note of the destruction in his surroundings.

As the Bell Band returned to Düsseldorf for a hastily scheduled return engagement, Bill had to rush to get to Paris by September 20 for his first recording session in nearly three years. Panassié supervised the recording, which was done for Vogue, the jazz label that Charles Delaunay and an entrepreneur named Léon Cabat had started several years earlier. Over the two days, Bill recorded twenty-five sides, all performed solo, accompanying himself on the acoustic guitar. Out of the hundreds of sessions in Bill's career as a recording artist, few had more of an impact than his two days at the Vogue studios.

The twenty-five songs represented the repertoire Bill had assembled over the past few years of performing for white audiences, first in the United States through People's Songs events and the "I Come for to Sing" revue, and then during his European tour. They would become the backbone of his performances for the rest of his career, and audiences on both continents would immediately recognize many of them as Big Bill songs. He had brought them together from a variety of sources, but the common theme was that he could perform them solo, without relying on the piano or rhythm section accompaniment that he had been using since the mid-1930s. Bill's transition away from working as a bandleader in the studio or performing in clubs as a member of a duo or trio, as he had been doing for years in Chicago, would soon become a crucial element in securing bookings in Great Britain.

The Vogue sessions also were Bill's first commercial recording of his song that directly addressed racism, "Black, Brown, and White Blues." Alan Lomax had recorded a version by Bill around the time of the *Blues in the Mississippi Night* taping, but it was only released on CD in 2003. In his autobiography, Bill described his unsuccessful efforts to interest American record companies in it, as executives asked him, "And why do you want to record such a song? . . . Nobody would buy it."[16] In contrast, Panassié assured Bill as soon as he heard it that Bill would be able to record it in France. "Black, Brown, and White Blues" became known as an expression of Bill's willingness to speak out against racial discrimination. Before the civil rights struggle in America emerged in the late 1950s and early 1960s to inspire anthems like "We Shall Overcome," Bill's song was an internationally recognized call for racial justice.

The September recordings were not only the template for Bill's set lists at his performances. They became the introduction to Big Bill Broonzy for many in Europe and Great Britain. As Bill toured over the next few years, the sides were issued and reissued in different formats, and often with updated packaging. The impact on aspiring musicians was often substantial. British blues and pop artist Long John Baldry recalled that, upon listening for the first time to one of Bill's recordings on Vogue, "I fell in love immediately. That for me was the turning point in my whole life. And then I was checking out Bill Broonzy on a regular basis after that."[17] Even after others had recorded versions of "John Henry," the arrival of a new compilation of the Vogue sides would prompt British record store managers to insist to prospective buyers, as a friend of Baldry's had done to him, "Oh, but you must listen to a proper rendition of the song."

On September 22, 1951, Bill traveled to London for two shows at Kingsway Hall. His appearance had required some maneuvering by promoter Herbert "Bert" Wilcox, who was acting as Bill's agent in Great Britain. A long-standing dispute between the British Musicians' Union and the American Federation of Musicians made it virtually impossible for American jazz musicians to perform there. Wilcox had identified a loophole that permitted Bill to appear as a "variety act," which meant that he would be allowed in if he performed as a soloist or was accompanied by British musicians.[18]

The most noteworthy feature of Bill's concerts at Kingsway Hall was the enthusiastic response he received from the modest number of people who attended. Blues historian Paul Oliver, who was at the afternoon show, wrote later of "the small crowd that clustered round [Bill] at the bottom of the steeply ramped seats," before going on to describe it as an "enraptured audience."[19] The headline for James Asman's column in the weekly newspaper *Musical Express* read "Frankly, I Am Disgusted," as the columnist lambasted British jazz fans for an afternoon concert that was "pitifully attended." Asman characterized Bill's performance as that of a

"great Blues artist" and "one of the finest living exponents of the Blues."
Attendance in the concert hall, known for its fine acoustics, improved to
half-full for the evening show.[20] The *Melody Maker* reviewer concluded
that "one of the least well-attended concerts of the last few years, this
was the best and most memorable as far as this writer is concerned."[21]

As jazz critic Stanley Dance summarized it, "Big Bill's repertoire is
well varied, his guitar playing delightful, and he swings in no mean fashion."[22] Bill's choice of songs included some he had just recorded over the
past two days in Paris, such as "John Henry" and "In the Evening," to
which he added others, such as "Key to the Highway" and a popular song
from 1936 titled "When Did You Leave Heaven?" In Paul Oliver's recol-
lection, the variety of songs Bill played meant that "the cluster of blues
enthusiasts was somewhat astonished," as they had been anticipating
"twelve-bar blues almost exclusively."[23]

Several elements converged to produce Bill's success at Kingsway Hall.
The two months he had spent touring in France and Germany had given
him the chance to refine his repertoire. In particular, the overwhelmingly positive response he and the Bell Band had received in Germany
would have assured him that there were receptive fans for him overseas.
Although he had offered a few brief introductory comments about songs
to his continental audiences, he could be more expansive in his remarks
to a fully English-speaking crowd. In addition, Alan Lomax drove down
from Scotland to serve as a combination emcee and interviewer for the
evening show, which meant that Bill was sharing the stage with a familiar figure, someone he knew and trusted.

Bill also demonstrated remarkable skill with the press. From his first
interviews in Great Britain, he was clear and consistent in establishing
who he was in several key ways. He portrayed himself as representing
a link to what he called "the real blues," which came from growing up
and living in rural settings where the music was integrated into daily
life. To learn the blues, he told one reporter, "you got to be born a Negro
in Mississippi and you got to grow up poor and on the land." He drew
a sharp distinction between urban and rural blues: "The blues ain't on
time, buddy. Did you ever see a farmer in a hurry? That's what's wrong
with them big city blues. They're all jazzed up and mean, the way city folk
themselves are. . . . Go to the city, and you get jazz, not blues."[24]

Bill also positioned himself as a historian of the blues. The songs the
writers knew as blues, Bill observed, "they used to call them *reels* back

in the last century when I was a boy. No one called them blues." He extended his analysis of the sources of the blues to include sacred songs as well: "We was prayin', spirituals, you know, and after a while they put new words to them and hollered them across the fields when they was feelin' low, and that's the blues."[25]

With an astute sense of what would resonate with jazz fans, Bill presented himself as one of the last artists in a line that was vanishing, because the conditions that produced them were changing. "But the real old time singers who worked in the fields," he stated, "there's almost none of them left now. I'm 58 and caretaker of a college now. You can't make a living with the real blues no longer, man."[26]

Bill also took advantage of these initial interviews to recommend other blues musicians to British writers and fans. The first artist he endorsed in Great Britain was Muddy Waters, and he did it in a way that linked Muddy directly to the rural conditions that produced the blues. In describing the "field hollers way down in Mississippi and Arkansas," he emphasized, "That's where you hear the blues, hollerin' across the fields at sundown." Having set that image in place, he lamented, "There's none of them left, expect maybe Muddy Water [sic]."[27]

Bill had crafted a persona for himself that would bring him international acclaim and steady work for the rest of his career. By highlighting the key elements of his rural origins, his firsthand knowledge of the musical sources of the blues, his membership in a finite and shrinking set of blues singers, and his desire to call attention to musicians whose work he could vouch for, Bill had secured a unique and powerful status. The decision he had made years before to add a decade to his age reinforced the other factors, as it gave legitimacy to his claim of childhood memories dating back to the nineteenth century.

The British jazz press found the combination of Bill's performances and his personality irresistible. Two writers who were allowed to attend a rehearsal with Bill each began their reviews by quoting Bill as he provided guidance to the young British pianist who would later accompany him onstage. Over the months and years that followed, Bill would similarly assume the role of instructor to several of the writers whose opinions and analyses helped to shape the tastes of British music fans.

Two days later, on September 24, Bill recorded four sides for the British label Melodisc. Because he was almost certainly still under contract to Mercury, he was listed on the label as "Chicago Bill" and on the contract as "William Johnson."[28] He received an advance of £20 ($56 at prevailing exchange rates), and Melodisc agreed to pay a royalty rate of 4 percent of the retail price. Two of the songs, "Five Feet Seven" and "Keep Your Hands Off Her," were ones he had recorded in February 1949 for Mercury, although this time he did it without the drummer who had backed him in Chicago.

A little more than two months after he came to Europe, Bill sailed back to the United States, leaving Southampton on September 25 on the French liner *Ile de France*. He had been applauded and cheered in France, Germany, and Great Britain. Leading figures in the jazz worlds of France and Great Britain had sought him out to interview him and had expressed keen interest in his opinions and his stories. He had recorded twenty-nine sides in three days in Paris and London, only eight fewer than the total number he had cut in the United States as a featured performer since 1945. If Bill had been leaning against the rail on one of the upper decks of the *Ile de France*, enjoying a cigarette as the ship headed west across the slate-gray North Atlantic, the thought of returning to Europe would have been an extremely enticing prospect.

Big Bill Broonzy's entry in the Bradley family records is under his real name, Lee, and shows that he was born in Arkansas on June 26, 1903. Tolbert Family Collection. Photo by Bob Riesman.

Bill and his mother, Mittie Belcher Bradley, and his youngest sister, Mary Bradley Dove, North Little Rock, late 1940s or early 1950s. They are sitting on the back step of the home of Bill's sister Lannie Bradley Wesley, at 412 West 30th Street. Michael van Isveldt Collection.

Bill (center of back row with light-colored hat) with family members, North Little Rock, Arkansas, 1947. His sister Lannie Wesley is on the left, and her granddaughter Jo Ann Jackson is the child in the white hat and jacket. Taken in front of Bill's mother's home at 411 West 30th Street. Yannick and Margo Bruynoghe Collection.

Bill with a jaunty hat and guitar, c. 1930s. Frank Driggs Collection.

Top row: Ernest (Little Son Joe) Lawlars, Bill (with guitar), Lester Melrose, Roosevelt Sykes, St. Louis Jimmy Oden; *below:* Washboard Sam, c. 1940s. Yannick and Margo Bruynoghe Collection.

Left: A rare photo of Bill's favorite piano player, Joshua Altheimer (standing at right). Bill is seated at left, and he identified the man standing above him as drummer Fred Williams. The man seated next to Bill is unknown. Late 1930s or 1940. Yannick and Margo Bruynoghe Collection.

Below: Lil Green and her band, photographed in Houston, Texas, c. 1941. *Left to right:* Simeon Henry (piano), Bill (guitar), Lil Green, Ransom Knowling (bass). Frank Driggs Collection. Photo by Teal Studio.

Bill on guitar, with Roosevelt Sykes on piano, c. 1940s. Yannick and Margo Bruynoghe Collection.

Bill playing at the 21 Club, located at 21 North Western Avenue in Chicago, with Charles Belcher on piano and Elga "Elgin" Edmonds on drums, mid- to late 1940s. Yannick and Margo Bruynoghe Collection.

Bill and Muddy Waters, Chicago, late 1940s or early 1950s. Yannick and Margo Bruynoghe Collection.

Sonny Boy Williamson and Bill, mid- to late 1940s. Yannick and Margo Bruynoghe Collection.

Left to right: Big Maceo Merriweather, Rose Allen Broonzy ("Texas Rose"), Bill, Lil Green, man identified only as "Jimmy," Lucille Merriweather, and drummer Tyrell Dixon, c. late 1940s. Lucy Kate Merriweather/Mike Rowe.

Hugues Panassié in front of shelves with stacks of records at his home in Montauban, France, 1949. Photos Tailhefer/ Médiathèque de Villefranche de Rouergue.

Bill smiling on his arrival in Brussels for the start of his first European tour. Photo by Yannick Bruynoghe, July 18, 1951. Yannick and Margo Bruynoghe Collection.

Bill at Kingsway Hall in London for his first British concert, September 22, 1951. *Left to right:* Alan Lomax, Bill, Max Jones, and Herbert "Bert" Wilcox. Max Jones Archive.

Bill performing, probably at the Doelenzaal, Amsterdam, late November 1955. Michael van Isveldt Collection.

"I Come for to Sing" group, Chicago, c. 1952. *Left to right:* Studs Terkel, Win Stracke, Bill, Larry Lane. Photograph by Stephen Deutch; iCHi-26824, Chicago History Museum.

Bill with Margo Bruynoghe walking in Paris, early 1953. Yannick and Margo Bruynoghe Collection.

Cab Calloway, Mahalia Jackson, and Bill in London, November 1952. © Walter Hanlon Archive / National Portrait Gallery, London, NPG CAP 00272.

Bill with Jean-Marie Masse, the head of the Hot Club of Limoges (France) and his two daughters, Sylvie and Agnes, and unidentified child, March 1953. Photograph by Michel Neyens, used with his permission. First published in *Le Livre d'Or du Hot-Club de Limoges ou l'histoire du jazz en Limousin* (1978), 10. Fonds Charles Delaunay, Département de l'Audiovisuel, Bibliothèque nationale de France.

Bill on the movie set of *Low Light and Blue Smoke*, Brussels, December 1955. Yannick and Margo Bruynoghe Collection.

Pim van Isveldt and Bill at recording session at the Hoog Wolde studio in Baarn, Holland, February 17, 1956. The man in the background behind them is Paul Breman. Photograph by Hans Buter/Maria Austria Instituut.

Opposite page, top:
Bill and Yannick Bruynoghe on the movie set of *Low Light and Blue Smoke*, Brussels, December 1955. Yannick and Margo Bruynoghe Collection.

Opposite page, bottom:
Gathering at London apartment of Paul and Valerie Oliver, February–March 1957, photographed by Paul Oliver. *Top row, left to right:* Alexis Korner (mandolin), Bobbie Korner, Beryl Bryden with arm around Bill, Derroll Adams (banjo). *Bottom row, left to right:* Ramblin' Jack Elliott (guitar), June Elliott, Valerie Oliver, Donald Kincaid (a friend of the Olivers), Brother John Sellers. Dave Bennett Collection.

Bill holds his fifteen-month-old son, Michael van Isveldt, Amsterdam, March 1957. Photograph by Hans Buter/Maria Austria Instituut.

Pete Seeger (banjo) and Bill (guitar) performing at Circle Pines Center in Michigan, July 6, 1957. Photo by John Glass.

Bill and Rose Lawson Broonzy, photographed in their apartment at 4706 South Parkway, by Yannick Bruynoghe, January 1958. Yannick and Margo Bruynoghe Collection.

Opening night at the Old Town School of Folk Music in Chicago, December 1, 1957. Bill, Frank Hamilton (guitar), Win Stracke (with glasses), Studs Terkel (leaning forward). iCHi-61967, Chicago History Museum.

Win Stracke and Bill at the Old Town School opening night, December 1, 1957. iCHi-61968, Chicago History Museum.

Win Stracke performing at Bill's funeral, August 19, 1958, at Metropolitan Funeral Parlors, 4445 South Parkway, Chicago. Photograph by Mickey Pallas, Collection Center for Creative Photography, University of Arizona, © 1995, The University of Arizona Foundation.

Pallbearers carrying Bill's coffin, Lincoln Cemetery, Blue Island, Illinois, August 19, 1958. *Left to right:* Win Stracke, Muddy Waters, Ransom Knowling (partially hidden), Studs Terkel, Chet Roble, Brother John Sellers, Tampa Red, Sunnyland Slim (only top of head visible), and Otis Spann. Photograph by Mickey Pallas, Collection Center for Creative Photography, University of Arizona, © 1995, The University of Arizona Foundation.

 "Be Proud of What You Are!"

Shortly after Bill returned to Chicago from his first European tour, he spent three days in November and December 1951 in the Mercury studios recording a total of twenty sides. His choices of songs and backing musicians neatly illustrated his efforts to straddle two musical worlds. All but four of the songs were from the solo acoustic repertoire he had been playing for white European audiences, and he had recorded many of them in Paris two months before. Bill performed these with only a bass player, Ransom Knowling, keeping the beat behind him. On all eight songs he recorded on one of the days, the recording included the sound of his foot tapping on the floor. This effect underscored the spare, stripped-down style of the sides, which showcased the range and intensity of his singing. In the cases of "Hey, Hey" and "John Henry," the sides also highlighted the power of his acoustic guitar playing.

During these Mercury sessions, Bill also recorded four songs in a style that was dramatically different from his folksinger mode, and one that was clearly targeted to an African American audience. On these cuts, he was backed by several of the top studio musicians in the Chicago blues world of the early 1950s. The group included Knowling on bass, saxophonists Oett "Sax" Mallard and Bill Casimir, drummer Judge Riley, and either Memphis Slim or Bob Call on piano.[1] If Bill had been tapping his foot on the floor during "Leavin' Day," "South Bound Train," "Tomorrow," or "You Changed," no listener could have heard it, because the sound would have been overwhelmed by the volume and drive of the rhythm section. These were the types of numbers that other black artists on Mercury were recording, and in the trade publications for the music business, Bill's Mercury records were listed with the new R&B releases.

Bill's performing schedule during this interlude between European trips reflects the same dual focus as his Mercury recordings. On two succeeding Saturdays, he played two very different South Side venues. On

December 1, he joined the "I Come for to Sing" revue for a return engagement at the University of Chicago's Mandel Hall, where the group had first played four years before. By now, as a review in the student newspaper observed, "the program consisted mainly of well-known songs, familiar to most of the audience," and "at the end of the performance . . . the concert was turned into a hootenanny." Bill was singled out as "a wonderful guitarist and probably the best blues singers [sic] in the country."[2]

A week later Bill was playing with his "House Rockers" about twenty blocks north of the university, at the Hollywood Rendezvous, located at 3849 Indiana Avenue. Although Bill had played the Rendezvous in years past, the weekend slot was probably available this time only because rising star Little Walter was out of town. Walter was riding high with his first hit, "Juke," and according to Billy Boy Arnold, "Whenever he was in town, he was there [at the Rendezvous] five–six nights a week."[3] Bill's protégés were ascending, and while he might have taken some pride in that, it was time for him to return to a continent where he would be the main attraction once again.

Bill sailed back to France at the end of December on the *Ile de France*. One of the first things he did when he arrived in Paris was to write a letter to Win Stracke, who was back in Chicago. Bill mentioned to Win that he had performed "for the navy on the ship" and enclosed a flyer for the "New Year's Eve Gala" at which he had been a featured artist. He also asked for Win's thoughts about the offer he had received for a two-year residency on board the well-appointed ocean liner, which he said would have paid him $450 a month, or the equivalent in 2010 of over $44,000 a year.[4]

The letter was among the many that Bill wrote to numerous friends and acquaintances on both sides of the Atlantic during the 1950s. He wrote frequently and fluidly, pouring his observations, questions, and concerns onto the page. Although he claimed that he had only learned to read and write later in life, noting at one point that the students at Iowa State had tutored him, he had written nine pages of recollections to Alan Lomax in the mid-1940s.[5]

The half-dozen letters that Bill sent to Win Stracke during his second European tour in the winter and spring of 1952 provide several tantalizing glimpses of Bill, as well as his friendship with Win. In the first letter, dated January 2, Bill began by addressing him as "Dear Mr. Starckie [*sic*]," but he soon shifted to a more familiar salutation, usually "Hello old pal." The subjects Bill covered ranged from personal matters to pro- · fessional choices, and it is clear that he trusted Win to handle both with discretion. The January 2 letter contained an oblique reference to "the business between me and you," which Bill requested that Win not mention to "Rose or Mrs. Glaser."[6] In another letter he asked Win to "see if anything is wrong with Rose," as she had not responded to the four letters that Bill had written her.[7]

As he tried to manage his business affairs while overseas, Bill often turned to Win for help and advice. On March 2 he noted that "they have released some of my old songs on different labels," including Columbia, and expressed his interest in being paid the publishing royalties due to him on their sales. After Lester Melrose, to whom the record companies had always paid Bill's publishing royalties, failed to respond to his inquiries, he asked Win if he would be willing to contact Melrose on his behalf. He provided a mailing address for Melrose, who had by this time retired from the music business and moved to Tucson, Arizona. In addition, he gave Win the mailing address for Hugues Panassié, as Vogue was one of the labels that had recently issued Bill's songs. Bill's instructions to Win were "if you think it is right to write [to] tell him about this it['s] OK with me. But you do what you think should be done about it, so I leave it up to you and the lawyer."[8]

Bill spent the first six weeks of this tour in France, and most of that time he was based in Paris. From January 16 until February 4, he had a steady gig at the Vieux-Colombier, where he opened for Sidney Bechet. The Left Bank club had become, in the words of one historian, the "home base" for Bechet, and he consistently drew large crowds of avid fans.[9] A reviewer for the *Melody Maker* who was present for Bill's opening night filed a report that praised Bill but pointed out the challenge he faced playing for the Parisian jazz fans.

In the reviewer's opinion, Bill's singing was "in that inimitable style of his which is the very essence of the kind of music we love." The audience, however, was composed of "long-haired existentialists who profess to know so much about jazz," and they "talked while Bill sang." Even though they gave Bill a hearty round of applause, they "were not really interested." This struck the writer as particularly unjust, because they then "screamed their heads off" for Bechet's performance, which he considered subpar, primarily because Bechet was struggling with ill health at the time. His judgment was that the crowd's "lack of discrimination" was "rather depressing," and that "Big Bill should have had a comparable reception."[10]

The Vieux-Colombier was also the setting for a unique informal gathering one night during Bill's residency that included jazz trumpeter Lee Collins. Collins, who had played as a teenager in New Orleans bands before World War I, had arrived in Paris shortly before Bill, whom he had known since the 1930s. In his autobiography, Collins described borrowing a trumpet after Bechet finished rehearsing his band. As he recalled, "I told Big Bill to play me some good old down-home blues, so he was playing and singing and I was backing him up with the trumpet." When, as Collins reported, "Bechet unpacked his clarinet and played along with us," the three expatriates brought decades of hard-earned musical wisdom to an unlikely jam session.[11]

Collins had been invited to travel to France by the American clarinetist Milton "Mezz" Mezzrow, whose personal and professional connections with Hugues Panassié dated back to his first sojourn in Paris in 1929. Mezzrow was a white Chicago-born clarinet player whose 1946 memoir, *Really the Blues*, describes his passion for jazz and his fascination with African American culture, which included living in Harlem with his black wife and his insistence on being placed with the black prisoners while serving a jail sentence for dealing marijuana. Panassié had brought Mezzrow over to play in France several times in the late 1940s and early 1950s, and Bill had spent some time with the clarinetist during his 1951 summer tour.

On February 5, 1952, Panassié presented a concert that included both Bill and Mezzrow's band at the Salle Pleyel, one of Paris's most distinguished concert halls, seating over two thousand people. Bill benefited from the grand setting, as a concert recording of his performance of seven songs documented a much more enthusiastic audience than at the Vieux-Colombier. Mezzrow's book had been filled with jazz hipster phrases, and it even included a glossary for non-hipsters, but his introductions of Bill's songs at Salle Pleyel that night were straightforward. "Bill tells me," Mezzrow announced at one point, "that for his next number, he's going to sing a protest number," and Bill then launched into "Black, Brown, and White Blues."[12] The thunderous applause when he finished was the loudest and most sustained of all the performances captured on the recording.

Chicago-based pianist Blind John Davis, who accompanied Bill for his concerts on the Continent during this tour, then joined Bill for three songs. Davis had been one of Lester Melrose's most frequently used studio pianists, and he had recorded with Bill on sessions going back to 1937. His presence at the Salle Pleyel made it possible for Bill to sing a rare recorded version of Leroy Carr's "How Long, How Long Blues." Bill once responded to a request for the song by declining to play it, saying that it didn't work with just a guitar because it needed the piano to fill the spaces between the singing lines.[13] His rendition of it that night in Paris included a moment when his voice cracked as he sang, "It's gonna be TOO late, baby," which gave an added emphasis to the song's powerful and emotional farewell to an unreciprocated love.

After two shows elsewhere in France and another shared billing with Mezzrow's band, this time in Liège, Belgium, Bill returned to Great Britain for a brief visit on February 20, 1952. He was in constant motion, giving four concerts in as many days, each in a different city. His arrival had been the subject of articles for several weeks in both British music weekly newspapers, in addition to the reviews and photos of his Paris appearances.

In contrast to his first visit to Great Britain five months before, Bill was not universally praised during this trip. His February 23 concert at the Usher Hall in Edinburgh received less than flattering reviews from the local press. Under the headline "Folk Singer Struck a Bad Patch," the reviewer for the *Evening Dispatch* declared, "There was no excusing a performance which for the most part was devoid of feeling, programme arrangement, and the high standards of artistry we have come to expect from Negro musicians." While agreeing with an attendee that that some audience members were "lacking in good manners," citing examples such as "laughter [and] noisy exits," the writer concluded that "the singer was accorded what seemed an unusually good reception in light of his performance."[14] The review in the *Scotsman* asserted that Bill "might well have appealed to his audience as much as Josh White, had he spoken less by way of introduction and played more by way of illustration."[15]

As both the concert promoter and a recording of the concert confirm, one significant challenge that Bill faced was that he had spent a number of hours before the show drinking, first in a bar across the street and then backstage. The backstage drinking was particularly ironic because the concert hall had a "no-alcohol" policy at the insistence of the family who had been the benefactors of the facility, despite their having made their fortune in the brewery business. While Bill's pacing in his song introductions was sluggish in the early going, he did become more animated as the evening went along, and even the critical reviewer for the *Evening Dispatch* praised his performance of "John Henry," saying, "Here was the Negro ballad as it should be." It is also possible that there was some skepticism from the Edinburgh writers about what they may have seen as the big-city hype coming from London about Bill. The *Evening Dispatch* writer suggested this in referring to Bill as an artist "practically unheralded by the lay Press but with glowing reviews from British and Continental jazz sources."[16]

When Bill performed the next afternoon at London's Cambridge Theatre, he was accompanied by the Crane River Jazz Band, a group whose origins exemplified the upsurge in interest in Great Britain in what became known as "trad jazz." As in the United States, France, and elsewhere, many British fans had identified the music and musicians of late nineteenth- and early twentieth-century New Orleans as the most significant in all of jazz, past or present. Beginning with George Webb's Dixielanders in 1943, jazz bands assembled throughout the country, dedicated to reproducing the instrumentation and arrangements that the often-amateur performers had absorbed from the 78s of Louis Armstrong, King Oliver, Jelly Roll Morton, and other revered figures. The phrase "trad jazz" was short for "traditional jazz," as opposed to the modernists, who embraced the innovations and explorations of swing and bebop musicians. Through recordings and live performances, trad jazz had become a part of the British jazz landscape by the early 1950s, as emerging talents such as trumpeter Humphrey Lyttelton, who had played in the Dixielanders, began to rise to top billing status.

The Crane River Jazz Band was generally recognized as among the most uncompromising in its efforts to hold fast to the principles and practices of early New Orleans music. This reflected the beliefs and personality of its co-founder and driving force, trumpeter Ken Colyer. Although Colyer had left the band by the time they played with Bill, the group still bore his imprint. Colyer's passionate interest in the social and historical conditions from which jazz emerged led him to join the Merchant Marine so that he could afford to travel to New Orleans. During his six-month residency there, he secured his reputation in Great Britain, first by playing with some of his musical heroes, and then for spending a month in jail pending deportation, because his visitor's visa had expired. The list of musicians a few years younger than Colyer who had played with him either formally or informally and who would go on to have a significant impact on the British music world of the later 1950s and '60s included Chris Barber and Alexis Korner. Each of them would also play a meaningful role in Bill's later trips to Britain.

The reviews in the national jazz press for the Cambridge Theatre show were highly favorable to Bill and illustrated the distinctive niche he had established for himself among some of the country's most influential jazz critics. Steve Race, in his column in the monthly *Jazz Journal*, began by stating flatly, "I loved listening to Broonzy at the Cambridge," and complimented him for "the incredible drive of his singing and playing." Race then identified a particular quality to Bill's presentation that took the concert-going experience to a heightened level, citing, "the healthy feeling of being in the presence of artistic purity, [which] made me feel more satisfied at the end of his show than I can remember feeling after almost any (jazz) concert."[17]

In the same issue, Derrick Stewart-Baxter used his monthly column, "Preachin' the Blues," to lay out his assessment of Bill's special talent. Opening with the judgment that "the London concert was, of course, magnificent," Stewart-Baxter stated that "the truth of the matter is, Big Bill is incapable of singing badly. His is the art of the true folk artist. At first hearing his art seems unconscious—but this is not strictly true—Bill has been singing his blues, worksongs and spirituals so long that he has developed a form of presentation (call it showmanship if you will) which really 'sells' his stuff."[18]

Using different words, both writers identified a similar attribute of Bill's work, as Race spoke of his "artistic purity," while Stewart-Baxter described him as a "true folk artist." This characterization of Bill ran in a direct line from John Hammond's note about him in the program for the first "From Spirituals to Swing" concert nearly fifteen years before that "between record dates he is a farm hand."[19] Hugues Panassié had reinforced this view of Bill in the articles and program notes that accompanied his first tour. When Bill had come to London five months before, he himself had emphasized the connection to rural origins both for himself and for the music he performed.

The intriguing dimension of Stewart-Baxter's comments was his recognition that Bill's performances were not "unconscious," that they in fact reflected a professional's craftsmanship. The writer noted with admiration how, onstage, Bill succeeded in winning over the audience, and he did not hesitate to describe this success in commercial terms, as he observed how Bill "'sells' his stuff." Although Stewart-Baxter attributed Bill's artistry in some part to his longevity, he acknowledged that Bill had "developed his presentation," and he rejected the idea that his performances were "unconscious." Taken together, what Race and Stewart-Baxter's comments suggested was a dual appreciation by British jazz critics of Bill as an artist: first as a musician whose playing was at a consistently high level; and second, as a performer who had worked to craft a presentation that would engage and entertain an audience.

When he returned to Paris, Bill settled into a routine of performing in the city's clubs and traveling to occasional concerts elsewhere in France and Belgium. Most of the tours included Blind John, as did at least some of the club gigs. It may have been fairly steady work, but as Bill wrote to Win Stracke in mid-April, "People want me to stay over here until September, but [there's] not enough work for me to stay over here." He described just about breaking even with income from three concerts a month and working "about 2 or 3 times a week" at a club. As for the cost of living, Bill noted that "everything is so high over here," and listed his expenses for rent, food, transportation, and laundry. The last was of particular importance because he had to have a clean shirt and suit to wear for performances.[20]

On March 19, 1952, Bill made what would turn out to be his final recordings for Vogue. The nine songs he recorded would be among the first of Bill's recordings to be issued in the relatively new 45-rpm format. Previously, all of Bill's materials had been released on ten-inch 78-rpm discs, with one song per side. Now, his records on Vogue and other labels would start to come out on smaller seven-inch discs, with two songs per side. The record jackets for the 45s soon began to reflect more of a focus on marketing, as they featured photos of Bill by leading jazz photographers such as Jean-Pierre Leloir in France and Walter Hanlon in Great Britain.

The recordings were taken directly from Bill's repertoire as a solo concert performer, and he played without any accompaniment. The most noteworthy feature of the session was that it included two spirituals, "Down by the Riverside" and "Stand Your Test in Judgement." Although he had been performing spirituals during both European tours, these

were the first ones he had recorded in a studio since the Chicago Sanctified Singers sessions for ARC of the mid-1930s. He sang both with con-
viction, and his rendition of "Stand Your Test in Judgement," with its
harsh and vivid imagery of having to "lay down and die, all by yourself,"
was especially impassioned. Whatever the circumstances were in which
Bill came to know the song, he sang it as if every memory it raised for
him was painful, and his driving guitar playing was like a Greek chorus
reminding him that he could not escape his fate.

In May 1952, while he was in Paris, Bill reconnected with Alan Lomax.
The folklorist was in the midst of a set of extended trips to rural areas
around Great Britain and continental Europe where he and others recorded local singers, both on audiotape and on film. Lomax had written
Woody Guthrie in late 1952 of his wish to accomplish two objectives: one
was to assemble "the folk music of the world all together in a big handsome set of thirty or forty long playing records," and the other was "to
do my big book on the Negro singers like Vera Hall and Doc [Reese] and
Big Bill which has been half finished." When he sat down with Bill and a
tape recorder in Bill's Paris hotel room, Lomax was likely collecting more
material to use in his proposed "big book."[21]

During the short performance and ensuing discussion with Lomax,
Bill was not alone. At some point during the months he had been based
in Paris, he had met a white French social worker named Jacqueline. By
the time Bill played "Only a Shanty in Old Shanty Town" for Lomax's
tape recorder, their romance had progressed far enough that he inserted
"Jackie" as an affectionate aside in one of the verses, and ended it by
singing playfully, "That was played for Jackie . . ." He was even more flir-
tatious in his rendition of "I Gets the Blues When It Rains," chuckling as
he sang, "I gets the blues when it pleuts." He pronounced his version of
the French verb for "rains" as if it rhymed with "blues."[22]

For the next hour, Bill and Lomax engaged in a wide-ranging conversation, during which Bill used Lomax's questions and comments as
jumping-off points for expressing his thoughts on numerous topics. All
of the issues they addressed related in some way to relations between
blacks and whites in the United States, and Bill's tone was often em-
phatic, even heated, as he made his points.

One overarching theme for Bill was the corrosive effects of racial
prejudice by whites against blacks and the ways in which it continued to
poison the lives of both blacks and whites. A crucial point for Bill was the

self-hatred that he identified in many African Americans, which stood out in contrast to the black people he had encountered in France. "These Negroes over here is lots different from the Negroes in America," he commented to Lomax. "They're proud of what they are. They're *glad* they're black. And my poor black brothers and sisters . . . in America, is sorry they're black." After Lomax agreed, Bill continued, "I know thousands of 'em will tell you that he wished he was yellow, or white, or something. . . . And I've heard 'em say it. I heard 'em say it. And that's the worst thing they can be. Because whatsoenever you are, you can't do nothing about it."[23]

When Lomax suggested, "If they weren't ashamed, they could win their freedom," Bill seized the moment. "If the black man of America loved one another like the Frenchman in France love one another, and die and stand up for one another, it wouldn't be no Jim Crow in America. No. It wouldn't be none. Because it wouldn't be nothing for Jim Crow for! Because he'd love his brother too well to forsaken his brother and go to the white man."

A particularly toxic element, in Bill's view, was the envy that less well-off African Americans felt toward those who had managed to establish themselves in professions and, in so doing, to rise to a middle-class status. As he put it, "The Negro is jealous of a Negro having a better break of living." In Bill's judgment, if the less well-off African American "loved his brother, they wouldn't bother him. It wouldn't be no Jim Crow. It would be kicked out. Altogether. But he don't love his brother. What'll he do? Take a knife and get behind, pop him in the back. See? That's it, that's the whole darned thing."

Bill's last comment was meant to some extent metaphorically, but he made it clear that the violence he was describing was all too real. "There's been more Negroes killed in America *by* Negroes than it ever was by white men. And I know that. And it's been more Negroes killed that people don't even know about, by Negroes, than ever any white man."

In Bill's view, it was vital to recognize that whites had established and reinforced the culture that not only tolerated but encouraged black-on-black violence. In response to Lomax's question about why "Negroes do so much fightin' and stabbin' and shootin' and all that," Bill used a dramatic vignette to illustrate what he meant: "They're *taught* to do that, *by* the white man. The white man tells 'em that. . . . The first thing they tell 'em when they come on the farm is, 'Do you know the rules of this place?' The first thing a Negro says, 'Well, no, sir, I don't.' [The white man] say, 'Well, I'll tell you the rules here.' See? 'If you keep yourself out the graveyard, I'll keep you out of jail.' See? So that means, you got to fight to stay there. And if you don't fight, [laughs] you goin', you goin' in the graveyard."

Bill underscored his argument with his own personal experience. "Well, that's true. That's true as you see me sittin' here. Those people, those people are *taught*. And if I hadn't have been a damn good fighter, and a *big* son of a gun, weighing two hundred and sixteen [pounds], I would have been in the graveyard a long time ago, because they tried it on me."

A few minutes later, Bill addressed head-on the powder-keg question of why black men and white women in America sought each other out for sexual relationships. In presenting his explanation, Bill began by noting that it is often an intentional choice by a black man, reasoning that "a Negro can have just as white a woman without bothering the white man's woman, because there are some white Negroes just as white as any white woman in the world." In describing a black man moving from the South to the North and choosing to seek out a white woman, he zeroed in on his motivation: "Why he do it? Because he knows he's doing something to hurt the white man! That's why he do it! Because the white man don't want him to have a white woman, and he say, 'Well, I'll hurt this son of a gun. I couldn't hurt him in Mississippi, but I'll hurt him here.' . . . They don't do it because he's so much in love with a white woman. He got just as white a woman as there is in the world! In his own race! He just do that to hurt the white man, because that's the only get-back he can get back at him."

Bill's explanation for what would make a white woman want to hurt a white man by entering into a relationship with a black man was that it was revenge for white men pursuing relationships with black women. In Bill's view, the white man "goes with . . . Negro women. He got kids by 'em. How do my Negro women get to be white? I didn't make no white babies. The white man made 'em by my Negro women. Wouldn't have never have been a light Negro if they'd just let me get 'em. Would he? All right, the white man got 'em. So the white woman know that. She knows that. And she get a baby by me."

Even as he acknowledged these discouraging factors and forces, Bill articulated a philosophy that insisted on the importance of self-respect for each individual. He told Lomax:

I think a man should be what he is. Regardless to what you are, or who you are, or where you come from. And that don't just go for a Negro. That go for every nationality in the world. Be *proud* of what you are! If you're black, be proud of that! If you're green, be proud of that! If you're white, be proud of that! [I] don't care what color you are, or who you are. And try to be so people in the world will say, "Well, that's, that fella, regardless to his color, whosoenever he is, he's all right." Don't, don't just try to be the lowest thing in the world because people say you's no good! Don't, don't, don't, don't pay that no attention! Ignore the man that says you're no good because you're black, or because you're some color, or you're some something. Be proud of what you are, and, and prove it to the people that, that you's intelligent! I don't give a darn what color you are, you can be intelligent! You can be a man, you can be decent!

There are several noteworthy features to this recorded conversation. The first is that it reflects the degree to which Bill trusted Alan Lomax. It was highly unusual in 1952 for a black man and a white man to be discussing relations between the two races with any degree of frankness, even if they were an ocean away from America. For Bill to express himself with such candor reflects the extent to which he not only felt comfortable with Lomax, but felt confident that he would not use Bill's comments in any way that could pose a threat to him or his family.

Second, Bill's comments took the form of vivid analyses of deeply painful conflicts within the black community. In describing some blacks in America as ashamed of the color of their skin, as well as envious of those among them who had had some measure of economic success, Bill acknowledged to Lomax divisions and perceptions that few had discussed with whites. He did not shy away from acknowledging the impact on his own career of the forces he described, as he spoke of the rejection by "the Negro that's [come north] from Mississippi, that knows the blues that I'm singing, he's ashamed of it when he hear it." Rather than being angry at losing his black audience, Bill focused on understanding why the newer migrant felt the way he did. In Bill's interpretation, the migrant had a keen desire to make a new life for himself, and "he don't want people to know that he come from Mississippi, . . . and was treated so bad, and was abused and pushed around, and done so bad."

Third, Bill's exhortation for each individual to be proud of himself provides a view of the part of his personality that impelled him to mentor younger musicians. While he may have used different words in other conversations, his core belief that everyone is capable of acting in a way that reflects self-respect shines through in his comments to Lomax. His insistence on each individual's capacity to find personal dignity, even in the face of discrimination and contempt, anticipated some of the strategy and tactics that emerged a decade later in the civil rights movement.

As Bill was winding up his stay in France, he was running into financial difficulties. He wrote Win Stracke in late April that the Hot Club of France owed him 125,000 francs, and that Mezz Mezzrow, despite his close friendship with Hugues Panassié, was having trouble getting paid as well. Because his primary contact at the HCF, the man with whom he had stayed when he had arrived in January, had left town, Bill was prepared to go to the American embassy for help. Bill cautioned Win not to mention his money problems to Rose or anyone else and added that he might have to ask Win to send him a boat ticket. Win responded quickly, sending him a ticket that cost $180 and that carried an open sailing date. Bill strode on board the *Liberté* in Le Havre on May 16 and, after five and a half months overseas, sailed back to America.

He shared his first gig back in Chicago over the weekend of May 30–31 at Silvio's Tavern with Blind John Davis, and the West Side club promoted the return of the European travelers. "Hay! Hay! [sic] Baby . . . The Blues are back in Town," the flyer announced, listing "The Blues King . . . Big Bill Broonzy and Blind John Davis."[24] According to harmonica player Billy Boy Arnold, who was then a teenager, Bill got a warm welcome from the hometown crowd. "So I came by that Sunday afternoon, it was like a cocktail party in the afternoon, about four o'clock in the afternoon," recalled Arnold, who knew Blind John Davis but who had never met Bill. Before Bill arrived, Blind John and guitarist Lazy Bill Lucas had started to warm up the crowd, whose members were also anticipating being part of a Sunday afternoon remote broadcast on radio station WOPA. Arnold remembered that he "was anxious to meet Big Bill because I'd heard so much about him, and he was late getting there. Blind John and Lazy Bill Lucas were playing, and they started the broadcast.

Then I saw this big giant of a guy come in the door. Silvio's was a long club, a great big club. I saw this great big giant of a guy come in the door, and he was standing there smiling, and people was hollering at him, and as he walked through the place he had to stop and talk with the people at the tables and at the bar, and then he came back and he looked up at the bandstand and they were playing, so he walked back up to the front, and then he came back a few minutes later and got his guitar and started singing on the radio.

In late June, Bill appeared at another West Side venue as one of several musicians, including Muddy Waters and pianist Sunnyland Slim, who were playing on a bill for which Memphis Slim was the top attraction. But it would be in early July that Bill would begin a weekly gig that would continue longer than any he ever held, and it would take him to the heart of downtown Chicago.

By the summer of 1952, Studs Terkel's career as the star of a locally produced TV show in Chicago had come to a premature end. The program, *Studs' Place*, had featured him as the proprietor of a small neighborhood restaurant, along with a set of colleagues that included Win Stracke and piano player Chet Roble. The show, which first appeared in 1949, was a prime example of the "Chicago school" of television, which was characterized by real-life settings and improvised dialogue. Despite its impact, the show had been canceled in 1951 as a result of Terkel's unwillingness to disavow his support for various left-wing political causes he had endorsed. As Terkel put it, "They wanted me to 'apologize.' . . . I said, 'no,' and they kicked me off the air."[25] Years later he would refer to himself and Stracke, in an ironic allusion to the widely publicized trial of the "Chicago Seven" who were accused of disrupting the 1968 Democratic Convention, as "the Chicago Two."[26]

As a former disc jockey and record columnist, one of the connections Terkel had made in the Chicago jazz world was with Frank Holzfeind, the owner of the Blue Note nightclub, located downtown at Clark and Madison. The Blue Note was as prestigious a venue for jazz as there was at the time in Chicago, featuring multi-week residencies by performers of the stature of Duke Ellington and Louis Armstrong. Because artists were restricted by union contracts from performing more than six nights a week, the club was generally closed on Monday nights. With Studs keeping an eye out for work wherever he could find it, and Holzfeind open to the possibility of generating some additional revenue, "I Come for to Sing" moved from the campus concert halls to the nightclub stage.

On July 7, 1952, the revue played its first show at the Blue Note, with Chet Roble joining the original group of Studs, Win, Bill, and Larry Lane. Beginning with the first show, the size of the audiences for "I Come for to Sing" was a pleasant surprise to Holzfeind. He was a congenial club owner who was respected by the musicians for his fair dealings, but also a clear-sighted businessman for whom, as he put it, the show had to make "reasonable monetary sense" to continue beyond its origins as "a happy little experiment."[27]

A particularly receptive constituency for the group turned out to be other musicians. The list of Blue Note performers who enjoyed the revue included Stan Kenton and Buddy Rich, and Benny Goodman "came to see the show not once, but twice."[28] The most public accolade from another artist came from Duke Ellington, who, according to Holzfeind, "asked permission to write a rave" for the nightclub's biweekly newsletter. In the article, Ellington praised the "wonderful little folk song revue" for its "rare gems of folklore woven together into a neat pattern by Studs Terkel." The bandleader and composer emphasized that "what we in our band do is all based on folklore, even if it sounds much more developed and mature by this time." He was particularly captivated by the way that "songs of such widespread origins" were "put together so they make such beautiful and entertaining sense."[29]

The arrival and extended run of the "I Come for to Sing" group in a leading downtown jazz club was an enormous leap forward for folk music in Chicago. The venues where folk music had been regularly performed up to that point had been mostly on or around college campuses. Nationally known artists such as Josh White had appeared at Orchestra Hall, but these performances were infrequent, and in fact White's 1946 concert had been sponsored by the now-defunct People's Songs. The presence of the folk-song revue at the Blue Note every Monday night, week after week, was a key factor in creating a larger audience for folk music.

One characteristic of the new downtown folk music fan base was that there were some affluent members. After the first year of the revue's run, the club's biweekly newsletter featured an article titled "Meet Our 'Fifteen-Timer' Club," which presented portraits of the Monday-night regulars. One of those mentioned included the business manager of *Seventeen* magazine, who was primarily a Dixieland fan but who had developed an "affection for Lawrence Lane's Elizabethan ballads [and] some of the frontier lullabies of Win Stracke." Another was a vice president of an advertising agency, who "doesn't wear sincere ties but he loves sincere songs, particularly if it's the earthy blues of Big Bill Broonzy, or the city street anthems of Chet Roble."[30] The unexpected nationwide success of the Weavers in 1950 had brought an awareness of folk music to a mass audience. Chicago residents and tourists could now see a quintet of experienced performers every week. The commercial viability and enduring appeal of "I Come for to Sing" was one of the first significant indicators that folk music was becoming a visible part of the city's cultural landscape.

For Bill, the regular slot at the Blue Note helped pay his bills. As the contracts stipulated for all the "I Come for to Sing" participants, he was paid $25 for each appearance, which in 2009 equaled $200, making it very much worth his while. If, as is likely, he supplemented those earnings with some kind of day job and an occasional appearance at a South or West Side tavern, he would probably have been stable financially for the summer and early fall.

It might have been a Monday evening sometime in October that Studs Terkel was describing when he wrote in his memoirs about a memorable night at the Blue Note:

> This night, the place is, for some inexplicable reason, jammed. Duke is in the house, too. He digs Big Bill. It is nine o'clock. Where is Bill? We're due to go on—now. I call the Broonzy home. His wife Rose answers.
>
> "He's on his way . . ." she says.
>
> "Good," I say, giving Frank the a-okay sign.
>
> ". . . to England," says Rose.[31]

When Bill disembarked in England on October 27, 1952, for his third visit there, the British music press was focused on the imminent arrival of another African American performer from the South Side of Chicago. "Mahalia—Greatest of Gospellers" read the headline in the *Melody Maker* that accompanied the article describing Mahalia Jackson's European debut in Paris.[32] Born in New Orleans, Jackson had moved to Chicago as a teenager, and after teaming up with the Rev. Thomas A. Dorsey, she became a leading figure in the gospel music world there. Jackson had come to the attention of white audiences in the late 1940s with her million-selling record "Move on Up a Little Higher." After meeting her during a 1949 trip to New York, Hugues Panassié had introduced Jackson's music to French audiences by playing her records on his French radio broadcasts. The photo in the *Melody Maker* of Jackson stepping off the plane at Paris's Orly Airport and being greeted by both Charles Delaunay and Mezz Mezzrow, no doubt acting as Panassié's stand-in, reflected a momentary détente between the two rivals, united by their joint passion for her music.

On the other side of the English Channel, Bill found himself in the midst of a controversy involving Jackson. The headline for the front-page story in the *Melody Maker* announcing his return to Great Britain read "No 'Sinful' Songs from Big Bill, Pleads Mahalia."[33] The article stated that "through promoter Bert Wilcox, Mahalia has requested Bill to keep off blues and 'sinful songs' during these concerts, and to concentrate on true folk songs." The writer described him as saying, "Please make it clear that I feel the same way as Mahalia about this. It wasn't my idea to go on her programme. In the States we never mix these things. I mean, if I was to do all blues and then she does her spirituals, it might look as if we were kind of fighting. That wouldn't do at all. I guess we must keep the two parts of the programme quite separate."[34]

The suggestion of a conflict between the "King of the Blues" and the "Gospel Queen" accomplished the promoters' purpose of achieving page-one coverage for the upcoming concerts. Mahalia was quoted the following week as saying that she was "very happy to have Bill on the concerts," adding that "there's no reason for any fuss. I was just hoping that he wouldn't do the lowdown blues, but those real country songs of his, they're fine."[35]

Even though some of the quotes attributed to Bill sounded nothing like him, they were consistent with views he expressed in interviews. As he told Studs Terkel several years later: "I just had that much respect for Christian people, I always have. And I still got that respect for Christian people. I never would sit down in front of Mahalia Jackson and sing a blues. The only time she heard me sing a blues I was on a stage. I never would sit down in [. . .] I would go to her dressing room and carry my guitar, if I sat there and played anything I'd play church songs. It's just the respect that I have for them because I know those people has got just as much chance to be right as I has to be right, too, with my way of thinking."[36]

Despite the efforts to drum up publicity, their four joint appearances were neither artistic nor financial successes. Mahalia performed despite having fallen ill before leaving the States. In fact, she had to cut her European tour short for a major operation shortly after completing her dates in England. At their concert in Oxford, Bill's late arrival forced Mahalia to go on as the opening act, and, obviously not feeling well, she only performed one thirty-minute set. In two different settings, including the prestigious Royal Albert Hall, the heat in the concert halls was barely working. In the raw weather of November in Britain, audiences and performers alike had to endure uncomfortably cold conditions. The half-full Albert Hall show reflected one critic's assessment that publicity was woefully inadequate, given that "the British public does NOT know either Mahalia or Big Bill."[37]

While the British public might not have been well acquainted with Bill, he had become a familiar figure in the British jazz world. In between concerts, he played for the "Jazz Dancing" sessions that trumpeter and bandleader Humphrey Lyttelton organized at the popular club at 100 Oxford Street.[38] Bill also sang "John Henry" and "The Midnight Special" on a BBC Radio special titled *Song of the Iron Road*, which presented "stories of the British and American railways and of the men who built them."[39] Joining Bill on the program were Lyttelton and his band, as well as singer and folklorist Ewan MacColl, who was becoming a major force in the emerging British folk music scene of the 1950s. When Bill performed with one of the leading trad jazz groups, the Christie Brothers Stompers, at a concert in Hove, *Jazz Journal* writer Derrick Stewart-Baxter interviewed Bill onstage. He then surprised Bill by presenting him with an abstract portrait of him, done in absentia by musician and artist Russell Quaye, who had also painted similarly unconventional portraits of Pearl Bailey and Ma Rainey. On the eve of his departure from Britain, the London Jazz Club held a farewell party in Bill's honor at 100 Oxford Street. The *Melody Maker* published a photo of him reading a newspaper on the train to Brussels with a downcast expression, under the headline "Bill Broonzy's Leaving Blues."[40]

Bill played one night in Brussels, accompanied by two Belgian jazz musicians and by pianist Lil Hardin Armstrong, who had been married at one time to Louis Armstrong. It was the first of several European appearances Bill made with Armstrong, who had played on her then-husband's Hot Five and Hot Seven recordings of the 1920s. A photo from the December 9 concert at the Théâtre Royal des Galeries shows Bill dressed impeccably in a dark double-breasted suit with a white pocket handkerchief, appropriate attire for a setting where audiences generally enjoyed ballets and operettas.[41]

From Brussels, Bill traveled to Paris. The French capital would serve as his home base for the next six months as he continued his relationship with Jacqueline and toured within France, as well as beyond its borders. It would also be where he cemented a friendship with a Belgian couple, whose keen interest in Bill, his music, and his stories would produce some of the most enduring elements of his legacy.

Too Many Isms

Yannick Bruynoghe was an unlikely rebel. His father was a prominent microbiologist at the University of Louvain, the prestigious Catholic institution located in the Belgian city where Yannick was born in 1924. His older brother, Guy, had followed directly in his father's footsteps, choosing not only to become a doctor, but also to specialize in the same field, and he held an appointment at the same university. Yannick's initial preference, if he had to become a doctor, was to become a psychologist or psychiatrist, but his father was not enchanted with that prospect. It was only after his father vetoed his younger son's wish to study musicology that Yannick agreed to study law.

In the aftermath of World War II, Yannick veered off the conventional path. He had been a jazz fan since Guy had brought him to a Duke Ellington concert in Brussels in 1939. Shortly after that, he traded his collection of classical records to his brother, receiving Guy's jazz records in return. He added to his collection by buying records during the final years of the war while stationed in Northern Ireland, where he was serving with a unit of the Belgian army then attached to the British army. His collecting efforts were made easier by his fluency in English, which he had acquired from being raised by a British nanny during his childhood. On his return to Belgium, he started a jazz magazine and began to correspond with Hugues Panassié in France and Stanley Dance in England, both leading figures in the European jazz world.

In 1947 Yannick traveled to New York City, where he stayed for two months, absorbing as much jazz as he could. While there, he began his lifelong hobby of amateur photography, often photographing jazz musicians. When he returned to Belgium, he started broadcasting a jazz program on the radio, and his name soon became known to the growing community of jazz fans who tuned in. What few of them realized was that although they were listening to Yannick's words and to the records he selected, the voice they heard was not his. Because, in his wife Margo's description, he was "very shy," he always arranged for someone else to read the script. As Margo put it, "People didn't know Yannick's voice, but they knew it was Yannick's show."[1]

The following year, Panassié tapped Yannick to select the Belgian musicians who would perform in the first postwar jazz festival held in France, which he was organizing in Nice in March 1948. Panassié was securing his control of the Hot Club of France, having engineered the ouster as secretary general of Charles Delaunay, his former colleague turned rival. Yannick had previously visited Panassié at his residence in Fontainebleau, near Paris, and he had become a trusted member of Panassié's European network.

Because Yannick was a reliable lieutenant, Panassié had given him the assignment of meeting Bill at the Brussels airport in the summer of 1951 and making sure the visiting bluesman got on the train to France for his first European performances. At the end of 1952, in his latest posting as an integral part of the Panassié team, Yannick was preparing to serve as manager for Mezz Mezzrow's band in their tour of Europe and North Africa in early 1953. By then, two significant changes had occurred since Yannick and Bill had first met in Belgium. For his part, Bill was now on his third overseas tour, and he was settling into his quarters in a Paris residential hotel for an extended European stay. And an attractive young Belgian woman had just broken off her engagement to someone else so that she could be with the broadcaster who was too shy to speak on the air.

When she turned twenty-one, Margo Vanbesien (pronounced van-buh-ZEEN) had left the Belgian town where she was raised and traveled to England. She was not getting along well with her father, and she was determined to learn English. Margo soon found work as a saleswoman in a large department store and began taking evening classes in English literature. By late 1952, she had mastered written and spoken English, had become engaged to a young man from Brussels who was serving in the Belgian army, and had relocated to Paris.

One evening, after he had climbed up the six flights of stairs to the unheated apartment that Margo shared with another young woman, "a tall fellow" knocked on the door. Margo recognized the visitor, who was delivering a note from her fiancé, as someone she had met briefly back in Belgium. When she invited Yannick to come in for coffee, he told her that he had two tickets to see Louis Armstrong perform that evening, and he invited her to accompany him to the concert. The seats turned out to be onstage, and Yannick and Margo extended the evening by traveling to Montmartre in search of a club that had been famous before the war, accompanied by trombonist Dickie Wells. Over the next forty-eight hours, they attended a conference on Louis Armstrong, heard jazz played in the cafés of Saint-Germain-des-Prés, and met guitarist Django Reinhardt.

After three days, Margo recalled, "I think the two of us both knew that we had met the right person." The only slightly challenging problem was that, at the time, each was engaged to be married to other people. This was quickly resolved when Yannick returned to Brussels and broke up with his fiancée, while Margo informed her fiancé that their engagement was off. While they would wait several years to get married, they were a couple from that point forward.

After Bill arrived in Paris in mid-December 1952, he and Yannick reconnected, and by the end of 1952 the two men were hard at work setting up a formal business relationship. Bill was eager to have someone handle all aspects of booking his concerts and making his travel arrangements. He was just coming off of a series of transactions with his British booking agent, Herbert "Bert" Wilcox, which had left him feeling enraged and exploited.

In a letter to Win Stracke, Bill described the sequence of events, which he began by typing in capital letters: "THIS IS WHAT MR. HERBERT WILCOX DON[E] TO BIG BILL." He wrote of having to pay rent of five pounds a week while living in Wilcox's home, paying cab and train fare for himself and Wilcox while traveling to and from concerts, and having to buy the tickets for the two of them to travel round-trip to Holland and Belgium. He went on to tell of being charged twice for the same set of expenses, as well as asserting that Wilcox had cashed a check for Bill from the Hot Club of Belgium. These all led Bill to conclude that he "never was treated by nobody like Mr. Wilcox treated me," and he questioned whether Wilcox "has a heart in him at all." He concluded by saying that he thought the agent "must have dollar signs for eyes."

In an interview given fifty years later, Wilcox explained that his business relationship with Bill was different from the standard arrangement he had with other performers. Whereas he generally acted as an agent and took a percentage of the fee that the venue paid the performer, he noted that "with Bill it was a different thing." Wilcox described paying Bill "fixed amounts of money," which he estimated at either 100 or 200 pounds a week, "plus all his expenses, plus living in my flat with my wife and I in London, rent-free. Everything was on me, you might say." In his judgment, "[Bill] did quite well." In addition, when he had seen that Bill "had a whole wad of money in his pocket," he described encouraging Bill to send the money back to the United States and said that he helped him make the necessary arrangements through a British bank. In Wilcox's view, the problem came because Bill sent the money to the account of a friend in Chicago, and the "so-called friend" had stolen the funds but told Bill he had never received the funds: "[Bill] sent it to the other man's account, who spent it." When Bill found out, "he was furious," and "thought that we were all tied up with this."[2]

Whatever in fact occurred, Bill's intense frustration with what he identified as unfair practices by Wilcox, on top of his decades-long outrage with Lester Melrose, made him determined to negotiate an arrangement with Yannick that would be certain to protect his interests. When he wrote Yannick on December 31, Bill was explicit in delineating his expectations for compensation and virtually every other aspect of their relationship. Discussing a prospective gig in France, he wanted to establish a standard rate of 35,000 francs per concert, which he calculated as equivalent to $100. He argued that "if [an]other country can pay 35,000 francs, France can pay it too."[3] Bill was particularly emphatic about charging a fee to anyone who wished to record one of his concerts. "I want this understood," he wrote, "if there is any tape recording, I want 10,000 francs for each place. I am holding you responsible for that." To reassure Yannick that he would operate in good faith, he added, "And don't worry about me taking any other jobs with other people."

Bill recognized the importance of formalizing their agreement, asking Yannick to "write up [an] agreement and put all of these things in it, and there won't be no misunderstand[ing] after, because we will both know the contract we signed. Not that I don't trust you, but this is business." The contract, which the two men signed in Paris on January 8, 1953, settled on a performance fee of 25,000 French francs. Yannick agreed to pay all "transportation and taxes," and, with the exception of "night-club work in Paris," Bill would "accept no engagement of any kind in Europe" without Yannick's agreement.[4] The contract, which would expire on May

10, 1953, gave Yannick authorization to book Bill for appearances in concerts, radio, and television, as well as the right to sign contracts in Bill's name.[5]

Yannick was able to make the arrangement work because of his contacts in the Hot Club of France network. He booked Bill primarily through the various Hot Clubs in France and elsewhere, such as Antwerp. He also made sure that the concert organizers paid for Bill's transportation and hotel expenses. If they knew the promoter, Yannick and Margo would request that there be a bottle of whiskey waiting for Bill in his hotel room. As Margo described it, "We [didn't] get any commissions. We didn't play the role of manager. But we didn't like the idea of cheating the artists, because the artist always got cheated somewhere."[6]

During this same period, as negotiations evolved into conversations, Yannick recognized that he and Margo were hearing a master storyteller at work, and that they could play a central role in preserving the tales. "The idea of writing the book came very quickly to Yannick's mind because [Bill] was telling so many stories," Margo recalled. "Because he was talking about his uncle Jerry, and all the many other things that happened. . . . And so Yannick must have said 'Put that down.' So [Bill] did, but very slowly."[7]

Bill responded favorably to the prospect of working with the couple to turn his stories into a book. At the end of December, while Yannick was back in Belgium, Bill wrote him to discuss the joint venture. He was thinking about the business side of the project, not only envisioning a formal agreement for splitting any earnings, but also suggesting a provision that would direct the royalties to Yannick "when I am in the U.S.A. or [if] something happens to me." He was eager to get started on the actual writing: "Don't you think me and Margo could be typing some of these things down because you can't read my writing so good?"[8]

Because Margo was in Paris, Yannick asked her to encourage Bill to write regularly. The role suited her well, as she found Bill's stories captivating, and she was eager to ensure that they would reach a larger audience. With her practical and organized approach to life, which later served her well when she ran an art gallery in Brussels, she would check in regularly with Bill to encourage him and monitor his progress. Bill, for his part, enjoyed Margo's company, writing Yannick that "she is like a sister to me . . . she is good to me, and a good-hearted person."[9]

From her unique vantage point, Margo had the chance to observe how Bill adjusted to living in a place where so much was unfamiliar to him. "He liked to get up early and walk," she recalled. "He loved to go through the streets, and [find] his way through Paris. . . . He liked to discover little cafés." Noting that Bill's combination of early rising and exploring on foot was unlike the preferences of most of the jazz musicians she knew, Margo believed that "he was a great observer. He wanted to be able to find his way by himself."[10]

Her interactions with Bill taught Margo about aspects of racism that most whites in the United States would have been unaware of. One day he had just returned from shopping and proudly showed her the new shoes he had purchased, which were still in the box. When she asked whether they were comfortable, Bill replied that he didn't know. After Margo expressed her puzzlement that he hadn't tried them on in the store, Bill informed her, "Oh, no. We're not allowed to do that in the States." After she and Yannick visited Bill in Chicago in 1957, Margo concluded that while his description was accurate, he was likely describing the customs of Arkansas or Mississippi, rather than those of Chicago.

It took some detective work by Margo for her to understand one aspect of Bill's eating preferences. He had an excellent appetite, and numerous accounts survive of the substantial amounts he consumed at memorable breakfasts and dinners during his European tours. After eating with him in restaurants for some time, Margo noticed that "he would never, never, never order a steak when he was in a restaurant," favoring instead dishes such as rice and beans, fried chicken, or ribs. When she asked him about it, Bill replied that it was because he was sure that he would be eating horse meat. Even after Margo explained that the menus in French restaurants that served horse meat listed it plainly, Bill still refused to order a steak. It was only when she returned years later to the site of the Hotel Lévêque at 29 rue Cler, where Bill stayed in those years, that the sign above the butcher shop across the street caught her eye. She had never before noticed the enormous horse's head, and she then realized that every time Bill left the hotel, he was reminded of his concern about the true content of French steaks.[11]

It was in pursuit of food that Bill encountered another expatriate African American one evening with Yannick and Margo. They had gone to a restaurant called Haynes, which had opened a few years before and had soon become, as one historian has described it, "one of the key establishments of African American life in postwar Paris."[12] The African American owner, cook, and namesake was Leroy Haynes, a former college football player who had served in the U.S. Army in World War II. Haynes had headed to Paris to pursue graduate studies and then discovered that he needed additional income to survive there. Along with his French wife, Haynes prepared, as Margo recalled, "real soul food, the *real* soul food, beans and rice, fried chicken, and chitlins, mashed potatoes and corn bread."[13] The restaurant's regular clientele included African Americans who were living in and traveling through Paris, as well as white Europeans who wanted to sample down-home cooking.

The writer Richard Wright, who had been based in Paris since the late 1940s, was a regular customer, enjoying a friendship with Leroy Haynes as well as the food. Yannick and Margo went frequently as well, as it was a favorite spot for the jazz lovers in the Hot Club of France, as well as for musicians such as Mezz Mezzrow. One night when Bill accompanied Yannick and Margo, they had dinner with Wright, whom they had met there previously. On the way back to Bill's hotel, they asked Bill what he thought of the well-known writer, who had been a Communist Party member in the 1930s and who, even after breaking with the party, had continued to write and speak out on controversial political topics. Bill delivered a terse assessment: "Too many isms."

Bill's comment reflected his cautious approach to politics. By 1953, many of the white American performers he had worked with since the mid-1940s had encountered significant difficulties in their careers as a result of their political beliefs. Alan Lomax had left the United States for an extended residency in Great Britain and Europe, Studs Terkel had lost his TV program in Chicago because of blacklisting, and Pete Seeger and his fellow members of the Weavers had plummeted from stars to pariahs as a result of accusations about their past political activities. Bill would almost certainly have been aware of Josh White's difficulties in the wake of his testimony before the House Un-American Activities Committee in 1950. White's name had been included in a list of 115 possible Communist sympathizers by a virulently anti-Communist publication called *Red Channels*. In attempting to find a middle ground between "naming names" of alleged Communists and risking the ire of anti-Communists by refusing to accept the committee's authority, White had only succeeded in becoming simultaneously a target for angry leftists and a reluctant example of a remorseful entertainer who had been duped by the Communists.[14]

While Bill was forthright in his opposition to segregation and racial injustice, he conveyed his beliefs in his songs and, later, in his autobiography. He did not express his views by participating in organized political activities or events. In his own way, Bill found the middle ground that had eluded Josh White as a result of White's first being listed in Red Channels and then choosing to testify before the congressional committee. Until his death in 1958, Bill continued to perform on stages with Seeger in Chicago and elsewhere, and he appeared with Terkel as part of "I Come for to Sing" and on Terkel's Chicago radio show. After Win Stracke's TV career in Chicago suffered the effects of blacklisting, Bill performed with him as well. Regardless of whether he knew about Richard Wright's past Communist Party membership or the author's present-day criticism of racism in the America he had chosen to leave, Bill had developed his own worldview independent of the ideological battles Wright had been fighting for several decades.

During the six months Bill was based in Paris from the end of 1952 until mid-May 1953, he toured several times within France and beyond it as well. He wrote Win Stracke that he played in Iceland in December, where he was struck by how dark it was and then learned that it is "six months night and six months day there."[15] A few weeks after playing a show in Louvain, Belgium, almost certainly arranged with help from Yannick, Bill traveled with Mezzrow's band to play in North Africa, appearing in both Algeria and Morocco. The two countries were still under French rule, and the Hot Club of France had either branches or contacts in each of them. The jazz fans at the Empire Room in Oran, Algeria, greeted Bill warmly, and the newspaper review contrasted Bill, whom the writer likened to a "former 400 meter Olympic champion," with Mezzrow, who, "with his glasses and bald forehead, corresponds exactly with the image of a meticulous attorney."[16]

On his return to Paris in mid-January, Bill wrote Win Stracke that he was playing "2 places every night," and that he was planning to cut back at the Ringside Club and just play at the Metro Jazz Club.[17] After maintaining his Parisian club residency and making a short tour of central France, Bill arrived in Holland at the end of February for a five-day stay. It was a country with which he would develop particularly strong connections, initially in his work and later in his personal life.

In Holland young jazz lovers had been captivated by jazz and its origins in the same way as had fans in the United States, France, and Great Britain after World War II. Bands such as the Dutch Swing College Band had begun forming in the mid-1940s, and concerts, radio broadcasts, and listening parties soon became part of the Dutch music scene. Bill had flown in from England the previous November for a brief visit during which he made two appearances in two days. When the members of The Hague Jazz Club had awarded him their second honorary membership during his brief stay, he was in good company, as the first had been given to Sidney Bechet.

Michiel de Ruyter, a Dutch musician and music writer in his mid-twenties who had learned to play the clarinet while recovering from polio as a teenager during the war, had been at the November event in The Hague. When De Ruyter heard early in 1953 that the first bluesman he had met was returning to Holland, he was quick to contact the concert organizers. As he later wrote to Bill, "[I] told 'em that I should be the man to introduce you to the public, as this public didn't know a thing about blues."[18] Through his radio broadcasts, his writing, and his work as an emcee, De Ruyter played a significant role in establishing Bill as a familiar figure in the Dutch jazz world. Bill likely recognized some similarities with Alan Lomax and Studs Terkel in De Ruyter's approach, as the wheelchair-bound commentator with the husky voice would give listeners background information on the songs Bill performed, along with, as he put it, descriptions of "the folks that made this music."[19]

Bill had arrived this time in a country that was still reeling from the impact of what has been called "the country's most terrible natural disaster of the 20th century."[20] Almost two thousand people had perished during the Zeeland floods at the end of January 1953. During the second of two concerts he gave in Amsterdam during his visit, Bill spoke to the audience in intensely personal terms as he introduced Bessie Smith's "Backwater Blues," by then a staple of his repertoire:

In 19-and-27 . . . I was down there at the time and it was a terrible flood. . . . And the whole city of . . . Scotts, Mississippi, and that's where I was born, it wasn't a house left that you could go into because the water was over the whole entire neighborhood. . . . It was fifteen hundred of my people lost their lives in that flood. Some of 'em didn't get drownded in the water but they was what we call marooned. I mean they was off on a hill and the government couldn't get to them to give them food or nothing to eat, and they starved to death up there on those hills. And I said that because I want you to know that everyone and whosoever that was in a flood here, you know I know what you went through with it, because I went through with it myself. My mother, my father, my sisters and brothers, and I had 16 of them, sisters and brothers. And all of us was sitting on housetops waiting for somebody to come by and pick us up and take us to safety, which they did.[21]

Based on all available information about Bill, it is highly unlikely that he or any of his immediate family experienced what he described so vividly. Yet what is striking is his desire to acknowledge the distress that strangers were experiencing in a country he hardly knew. Bill's wish to provide some comfort in the wake of a calamity, combined with one of his most heartfelt renditions of a blues about a catastrophic flood, was both unexpected and most welcome. A review of his appearance the following night at a benefit concert for a disaster relief fund described Bill as someone who "has become more of a citizen than a visitor."[22]

When he returned to Paris, Bill began a correspondence with De Ruyter. These letters, along with ones he wrote to other European correspondents, shed some light on how Bill was able to adapt to his extended stays overseas. One noteworthy aspect is how quickly and easily Bill established a comfortable level of intimacy and warmth with his European friends. His first letter to De Ruyter began "Hello, old pal," and the second, probably written a week or so later, opened with "Hello, my dear brother and friend."[23] In addition, over the course of the two letters, Bill apologized for his behavior at a gathering at De Ruyter's home and explained in some detail his unintentional entanglement with a woman who was simultaneously pursuing both Bill and a married man who was active in the Dutch music scene. Bill asked De Ruyter's help in explaining the situation to their married friend and in particular to make it clear that "it was all my fault [because] I didn't know and went just a little too far."[24]

The letters to De Ruyter bear a close resemblance to Bill's correspondence with a French chemical engineer and Hot Club of France member named André Vasset. Bill had met Vasset during his first visit to France in 1951 and had stayed with his family in Clermont-Ferrand, in southern France, after a concert there. He had written to Vasset when he returned to Chicago after his first trip, and by early 1953 he was also referring to Vasset as "brother." Bill went so far, when he described his intention of getting married to his French girlfriend, Jacqueline, as to tell Vasset that "she is going to be your sister pretty soon now."[25] In several different letters, Bill had written longingly of Vasset's mother's delicious beans and praised his father's tasty homemade wine.

In order to succeed professionally in this period, Bill had to figure out how to live for months at a time far from his family and in countries whose currency, food, language, and customs were unfamiliar. Unlike most of the American jazz musicians who would tour with their fellow band members, Bill was working almost exclusively as a solo performer and therefore without kindred spirits facing similar cultural challenges in their lives offstage. Bill coped with these dilemmas and uncertainties by forging bonds with a number of the people he encountered, as well as their families, and he reinforced these connections through regular letter writing. For many of these white Europeans, Bill was probably the first African American they had known as more than an acquaintance, and almost certainly the first one who had called them "brother." His correspondents were pleased to reciprocate, and these exchanges sustained the friendships during his extended absences while in the United States or touring elsewhere.

In early May, Bill returned to Germany to play at the first German Jazz Festival, held in Frankfurt.[26] One of the organizers was Horst Lippmann, whom he had met in 1951 when he was there with the Graeme Bell band. But the person in the German jazz scene with whom Bill forged the closest bond was a friend and occasional bandmate of Lippmann's, a German radio broadcaster and jazz piano player in his early thirties named Günter Boas.

Born in 1920, Boas had his first exposure to jazz at age eight, when a lodger in his parents' home who was a student of the artist Paul Klee gave him a copy of Louis Armstrong's "Basin Street Blues." During a trip with his father to Paris for the 1937 World Exposition, he met Hugues Panassié, with whom he had been corresponding and who brought him to the initial recording session for the Swing record label. After Boas's brief tour of duty as an orderly in a military hospital, his landlady informed the local Nazi authorities that her tenant had been listening to illegal broadcasts of jazz and the BBC. Boas was sent to a Nazi labor camp in Kahla, which he was able to endure because the camp's chief doctor, a former professor of his, had him assigned as his personal aide. After the end of the war, Boas moved to Frankfurt, and soon his radio program *Blues for Monday*, was a weekly fixture on the Armed Forces Network. Most of the two thousand jazz and blues records in Boas's collection had not survived a wartime air raid, but he began to rebuild it as he reached out to collectors and fans in other countries in the aftermath of the war. A talented pianist, Boas met Lippmann in Frankfurt, and the younger man sometimes played bass or drums in one of Boas's combos, which featured names such as the Two Beat Stompers.[27]

Boas probably met Bill for the first time during the Bell band's visit to Frankfurt for the 1951 concert, at which his friend and fellow jazz enthusiast Olaf Hudtwalker served as emcee. By early 1953, Bill was writing Boas from Paris, thanking him for "my membership card" and saying he was "glad to be a member of the club."[28] This was a reference to the Hot Club of Frankfurt, which, although it lacked a formal affiliation with Panassié's organization, performed very similar functions. Bill specifically asked Boas to "arrange some concerts in Germany," because "I sure do want to come to Germany before I come home."[29] His request likely played a part in Bill's appearance at the jazz festival, held at the Althoffbau on May 4, 1953.[30]

Bill would continue to correspond with Boas after he returned to the States, and he was particularly grateful for Günter's help in arranging for him to stay at the home of another family. Bill expressed his appreciation by making sure that other blues artists knew about the thoughtful welcome that Boas had provided. A decade later, when blues musicians came to Germany on the American Folk Blues Festival tours of the 1960s that Lippmann organized, along with Fritz Rau and Willie Dixon, the artists greeted Boas warmly. Boas's wife, Lore, recalled that "when [Boas] met all these blues guys, who hadn't been over here before," they would exclaim, "Oh, you're Big Bill's friend!" As Lore noted, "Big Bill must have talked about him quite a bit."[31]

Almost two weeks later, after playing the first concert by a blues artist in Spain for the Hot Club of Barcelona, Bill took an Air France flight back to the United States. This time, instead of a residency at Silvio's, Bill headed for a Chicago recording studio in the weeks that followed. The solo artist who had effectively become the ambassador of the blues overseas was about to record with a couple of old friends for the last time.[32]

By the late spring of 1953, Leonard and Phil Chess had established themselves as forces to be reckoned with in the Chicago blues world. Their record labels—which included Chess, Checker, and later Argo—were becoming known as a source of songs that regularly hovered near the top of the R&B charts in national music magazines. The artists whose records they were recording or releasing included Muddy Waters, Little Walter, and Howlin' Wolf. At the same time, Willie Dixon was settling in to his multiple roles of songwriter, bassist, and session organizer for the Chess brothers.

As Nadine Cohodas has described in her book *Spinning Blues into Gold*, the Chess brothers' goal was to make hit records, and, as they told one music magazine, "The key to a hit is to give the people what they want to hear."[33] In her assessment, "The brothers didn't always guess right, but Leonard was willing to try anything." One illustration she gave of this philosophy in action was of Leonard Chess's decision to record Bill's longtime musical colleague Washboard Sam after meeting him at Chicago's Midway Airport.[34] Perhaps Chess decided to add Sam to a session that he had previously arranged with Bill, or maybe Bill and Sam both benefited from the entrepreneur's willingness to take a chance on recording stars of the previous decades. Either way, Bill and Sam between them recorded a total of twelve songs for Chess Records in late May or early June.

The two veteran blues artists were joined by three experienced Chicago sidemen for what was likely one extended session. Guitarist Lee Cooper was once described by pianist Sunnyland Slim as "one of them old soul guitar players," while bassist Big Crawford had played on some of Muddy's first Chicago recordings and with Memphis Slim before that.[35] Memphis Slim himself sat in on piano for Sam's version of Bill's 1940 song "All by Myself." Bill's singing was energetic on the fast numbers and soulful on the slower ones, and Sam's washboard, which was making one of the very few appearances by the instrument on a Chess recording, combined with Crawford's thumping bass to form a solid rhythm section. Bill demonstrated that his songwriting skills had not diminished, as he sang in "Romance without Finance" that "Now look here, baby, I want to give you a hint / You can have romance, just give me those dead presidents." He drove the point home when he concluded that "Romance without finance don't mean a thing, now, can't you see? / Yeah, you got to have finance, baby, if you want to romance with me."[36]

The lyrics to his song "Jacqueline" (which Bill pronounced, in the French style, "Zhack-LEEN") provide a window into his feelings for the woman he had left behind only days before. "She's got my heart / Someday she'll have my name," Bill proudly proclaimed, as he imagined how "we'll have pictures made together / And put in the same frame."[37] The expressions of love that he sang reflected how he genuinely felt about the real-life Jacqueline. He had written André Vasset while he was still in France that Jacqueline "is all in this world to me," and he had stated in several of his letters to Vasset his expectation that they would get married "soon."[38] Jacqueline had underscored the extent to which they were, in fact, a couple in a postcard that Bill sent to Vasset in February. She had completed Bill's note by adding, in French, "We give a big hug to the Vasset family with all our heart."[39]

Even as Bill was recording his musical tribute to Jacqueline, trouble was brewing in their transatlantic relationship. In June Bill wrote Yannick Bruynoghe that someone had told Jacqueline that he "had forgotten about her" since he had returned to Chicago. Things took a turn for the worse when Jacqueline informed him that if he came back to Paris, her father would kill him.[40] For the next two years, as Bill corresponded with Yannick and Vasset while he remained in the United States, he implored his friends to contact Jacqueline on his behalf to persuade her of his commitment. In November 1953, he asked Vasset to "please write to Jacqueline for me and tell her I do love her, and if I get back to France I will marry her."[41] He added that she had not been answering his letters, a concern he was soon expressing in nearly every letter. While sending Yannick some song lyrics for the book project, Bill wondered "why people try to put her against me, and tell her I am not coming back to France."[42] By the spring of 1954, he was imploring Yannick to "tell Jacqueline I still love her no matter what she thinks of me."[43]

In the last two surviving letters from Bill to Vasset in which he mentions Jacqueline, Bill identified two factors that surely played a role in bringing their relationship to an end. At the end of December 1954, Bill wrote, "Brother, don't forget to tell Jacqueline that I do still love her. I don't care what nobody says about me being a Negro. I still love Jacqueline, she is my heart."[44] Whether he was referring to her father or other friends or family, Jacqueline was clearly feeling pressure from some source for being in an interracial relationship. In March 1955 Bill revealed to his friend that "[Jacqueline] had went to the doctor to get rid of the baby before I left, and the doctor told me she would never have another baby because he had fixed her so she never would have a baby." He went on to acknowledge that "I was the cause of what happened to her," and continued, "I do want to make up to her some way if I can because I love her very much. Brother, please believe me, I do love her and do wish she was with me. I have cried about her so many nights."[45]

Although Bill finally returned to France in 1956, there is no indication that he and Jacqueline ever saw each other again. People who were in touch with Jacqueline decades later gave differing accounts of her perspective on the time she spent with Bill. Vasset reported that while she "suffered greatly" when the relationship ended, she had no wish to discuss Bill in the years that followed.[46] Margo Bruynoghe, who spoke with Jacqueline near the time of her death in 2001, said that Jacqueline expressed regret at not having followed Bill back to the United States.[47] What is clear is that the powerful feelings Bill had for her were sustained over several years of being separated not only by distance but painful and complex issues. His relationship with Jacqueline was one that affected and engaged him deeply, and the image of him crying the tears of guilt and pain that he described to Vasset is a sad and credible one.

The session at Chess produced what turned out to be Bill's final recordings for primarily African American audiences. The contract that he had received from Leonard Chess, which was executed in the name of the Aristocrat Record Corporation—the original corporate entity for Chess Records—had specified a minimum of eight sides, and committed Bill to record exclusively for Chess for a one-year duration.[48] He would continue to be a presence in the blues clubs and taverns on Chicago's South and West Sides, but his recordings after the Chess sessions, both in the United States and in Europe, were made for and marketed to white record buyers.

Bill soon began to reach Chicago audiences for his folk-oriented acoustic music in a new way. On July 23, 1953, Studs Terkel invited Bill to appear on his interview program on radio station WFMT. Ever since his TV show *Studs' Place* had been discontinued in 1951 and opportunities had dried up because of his blacklisting, Studs had found it hard to find work. He had been characteristically entrepreneurial, and in the summer of 1952, he had appeared with Win Stracke in a community theater production of John Steinbeck's *Of Mice and Men* in nearby northwestern Indiana.[49] Not long after that, he persuaded Bernard and Rita Jacobs, who had recently bought WFMT, that he would be happy to host a show for free. This was an attractive proposition for the new owners, perhaps because of Studs's reputation as the knowledgeable host of *The Wax Museum* show a few years before, but especially because they had no funds at that moment to pay him.[50]

By the time Bill sat down with Studs in the WFMT studios, the two men had been performing together for half a dozen years in the "I Come for to Sing" group. The radio interview format gave both men the latitude to expand upon the roles each had established in the revue. Bill could draw on the set of stories he had been telling to European audiences to introduce songs, as well as the ones he was writing down and mailing to Yannick in Belgium to be included in his autobiography. Because Studs was participating in a dialogue, rather than simply serving as the narrator for a stage show, he could ask follow-up questions of Bill as he explored the origins and themes of the songs Bill played and sang.[51]

Although a relatively small number of Chicagoans were listening to WFMT in 1953, they tended to be people who were passionate about their cultural interests. An FM station when that was far from a popular spot on the broadcast spectrum, WFMT primarily aired what broadcaster and executive Ray Nordstrand later described as "serious music and the spoken arts," while *High Fidelity* magazine described it as "Chicago's ivory tower station."[52] As the station expanded its programming from ten to eighteen hours a day, Terkel's visibility in Chicago began to increase. His show, which was soon upgraded from weekly to daily, became a reference point on the city's cultural landscape.

A few months after his first appearance on Studs's radio show, Bill performed during the debut of the *Midnight Special*, a new Saturday night program on WFMT. The show's creator and host was Mike Nichols, who not long before had been an undergraduate at the University of Chicago. The initial broadcast was done live from the Hotel Guyon on Chicago's West Side, where Bill and Nichols were joined by banjoist Fleming Brown. According to Ray Nordstrand, it was Brown who contributed the show's title as a reference to the song that was generally associated with Lead Belly. It is not hard to imagine Bill sitting with his guitar in the ballroom of the run-down hotel, being told the name of the show and smiling to himself as he recalled his energetic fiddling in a Chicago recording studio during a raucous rendition of "The Midnight Special" nearly twenty years before.

Over the next several years, the *Midnight Special* became a trusted and authoritative source for the growing numbers of people with an interest in folk music in Chicago. Fans could tune in to hear recordings by new artists and traditional musicians, to find out who was coming to town and where and when they would be playing, and to hear live performances. Nichols found he had a talent for improvisational comedy through his work with a local group called the Compass Players, which evolved by the end of the decade into Chicago's influential Second City troupe. When Nichols headed to New York in 1956, the move set him on a course that brought him national prominence, first as a performer, and later as the director of movies such as *The Graduate*. After Nichols's departure, programmer Norm Pellegrini, soon joined by Ray Nordstrand, took over the announcing duties, which they shared for several decades. The combination of occasional appearances by folk musicians on Terkel's show and the weekly broadcast of the *Midnight Special* ensured that WFMT became the primary radio home for folk music in Chicago.[53]

As he was becoming a familiar voice of folk music for Chicago radio audiences who were primarily white, Bill was using his name recognition among black Chicagoans to pursue a business venture on the South Side. He wrote to Yannick Bruynoghe in early October 1953: "I bought me a tavern here in Chicago."[54] It was a joint venture, as its name indicated: "Big Bill and Moore's Lounge." The tavern was located at 3634 South Cottage Grove Avenue, not far from several other blues clubs, and although Bill was not active in the politics of the black community, his business partner, Josephine Moore, clearly was. The business card they printed up identified her not only as the proprietor, but also as a precinct captain in the city's Second Ward. The card also listed the alderman, which in Chicago meant the elected representative of the ward on the city's fifty-member city council, and the ward committeeman, also an elected official who, in some cases, wielded more power than the alderman. In this case, the ward committeeman was William L. Dawson, who over several decades established himself as "boss of the black sub-machine in Chicago," controlling the predominantly African American wards on the South Side.[55] With the additional mention on the card of the name of the district's representative to the state legislature, it is fair to assume that Big Bill and Moore's Lounge had little difficulty obtaining the license to serve the "Choice Whiskies, Wine, Beer, and Cordials" they advertised.

Harmonica player Billy Boy Arnold recalled that Big Bill and Moore's was known for its Sunday jam sessions. "Every Sunday they'd have a cocktail party where all the jam sessions were. And they had Muddy Waters, [guitarist] J. B. Lenoir, everybody." Arnold went there several times, and each time "everybody would go up and play, and then when everybody had played, Big Bill would come up and then play with the band. It was his band. . . . He had a piano, guitar, drums, maybe a sax."

While, in Arnold's words, "all the blues singers, all the musicians hung out there," the artists whom Bill had mentored were now getting the weekend residencies at the top clubs, and black record buyers were purchasing their recordings. Even as their stars were eclipsing Bill's, they still made a point of stopping by his jam sessions. J. B. Lenoir, whose "Mama Talk to Your Daughter" would soon be near the top of *Billboard*'s R&B chart, described him in glowing terms: "Big Bill[,] he take me as his son, and I played with him just as long as I wanted to play."[56]

During this period, Bill declined an offer to record with at least one up-and-coming African American talent. Billy Boy Arnold had taken harmonica lessons from Bill's friend and musical colleague Sonny Boy Williamson, and he considered the 1930s and '40s recordings that Bill and Sonny Boy had made separately and together to be among the finest he had heard. Now nearing age twenty, Arnold approached Bill with a proposal that they record together, hoping also to bring in pianist Blind John Davis, who had played with both Bill and Sonny Boy. But Bill declined, telling him, "You don't need me to make a record with you." Instead, he encouraged Arnold to record with the Aces, who were then the dynamic backup band for Little Walter, the harmonica virtuoso who was rising to the top of the Chicago blues scene. Arnold was disappointed, but he saw that Bill was clear-sighted about his commercial prospects as a recording artist for African American audiences. In Arnold's words, Bill "had realized that his guitar playing wasn't what was happening."[57]

 *Low Light and Blue Smoke*

When Bill visited his family in North Little Rock in the 1950s, it was cause for celebration. He would drive down from Chicago, and when his Cadillac would pull up in front of his sister Lannie Wesley's home at 412 West 30th Street, Lannie's granddaughter Jo Ann Jackson remembered, "Everybody in the area would know when Big Bill Broonzy came home."[1] There were plenty of relatives in the neighborhood, starting with Lannie and her husband, Mack Wesley, plus their children and grandchildren. Bill's mother Mittie lived right across the street, along with Bill's older sisters, Gustavia Dozier and Sallie Taffie, and his older brother Frank Bradley and his wife, Bertha, were only a few blocks away. Bill would distribute the gifts that he had brought for the children, and after they'd eaten, he would take out his guitar and play and sing for them. The kids loved it when he'd play "Hey, Hey," because then they could get up and dance. Jo Ann recalled that for that song, "Everybody'd be jitterbugging."[2]

Many of Bill's Arkansas relatives were working in jobs that just about enabled them to make ends meet. By this time, his sister Gustavia had become the janitor at the local elementary school, while Lannie Wesley was working as a beautician and did some quilting on the side. Although Mack Wesley's job as a laborer for the Missouri Pacific Railroad did not pay very well, it had the valuable fringe benefit of free train travel. Because of this, Lannie and her husband would visit Bill in Chicago with their children and grandchildren every other summer, alternating with the relatives in Mack Wesley's hometown of Cincinnati.

Bill's family was threatened with financial disaster in April 1954. In an attempt to help the family finances by raising some cotton and corn as cash crops, his brother Frank had taken out a loan, using the house his mother and sisters lived in as collateral. When the crops failed because of a drought, Bill's mother was facing the prospect of eviction if the lenders were not repaid. Fearful for his mother's well-being, Bill raced down to North Little Rock. Bill wrote Yannick Bruynoghe before he left that "because I ain't got no money to pay the debt with," he was bracing for having to work in a setting where it "will be just like being in jail. I know because I did it once before." He was prepared to do it because "I will do anything to keep my mother from being put out in the fields."[3]

Somehow, by the time Bill had returned to Chicago two weeks later, the situation had been resolved, and Bill's mother was able to keep her home. Without sharing any specifics about the way the crisis had been defused, Bill reported to Yannick that "everything is all right now, and I am back in Chicago."[4] During all the years that Bill made his visits to North Little Rock, it was the most significant family emergency in which he was involved. Bill made a point of staying in touch with Lannie, and he would write her regularly when he was in Chicago or traveling overseas. Because she could not read or write, Lannie enlisted her young but literate granddaughters, Jo Ann and Rosie, to read Bill's letters to her and to put her replies down on paper.

Lannie's son, Frank Wesley, remembered that when his uncle Bill was visiting, he would seek out the company of Frank's father and Lannie's husband, Mack. "My uncle Bill and my daddy were real good friends," recalled Frank. Although Frank was too young to accompany them, he knew that his father and uncle would be out "hunting . . . and gambling and drinking, and chasing women, and everything." Frank also was present once when Bill turned a broom of his mother's into a homemade instrument: "He took a broom, that wire holder broom . . . [and] took that wire off a broom and nailed one end up high on the side of the house, and the other end down low, and took tin cans, milk cans, and pushed them . . . and he'd start playing on that."[5] The rudimentary instrument, sometimes called a "diddley bow," was common throughout the South in the early twentieth century. Bill had clearly not forgotten the skills he had acquired during his rural childhood in Lake Dick.

With his mother safely established in her home again, Bill could turn his attention to earning a living as a musician in Chicago. Already in 1954 he had performed twice at the University of Chicago with Pete Seeger, once on a joint bill in late January, and then two months later as an unadvertised guest, joining Seeger during an early April concert at the university's Mandel Hall. The day after the April event, Bill and Pete appeared together on Studs Terkel's Sunday morning show on WFMT, where Terkel introduced Seeger as "one of the true virtuosos of the five-string banjo in this country" and Bill as "the king of blues singers."[6] It was a lively hour, during which Studs described Bill playing some barrel-house piano at a recent "I Come for to Sing" gig, and the two musicians traded folk songs, spirituals, and observations with Studs.

About a year later, Terkel succeeded in making an arrangement with Moses "Moe" Asch, the owner and guiding force of Folkways Records in New York, to release a tape of the session as an LP. Asch had established a reputation over the previous fifteen years for releasing recordings that he believed deserved to be heard, regardless of whether they would sell many copies. In particular, mainstays of the Folkways catalogue by the mid-1950s included Lead Belly, Woody Guthrie, and Pete Seeger. Asch could safely assume that the record buyers who purchased those records, generally white and often liberal-to-left in their political views, would be interested in hearing Terkel's conversation with the two musicians. The album would be the first appearance on Folkways by Bill and Studs, and would help to raise the national profile for both men as the cachet associated with Folkways Records increased through the decade.

In June 1954 Bill was hired for a job that was unlike any other he had ever held in his long and varied employment career. For the duration of the summer, he was the assistant cook at a summer camp in western Michigan. By all accounts, he was not a conventional assistant cook, but Circle Pines Center was not a conventional summer camp. It had been founded in 1938 as a cooperative, and its members drew their values and principles from a variety of different traditions, ranging from labor union activism to Quaker work camps and Danish folk schools. Located on nearly three hundred acres of farmland about twenty miles north of Kalamazoo, the center was dedicated to demonstrating and teaching, as the bylaws put it, "the superior advantages of cooperation as a way of life."[7] Programs and activities were offered year-round, and the summer camp for children was a key source of revenue, as well as an excellent opportunity to convey the goals and methods of cooperative living to the next generation.

The connections through which Bill found work at Circle Pines ran through Studs Terkel. As one Circle Piner recalled, "Everyone we knew, knew Studs."[8] More than a few Circle Pines members were active in liberal or left-leaning political causes, and workshops held at the center in this period addressed topics such as "Problems and Progress in Desegregation" and "Safeguarding Our Civil Liberties."[9] Once camp was under way, Bill immediately found himself much in demand as a performer. Like Lead Belly, he was comfortable playing for children, and the campers were soon calling out requests for "John Henry" and "St. Louis Blues." During the summer, Bill developed a catchphrase that found its way into several end-of-camp write-ups and was preserved on a tape of a Chicago house concert for Circle Piners held the following month. His "Ahh—shaddup!"—which he exclaimed with mock exasperation and which was received with glee by the campers—reflected his successful adaptation to camp life. One staff member summarized Bill's tenure that summer by saying that "he wasn't a terribly good cook, but he was a marvelous musician."[10]

The warm welcome that Bill received at Circle Pines made an impression on him. The following year, he sent André Vasset a photo of the farmhouse, which was the main building at the center. He described Circle Pines as "a summer camp in Michigan where all people can go and be treated the same," and asked his French friend to do what he could to have it included in his forthcoming autobiography.[11]

By early 1955 Yannick and Margo Bruynoghe were in the late stages of turning Bill's writings into a manuscript they could send to prospective publishers. The couple had married and settled in Brussels, where Yannick worked for the newly established Belgian state television network. With a keen interest in movies, he soon found himself hosting the *Midnight Movie Club*, selecting foreign films that were broadcast to a small but loyal audience after ten o'clock at night. When Yannick was not at the TV station, he was spending considerable amounts of time working with his wife to locate the threads that connected the many segments Bill had provided to them.

The first step was to decipher what Bill had written. He did not use punctuation marks, he would sprinkle capital letters throughout the text, and his spelling was idiosyncratic. The key, Margo discovered, was that "you have to read it out loud."[12] In general, Bill set down on the page the written form of what he would say if he were speaking, rendered with as much phonetic accuracy as he could muster. He had written some sections on small notebook pages in pencil so that he could erase and correct any errors, while others were written in pen, often on both sides of thin airmail papers, making the reading even more challenging. With each of the Bruynoghes reading separately, and then the two of them comparing notes and sounding out the difficult phrases, they were able to type up the material.

Their next step was to identify what was usable, and then, because Bill had occasionally repeated some or all of a story, to select the best version among more than one option. Bill had been writing in his room in Paris at the residential hotel at 29 rue Cler, as well as in the various locations in Chicago where he stayed when he was based there. Yannick had instructed Bill to "write it down as it came to him," and so for months he had done just that.[13] Because he had handed or sent the writings to the Bruynoghes as he went along, they were the ones who assembled the full set of materials and made the editorial choices.

Once they decided on the writings they would use, Yannick and Margo organized the material into three general sections: Bill's life, his songs, and his friends. These were fluid boundaries, and there were elements of each in all three chapters. Initially, Bill had wanted to call the book *The Truth about the Blues*, and he had suggested to Yannick at one point the idea of copyrighting the title in advance of publication.[14] After some consideration, the Bruynoghes settled on *Big Bill Blues* and began to look for a publisher.

Their initial efforts, to their bewilderment, were completely unsuccessful. None of the publishers Yannick contacted in Great Britain was interested in the book. The Bruynoghes, though deeply disappointed, were determined to get Bill's story in print. "At one point we were both desperate," remembered Margo, "because we promised [Bill] it would be published, and the publishers didn't want it."[15] Hoping that a French publisher might see some commercial possibilities, Yannick contacted potential firms there while he, with Margo's assistance, struggled with the difficult challenge of translating the manuscript into French.

Ultimately, Margo recalled, they found in Belgium "an old publisher who was at the end of his career," whom she described as "absent-minded, sort of a maverick . . . not organized at all."[16] His finances were so tenuous that Yannick had to pay him in advance so that he could print copies of the book. The first printing of *Big Bill Blues*, in mid-1955, was a commercial flop. Even with modest expectations, fewer copies were sold than they had anticipated. A door opened in England when Yannick reached out to British music critic Stanley Dance, whom he had known for nearly a decade. With an entrée provided by Dance, a respected and influential figure in international jazz circles, the British publisher Cassell and Company agreed to publish an English-language edition. Cassell made several changes to the original edition, which included contracting with Paul Oliver for several drawings, eliminating an introductory essay by Hugues Panassié, and adding a foreword by Stanley Dance, as well as a discography by Albert McCarthy. When it was released in the fall of 1955, the Cassell edition became the standard version of *Big Bill Blues* for nearly a decade.

One way to think about *Big Bill Blues* is to approach it as if the material had come from a writer's notebook, written with the understanding that a friend would edit the contents for publication. Bill took to heart Yannick's direction to "write it down as it came to him," and he set down his thoughts on a wide range of subjects. From childhood memories to observations on current social trends, from stories he insisted were accurate to tales he acknowledged were unbelievable, the literary talent he had revealed first to Alan Lomax and then to Albert Walker, the English professor at Iowa State, came into full flower.

A key feature of the book was that it was primarily intended for a white audience. Bill's opening sentence reads, "The reason I'm writing this book is because I think that everybody would like to know the real truth about the Negroes singing and playing in Mississippi."[17] While it is unstated, it is clear that the "everybody" he is referring to are the white fans of jazz, blues, and folk music that he had reached over the past decade. Bill had been rehearsing for this role in many ways: in his oral history and discussions with Alan Lomax, his time spent with Hugues Panassié, his encounters with the British jazz press, and his interviews with Studs Terkel.

When he jotted down his thoughts for the Bruynoghes, Bill knew that a number of African American jazz musicians had already documented their histories through articles, interviews, and books. Many of them—such as Jelly Roll Morton, Louis Armstrong, and Bunk Johnson—had come from urban areas in or around New Orleans. He recognized that what made him distinctive to his white interviewers and listeners was that he was a blues musician, or, as he liked to refer to himself, a blues singer. This meant that he would be presenting fresh and original perspectives to his readers when he wrote about his childhood in Mississippi and Arkansas, his familiarity with rural African American customs, and his personal relationships with other blues artists.

In *Big Bill Blues*, Bill's considerable powers of imagination guided and shaped his descriptions and observations. He used tall tales, folk tales, and anecdotes with comic exaggerations to illustrate many of his points. When he argued that the blues was still very much alive as a musical genre, he told of a turtle that had continued to crawl around for a while after his uncle had decapitated it with an ax. Quoting his uncle's pronouncement that "there's a turtle that's dead and don't know it," Bill drew the conclusion, "And that's the way a lot of people is today: they got the blues and don't know it."[18] He lampooned white southern police officers in a yarn about his uncle and a friend being stopped after driving across a state line with a stolen black hog. The two thieves evaded detection by putting a hat and coat on the pig, and seating it between them. After the animal responded to the policeman's verbal and physical prodding by grunting, the officer decided to let them go after concluding that the passenger, "that Negro in the middle, the grunting Negro, he's about the ugliest Negro I've ever seen in my life."[19] Bill's account of how he came to write his song "Looking Up at Down" featured a vivid description of how a crop failure due to a devastating drought had forced him to work underground in a coal mine. The title, according to Bill, came from his assignment to dig in a pit that was located twenty feet below the other miners.

Bill's ironic wit and his skill in turning a memorable phrase leavened many of the segments in the book. When he wrote of Mr. White, the white Arkansas farmer who refused to have anything on his farm that was black in color, Bill noted that although he "didn't like Negroes at all," the farmer would give the local black residents the unwanted animals, as well as surplus fruits and vegetables. Bill described Mr. White's unwillingness to accept any expression of gratitude in return, commenting that he "didn't take nothing from a Negro, not even a thank-you."[20] In describing his inspiration for the various verses of "Black, Brown, and White Blues," he told of standing in an employment line with fifty white job seekers and one other African American, a woman. After they had been there for hours, the manager explained to the two of them that they had been rejected because Negroes were not being hired that day. When the woman, who was from the South, expressed surprise at finding discrimination in the North, Bill told her, "All over the USA, it's the same soup, but it's just served in a different way."[21]

In a section on the challenges facing a bandleader in dealing with the vices of musicians, Bill compared the relative drawbacks of working with a musician who drinks whiskey versus one who smokes marijuana. He concluded that he would rather hire a marijuana smoker, based on his frustrations in dealing with whiskey drinkers. Bill supported his argument by telling of being berated by a several drunken musicians at a session who insisted, "That ain't the way that blues goes!" In an aside to the reader, Bill noted, "They would tell me that and I had written the song myself."[22]

Through Bill's profiles of various musicians, *Big Bill Blues* has had an enduring effect, for better and for worse, on efforts to document blues history. When the book was first published, information on many of the artists Bill described was scarce. *Big Bill Blues* provided a logical starting point for anyone interested in learning about musicians such as Big Maceo Merriweather, Tampa Red, Sonny Boy Williamson, and Lil Green. In his colorful and lively descriptions, Bill was specific in identifying the year, or even the actual date, of events ranging from recording sessions to someone's birth or death. A revised edition of the book issued in 1964 included a page of notes by Yannick Bruynoghe, in which he identified where he thought Bill was in error and added what he believed to be the correct information. One of the most noteworthy examples was Bill's statement that guitarist and songwriter Sleepy John Estes was "just about eighty-seven years old now," an assertion that turned out to be off by over thirty years, as Estes was fifty-six when the book was published.

Although some of his dates were wrong, Bill succeeded in presenting compelling portraits of his friends and colleagues. He wrote of the decline of singer Peter Clayton, who recorded as "Doctor Clayton," in the wake of the deaths of his wife and children in a house fire, telling how "he wore tennis shoes in winter time and slept on pool tables and in alleys and basements, anywhere he could."[23] In characterizing Sonny Boy Williamson, Bill wrote about the significant role that his wife, Lacey Belle, "a very nice girl," played in his life: "I say she was a mother and a wife to him. She helped him writing his songs and helped him to learn how to sing them. She could rhyme a song."[24]

Bill's profile of guitarist, singer, and songwriter Memphis Minnie (born Lizzie Douglas) contained what has become an often-cited account of a contest between the two musicians. The high esteem in which Bill held Minnie is evident in his descriptions of her in the book as a musician who "can pick a guitar and sing as good as any man I've ever heard," and his praise for how she "can make a guitar speak words, she can make a guitar cry, moan, talk and whistle the blues."[25] Bill provided a detailed description of what he characterized as "the first contest between blues singers that was ever given in the USA, in 1933, on my birthday, June 26." He told how the two competed before a packed house in a Chicago tavern, under the scrutiny of the three judges, whom he identified as Sleepy John Estes, Tampa Red, and songwriter and pianist Richard Jones, composer of the blues standard "Trouble in Mind." When Minnie's performance had won her the prize of two bottles of liquor, Bill reported that he stole the bottle of whiskey and ran off.

In fact, there was an actual contest that took place between Bill and Memphis Minnie. According to an ad in the *Chicago Defender*, it was held at the 708 Club on Sunday, November 6, 1949, between 3 and 8 p.m. The 708 Club, located on the South Side at East 47th Street, had become one of the leading venues for blues in Chicago. There were, as Bill had said, three judges: Sunnyland Slim, Muddy Waters, and Jimmy Rogers. Once the contest was over, the ad promised that Minnie and her co-star, Little Son Joe, would be the featured performers "'Till Closing."[26]

The relationship between Bill's version and the known facts about the contest is representative of many of the stories Bill told in *Big Bill Blues* and elsewhere. He began with something that actually did happen, and then created a tale that conveyed the key elements of the story in ways he believed would hold the attention of the listener or the reader. Bill focused on flavor rather than facts as he created indelible characters, addressed social issues, and told memorable stories. American writers from Mark Twain to Ring Lardner had used similar approaches and devices, and Bill drew on some of the same wellsprings for his inspiration that they had for theirs. The Bruynoghes may have selected the title, but *Big Bill Blues* showcases Bill's efforts, as he had originally intended and using his own definition, to tell "the truth about the blues."

In late October 1955, Bill returned to Great Britain. Since his summer at Circle Pines the previous year, he had been performing regularly in a variety of settings in Chicago. In addition to the open-ended run of the "I Come for to Sing" revue, he had appeared at Mandel Hall at the University of Chicago in October 1954 with Pete Seeger and harmonica ace Sonny Terry, and then had returned to the same stage in May 1955 for a benefit concert for Circle Pines with Studs Terkel, Fleming Brown, and children's singer Ella Jenkins. When Terkel interviewed Bill on WFMT just before his departure for England, Studs had proudly announced to his listeners that he was holding a copy of the French-language edition of *Big Bill Blues*.[27]

By the time Bill arrived in Great Britain, many British jazz and blues fans had already read portions of his autobiography. The British weekly newspaper *Melody Maker* had run a five-part condensed serial version of the book in August and September, with each installment taking up the better part of a page, including drawings by guitarist and cartoonist Diz Disley. Bill performed at a cocktail party in London on October 26 that Cassell arranged to mark the book's publication, which one attendee reported drew "a curiously mixed assembly of musicians, critics, literary men and their respective ladies."[28] Ads for *Big Bill Blues* began to appear in the *Melody Maker* and *Jazz Journal*, and reviewers compared it favorably with recent memoirs of jazz musicians, such as Mezz Mezzrow's autobiography *Really the Blues* and Alan Lomax's oral history of Jelly Roll Morton, *Mister Jelly Roll*.[29]

As Bill began touring during his fourth visit to the United Kingdom, a musical style called skiffle was just starting to galvanize young audiences in Great Britain. The essential elements of skiffle were an ensemble of four to six musicians playing acoustic instruments such as guitars, washboards, and homemade one-string bass, and singing a repertoire drawn from American folk music, old-time country, and blues, especially from Lead Belly.[30] The genre's first hit was Lead Belly's song "Rock Island Line," sung by Lonnie Donegan, a young Scottish banjo player and guitarist. Donegan quickly became skiffle's most-recognized individual star, with a string of successful records. Soon other performers such as the Vipers, the Chas McDevitt Group with singer Nancy Whiskey, and Johnny Duncan achieved popular success.

The person who played the most crucial role in Lonnie Donegan's unlikely ascent to stardom was Chris Barber, a bandleader who had attended a London music conservatory after twice failing his exams to become an actuary. Barber had graduated having mastered both trombone and bass, and, with a passion for jazz and blues that he pursued avidly as a record collector, he had been playing in and often leading a set of bands performing primarily traditional jazz since the late 1940s. By 1954 Barber was leading the Chris Barber Jazz Band, a group that included Donegan. The ensemble had developed a tradition of a skiffle set during intermissions, in which a subset of band members put down their brass instruments and played a set of American folk tunes.[31] When the band had the chance to record an LP for Decca, Barber insisted on including four songs in the style of the intermission set (or "interval," in the British phrase), one of which featured Donegan singing "Rock Island Line."

Years later Barber spoke of a missed opportunity for Bill in the wake of the stunning success of the Donegan record. As the Decca LP began to sell well, Barber—who, despite his actuarial shortcomings, had a head for business—made a deal with an equally enterprising British record producer named Denis Preston. Preston had set up an arrangement to produce a number of records for Nixa Records, a division of Pye, the British radio manufacturer. As both a record collector and an active contributor to the British jazz scene, Barber was very familiar with Bill's music, and the Barber band performed with Bill several times during this tour. When the bandleader recommended to Preston that he should record Bill being backed by the Donegan/Barber skiffle group, the producer declined. According to Barber, Preston believed that Bill should record with "real musicians like he would be [recording with] in America!"[32] Instead of the skiffle group, Preston set up a session for Bill with musicians whom Barber later described as "modern jazz players" who "didn't understand playing rhythm and blues."[33] In his view, "Big Bill could have had giant hit records. Worldwide! I'm quite sure. Because Lonnie Donegan would have carried him off."[34]

The rise of skiffle may not have brought Bill a hit record, but it did enhance his popularity among the emerging talents. Chas McDevitt, whose skiffle group was the first to cross the Atlantic to play the *Ed Sullivan Show*, reported that in arranging his band's rendition of "John Henry," "it was Bill's version that we favoured."[35] From Bill's perspective, he could benefit from the success of skiffle. "If Lonnie or any of them like to take my best songs and record them, and maybe sell a million of 'em, I'll be proud," he told Max Jones and Sinclair Traill of the *Melody Maker* once the skiffle phenomenon was well under way. "And if they do that, and my wife or children get some money out of it, I couldn't ask for more than that."[36]

It was through Max Jones, the well-respected jazz and blues critic for the *Melody Maker*, that Bill became a guest in the home of guitarist and broadcaster Alexis Korner during his time in London. Korner and his wife, Roberta (known as Bobbie), were both knowledgeable blues fans who attended Bill's Kingsway Hall debut in 1951. Bobbie recalled that "we were aware of the fact that things weren't always terribly nice for black musicians in hotels, so we thought maybe he'd like to stay [with us]."[37] When they asked Jones for his thoughts, he encouraged the Korners to extend Bill an invitation and gave them Bill's phone number at his hotel. When they called, "he came right over."[38]

Alexis Korner had first become captivated by blues and jazz when he heard the boogie-woogie piano of Chicagoan Jimmy Yancey and others on a 78 record he bought as a teenager during World War II. He picked up the guitar while serving in the British Army after the war, and after hearing Lead Belly in Paris in 1949, he played in Chris Barber's amateur band, the Bluebirds. The band's name reflected Barber and Korner's keen interest in the sessions for that record label done in the 1930s and '40s by artists such as Bill, Tampa Red, and Big Maceo.[39] It would be hard to overstate the level of esteem in which Korner held Bill. He once commented that "I've come as close to worshipping Bill Broonzy as I've ever worshipped anyone in my somewhat unworshipful life."[40] Korner would become one of Bill's most ardent supporters in Great Britain, using his formidable persuasive skills to praise his work in liner notes, magazine and newspaper articles, and radio broadcasts.

During his stay with the Korners, Bill provided them with a glimpse of how seriously he took his craft as a musician. The couple's daughter was three and a half years old at the time, and Bill would sing to her at bedtime. Korner was astonished to discover that "he would never, ever go in without practising first. He would sit in his room and he'd practise the two songs he was going to sing her. And what's more, he would practise alternate verses, in case he forgot the right ones."[41] British music critic Derrick Stewart-Baxter had recognized four years before that Bill had put considerable thought into his presentation on the concert stage, but few would have guessed that his preparations extended to performances of lullabies to an audience of one child.

The Korners' concerns about Bill's experience with British hotels turned out to be prescient. The *Melody Maker* carried an account of the welcome he received in Nottingham on November 4, when Bill arrived at the hotel where he was scheduled to stay after his performance that evening. As the representative of Bill's booking agent, who was traveling with him, told the *Melody Maker*, "We stayed at the same hotel some days previously without complaint. The trouble on Friday started when we entered the hotel. The hall porter said, 'We do not accept coloured people here.' Naturally, Bill was very upset and walked out."[42] The agent then spoke with the "manageress, who corroborated the porter's statement and implied that Bill had been admitted to the hotel previously in error." Although "in the end she agreed to put us up," the agent and Bill chose to stay elsewhere. When the *Melody Maker* reporter contacted a hotel representative, he was first told that the reservation had not been confirmed, that the hotel had been full, and "that there was no colour bar in force." Soon after that, Bill's agent received a written apology addressed to Bill from the hotel manager.[43]

The Nottingham hotel incident was a rare one for Bill's overseas tours, because it involved a published account of an instance in which Bill was confronted directly by racial prejudice. In the postwar years, immigration of non-white people to Great Britain increased significantly, especially from British colonies in the Caribbean. Bill's experience in Nottingham likely reflected rising racial tensions there, as three years later the city was the site of an evening of fighting in the streets between white and non-white residents, followed a week later by the appearance of "thousands of white people . . . on the streets, shouting 'Let's get the blacks!'"[44]

Overall, it was an eventful month in Britain for Bill. In addition to the Nottingham hotel incident and the recording session, he performed on November 5 with the Chris Barber Band at the Royal Festival Hall, one of the country's most prestigious venues. The *Melody Maker* reported that by the end of his show there, Bill "had three thousand people shouting for more."[45] During a gig at Humphrey Lyttelton's club at 100 Oxford Street, Bill brought Josh White up out of the audience to perform, which resulted in a page-one photo of the two artists in the next issue of the *Melody Maker*, under the headline "Famous Blues Singers Unite."[46] Just before he left for Belgium, Bill appeared for the first time on British television on November 15, performing "Keep Your Hands Off It" and "Trouble in Mind" on the *Downbeat* program on Britain's newly launched commercial TV channel. The show was produced by Richard Lester, who a decade later would direct the Beatles' movies *A Hard Day's Night* and *Help!* A reviewer complimented Lester for his success with the several musical segments, noting favorably his approach of "offering jazz without any gimmicks," and also praised Bill for his ability to perform "unaware of the TV cameras."[47]

After just over a week of appearances in Belgium, Bill arrived in Holland. His schedule included concerts every night, plus a TV broadcast for the Dutch program *Jazz Sociëteit*, and he recorded a radio interview with his friend Michiel de Ruyter for later broadcast. On November 28, the second night of a two-night run at the Doelenzaal in Amsterdam, Bill was in his dressing room before the evening's concert when a tall woman in her mid-twenties walked in, accompanied by a photographer friend who had invited her backstage. Bill, who was opening his guitar case, first stared at her "from top to toe," and then blurted out, "Jesus Christ!" He soon recovered his composure, handed her several of his personal items, including his watch, and urged her to wait in the dressing room for him until after the show. When he returned and the pair walked out into the street, Bill saw a vendor selling flowers, and he insisted on buying all she had and then presented them to his delighted companion.

The woman's name was Pim van Isveldt. Pictures of Pim from the mid-fifties show her wearing her hair in a short but stylish cut, and dressed in simple outfits that she accented with a scarf or with earrings and necklaces that suggested her artistic sensibility. She was a native of Amsterdam and the daughter of a laborer for the city tram system and his wife. When she met Bill, Pim was working as a costume designer for the Municipal Theater in Amsterdam. Her interest in American folk music had been piqued the year before, when she had first heard a Lead Belly record.

Bill was clearly smitten from their first meeting, and the feeling was mutual. Pim, in her words, was "crazy about that man."[48] She gave him her phone number at work, as she had no phone at home, and she immediately accepted Bill's invitations to accompany him to social gatherings with his friends in the Amsterdam jazz world. The night after they met, they were together at the home of Michiel de Ruyter and his wife. De Ruyter had also invited several colleagues, including Paul Breman, a bookseller whose avid interest in African American culture extended beyond music to literature. While still a university student several years before, Breman had published translations in a leading Dutch literary magazine of the works of the poets Langston Hughes and Waring Cuney, as well as W. E. B. DuBois. Breman, who was knowledgeable about jazz and blues, later wrote one of the first books in Dutch about blues. In particular, Breman saw the music and the musicians in the context of larger cultural and political forces.[49]

A tape that survives from the gathering at the De Ruyters's home contains both an informal set of performances by Bill and about forty minutes of conversation. The eleven songs he played included a number of popular songs in a romantic vein, ranging from George Gershwin's "Somebody Loves Me" and the 1920s standard "Ain't She Sweet" to "When Did You Leave Heaven?," co-written by composer Richard Whiting. While the unhurried single-string lead Bill played on "I Love You So Much" had a distinctly tender quality, likely directed to Pim, he also made a point of acknowledging the hospitality of the hosts, dedicating the instrumental "The Isle of Capri" to De Ruyter's wife.

As the post-performance conversations unfolded, alcohol was flowing freely among the relaxed and congenial group. When one participant protested at being described as drunk, Bill's response was to comment about him to the others, "I think he quit drinking. He won't live very long after this."[50] Not long after, he announced after audibly taking a drink, "Oh, brother. I got drunk last night, I'm going to do the same damn thing tonight," which evoked general laughter in the room.[51] A few minutes later, after unsteadily giving out his home address to a potential correspondent, he entered into an extended and often passionate discussion of race with Paul Breman.

While the spark for their exchange is not entirely clear from the tape, it may have been prompted by Bill's declaration that he would be returning to Holland "one of these days." Breman seems to have decided to tease Bill by pointing out that he was not fully acknowledging that a primary motivation for his return visit would be to see Pim, the woman with whom he was so obviously taken. When Breman, in jest, accused Bill of being a liar, Bill quickly pointed out that while he and Breman could each say what they wished to say, the two would likely feel differently because of the different experiences they would bring to the discussion because one was black and the other white. Breman disagreed, and when Bill asked him whether he thought "everybody in the world is just the same," Breman told him that he did. Bill's immediate response was "You're crazy," and he insisted to the young Dutch intellectual that "you *can not* be like me."

Over the next half hour, Bill spoke emphatically about some of the ways in which he believed that "a black man's life is different from a white man's life." His statements illustrated why he believed that a black man "don't live like a white man. He can't!" His comments ranged from his own experiences touring Europe to his observations about other African Americans who had found success in different fields. He spoke about traveling "where they don't accept me . . . some places in England and some places in other places that I've been, France, and different places where they didn't accept me as a black man." As he had done in his discussion three years before with Alan Lomax, he lamented that "there's some people in the world, they just don't want to be a Negro." While he noted that some of them had attained high rank in the U.S. military and in the U.S. government, he pointed out that for any of them, in the eyes of the white world, "what the heck, he's still a Negro." In commenting about the prejudice of those with status conferred by both skin color and wealth, he took a long view: "It don't mean a darn thing to be above folks, to be elevated, to be above people. It don't mean a thing. Because when that day come that you die, they put you in the same place as they put me. Know what I mean? You're a dead duck, that's all."

After the discussion had shifted to other topics for a while, Bill again engaged Paul Breman directly, telling him, "You know, people like me and you should get together more often." As he described his earlier comments, "Maybe I popped off a little bit too much, but I was trying to explain to you exactly the truth." Bill then, in a series of statements and questions to Breman, asserted unequivocally his view that "this is a white man's world. It's not a black man's world." When Breman replied that he was not sure he agreed, because there was the possibility of change through the mixing of the races, Bill disagreed, stating, "It will never be a black man's world the same as it is a white man's world now." Breman replied that he believed that "it will become another world, and it will not stay a white world."

Bill's response conveyed a much bleaker view of race relations than he had previously indicated, either publicly or privately. His initial comment to Breman was that "it will always be a white man above a Negro, a black man." Bill then clarified his next remarks by telling him, "I'm not saying *you*, but I'm saying this *to you* because you're a white man. You don't ever expect me to ever forgive you for what you've done to my people in, in life." When Breman said that he did not, Bill went on: "All right. The Germans, what they done to the Jews, the English, what they done to the Africans, the Americans, what they done to me and my people in lifetime . . . what they're still doing. You think I can forget that? No." He then qualified his comments, saying "I don't mean me," and added, "They can destroy me . . . but there are so many more that they can't. That many black people in the world, they're still going to have that hatred. Not against you, but for the Americans and the English." In Bill's view, "That's going to be, brother, and don't think it ain't. As long as life lasts."

Bill's comments that night in Holland were unique among all his public and private statements about racial equality in the degree of pessimism he expressed for the future. It is hard to know why Bill decided to be uncharacteristically blunt in talking with the group of white admirers. It may have been because he had consumed a lot of alcohol, or because he let down his guard as he was caught up in the emotions of a rapidly blossoming romance. He might have felt that even in the event that anyone present had chosen to broadcast his comments beyond that room, it was unlikely that he or his career would suffer. Perhaps he simply hit a point of frustration after keeping his feelings in check for so long. Whatever the reason, his listeners heard him provide an unusual level of insight into the worldview of a black American. When his Dutch admirers heard about a bus boycott that began a few days later in Montgomery, Alabama, perhaps they gained some understanding of the frustration that caused black citizens to risk their freedom, even though the odds of success were slim, in the hope that they might be able to effect some lasting change.

Although Bill headed to Belgium shortly after that evening, he began what would continue to be a regular correspondence with Pim. Even into his final illness several years later, he wrote her frequently from wherever he was, either in Europe or the United States. When he met Pim, she had a five-year-old son, Jeroen.[52] Bill would bring him presents when he visited, and photos show Jeroen sitting on Bill's lap with the two of them happily banging on a child's drum together.

When Bill arrived in Brussels in early December, the Bruynoghes had a project lined up for him. A friend of Yannick's, a filmmaker named Jean Delire, was a blues fan and was eager to make a film featuring a blues musician. Yannick suggested Bill as the subject, pointing out that it would keep expenses down if they filmed Bill during his visit to Brussels. Delire enthusiastically agreed, and Yannick brought in a colleague from his job at the television station, Jacques Boigelot, to write the script. The need to raise money for the movie dictated the length and format: it had to be a short film rather than full-length, and it could not be a documentary, which they believed would have no commercial appeal. Because the film "had to have a little story to tell," in Margo's words, it would not simply present a performance by Bill, but it would include some interaction between him and a young woman in the audience.[53] For the Bruynoghes, the storyline was secondary, because what was "essential was Big Bill."[54]

The events in the movie *Low Light and Blue Smoke: Big Bill Blues* can be summarized briefly. Bill enters a small club, in which a New Orleans–style band is finishing a set, and during the intermission he plays four songs for an appreciative audience. He interacts several times with a woman wearing a leopard-print coat who lingers near the piano at the side of the stage, and although the two never speak, she finds him intriguing, and he does nothing to discourage her interest. After he plays his last song, the band returns, and he packs up his guitar and leaves the club.

From the opening shot, the film reflects Jean Delire's intent to use atmospheric effects to emphasize certain aspects of Bill's life as a bluesman. A central theme is that he is a solitary, self-reliant figure. He arrives alone in a light drizzle, carrying his guitar case as he walks slowly up the stairs to the club. In contrast to the jazz musicians, who play as an ensemble, he performs unaccompanied, and when he leaves, he retraces his steps as he walks by himself down the stairs and into the rainy evening.[55] In addition, the camera angles and lighting underscore the dramatic nature of Bill's performance. In many shots, he is sitting under an overhead lamp with a single bulb, and with the camera positioned below him, the viewer sees Bill singing with his eyes closed as cigarette smoke curls behind his head.

The nearly seventeen-minute film achieved critical success after its 1956 release, winning the Silver Bear award for Short Documentary at the 1957 Berlin Film Festival. While it was shown in a few clubs and on Belgian TV, it never generated much of a financial return. *Low Light and Blue Smoke* did, however, have an enduring impact in Great Britain. Specifically, it played a key role for several young British musicians in shaping their perceptions of blues artists. Eric Clapton, who saw it on British television not long after it was made, recalled watching "this piece of footage which is now quite famous, of [Bill] in the French nightclub with the swinging light, and he was playing 'Hey, Hey.'" It brought the teenaged guitarist up short: "I had never seen anything like it before. . . . It nailed me, really."[56] Ray Davies called the film "one of the seminal video clips, one of the greatest videos ever shot, I think, in the documentary style." For Davies, the way the movie portrayed Bill "evokes so much of what the 'bluesman' is about—the journeyman, the singer-songwriter."[57] Keith Richards, in expressing his regret that he never saw Bill live, described the "great film of him singing 'When Did You Leave Heaven' in a little club in Belgium." His view of the movie was that "it was a classic video before its time."[58]

Bill ended his tour by recording half a dozen songs in a session in the Bruynoghes' apartment, and then sailed back to New York, again on the *Ile de France*. His stay in the United States was brief, and after spending Christmas and New Year's in Arkansas and making an appearance at Silvio's in mid-January, he returned to Europe in early February.[59]

Once Bill arrived in Paris, Pim joined him there. It was hard for her to get the time off from work, but with her parents available to look after Jeroen, she was able to make a short trip. In Paris, Bill introduced Pim to Trixie Stevens, the wife of British jazz pianist David Stevens. Bill had met the couple when he was staying with Alexis and Bobbie Korner; Stevens and Korner had been friends since they began playing together in the early 1950s. Trixie Stevens, who had traveled to Paris at Bill's invitation to join them there, recalled that Pim had been wary of her at first, apparently concerned that Bill was introducing his British girlfriend to his Dutch girlfriend, but when she saw that this was not the case, the two women became friends. Pim was clearly mindful of Bill's reputation as a ladies' man, and she acknowledged that she felt jealous when she watched the sequence in *Low Light and Blue Smoke* in which Bill flirted with the woman in the club.[60]

Working on a hectic schedule that resembled some of his busy periods in the 1930s, Bill was soon recording in studios in two different countries in eight days. In Paris on February 10, he recorded seven songs for Columbia, backed by jazz drummer Carl "Kansas" Fields, who had been playing in Europe for several years with Mezz Mezzrow and others. By the seventeenth he had returned to Holland, where Michiel de Ruyter had arranged for a solo session for the Philips label. The ten songs he recorded at the Hoog Wolde studio in Baarn, about twenty-five miles southwest of Amsterdam, resulted in one of his first LP releases.[61]

Bill spent the spring touring through several European countries. The prominent French jazz photographer Jean-Pierre Leloir photographed his performance in Paris on March 19, and images from that session later appeared on a number of Bill's EP and LP covers. During a brief return visit to Germany in early April, he performed in Hamburg with Humphrey Lyttelton and Lil Hardin Armstrong. In the course of his two-week stay in Denmark in late April and early May, Bill played for several nights in a Copenhagen jazz club called the Club Montmartre. The owner of Storyville Records, Karl-Emil Knudsen, arranged for live recordings, and Storyville released a series of EPs, LPs, and, later, CDs of Bill performing over the course of three evenings for the Danish jazz and blues fans. The LPs were released shortly after Bill's death in 1958, and for several decades they were among the few commercially available LP-length recordings of Bill performing for European audiences. They presented him singing not only his familiar repertoire of blues, folk songs, and spirituals, but also adding a cover of Tennessee Ernie Ford's recent hit "Sixteen Tons."

In his between-songs comments, Bill made a point of identifying for the Club Montmartre crowd "the greatest blues singers in America today." His list included "Smokey Hogg, Lightnin' Hopkins, John Lee Hooker, Brownie McGhee, Howlin' Wolf, Eddie Boyd, and Elmore James." Bill anticipated a time when "someday, they might get a chance to get over here, and you'll hear them." He then distilled his list down to those whom he called "the greatest in the States," a roster made up of Muddy Waters, whom he referred to as "a great man," Hogg, Hooker, and Hopkins.[62] Later, he introduced "Goodnight Irene" by saying, "I'll sing this simply because, I don't know, maybe you'll never see me again. . . . I hope I can get back again. But if I don't, there'll be another fella come along that's a little bit greater than me. There always is, you know."[63] Bill clearly recognized that the position he had fashioned for himself of ambassador of the blues provided him with the opportunity to promote the careers of a cohort of younger musicians. His effective advance work would pay off, when the artists he mentioned, and many others, would soon begin to tour overseas for appreciative audiences.

In early June, after playing seven concerts in ten days in France, Bill made his only visit to Italy. He had been invited there to perform on the Italian television station RAI, which had been in existence for only a couple of years. The trip had some logistical challenges, ranging from Bill's arrival in Milan a day earlier than expected to the technical problems at the television station that extended his stay to nearly a week, but Bill still managed to record a dozen or so songs for RAI. He was welcomed by a small group of jazz fans who brought him to the Hot Club of Milan so that he could supplement whatever he was paid for his TV appearance. They also invited Bill to perform in their homes, and some of the songs he played at the home of ethnomusicologist Roberto Leydi were later released commercially.[64]

Gianni Tollara, who went on to become a successful concert promoter, was one of the jazz fans who spent time with Bill in Milan. Tollara recalled years later that during his visit, Bill was carrying with him a newspaper article he had cut out. The article described the lynching of a young boy "who was only 12 or 13 years old," and who "had been hung from a tree with a length of wire."[65] Tollara noted that "that lynching shocked people in Italy, too." Bill told Tollara that he had brought the clipping to show Europeans a particularly egregious example of the treatment to which black southerners were often subjected, with local white authorities frequently complicit. Although in Tollara's telling the facts were slightly off, the story was surely that of the murder in Mississippi the previous summer of fourteen-year-old Emmett Till.[66]

On June 21, 1956, Bill boarded the *Queen Elizabeth*, then the world's largest ocean liner, in Cherbourg, France, for his return to the United States. He had been in Europe for five months, and, since his first trip in the summer of 1951, he had spent a cumulative total of nearly two years abroad, spread over five separate tours. Despite his extended absences from Chicago, or perhaps because of the pent-up demand that they generated for his services, he could anticipate that there would be work for him as a musician on his return home.

"A Requiem for the Blues"

On July 11, 1956, Bill married Rose Lawson in Chicago.[1] She was almost exactly one year younger than he was, having been born on June 25, 1904, in Georgia. In contrast to Bill's itinerant lifestyle—even when he was staying in Chicago he gave a series of different return addresses to his European correspondents—Rose was inclined to stay put. When she had applied for Social Security in 1936, she gave the address of the same apartment building she was living in twenty years later: 4706 South Parkway. She was also working for the same North Side employer twenty years later, still holding down a position at the Hotel Lincoln at 1816 North Clark Street.

Bill's grandnieces Jo Ann Jackson and Rosie Tolbert remember traveling to Chicago during the 1950s to visit their Uncle Bill and this Rose Broonzy, as distinct from her predecessor, "Texas Rose." While Rose Lawson had been a consistent presence in his life dating back several years, it is not clear why Bill decided to marry her at this particular time. One motivating factor may have been Rose's desire to formalize their status after becoming aware of Bill's relationship with Pim van Isveldt. If that was her intent, the results were mixed, as his regular letter-writing and his visit to Holland the following year reinforced his ongoing commitment to Pim. At the same time, during the periods when he was in Chicago, Bill and Rose seem to have enjoyed a relatively stable marriage, welcoming relatives, friends, and visitors to their small but comfortable apartment, located at the bustling South Side intersection of Forty-seventh Street and South Parkway.

Although they were living across the street from the Regal Theater, which was then hosting some of the nation's top black jazz artists, Bill was performing at venues where the audience consisted primarily of white folk music fans. Folk music's popularity in Chicago was surging, and WFMT's showcase for folk music, *The Midnight Special*, was expanding to a two-hour show. In September Bill played at the Gate of Horn, a club that had just opened two months before on the North Side, in the basement of the old Rice Hotel at Chicago Avenue and Dearborn Street.[2] The goal of the owners, entrepreneur Albert Grossman and journalist Les Brown, was to attract folk music fans, and some of their inspiration had come from attending a concert featuring Bill and banjoist Fleming Brown. In Les Brown's words, "A certain kind of person went to those concerts that we didn't see at nightclubs and jazz clubs and other places like that. We thought that was a niche."[3]

On October 25, Bill performed with Pete Seeger at Cahn Auditorium at Northwestern University, located in the residential suburb of Evanston just north of Chicago. Folk musicians were discovering that they could count on large and enthusiastic crowds when they played at a growing number of college campuses across the country. Seeger, who had been forced by the blacklisting of the Weavers to support his family by playing primarily for children at schools and summer camps, had been cultivating college audiences over the past several years. Bill had performed at numerous college campuses as a member of the "I Come for to Sing" revue, including a 1950 appearance at Northwestern.[4]

The Northwestern concert was noteworthy for several reasons. It marked a milestone for WFMT because it represented the first concert held in the Chicago area that the radio station taped for future broadcast.[5] In the years to come, WFMT would record hundreds of concerts by folk and classical artists. In the case of the Northwestern show, some of the material was later released on an LP by Folkways, in conjunction with Verve. For years, *Big Bill Broonzy and Pete Seeger in Concert* was the only commercially available recording of Bill performing live for an American concert audience. It captured him clearly comfortable with Seeger, as he kept up a running gag about making sure to sit down whenever Pete started his pre-song comments, and Bill was energetic in presenting his repertoire to the very appreciative crowd. The recording also documented one of Bill's most-quoted observations. As he was introducing his version of the spiritual "This Train," he observed, "I like all songs, you know, and some people call this a folk song. Well, all the songs that I ever heard in my life was folk songs. I never heard horses sing none of 'em yet."[6] Bill's inclusive pronouncement has been invoked many times since then in discussions about what constitutes folk music.[7]

Three weeks later, in mid-November, Bill sat down with Studs Terkel for what was effectively his annual interview on Terkel's WFMT show. At one point during the course of their hour-long conversation, in discussing how audiences might respond to "This Train," Bill reflected on one of his biggest challenges as a musician. "The hardest thing in the world to try to do," he told Terkel, "is try to explain your . . . way of feeling about different things." He noted that if someone who was unfamiliar with the details of the experience of African Americans in the South heard blues or spirituals that described how "they had been really tortured and done around and pushed around," he or she would be unlikely to grasp what the song was trying to convey. Bill then reflected on his own limitations:

> I realize it now because I been in places where people do sing serious songs of what happened to them in their lives. Well, it didn't happen to me. I have never had a bomb to drop in Chicago. . . . There was no bomb dropped here, never was no bomb dropped in Mississippi, nothing like that. What [do] I know about a bomb? Only time I see a bomb is a picture of it. I never saw one, really, in my life. Never had my hand on one. But those people over there, they know what it mean, they see a plane, hear a plane coming over late hours at night and somethin' fall and destroy their homes. Never nothin' like that happen to me.[8]

Bill had not forgotten the residual examples of the war's devastation he had observed during his walks around European cities, and especially during the night he had spent in Germany in 1951 in an underground hotel that had been an air-raid shelter only a few years before. Bill was candid in acknowledging his own limitations in responding to music that was shaped by a trauma far from his own experience, even given the considerable powers of his imagination. He also acknowledged that the same limitations could hold true for anyone hearing his music who had not grown up in an African American community in the rural South in the early twentieth century.

After closing out 1956 with a mid-December appearance with Terkel, Win Stracke, and folksinger Gerry Armstrong at a "Roosevelt Hoot" at Chicago's Roosevelt University, Bill sailed to Great Britain in early February 1957. He was joined on this tour by Brother John Sellers, an African American singer in his early thirties who performed both sacred and secular material, and whose 1954 recording session for Vanguard had been supervised by John Hammond. Their first performance was on February 16 at the Royal Festival Hall, and Bill fared better than Sellers, whose British debut was marred by technical problems and poor coordination with the band of British musicians. Critic Max Jones's Dickensian summary of the Sellers portion was that "it is best to draw a veil over that part of the proceedings," but he praised Bill, noting that in the joint finale, "the crowd roared for more, and particularly more Bill," adding that "British audiences feel really affectionate toward Broonzy."[9]

Bill and Brother John immediately set off on a tour of England and Scotland, playing sixteen dates in nineteen days, most of them with the Chris Barber Band. It was the first in a series of tours that Barber and his agent were able to arrange for visiting blues and jazz artists. Barber had by this time achieved what a *Melody Maker* profile called a level of "phenomenal success," and in the article he acknowledged that "it's wonderful to be able to play jazz and get paid so well for it."[10] Over the next few years, audiences all over Great Britain were able to see Bill, Sister Rosetta Tharpe, Louis Jordan, Sonny Terry and Brownie McGhee, and Muddy Waters and Otis Spann, each performing on a bill with the Chris Barber Band. Their appearances all directly resulted from Barber's decision to use his earnings to finance their tours.

A separate London-based entrepreneurial venture served as an incubator that nurtured the growth of both the British blues scene and the British folk music revival. The Barrelhouse and Blues Club was started around the time Bill arrived for his fifth visit to Great Britain by Alexis Korner and Cyril Davies, a twelve-string guitarist and harmonica player. Davies, who shared Korner's consuming passion for blues, had been presenting a well-attended skiffle night on Thursday evenings in a room over the Roundhouse pub on Wardour Street. Korner later described the Roundhouse's transition from skiffle to blues: "One day, Cyril said to me, 'I'm fed up with all this skiffle rubbish, I want to open a blues club, will you run it with me?' I said yes."[11]

In the early days of the Barrelhouse and Blues Club, Bobbie Korner recalled, there were "more musicians than punters [customers]."[12] Davies and Alexis Korner would perform as a duo, and they would then invite other musicians to sit in. News of Bill's presence there, when he stopped by to play, helped to spread the word about the fledgling operation. Only a relatively small number of people would have identified themselves at that time as blues fans. As Bobbie Korner remembered, "We were still thunderstruck that other people liked blues."[13]

A tall, lanky teenaged guitarist named John Baldry soon became a regular at the Roundhouse, both as an audience member and as a performer. Baldry, who would add an adjective to his name and become Long John Baldry, drew his repertoire from sources such as Bill and Lead Belly. British folksinger Martin Carthy remembered attending a Baldry performance at the Roundhouse, where "he sang one of the field hollers from the Lomax recordings, and it was breathtaking."[14] Eric Clapton recalled seeing Baldry sing and play twelve-string guitar not long after and has described him as "phenomenal."[15]

During this period Davy Graham, another British guitarist not yet twenty years old, had been teaching himself to play "House Rent Stomp," the instrumental that Bill had recorded for the French Vogue label in 1951. Journalist and skiffle player John Pilgrim first heard Graham perform in a Soho flat for an informal gathering of musicians one afternoon in the late 1950s. When Graham played his version of Bill's song, Pilgrim and his fellow skifflers instantly recognized the young guitarist's uncommon ability to play the difficult piece with both precision and feeling. In Pilgrim's words, "We knew the world was changed, and we were finished."[16]

In the early 1960s, in Carthy's words, Graham became "an important figure to all British [acoustic] guitar players . . . *the* groundbreaking player."[17] He would go on to compose "Anji," an instrumental piece that became the litmus test in the United Kingdom for guitarists seeking bookings in folk music clubs, and which Paul Simon brought to U.S. audiences in the mid-1960s. Graham's innovations included incorporating elements into his guitar playing from extraordinarily diverse sources, ranging from American jazz to the musical traditions of India and North Africa, as well as discovering a guitar tuning that enabled players to play Scottish and Irish music with greater ease and imagination.

Three of the leading figures in the British folk revival of the 1960s and '70s who have praised Graham as a transformative force—guitarists Martin Carthy, Bert Jansch, and John Renbourn—have also identified Bill as a significant and early inspiration. Carthy would later play with the electrified folk group Steeleye Span, and in the Waterson:Carthy group with his wife, Norma Waterson, and their daughter Eliza Carthy. For Martin Carthy, hearing Bill's guitar playing on instrumentals such as

"Guitar Shuffle" was "just a revelation." He was "absolutely blown away" by it, because "it was driving as hell, it swung like mad, and it was extraordinarily passionate stuff." A particular technique of Bill's that Carthy incorporated into his own playing was the use of the thumb on his right hand, or strumming hand, to give "this very heavy accent on the bass strings." With its "percussive effect," Bill's use of his thumb provided Carthy, and other British guitar players who studied him, with one of the first models they had for keeping a powerful beat on the lower strings while playing the melody on the higher strings.[18]

Bert Jansch, who grew up in Edinburgh, had his first exposure to Bill when he watched a segment from *Low Light and Blue Smoke* on Scottish television. He later bought an EP of Bill's songs in a record store and "spent a year trying to play this stuff," fascinated by the idea that "the rhythms seemed to be held down by the thumb."[19] Jansch first came to prominence as a solo performer, and then as a member of the group Pentangle, which he formed with several other musicians versed in the British folk tradition, including John Renbourn. Renbourn had learned to play Bill's music from listening to his records, as well as studying musicians who had incorporated Bill's style into their own playing, such as Davy Graham. He also tracked down and observed guitarist Wizz Jones, whose footloose lifestyle earned him the reputation of a "pre-hippie," but who had mastered Bill's thumb-stroke.[20] Renbourn has gone on to an acclaimed career as a solo and ensemble performer, but he recalled how he initially "wanted to be like Big Bill and like Wizz," because "that was the way, you had to play with that thumb, the dead thumb, that was considered really important."[21]

Bill concluded his British tour by returning to London, where he appeared on the new TV variety show *Six-Five Special*. One of the program's producers was Jack Good, who produced a 1964 British TV special for the Beatles, and then moved to the United States in the mid-1960s to develop the rock-and-roll series *Shindig*.[22] Because *Six-Five Special* was one of the first programs on British TV geared to a teenage audience, the guests, in addition to Bill, included the Vipers skiffle group and pop star Tommy Steele. Bill chatted with co-host Jo Douglas about how blues developed from spirituals, playing "I'm Going to Tell God How I'm Treated," and then introduced "Take This Hammer" by telling her how his 107-year-old uncle had known Casey Jones.[23] After a final British concert on March 10 with Brother John Sellers and Sandy Brown's Jazz Band at the Stoll Theatre in London's West End, Bill headed to Holland.

When he arrived in Amsterdam, Bill reunited with Pim and met Arnold Michael van Isveldt, the son he had fathered with her. Michael had been born on December 4, 1956. Pim had selected Michael's first name in honor of her father, at her parents' request. During her pregnancy, Bill had written her about his preferences for "the name of our baby," suggesting "Pim Lee Broonzy" for a girl, and "William Lee Conley Broonzy" for a boy, who would have the nickname "Little Bill."[24] In the same note, Bill had indicated to Pim how he felt about their relationship, signing it: "To a wonderful woman and a sweet girl and a good wife. Best of everything from [your] husband[,] Big Bill Broonzy." He added "10,000 kisses to Pim."[25]

Bill did not keep these feelings to himself. He told a reporter from the *Melody Maker* at a press reception upon his arrival in Great Britain the month before that he was "going to Holland to marry a Dutch girl."[26] Similarly, during his stay in Amsterdam, the Dutch jazz photographer Hans Buter accompanied Bill, Pim, Jeroen, Michael, and Pim's younger sister as they strolled through their neighborhood. The images show Bill smiling while he pushed the pram with four-month-old Michael down the sidewalk, with Jeroen serving as a drum major as he led the procession.

The information that Bill shared with Pim about his marital status can best be described as selectively factual. He gave her a copy of the 1951 divorce decree that confirmed the end of his marriage to Rose Allen Broonzy, or "Texas Rose." He apparently believed that this would be persuasive evidence to Pim that he was single, and that his private and public announcements of his wish to marry her would be credible. It was only at some point later, and very likely after Michael was born, that Pim learned that he had married two different women named Rose.[27]

Exactly how Bill imagined that he would maintain his role as Rose Lawson Broonzy's husband on one continent while continuing his relationship with Pim and fulfilling his responsibilities as Michael's father on another is not clear. The photos that Hans Buter took of Bill's Dutch family at home showed Bill tenderly cradling Michael in the crook of his left arm, beaming at his infant son, while his right arm rested on his guitar. Other shots captured Bill embracing Pim's younger sister and Jeroen, as well as being playfully affectionate with Pim. In all likelihood,

Bill's strategy was to continue the status quo, on the basis that a consistent stream of European concert dates and recording sessions would enable him to maintain a regular presence in his two domestic worlds four thousand miles apart.

In early April, Bill returned to Rose and Chicago, arriving in New York on the liner *Liberté* on April 8. The next month, he joined guitarist Brownie McGhee and harmonica player Sonny Terry for a freewheeling late-night session with Studs Terkel in the studios of WFMT. The other two musicians were in Chicago performing in a production of the Tennessee Williams play *Cat on a Hot Tin Roof*, and Bill's career had overlapped in several ways with each of them. Both Bill and Sonny had appeared at the first two "From Spirituals to Swing" concerts in the late 1930s, and in the 1940s Brownie and Sonny had performed at People's Songs hoots in New York. In 1947 Brownie had made the first recording of Bill's "Black, Brown, and White Blues."

During the recorded conversation and performances, Brownie and Sonny used Terkel's questions about how they had become blues artists as a way to introduce themselves to the Chicago listening audience. The recording was broadcast during his regular *Almanac* show the following night on WFMT, and Terkel also succeeded in persuading Moe Asch at Folkways that it was worth releasing as an LP. During the session, Bill assumed the role of discussion leader and, to illustrate his point that "blues is a steal from spirituals," requested that each of the musicians perform a spiritual.[28] The recording provided a rare opportunity for 1950s audiences to hear Bill perform with both a second guitarist and a harmonica player, an event that was especially important because each of them was an extraordinarily talented artist. Their joint performance on "Key to the Highway" enabled all three musicians to make superb individual contributions while allowing the others to shine. As in the gathering that had produced the *Blues in the Mississippi Night* recording a decade before, Bill used his stature as leader to ensure that the session would offer his colleagues exposure as well.

Two months later, over the Fourth of July weekend, Bill returned to Circle Pines Center in Michigan. This time, instead of a summer-long job in the kitchen, he had been invited with Pete Seeger to appear as artists-in-residence over the long weekend. During the Saturday-night concert they gave, Seeger called attention to the prominent role that Bill's thumb played in his guitar playing. After Bill finished the driving blues

"Willie Mae," Seeger commented, "That's an awful good kind of guitar picking," and requested that he "show 'em the way you keep your thumb hitting the bass." When Bill obliged him, Seeger noted, "His thumb never changes. Just like a rock." Bill acknowledged that it effectively served as the rhythm section for a solo guitarist: "[It's] the same as a drum keeps going when the band's playing. And the horns be going one way, and this way and that way, but they all come back to where that drummer's going, with that one beat."

Seeger then made a statement that was uncannily accurate in what it anticipated: "Bill, maybe someday a music school's gonna teach that way, but right now there's nobody in the country that, that knows how to play that unless they were to listen to you and study it."[29] Less than six months later, precisely such an institution would emerge in Chicago. It would provide the instruction that Seeger had imagined, and Bill would be present at its opening.

Before he left Circle Pines, Seeger filmed Bill playing and singing segments of several songs. Two years before, he had purchased a used sixteen-millimeter movie camera that made it possible for the operator to record sound as well as moving images. Seeger would bring it with him when he and his family were traveling so that they could, in his words, "preserve what we saw and heard."[30] Bill was among the first performers Seeger filmed, a group that later included Sonny Terry, Canadian fiddler Jean Carignan, and prisoners at the Texas State Penitentiary.

Seeger shot the footage on a warm and sunny July day as Bill sat on the front porch of the wood-framed farmhouse at Circle Pines. As he strummed and sang in a short-sleeved shirt, Bill was clearly in a rural setting, and at times the footage has been incorrectly, if understandably, identified as having been shot in the South. He appeared relaxed, as these were truly home movies being filmed by a colleague with whom he had often worked in recent years. In several of the songs, Seeger alternated between focusing the camera on Bill's left hand while he played chords and single notes on the guitar neck, and concentrating on his right hand, especially on his ability to pluck the higher strings while keeping the steady beat with his thumb on the bass strings. The footage of Bill was stored in Seeger's barn for many years, until guitarist Stefan Grossman took the initiative to review it and prepare it for release on video and then on DVD. Ever since, fans of Bill's, particularly musicians curious to learn the specifics of his technique, have had the chance to study what amounted to one of the first instructional videos ever made of a blues musician.

───────────────────────────────────

As he traveled back to Chicago from Circle Pines, Bill was facing the imminent prospect of major surgery. He regularly smoked cigarettes and had been suffering for some time from a deep and persistent cough, which is audible in his live recordings. After he returned from his most recent European tour in April, he had sought medical attention, and his doctor had recommended that he have a lung operation. Bill's request for Pete Seeger to film him playing at Circle Pines had been motivated by his anticipation of the surgery. "Well, you'd better record me now," Seeger later recalled Bill telling him, "because tomorrow, I'm going under the knife. And I don't know if I'll ever sing again."[31]

Bill's impending surgery had also spurred a Cleveland-based disc jockey named Bill Randle into arranging a recording session he had been thinking about for some time. Randle had been identified in a *Time* magazine profile two years before as "the top U.S. deejay." The article had described his talent for predicting which songs would become hits, as well as his $100,000 annual salary.[32] He became prominent by commuting to New York every week for a program aired over the CBS radio network. Randle had also been one of the first DJs outside the South to recognize Elvis Presley's talent, and he introduced Presley's first appearance on national television in January 1956, during a broadcast of CBS's *Stage Show*.[33]

In addition to his acumen in spotting rock-and-roll singers and songs in advance of their success, Randle was keenly interested in other musical styles, including jazz, gospel, and blues. At the time, he was also enrolled in a graduate program in sociology at Cleveland's Western Reserve (later Case Western Reserve) University, in which he was studying "the impact of urban milieus on rural folkways." He decided to use an assignment for a seminar paper as a springboard for taking "an individual performer and [doing] an in-depth study of him. The performer was Big Bill Broonzy."[34]

Bill Randle was uniquely positioned to arrange for the recording session. The convergence of his formal academic studies, his passion for blues in general—especially his belief that Bill was "the greatest blues singer of all time"—and his awareness of Bill's uncertain health status all compelled him to act swiftly.[35] His extensive contacts in the music business and his ability to finance the session ensured that the recordings were done at a high level of technical quality. Randle had contacted Bill through Studs Terkel and decided to hire Terkel to share the interviewing duties. He booked the studio time at Universal Recording Studios, where recording engineer and inventor Bill Putnam owned and operated what has been described as "the preeminent studio in Chicago in the 1950s."[36]

Bill arrived at the downtown Chicago studio late in the day on Friday, July 12. Terkel set the tone for the session at the outset because Randle was delayed by bad weather. As the tape began to run, Studs told Bill, "Anything you want to say about a song . . . anything connected with it or anything that comes to your mind as you're singing it, you just go ahead and do it."[37] By the time Bill indicated on Sunday night that he was ready to wrap it up, the sessions had generated about nine hours of conversation and performance. He had played, as he said at the end, "practically everything I know," told dozens of stories, and offered his observations on a wide range of topics.[38]

When Randle was finally able to find the time to edit the tapes several years later, the result was a five-LP set titled *The Big Bill Broonzy Story*, containing over three hours of material. Not surprisingly, there were overlaps between the contents of Bill's autobiography, *Big Bill Blues,* and the stories he told in *The Big Bill Broonzy Story.* In particular, his commentaries in both the book and the LP set prominently featured his uncle Jerry Belcher as an early musical influence and as a purveyor of wisdom. The two works can be seen as complementary pieces, in which Bill used the respective advantages of each medium to convey his points.

The most striking difference between the two works was Bill's presentation in *The Big Bill Broonzy Story* of his friends and musical colleagues. During one half-hour segment, Bill played selections by Tampa Red, Jim Jackson, Leroy Carr, Big Maceo Merriweather, Richard Jones, and Lead Belly, introducing each one with a few observations. While he had discussed each of them in *Big Bill Blues,* he could illustrate their significance in a more powerful way by performing their songs.

The timing of the recording session also gave Bill a theme he repeated about several of the musicians who were no longer living. Bill was clearly mindful of his own mortality as he braced for the surgery. When he introduced Leroy Carr's "In the Evening (When the Sun Goes Down)," he observed, "I don't think he'll ever die, because a song like this don't die."[39] His elegiac tone continued when he spoke of Big Maceo Merriweather's "Worried Life Blues," and it deepened as he came to Richard Jones's "Trouble in Mind." "A song like this," Bill said, "that these guys [have written], they still live in the minds and the hearts of all blues singers."[40] After listing a few songwriters he had already mentioned, he added, "Well, Big Bill, too. They got some of us in there. So that's why I sing these songs, because I—these fellas is dead, and I am alive and I can sing 'em."[41]

Bill was also in a reflective mood as he considered his status as "a real blues singer." When Terkel asked him about the trend in popular music of using some of the vocal techniques used in the black churches, or "spirituals sung in juke boxes," Bill acknowledged that "the young people like it better."[42] The older style that Bill played "carries them back to horse-and-buggy days and slavery times, and they don't want to think about that."[43] When Terkel asked directly, "Is that why some Negroes don't like blues?" Bill immediately responded, "Yeah, some—most of 'em, it's the majority of younger Negroes." To Terkel's surprise, Bill praised Elvis Presley for his success in "singing blues now. . . . [H]e's singing the same thing I'm singing now, and he knows it. . . . [W]hen I was a kid, I used to hear them call it 'rockin' the blues'—well, that's what he's doing now."[44] In fact, Bill was right on target, as Presley later identified Bill specifically as an influence: "I dug the real low-down Mississippi singers, mostly Big Bill Broonzy and Big Boy Crudup." Presley added that his interest came at a price: "They would scold me at home for listening to them"[45]

As the Bruynoghes had done in trimming Bill's writings for publication, Bill Randle omitted significant chunks of the session in editing the tapes for commercial release. One segment that did not make the final cut was Bill's performance of what he called the "Dirty Dozens," a well-established tradition in the African American community of creative insults. He sang a number of verses, employing the melody he had used two decades before for his song "Truckin' Little Woman," and inserting the phrase "mother for ya" in the chorus as a sanitized alternative to what he called "the word we use for it."[46] In addition, three hours of unused material included songs and conversation with Sonny Terry and Brownie McGhee, whose visit on Sunday produced an extended version of the session they had done with Bill and Studs Terkel at WFMT two months before. The sequence with Sonny and Brownie included Brownie's description of the high regard that A. P. Carter, of country music's renowned Carter Family, had for Bill's song "Just a Dream." According to McGhee, A. P. Carter would travel to Brownie's home, and when they discussed music, A. P. would say that he "loved that song because it started out with a story. 'Well, he told me, it's got laughter in it, got a little tears in it, it's got color, it's got life.' And so he liked that."[47]

One of the most fascinating of the omitted sections is the final half hour of the Sunday-night session. It came after Sonny and Brownie had departed, leaving Bill and Studs Terkel in the studio. Terkel, anticipating that this conversation would bring the three-day marathon to a close, asked Bill for his impressions of his travels abroad, and specifically for his thoughts on the trip he had made to Senegal, in West Africa. As Bill described it, his visit would likely have taken place in early 1953, when he toured in Morocco and Algeria. After performing in Algiers and Casablanca, he told Terkel, he traveled to Dakar, the capital of Senegal and its largest city.[48]

Bill told Terkel of an encounter in which he almost came to blows with a Senegalese man over a disagreement while drinking. He was dissuaded from hitting the man by a mutual Senegalese friend, who shortly thereafter excused himself to go with Bill's potential sparring partner to pull a car out of the mud. "And so them two picked up this car with the man sitting in it, and carried and put it up on the highway." After witnessing this display of strength, Bill noted that he "got to thinking and wondering, now, if I'd've hit that guy, I wonder what would have happened to me, if he can carry a car that big?"[49]

More than simply a setting for his tales, Bill felt a sense of connection with the West African country and its people, as well as its music. He told of meeting a man who spelled his name "Broonzie," and, as Bill considered the history of the slave trade, he arrived at the conclusion that "I think, really, my foreparents come from there."[50] He played and sang a fragment of a mournful song that he had heard there that had "sounded something like" a blues, but he noted that because it was in a minor key, he was not able to reproduce it accurately. Bill brought the session to a close by singing a final version of "The Glory of Love." If he had seen the three days as a chance to document his life and his work, his concluding reflections took him as far back to his roots as he could have imagined tracing them.

Bill Randle, after being approached by the jazz label Verve, decided that the company would be an excellent choice for issuing the recordings. He saw Norman Granz as a label owner who appreciated the value of the material. Granz was a jazz impresario and founder of the successful *Jazz at the Philharmonic* series of concert tours featuring some of the world's top jazz artists. Randle also recognized that Verve could afford to issue and distribute a multi-LP set to an international audience.[51] When it was finally released in early 1961, *The Big Bill Broonzy Story* met with critical acclaim. John S. Wilson, the jazz critic for the *New York Times*, compared it favorably with Alan Lomax's 1938 recordings of Jelly Roll Morton for the Library of Congress and praised Bill for providing "a unique panorama of the relatively unexplored post-Twenties blues world."[52]

Soon after the Randle sessions—in several accounts, the day after—Bill underwent the scheduled surgery. In an article published several years later, Yannick Bruynoghe recalled, "You wrote to me: 'They have cut my lung.' They cut your vocal chords [*sic*], too."[53]

Suddenly, Bill had become, as Yannick ironically observed, a "blues singer with no voice."[54] He was able to speak no louder than a hoarse whisper, and the doctors had found cancer in his lungs. Fortunately, Rose had her job at the Hotel Lincoln, which had likely been the primary support of their household for most of the time they had been together. Nevertheless, the combination of increased expenses for Bill's medical care and the reduction in income due to his illness put a considerable strain on their finances.

On November 27, the night before Thanksgiving, a set of Bill's friends and admirers organized a benefit concert for him at Temple KAM, located about a mile from Bill and Rose's apartment. It was unlike any previous gathering of musicians that had occurred in Chicago. The list of performers included Chicago blues artists, musicians from the rapidly developing Chicago folk music scene, gospel star Mahalia Jackson, and nationally known folk artists Pete Seeger and Odetta. Radio station WFMT played a vital role in promoting the event, and the fifteen hundred seats sold out by mail order in advance.[55]

The evening, with Studs Terkel serving as emcee, began with an entrance by bagpiper George Armstrong, followed by his wife, folksinger Gerry Armstrong. The contingent of blues performers included pianists Sunnyland Slim and Little Brother Montgomery, as well as guitarist

J. B. Lenoir, who stood out for his "zebra-patterned jacket and electric guitar."[56] Terkel read telegrams from Muddy Waters and Memphis Slim, as well as letters from well-wishers in Belgium, Holland, and Great Britain, and the audience included Tampa Red.[57] The performers included three Chicago musicians, in addition to Terkel, who had appeared with Bill in the "I Come for to Sing" revue: Fleming Brown, Larry Lane, and Win Stracke. Children's singer Ella Jenkins led the audience in chanting "Get well, Bill," as she provided the rhythm with a conga drum.[58] Other Chicago-based folk artists who performed were banjoist Bob Gibson, who was a regular attraction at the Gate of Horn, and guitarist Frank Hamilton.

In the second half of the concert, Odetta sang a selection of songs with sufficient authority and volume to cause one reviewer to note that she "didn't need the loudspeaker system at all."[59] The singer, who was on her way to becoming one of the most acclaimed performers in the American folk music revival of the late 1950s and '60s, had enjoyed a four-month run at the Gate of Horn the previous year. She later recalled how warmly Bill and Josh White had greeted her during her residency there, and how much she appreciated their thoughtfulness in coming "just to make sure their baby sister was going to be all right."[60] Pete Seeger, who had flown in from California for the concert, contributed several songs, including Lead Belly's "Bourgeois Blues" and a banjo solo.

The emotional crescendo of the nearly three-hour concert came with Mahalia Jackson's performance. After opening with two spirituals, "Steal Away to Jesus" and "I'm on My Way," Jackson spoke of appearing overseas with Bill in 1952, and then invited him to join her. When Bill, "obviously moved, walked onstage to a standing ovation," she sang "Just a Closer Walk with Thee."[61] Jackson followed that with "When the Saints Go Marching In," but when she "called Bill to the microphone," the *Sun-Times* reporter wrote, "he couldn't sing." The Queen of Gospel, who was well versed in engaging congregations when emotions were running high, then "instructed the audience in how to clap time, then struck out 'Down by the Riverside,'" as all the performers joined in.

At the conclusion of the song, Bill approached the microphone. One observer noted that "his big frame was shrunk in his double-breasted suit, [and] his hair was graying." He said two barely audible sentences: "I do thank you all. That's all I can do."[62] The evening achieved its purpose in providing financial assistance to Bill, raising about $2,500 for him. The money was certainly a timely and welcome infusion of income, and the outpouring of respect and affection from the range of performers likely had a tonic effect on him as well.[63]

Beyond the beneficial impact it had on Bill, the concert also made a powerful statement about the status of folk music in Chicago in late 1957. The majority of the performers were musicians who were working regularly in Chicago. Folk music fans, whose numbers were swelling, were familiar with them through their appearances at venues like the Gate of Horn, as well as by hearing them on WFMT, either on *The Midnight Special* or on *Studs Terkel's Almanac*. In addition, performers with national followings, like Pete Seeger and Odetta, were now regular visitors to Chicago, where they could be assured of sizable and enthusiastic audiences.

Four days after the benefit concert for Bill, on December 1, 1957, an institution dedicated to teaching people to play folk music opened its doors in Chicago. The specific sequence of events that led to the creation of the Old Town School of Folk Music had begun earlier that year when Win Stracke heard Frank Hamilton, a guitarist who had recently arrived from California, perform at the Gate of Horn. Stracke thought Hamilton had demonstrated considerable talent, as did Dawn Greening, a housewife from suburban Oak Park whose newfound passion for folk music had drawn her into regular attendance at the Gate's concerts. When Greening learned that Hamilton hoped to remain in Chicago but needed a regular source of income, she invited him to give group music classes in her Oak Park home. Stracke had met Greening at the Gate, and, looking to "improve my finger work" on the guitar, he began attending the classes Hamilton was teaching.[64]

In Stracke's judgment, Hamilton was an unusually talented teacher, not only for "the playful joyousness that he brought to any kind of traditional music," but for his skill in guiding a group of students at differing levels of musical ability.[65] Hamilton had learned his group teaching techniques in California from Bess Lomax Hawes, Alan Lomax's sister, who had pursued a career in music education. As Stracke later recalled, after attending the classes for several weeks, "it occurred to me, as it had many times previously, that Chicago could do well with a school devoted to folk music."[66] This time he had found a teacher whose skills he had benefited from firsthand in the Greenings' dining room. When Hamilton agreed to Win's suggestion that he oversee the instruction at "a school in which he would use the dining room approach, but for larger classes . . . Frank agreed, and the project was on."[67] Win then invited Gertrude Soltker to serve as the school's administrator, having first been impressed by her organizational skills two decades before at the Chicago Repertory Group.[68]

Although he could not sing, Bill was a featured performer at the opening of the Old Town School of Folk Music on December 1. Win later reported that "several hundred prospective students" attended the event.[69] He had found space for the school in the Immigrant State Bank Building at 333 West North Avenue, located in the Old Town neighborhood, which inspired the school's name. Bill's portion of the program provided the most dramatic teaching—and marketing—moment. Wearing his dark double-breasted suit, he played a blues piece under the watchful eye of Frank Hamilton, who then proceeded to diagram "Bill's intricate right hand style in written tablature on a blackboard."[70] Hamilton used the notation first to reproduce the piece himself, and then to guide a small group of students through the piece. After Win and Frank led the room in a sing-along, dozens registered for classes. Soon Hamilton could report an enrollment of about 125 students learning guitar and five-string banjo, as well as "an additional 30 for a Friday night lecture series delivered by Studs Terkel on American Folklore and music."[71]

Not long after opening night, Bill returned to the Old Town School for the U.S. debut of *Low Light and Blue Smoke*, the short film that Yannick Bruynoghe had produced that featured him playing in Belgium. Yannick and Margo had stopped to spend time with Bill in Chicago as part of a three-month trip to New York and the West Coast, and they had brought a copy of the film so that he could see it for the first time. Win and Studs Terkel were also present at the showing, and Margo recalled that Bill was "very pleased" with the movie.[72]

Despite his illness, Bill brought the Bruynoghes to numerous blues and jazz clubs on the South and West Sides, transporting them in his aging Cadillac. If they were not the first European visitors to most of the venues they visited, they were certainly among the first to photograph the musicians. After Bill greeted the Bruynoghes in his and Rose's apartment with a small group of friends that included Memphis Slim, Little Brother Montgomery, and Tampa Red, he brought them to the 708 Club to see Howlin' Wolf and his band. Yannick's photos show Wolf singing while standing on the bar, and he later recalled that "hearing [Wolf] live, so lively, so rough, so wild" meant that "as a first night in a Chicago blues joint . . . it was a real shock!"[73]

Over the course of their visit, Bill took Yannick and Margo to see and photograph many of the top performers in the Chicago blues world, including Muddy Waters, Little Walter, Elmore James, Robert Junior Lockwood, Eddie Boyd, Sunnyland Slim, and Jimmy Rogers, as well as the talented musicians in Muddy's band, such as Otis Spann and James Cotton. With Bill as a guide, they also heard emerging artists such as Otis Rush and Magic Sam, with Willie Dixon backing him on bass. Because Yannick was an avid record collector, he asked both Bill and Muddy for recommendations on where to buy old 78s. Their suggestions brought the couple to Maxwell Street, which reminded Margo of "some places I've seen in Belgium one time after a bomb raid."[74] When Yannick located the shop Muddy had recommended, he bought "about 1000 records," which he shipped back to Belgium. Yannick also later recalled that Muddy told him that he "would love to travel to Europe, but he felt a little bit scared."[75] After "three weeks of nightly visits" to jazz and blues clubs, the Bruynoghes departed early in January 1958 for San Francisco, where Yannick, at the request of writer and producer Stanley Dance, began to organize an early February recording session for jazz pianist Earl Hines.[76]

As the new year began, reports of Bill's condition were reaching key people in the British jazz world. After Brother John Sellers had written critic Max Jones that Bill was scheduled for another operation on his lung, the headline in the *Melody Maker* read: "Bill Broonzy May Never Sing Again."[77] Two weeks later, another front-page story announced that "Britain's top skiffle and jazz stars" were planning a benefit concert for Bill at the London Coliseum on March 9.[78] At the initiative of Alexis Korner and pianist David Stevens, a committee composed of several influential individuals, including the editors of the *Melody Maker* newspaper and *Jazz Journal* magazine, took charge of the event. The prominent trumpeter and bandleader Humphrey Lyttelton wrote an article for *Melody Maker* praising Bill as "a true folk-artist" and exhorting "the jazz world" to "show itself ready to offer him its gratitude."[79] The same edition informed readers that a second, separately organized benefit show was also being arranged for March 15 at the Dominion Theatre, featuring Lonnie Donegan and the Chris Barber and Ken Colyer bands.

Bill and his illness were regularly covered in the *Melody Maker* in the weeks leading up to the events. British jazz fans could read an excerpt from a letter from Bill, in which he informed them that his first two operations had cost $2,500, and that his current treatments cost $75 a week.[80] A profile by Chicago-based writer Bernie Asbell, who had known Bill since the days of People's Songs, described how "when he opens his mouth to talk, Big Bill Broonzy isn't there. There's only a whisper of the man."[81]

Those attending the March 9 concert at the Coliseum received a handsome twenty-eight-page booklet with articles about Bill, photos and drawings of him, quotes from his autobiography, a list of all of his records that were currently available in Great Britain, and ads from record companies and record store owners wishing him well. An uncredited essay titled "A Man Must Live" noted that this was "the first time that a benefit concert has been organized in Britain for an American musician." It also identified the November benefit concert at Temple KAM as a direct inspiration for the event. The list of performers included the promised set of skiffle and jazz stars, from Chas McDevitt and Johnny Duncan to Humphrey Lyttelton and Johnny Dankworth, and Alan Lomax served as one of the emcees. Although touring American gospel guitarist and singer Sister Rosetta Tharpe was restricted from performing due to an expired work permit, she "squeezed through the curtain to pay her respects to the artistry of Broonzy."[82] The March 15 show at the Dominion Theatre was billed as a "Midnight Matinee" and featured a rare reunion of Lonnie Donegan, Chris Barber, and Ken Colyer.[83]

Bill's final performance took place the day before the Midnight Matinee. He had made an appearance back in January at the Old Town School, accompanying Mahalia Jackson and her pianist, Mildred Falls, along with the Weavers (then touring without Pete Seeger). On Friday evening March 14, he came to Ida Noyes Hall at the University of Chicago for a square dance being held by the University of Chicago Students for Circle Pines. During the intermission, the Circle Pines newsletter reported, "as a special surprise, Big Bill Broomzey [sic] played some of his famous blues on the guitar."[84]

Even though reports of the well-attended concerts lifted Bill's spirits, his condition continued to decline. In a letter to Max Jones published in the *Melody Maker*, Bill asked him to "Please tell everyone in England I would like to write to every one of them, but I can't see too good and have a hard time writing letters." He added, "I will be glad to get the money because I do need it because I got just seven dollars left in the bank."[85]

Bill also gave an endorsement to Sonny Terry and Brownie McGhee, for whom Great Britain would be their initial stop on their first overseas tour. He praised them as "two good boys [who] can really play and sing the blues."[86] Brownie, for his part, identified Bill's urging them to make the trip as a crucial factor in their decision to go.[87] The duo was warmly received, performing at the Royal Festival Hall, and then touring and recording with the Chris Barber Band. When the pair visited Günter Boas in Germany, they went into a shop that offered do-it-yourself record-making technology, and recorded a get-well message for Bill. Brownie began by asking Sonny, "This is dedicated to Big Bill, isn't it?" Sonny replied, "Yes, it is, Brownie McGhee," and proceeded to sing a one-verse blues telling how "Big Bill wanted us to come overseas," assuring them, "You know the people over there . . . they will like you and Brownie McGhee." Brownie signed off by saying, "This is being recorded, Bill. Hope you get better. Everybody over here wants to see you again. Everybody. Everybody wants to see you again."[88]

As the summer progressed, Bill's health deteriorated further. Win Stracke wrote Yannick Bruynoghe in late July that Bill had undergone a brain operation and that the cancer was spreading. Two weeks later, on August 12, Win wrote Yannick again, this time to say that "Big Bill is dying," reporting that "he has almost completely lost his sight, is down to about eighty-five pounds, has severe head pains, and is under constant sedation."[89] Bill died three days later in the early morning, riding with Rose in the ambulance that Win had called to take him to Billings Hospital.

Over the next few days, Bill's friends mobilized to remember him in public and private ways. Win and Brother John Sellers went with Rose to select a grave site for Bill in Lincoln Cemetery. They chose a lot that was "close to the entrance," Win wrote Yannick, "where the grave could be easily located" by the fans of Bill that he hoped would come over time "from all over the world."[90] Studs Terkel broadcast a memorial radio program on WFMT that included material from the as-yet-unreleased Randle sessions. Telegrams arrived from blues musicians (Mr. and Mrs. Muddy Waters, Big Maceo Merriweather's widow Lucille, guitarist Earl Hooker and family), from jazz musicians (trumpeter Lee Collins and his wife), from across the ocean (the Antwerp Jazz Club), and from Bill's own neighborhood (his former business partner Josephine Moore and her family).[91]

Several of Bill's family members traveled to Chicago for the services. His younger sisters Lannie Wesley and Mary Dove had come to stay with him and Rose in the days prior to his death. Lannie had been calling so frequently during Bill's illness that her phone service in North Little Rock had been cut off because she could not afford to pay the bill.[92] Lannie's granddaughter, Jo Ann Jackson, who came up from Arkansas for the services, had spent the previous summer with Bill and Rose in the weeks after Bill's first surgery. At that time, she had helped to care for her great-uncle, reading to him and talking with him.[93] She remembered the crush of musicians coming by the apartment in the days after Bill died—Howlin' Wolf, Muddy Waters, Memphis Slim, so many that she, as a young teenager, spent most of her time playing with the infant daughter of Little Walter, who was living across the hallway.

During the funeral, and in articles published in a variety of publications, some who eulogized Bill emphasized his personal attributes. Studs Terkel pointed out that Bill "always carried with him a sense of self-respect, as easily and as gracefully as he carried his guitar."[94] A physician who cared for him wrote, "Though his body was ravaged with disease, his mind heavy with pain, he somehow retained a spirit which made the task of those ministering to him doubly wonderful and at the same time more awesome."[95]

Other remembrances focused on him as a figure whose life and work reflected larger themes in African American life. *Time* magazine in its obituary declared that "Big Bill's blues were the simple, freewheeling poetry of fresh-plowed earth and cotton fields . . . [h]is blues were the big city too, its tenements, its bread lines. . . ." The article concluded that "his legacy was a battered suitcase, a few pictures, two guitars, and 200-odd recordings in which he preserved a part of his country—the best of the blues."[96]

Ebony magazine ran a two-page photo-editorial with the headline "Weep No More." Opposite a photo of Bill posing in a casual open-necked shirt with his guitar and a cigarette in his mouth, the editorial memorialized Bill as "one of the last of the shouting blues singers." It quoted Bill's comments from the Randle sessions, when he was describing the significant role that spirituals had historically played for black Americans who suffered injustices without legal recourse: "Back in my day, people didn't know nothing else to do but cry. They couldn't say about things that hurt 'em. But now they talks and gets lawyers. They don't cry no more." In

Ebony's view, although "the sorrows and sufferings of the Negro which Bill Broonzy says produced the blues have not disappeared," the response of present-day black Americans had become that of "an aroused race." It noted with pride that "Negroes today talk the language of law," and praised the younger generation of African Americans for launching a "children's crusade . . . for their tomorrow." Bill's death represented "a requiem for the blues," and for "the moral climate that produced Big Bill and the blues."[97]

Two careful observers of Bill's musical skills remembered him by celebrating his artistry as a musician. Two months after Bill's death, jazz critic Whitney Balliett wrote an appreciation of the blues in general and Bill's work in particular for the *New Yorker*. Balliett devoted the same level of attentiveness in his essay to Bill's playing as he normally did to the jazz giants about whom he usually wrote. In analyzing Bill's singing of "Trouble in Mind," he praised Bill for his "continual awareness of dynamics, dramatics, and shifting rhythm that is faultless." He presented a detailed description of Bill's performance of "Southbound Train," which he summarized as "incomparable." Balliett wrote in conclusion, "Indeed, the balance between voice and guitar, form and content, and emotion and restraint is perfect."[98]

Alexis Korner wrote to Win Stracke when he heard of Bill's death that "it must be difficult for you, in Chicago, to understand what the blues mean to some of us over here." By way of explanation, he stressed that "for Bobbie (my wife) and myself it has been one of the most important parts of our lives—and Bill was all of the Old Blues to us. There was never anyone who made a guitar ring the blues like Bill." Then, in assessing him as a performer, Korner wrote, "there was never anyone who achieved a more complete entity of voice and guitar."[99]

EPILOGUE

After Bill's death, the horizons of the blues world expanded dramatically. The number of American blues performers traveling overseas soon swelled, and through the 1960s and '70s European and British audiences responded enthusiastically to their appearances in a steady stream of concerts and tours. Bill had played a vital role in shaping this growth. Over the course of his six tours abroad, he had used his musical talents and his storytelling skills to promote both himself and others. His success in capturing the imaginations of jazz fans as one of the last of "the real old time singers who worked in the fields" enabled him to whet their appetites for the musicians he endorsed by name, from Muddy Waters to John Lee Hooker.[1] His persuasiveness and credibility when he told his fellow blues musicians about the warm reception he had received abroad helped them to overcome their concerns about traveling thousands of miles to perform in unfamiliar environments. In addition, his extended residencies in Europe demonstrated to his colleagues that performing there was a financially viable proposition.

Bill's visibility in the United States remained high into the early 1960s. In 1961 Norman Granz's Verve label released the five-LP set drawn from Bill Randle's recordings, *The Big Bill Broonzy Story*. Two leading American jazz critics, Ralph J. Gleason and Nat Hentoff, offered high praise for the recordings and for Bill, with Hentoff describing him as "a major figure in blues history."[2] Bill also appeared prominently in *The Country Blues*, Samuel B. Charters's groundbreaking 1959 study of the lives and contributions of significant blues artists. Devoting a chapter to Bill, Charters emphasized his importance during the decades when he was recording primarily for black audiences and declared that "as a warm, entertaining blues singer he had no equal."[3]

As the decade progressed, however, several factors elevated other blues artists and blues styles into prominence. A new generation of white blues fans discovered Robert Johnson when Columbia Records issued the 1961 LP *Robert Johnson: King of the Delta Blues Singers*, and over time white musicians incorporated Johnson's songs into their repertoires. Venues presenting rock musicians began to book artists such as Muddy Waters, B.B. King, and Howlin' Wolf, and blues bands playing a loud, electrified sound rose in popularity. In addition, a set of African American musicians who played acoustic blues and who had not performed or recorded for decades were located through the often-dogged efforts of young admirers. The newly rejuvenated careers of "rediscovered" bluesmen such as Son House, Mississippi John Hurt, and Skip James brought their unique styles of acoustic blues to new listeners through concerts and records.

As African Americans became more politically and culturally assertive during the 1960s, some commentators in the United States criticized Bill for being a blues artist who had modified his repertoire to appeal to white audiences. In his 1966 book *Urban Blues*, Charles Keil characterized Bill, along with Sonny Terry and Brownie McGhee, as finding "it convenient to let themselves be labeled country singers, primitives, or folk singers, unhooking their electric amplification and cleaning up their diction a bit to fit the new roles demanded of them." Keil grouped Bill with Josh White as "city bluesmen who have remodeled their presentation to meet pseudo-country standards as defined by the various folk impresarios."[4]

In Great Britain, some disillusionment with Bill set in as well. A 1968 essay by author and broadcaster Charlie Gillett referred to Bill and Brownie McGhee as "slick entertainers," and after describing his initial belief that "Black, Brown, and White Blues" was "the anthem of Negro protest," he stated, "We didn't know then that most Negroes at the time had never heard of Broonzy or his song." Gillett continued, "If they listened to the blues at all, they listened to B.B. King and Muddy Waters."[5] Bill's status also suffered from the combined effects of the presence of the "rediscovered" bluesmen and a perception that he had described himself as the last of the blues singers. Although he had never expressed it exactly that way, the reappearance of the long-absent artists, and the inaccuracies in pronouncements he had made in *Big Bill Blues* and elsewhere, took some of the luster off his reputation.[6]

Although popular tastes in blues shifted in the direction of other artists, Bill remained an essential reference point for some of the most successful rock musicians to emerge from Great Britain. Among them were Eric Clapton, Pete Townshend, and Ray Davies. Although Clapton had heard other blues artists before, he remembered that "Big Bill was the one that got to me on another level, above everybody else, because he was just an extremely good technician. He was a great player."[7] For Clapton, Bill "became like a role model for me, in terms of how to play the acoustic guitar."[8] He was rigorous in his approach as he taught himself to fingerpick in Bill's style. Playing along with Bill's records and then recording his own versions on a tape recorder, he would keep practicing until he could reproduce the pieces to his exacting standards. In his view, "Everything [Bill] did, it was almost mathematically perfect."[9]

Over time, two of Bill's songs became standard elements in Clapton's repertoire. "Hey, Hey" had resonated for him ever since he first saw Bill playing it in the segment from *Low Light and Blue Smoke*. "Maybe if I'd just heard it, it might not have had the same effect," Clapton once observed. "But to see footage of Broonzy playing 'Hey Hey,' this was a real blues artist and I felt like I was looking into heaven."[10] The other song was "Key to the Highway," which he had brought to an international audience with the version recorded by Derek and the Dominos in 1970. The song held a particular meaning for him because it was "the one that I thought somehow would, like 'Crossroads,' capture the whole journey of being a musician and a traveling journeyman."[11]

Pete Townshend of the Who had first become aware of Bill through references to him by skiffle star Lonnie Donegan, as well as comments made by some of the British trad jazz artists. As Townshend recalled, "I loved him first and foremost for his voice. But I also had never heard true basic blues guitar (where the instrument might be tuned to an open chord) and that was a revelation." He acknowledged that Bill's impact "got a little lost when a few years later we became submerged in all that great music from the Delta and the South." Townshend had grown up listening to the jazz standards his father played as a member of a swing band, and "so I knew good music, but not blues, folk-blues, or soul music." It was "when I first heard Big Bill" that he realized, "I knew I was listening to the music behind the music."[12]

Ray Davies of the Kinks once held up a Big Bill album for an interviewer and declared, "Without this man, I don't think I would have done what I did."[13] Growing up in north London, he and his brother Dave would listen to their "early guitar heroes," a list that included figures such as Chuck Berry, Charlie Christian, James Burton, and Lead Belly. "But to me," he underscored, "the greatest of all these guitar players was . . . Big Bill Broonzy," and Bill's music helped to inspire Davies's composition, and the Kinks' first hit, "You Really Got Me."[14] In contrast to Eric Clapton's fascination with Bill's precision, part of Bill's appeal to Davies was that he "loved the rough edges and the mistakes, and it made me realize that you don't need to be a virtuoso muso to make good music."[15] He was "astounded by [Bill's] playing," which he described as "although acoustic, was really electronic in its dynamic."[16] In a comment that sums up the perspective of many of Bill's fans, Davies observed that Bill "became like a talisman to me in what I believed him to be, and what I got from his playing."[17]

It was Eric Clapton who made it possible for Muddy Waters to meet Bill's son, Michael van Isveldt. In 1979 Clapton was touring in Europe, and Muddy was the opening act. Pim and Michael heard from friends that a late-night jazz radio program had offered tickets and backstage passes to Big Bill Broonzy's son for the show at Amsterdam's Jaap Eden Hal, as Muddy had been told that he was living somewhere in Holland. They called the radio station, identified themselves and their connection to Bill, and wound up meeting Muddy backstage before the show.

Michael, who was then twenty-two years old, later described how Muddy had "embraced me, and then held my hand for about a minute or so." He remembered that Muddy "really had tears in his eyes, and told me that he learned everything from my father, and that I looked exactly like him." They spoke for about ten minutes, and then Michael and Pim took their seats at the front of the house. When Muddy played "Key to the Highway" during his set, Michael recalled that he introduced it by saying, "This song is from Big Bill Broonzy, the greatest blues singer who ever lived, and this one is for his son who is in the audience tonight!"[18]

Not long after Bill's death, Muddy had recorded what was likely the first blues tribute album. *Muddy Waters Sings Big Bill Broonzy* features ten songs originally recorded by Bill, performed by two of his pallbearers (Muddy and Otis Spann), and including harp player James Cotton, who had attended his funeral. Their versions are harder-edged than Bill's had been, with Muddy's vocals ranging from growling to shouting. As a result, songs such as "When I Get to Thinkin'" become showcases both for Bill's caustic writing ("When I get to thinkin', you know it makes my poor heart ache / You know I ain't doing nothin', but fattenin' frogs for snakes") and Muddy's expressive power. While the project might have been an effort by Chess Records to attract fans of Bill's who wouldn't usually have bought an LP of electric Chicago blues, it is impossible to imagine Muddy treating the recording sessions as anything other than a chance to honor Bill. "'Do your thing, stay with it, man; if you stay with it, you goin' to make it,'" Muddy once recalled Bill telling him. "Mostly," he concluded, "I try to be like him."[19]

Over time, other individuals and institutions prominent in the fields of blues and folk music have kept alive the memory and significance of Bill's life and work. *Living Blues* magazine showcased Bill and the Bruynoghes in a 1982 issue that presented rare materials from Yannick and Margo's collection. Featuring a cover photo of Bill shaking hands with Muddy Waters, the issue contained numerous unpublished segments of Bill's writings to the Bruynoghes. It also reproduced a letter to them from the American author Henry Miller, which noted that Miller was "immediately enthralled" upon reading *Big Bill Blues*.[20] The issue was the most extensive compilation of new material relating to Bill that had appeared since his death nearly twenty-five years before. It also illustrated the significance of the Bruynoghes, in their roles as Bill's friends, editors, and now curators, as well as for their own pioneering work in documenting the Chicago blues scene of the late 1950s.[21]

The Old Town School of Folk Music has done more than any other institution to honor Bill over the years in a variety of ways. When a successful fund-raising campaign allowed the school to renovate its performance space in the mid-1980s, the hall was named the Big Bill Broonzy Concert Hall. For several decades, the school has presented Big Bill Broonzy tribute concerts, which have featured appearances by blues musicians of the caliber of Buddy Guy, Billy Boy Arnold, and Guy Davis. The school also has served as a reliquary for a number of items of Bill's, including his Local 208 union card and his Martin 000-28 guitar.

Both Alan Lomax and Studs Terkel incorporated Bill into books and commentaries that have reached audiences around the world. When Lomax wrote his award-winning 1993 book *The Land Where the Blues Began*, he drew on the substantial amount of material he had collected from Bill. The chapter titled "Big Bill of the Blues" used portions of the oral history he had done of Bill in the mid-1940s, as well as segments of letters and autobiography that Bill had written to Lomax. When combined with Bill's autobiography, *Big Bill Blues*, Lomax's book offered readers a fairly thorough version of Bill's description of his life from birth into middle age.

The first extended piece that Studs Terkel wrote about Bill, beyond liner notes for Folkways albums, was a 1958 essay titled "Big Bill's Last Session." In it, Terkel used a series of vignettes of the three days of the Randle sessions to present a memorable portrait of Bill, illustrated with quotes of Bill's singing and commentaries. Over the course of his long and productive career, Terkel would often refer to Bill in his anecdotes and asides, frequently underscoring Bill's stature among blues musicians, and relishing the examples of Bill's "razor-keen wit and deft turn of irony."[22]

Of all the Chicago blues musicians, Willie Dixon took on a set of roles that were most similar to those that Bill had assumed. Like Bill, Dixon was a prolific and talented songwriter, as well as a much-recorded musician who had been based in Chicago for decades. These attributes meant that he could serve as a talent scout and session coordinator for Leonard and Phil Chess in ways that resembled how Lester Melrose had called upon Bill. Dixon brought his own charismatic and persuasive style to these endeavors and particularly to the American Folk Blues Festivals, where his savvy and drive were vital elements in sustaining a commercially successful connection between U.S. blues musicians and European audiences. He likely saw Bill less as a role model than as a similarly situated entrepreneur who had opened up a new market overseas. At the same time, he acknowledged Bill as a mentor in one respect, identifying him as the musician who gave him "the encouragement to venture into the field of writing songs." After Bill's death, Dixon wrote, "It is great to say that I have worked with the best of the blues in the person of Big Bill Broonzy."[23]

Over half a century after his passing, uncertainty still surrounds one significant dimension of Bill's life: his status as a father. Despite Bill's occasional references to other children, only Michael van Isveldt has been unambiguously identified as his child. In his Dutch family, Bill's memory has been well preserved. Pim, who died in 2005, spoke of telling Michael's children about how their grandfather was "always singing." When she talked to her grandchildren about Bill, she would use the affectionate Dutch word for grandfather: "Opa Bill."[24]

Bill provided descriptions of several of his children on a number of occasions in the 1950s. He told a Dutch audience on his first trip there in late 1952, "I am married and have five children and seven grandchildren and maybe even more when I return [to the United States]."[25] He provided more detail to a Dutch jazz newsletter during his 1953 visit to Holland: "Bill is married to a Creole woman and has five children. Eveleen, who's very religious, Harriet and Catharine, the youngest who just got permission to get married and who can drink jenever [gin] just as well as her dad. Then there are the boys William and Willie. He loves musing about the time the children were little and would go to bed. He would put their 'nighties' on and pray: Precious Lord, Take My Hands, and every child would repeat every sentence and end with: To You the Lord May Keep." [26] He spoke specifically of one child in his comments to an Amsterdam audience during the same visit: "I have one kid that I got that will go south with me, and that's Harriett. And she's so much like me, at least I think that. But the rest of them, they won't go south because they don't like discrimination, you know."[27]

When Bill filled out a questionnaire for a folk music researcher in 1955, he wrote in response to the question about children that he had "3 in Ark [and] 2 in Chicago Ill." He also provided a photo of himself playing the guitar sitting on a bench outdoors next to a young man who looks to be in his mid- to late teens, perhaps a little older. The caption he wrote identified the pair as "Son, William—Big Bill." In addition, in making a point about France to Studs Terkel in an interview during the Randle sessions, he commented that "my son was over there during the war in 1940, '41, and '42."[28]

Billy Boy Arnold remembered being in Big Bill and Moore's Lounge, the club on the South Side that Bill co-owned in 1953–54, on an occasion when Bill came in with people he identified as his son and grandson. As Arnold described it, "When he and Ms. Moore had this club, he had a son, tall son, looked just like him, and he had a baby, the son had a baby, Big Bill was showing [and saying], 'This is my grandbaby.'" Also, although Arnold did not attend Bill's funeral, he was told by someone who was there that "Big Bill's daughter was crying, saying, 'Daddy, I'm sorry, I'm sorry.'" This was likely Rose Lawson Broonzy's daughter, Hattie Harrell (1921–1984), whom Bill's grandnieces Jo Ann Jackson and Rosie Tolbert both remember from their trips to visit Bill and Rose in Chicago. The funeral photos clearly show that Hattie Harrell was at the service, sitting with her mother and Bill's sister Lannie Wesley.[29]

Bill's nephew Frank Wesley, Lannie Wesley's son, described arranging to sit at his uncle's funeral service with a daughter of Bill's named Catherine: "I went to the back and got, what's that girl, Catherine, I think her name [was], and went up to the front with me. . . . [I]f you see me [in the funeral photos], the girl that's sitting beside me would be his daughter. . . . [S]he was my cousin." He recalled that she worked at a hospital in Chicago, and that she was "about 6 or 7 years older than me," which would give a birth date for her of 1926 or 1927.[30] It is possible that she might be the Catherine whom Bill had mentioned in the Dutch jazz newsletter.

Despite these tantalizing clues, a full reckoning of the number and identities of Big Bill Broonzy's children beyond Michael van Isveldt remains, for now, an unfinished task. His grave site, by contrast, reflects the realities of his last marriage. Rose Lawson Broonzy died in Arkansas in 1997, and a graveside service was held at Lincoln Cemetery, just outside Chicago, in the plot where Bill was buried. Rose and her daughter, Hattie, share a joint gravestone, on which is carved the date of Rose's birth (although not her date of death), as well as Hattie's birth and death dates. There are two additional inscriptions on the joint gravestone: "Mother and Daughter" and "Together Forever." On Bill's separate grave, about a foot away, is carved "William L. Broonzy—Big Bill," as well as "1893–1958." The inscription above this information reads simply, "Husband."[31]

On January 20, 2009, Barack Hussein Obama took the oath of office as the forty-fourth president, and first African American president, of the United States. It had been seventy years since Bill had sung to an overflow audience at Carnegie Hall about imagining that he was in the White House, sitting in the president's chair, only to wake up and find that it was just a dream. And almost forty-five years after Bill had argued strenuously that "it will never be a black man's world," an African American had become arguably the most powerful person on the planet. If Bill had been alive to watch the ceremony, he would almost certainly have been delighted to be proven wrong as a prophet.

If he had continued to listen to the closing prayer delivered by the Reverend Joseph Lowery, he would probably have been even more surprised to hear some of his own words echoed in the minister's benediction. Bill would have heard a prayer "for that day when black will not be asked to get back, when brown can stick around, when yellow will be mellow, when the red man can get ahead, man, and when white will embrace what is right."[32] The words may not have been exactly the same, and Reverend Lowery may not have consciously quoted from Bill's song, as some of the phrases had been in use in African American circles before Bill incorporated them into his "Black, Brown, and White Blues."[33] But fifty years after his funeral, billions of people around the globe were hearing the rhythmic cadences and well-crafted insights with which Bill had captivated music fans, first in the United States, and then far beyond its borders.

AFTERWORD

As for me, I would love to pick up a book and read a story about Big Bill Broonzy. I wouldn't care if it's just a story about how I live or how drunk I was the last time that they saw Big Bill. I would enjoy reading it because it could be true.
—Big Bill Broonzy, from the "Envoi" to *Big Bill Blues*

SELECTED DISCOGRAPHY

With the convenience and popularity of purchasing music in digital files online, writing a selected discography in 2010 feels a little like writing a comparative guide to rotary-dial telephones. Still, it seems fair to assume that if you're interested in listening to Big Bill Broonzy, you're likely to be curious about the groupings of songs and additional information about his life and work that CDs can offer.

Bill's prolific recording career spanned about thirty years, from the late 1920s through 1957. In very general terms, his recordings can be divided into two categories: the material for African American audiences (late 1920s through 1951) and the material primarily intended for white audiences (1951–57). While Bill did record some sides for black record buyers after 1951—notably for Chess Records in 1953—the vast majority of his recordings once he made his first trip to Europe in the summer of 1951 were for his newer white fans in North America and overseas.

LATE 1920S THROUGH 1951

There are two multi-CD sets that cover the vast majority of the recordings Bill made in this period, and either or both of them are worth acquiring if you want to own a comprehensive compilation. Document Records offers twelve individual CDs of Bill's *Complete Recorded Works* (DOCD 5050–5052, 5126–5133, and 6047), which cover the period 1927–47. JSP presents thirteen CDs packaged into three separate boxed sets: *All the Classic Sides, 1928–1937* (JSP 7718A-E); *Part 2, Chicago and New York, 1937–1940* (JSP 7750A-D); *Volume 3: The War and Postwar Years, 1940–1951* (JSP 7767A-D). The liner notes to both the Document and the JSP sets are informative and well written (Keith Briggs for Document, Neil Slaven for JSP), while the JSP set generally has the better sound.

One other multi-CD set, on the Masters of Jazz label and covering the years 1927–35, is noteworthy: *Big Bill Broonzy, Volumes 1–7* (MJCD 51, 56, 66, 96, 109, 132, 172). André Vasset produced them and wrote the notes, which present extensive historical and discographical information about Bill and his musical colleagues of that period. Unlike Document and JSP, the set includes recordings in which Bill appears as an accompanist, in addition to ones where he is a featured performer.

The two best single-CD collections of Bill's early recordings are the Yazoo releases, *The Young Big Bill Broonzy* (Yazoo 1011) and *Do That Guitar Rag* (Yazoo 1035). Between them, they represent a total of nearly thirty tracks of Bill performing both solo and in various groupings with musicians such as Georgia Tom Dorsey and Frank Brasswell. Listeners with a musicological bent will find the notes to both CDs to be of particular interest.

There are numerous single- and double-CD reissues of Bill's recordings prior to the early 1950s. Among the single CDs worth acquiring are *Good Time Tonight* (Columbia CK 46219), *Warm, Witty & Wise* (Columbia/Legacy CK 65517), and *Big Bill Broonzy* (Topaz 1038). Solid choices among the 2-CD sets include *Where the Blues Began* (Snapper SMDCD 248) and *Chicago: 1937–1945* (Frémeaux & Associés 252). For single CDs covering his U.S. studio recordings from 1949–53, all of Bill's fine 1951 Mercury recordings are on *Black Brown and White* (Mercury 842 743-2), while *Rockin' in Chicago, 1949–1953* (CR BAND 16) presents his 1949 Mercury sides, some of the 1951 cuts, and most of the 1953 Chess sides on which he appeared.

THE YEARS 1951–57

Bill's 1950s recordings fall into two groups: the material he recorded in Europe and the recordings he made in the United States. For his European years, an excellent starting point would be the set of recordings he made for Vogue in September 1951, which are included in the 3-CD compilation *The Complete Vogue Recordings* (Sony BMG 82876643512). The 2-CD set *Amsterdam Live Concerts, 1953* (Munich MRCD 275) is essential for several reasons: the high quality of Bill's performances and of the tape recordings that preserved them, and for the superb notes by Dutch blues scholar Guido van Rijn, along with the handsomely presented photos.

Bill's recordings for white audiences in the United States in the 1950s were primarily released by Moses Asch's label, Folkways Records. The single CD *Trouble in Mind* (Smithsonian Folkways SFW 40131) presents a well-chosen variety of selections by Bill from studio sessions, conversations on Studs Terkel's WFMT radio show, and his 1956 concert with Pete Seeger. If the contents and first-rate notes by Jeff Place and Anthony Seeger whet your appetite for more, Smithsonian Folkways offers custom-burned CDs—as well as digital downloads—that replicate the Folkways LPs from which most of the tracks on *Trouble in Mind* were drawn.

In the words of Bill Randle, who supervised its production, *The Big Bill Broonzy Story* (Verve 314 547 555-2) represented Big Bill Broonzy's "last will and testament." The three-disc set presents more than three hours of Bill talking, reminiscing, singing, and playing during his final recording session in 1957. It is a remarkable listening experience, and well worth the investment of time and money.

Two other CD reissues that include contributions from Bill are worth considering. The *Blues in the Mississippi Night* session has been most recently released by Rounder (Rounder CD 82161-1860-2) as part of the Alan Lomax Collection. The liner notes include a transcription of the 1947 discussion among Bill, Memphis Slim, and Sonny Boy Williamson that was recorded by Alan Lomax, and it also includes the earliest known recording of Bill singing "Black, Brown, and White Blues." And if you are curious about Bill's appearances at the "From Spirituals to Swing" events, the 3-CD box set *From Spirituals to Swing: 1938 & 1939 Carnegie Hall Concerts* (Vanguard 169/71-2) presents his performances, along with those of the dozens of blues, jazz, and gospel artists who appeared during the two concerts.

BILL ON FILM

There are two filmed sequences of Bill playing and singing that are commercially available.

Low Light and Blue Smoke: Big Bill Blues. Filmed in Brussels in December 1955 and released in 1956. Approximately sixteen minutes long. Directed by Jean Delire; written by Jacques Boigelot; produced by Yannick Bruynoghe. Winner of the Silver Bear award, Berlin Film Festival, 1957. Features Bill playing guitar and singing four songs: "When Did You Leave Heaven?," "Just a Dream," "House Rent Stomp" (actually an instrumental version of "Hey Hey"), and "Saturday Night Blues." The full version of the movie is available on VHS on Yazoo 518, *Masters of the Country Blues: Big Bill Broonzy and Roosevelt Sykes*, and although there is also a DVD version with the same title and Yazoo catalogue number, it only contains the performances and not the entire film. The film has been posted on Google Video.

Pete Seeger's footage of Big Bill Broonzy. Filmed at Circle Pines Center in Cloverdale, Michigan, on July 6, 1957. Approximately eight minutes long. Features Bill playing and singing five songs: "Worried Man Blues" (sometimes listed as "Stump Blues"), "Hey Hey" (sometimes listed as "Guitar Shuffle"), "How You Want It Done," "John Henry," and "Blues in E." "How You Want It Done" and "Blues in E" are noteworthy because Bill clearly uses a flat pick in playing them. All five of these songs are available on VHS and DVD on Vestapol 13042, *A Musical Journey: The Films of Pete, Toshi & Dan Seeger, 1957–1964*, with informative notes by Mary Katherine Aldin that include Pete Seeger's recollections. The footage is also available on VHS and DVD on Yazoo 518, *Masters of the Country Blues: Big Bill Broonzy and Roosevelt Sykes*. Most of these segments have appeared on YouTube and Google Video, under a variety of song titles.

There are also two brief video segments with audio, each approximately two minutes long, at the beginning and end of the DVD of *The Guitar of Big Bill Broonzy* (Guitar Workshop, 802), an instructional video by Woody Mann. The first, at the very beginning of the DVD, shows Bill performing "Trouble in Mind," while in the second he performs "Backwater Blues." Although there are no specific dates or locations given either in the DVD or the accompanying booklet, Mann says in introducing "Backwater Blues" that "it's from a European video that's very rare." My guess is that both segments may well be from Bill's appearances on RAI, the Italian television network, during his visit to Milan in June 1956. André Vasset, in his section on "Film" in his memoir of Bill, *Black Brother*, specifically mentions him performing both "Trouble in Mind" and "Backwater Blues" during his appearance on RAI.

It is worth noting here that, despite what at least one blues reference volume asserts, Bill did not appear in a film titled *Swingin' the Dream* in 1939. There was a theatrical production by that name that played briefly in New York City in 1939. It was a musical version of Shakespeare's *A Midsummer Night's Dream*, starring Louis Armstrong and Butterfly McQueen, with music composed by Count Basie and Benny Goodman. The show closed after thirteen performances, and there is no surviving record of a film version.

NOTES

Chapter One

The bibliography can be found online at http//www.press.uchicago.edu/books/riesman.

1. Win Stracke to Yannick Bruynoghe, August 12 and 17, 1958, collection of Margo Bruynoghe.

2. Stracke to Bruynoghe, August 17, 1958.

3. Stracke to Bruynoghe, August 12, 1958.

4. M. W. Newman, "Big Bill's Chariot Swings Low," *Chicago Daily News*, August 20, 1958; Hoke Norris, "Big Bill Sings One More Time of His Sweet Chariot," *Chicago Sun-Times*, August 20, 1958, 3.

5. Ibid.

6. Stracke to Bruynoghe, August 17 and 30, 1958.

7. Stracke to Bruynoghe, August 30, 1958.

8. The identification of Knowling, whose face is not visible in the photo described in the text, was made after comparing his image in other photos taken that day by Mickey Pallas with confirmed photos of Knowling. As Knowling was African American, there were only three white pallbearers (Stracke, Terkel, and Roble), rather than the four that Win had anticipated in his letter of August 17 to Yannick Bruynoghe.

9. On Ransom Knowling's 1938 Social Security application, he stated that he was born on June 30, 1908, in Vicksburg, Mississippi. Recent census research by blues researchers Bob Eagle and Jim O'Neal has also identified Knowling as living in Vicksburg during his early years.

Chapter Two

1. The entry for Frank Bradley in the family record of births lists him as "F.B. Bradley."

2. On the marriage license for Frank Bradley and Anna Lou Sparks, dated August 18, 1882, Bradley's age is given as twenty-one. On the marriage license for Frank Bradley and Mattie [*sic*] Belcher dated December 26, 1889, Frank's age is given as twenty-eight. (Marriage licenses in Jefferson County Marriage Records, Arkansas History Commission, Little Rock, Arkansas.) In the 1900 U.S. census, Frank Bradley was counted in June 1900 (no specific day of the month given) in Enumeration District 98, Vaugine Township, Jefferson County, Arkansas. His age was listed as thirty-eight, with a birth date of November 1861, and both he and his parents were listed as having been born in South Carolina. In the 1910 Census, Frank Bradley was counted on April 15, 1910, in Enumeration District 104, Plum Bayou Township, Jefferson County, Arkansas. His age was listed as forty-eight, and the 1910 census form did not ask for year or month of birth. Again,

both he and his parents were listed as having been born in South Carolina. On February 9, 1920, Frank Bradley was counted in the 1920 census in Enumeration District 127, Plum Bayou Township, Jefferson County, Arkansas, and his age was listed as fifty-six. The only information listed in the 1920 census regarding the birthplaces of Frank and his parents was "United States."

There is very little information available in primary source materials about Frank Bradley's parents. In the Bradley family record for deaths, there is an entry for Mary Bradley, listed as "mother," with a date of December 12, 1881. Blues researcher Bob Eagle has identified entries in the 1870 and 1880 censuses for Frank Bradleys who were counted in South Carolina and whose ages roughly match up with that of Bill's father. The 1870 census for Sumter Township in Sumter County, South Carolina, counted a fourteen-year-old farm laborer who was the son of Henry and Elsey Bradley, and all three, as well as the couple's other four children, had been born in South Carolina. The 1880 census for Concord Township in Sumter County, South Carolina, counted a twenty-four-year-old laborer who was married to a twenty-five-year-old housekeeper, and both had been born in South Carolina. Without additional supporting evidence, there is no way to know whether these individuals had any connection to Bill's father.

3. On the 1889 marriage license, Mittie Belcher Bradley's age is given as twenty. Mittie Bradley was counted in the same 1900 census as was her husband Frank, with her birth date listed as January 1873. Her age was given as thirty-seven, which was a computational error, as the age matching her given birth year would have been twenty-seven. She reported having been born in Arkansas, as were her parents. She and Frank had been married for ten years, and she had five children, all living. The presumption that Rachel was the first child born to Mittie is based on the count of Rachel, James, Sallie, Frank Jr., and Gustavia as her five living children as of 1900.

Mittie Bradley was counted in the same 1910 census as was Frank, and her age was given as thirty-eight. Each was listed as being married for twenty years, with an indicator that it was Frank's second marriage and Mittie's first. Mittie reported that she had eight children, of whom seven were then living. Mittie and her parents were all reported to have been born in Arkansas. Mittie Bradley was counted as "Middie" in the same 1920 census as was Frank, her age was listed as forty-eight, and her birthplace was reported as Arkansas. Her father was listed as having been born in Georgia and her mother in South Carolina. Her 1956 death certificate states that she was born on March 1, 1884, in Arkansas, and that her parents were Jerry Belchaire and Caroline Jones. The informant for those data is listed as Frank Bradley, who was Bill's brother Frank Jr.

None of the family members I asked knew anything about either Jerry Belchaire or Caroline Jones, and no additional information about them that might connect them to Mittie Bradley could be located in census records. In the family death records, there is a listing for "Calaner Belcher [or Belchem]" with a death date of July 3, 1888. How, if at all, this person might be related to Mittie Bradley is not known.

4. According to the 1910 census, only seven of Mittie Bradley's eight children were living at the time of the census. A Heaster Bradley appears in the family birth records as having been born in Arkansas in 1895, but she was not enumerated in the 1900 census in which Mittie reported that she had five children, all living. The family death record has a listing for a Heaster Bradley with no date or year of death, although the listing follows one for someone who died in 1888 and precedes someone who died in 1919. It is possible that Heaster had been born in 1895 and died before the 1900 census, but that Mittie chose to wait until the 1910 census to report she had had a child who died. An

1895 birth date would have fit into the family pattern of births every two to four years that began in 1887 with Rachel and ended in 1909 with Mary.

5. "My Name is William Lee Conley Broonzy," *An Evening with Big Bill Broonzy*, vol. 2, (Storyville STCD 8017), track 9.

6. "Lannie" is the spelling that appears on Lannie Bradley Wesley's application for Social Security in 1942, as well as her 1981 death certificate. Bill spelled her name "Lanie" when he handwrote some recollections of his life for Alan Lomax in the mid-1940s. Lomax used the "Lanie" spelling in the section of his 1993 book *The Land Where the Blues Began* (New York: Delta, 1993) where he quoted Bill's writings (423), but he spelled her name "Laney" a few pages later (429–30) when he transcribed a story about her from an oral history he conducted with Bill.

7. Big Bill Broonzy and Yannick Bruynoghe, *Big Bill Blues: William Broonzy's Story as Told to Yannick Bruynoghe* (New York: Da Capo, 1992), 31–32.

8. Federal Writers' Project records, section on "General Topography," credited to "May P. Martin, P.B., F.E.C. 600," Arkansas History Commission, Little Rock, Arkansas.

9. Census data for Jefferson County 1890–1930, U.S. Census 1890–1930. Thanks to Timothy G. Nutt, Assistant Head of Special Collections at the University of Arkansas Libraries in Fayetteville, Arkansas.

	1890	1900	1910	1920	1930
White	10,951	11,146	15,038	20,824	27,003
Black	29,908	29,812	37,692	39,493	37,116
Other	22	14	4	13	35
Total	40,881	40,972	52,734	60,330	64,154
% Black	73.2%	72.8%	71.5%	65.5%	57.9%

". . . one of the largest groups of negroes in the State": Federal Writers' Project records, section on "Negro Population—Farmers," credited to "Arkansas Tours, Jefferson County, Bernice Bowden, Sept. 22, 1938," Arkansas History Commission, Little Rock, Arkansas.

10. "Negro Population—Farmers," Federal Writers' Project.

11. Sydney Nathans, "'Gotta Mind to Move, a Mind to Settle Down': African Americans and the Plantation Frontier," in *A Master's Due: Essays in Honor of David Herbert Donald*, ed. William J. Cooper Jr., Michael F. Holt, and John McCardell (Baton Rouge: Louisiana State University Press, 1985), 218, quoted in Leon Litwack, *Trouble in Mind: Black Southerners in the Age of Jim Crow* (New York: Vintage Books, 1999), 135; Robert Gordon, *Can't Be Satisfied: The Life and Times of Muddy Waters* (Boston: Little Brown, 2002), 6–9.

12. Tax Records for Jefferson County, 1900, Collection of Arkansas History Commission, Little Rock, Arkansas.

13. Broonzy oral history conducted by Alan Lomax, c. 1947, recording and forty-three-page transcript in Alan Lomax Collection, American Folklife Center, Library of Congress, segment TD100R03.

14. During the period when I was researching Big Bill Broonzy's origins, the Australian blues researcher Bob Eagle was also working on his own research into the same topic. Through his rigorous analysis of census records, he arrived at the same conclusion: that Big Bill Broonzy was the Lee Bradley who was enumerated in Jefferson County, Arkansas, in 1910 and 1920 as the son of Frank and Mittie Bradley. My thanks to Bob for his willingness to share the results of his work on Bill and his family.

15. Jo Ann Jackson and Rosie Tolbert, interview by author, January 22, 2004.

16. "Willie Mae" lyrics transcribed from *Big Bill Broonzy: Amsterdam Live Concerts 1953* (Munich Records, MRCD 275), live performance in Amsterdam, Holland, February 26, 1953.

17. A search of the Arkansas prison records from 1879–1933 does not contain any credible possibilities under the names Bradley or Broonzy. There is a listing for a Bill Belcher, a black male from Jefferson County who entered the system on August 15, 1923, but it is unlikely that he would have been incarcerated under a false name in his home county. It is also far more likely that he was in Chicago at that time, having been divorced two months before. Prison Records, Index to Prisoners, 1879–1933, Arkansas Department of Corrections, Roll 2, Arkansas History Commission, Little Rock, Arkansas.

18. The Bradley family death record in the collection of Rosie Tolbert lists death dates of February 16 [or 18?], 1926, for W. B. Bromzie, and December 16, 1926, for Mittie Bromzie. Despite the shared first name, the latter was not Bill's mother, Mittie Belcher Bradley, who died four decades later, on November 25, 1956.

19. Broonzy and Bruynoghe, *Big Bill Blues*, 32.

20. Nine-page handwritten communication from Big Bill Broonzy to Alan Lomax, and the accompanying five-page typed document with the heading, "Autobiographical pages from Big Bill Broonzy, handed Alan Lomax in pencil copy in October, 1946, and copied verbatim, ad literam by him." From Alan Lomax Collection, American Folklife Center, Library of Congress.

21. Paul Breman, interview by author, February 17, 2004.

22. *Big Bill Broonzy Interviewed by Studs Terkel* (Folkways F-3586), track 1.

23. Lomax, *Land Where the Blues Began*, 434.

24. Big Bill Broonzy, "Truth about the Blues," *Living Blues*, no. 55 (Winter 1982/83), 20. "When I came North and could not read or write and I got a job at the Iowa State College as janitor, every night it would be three or four of them [white female students] to come and teach me, because I told them I wanted to read and write and they would sit and show me."

25. Federal Writers' Project records, section on "Educational Facilities," Arkansas History Commission, Little Rock, Arkansas. The entry is credited to "Arkansas Tours, Jefferson County, Bernice Bowden, Sept. 22, 1938."

26. Federal Writers' Project records, section on "Ethnography," Arkansas History Commission, Little Rock, Arkansas, 2–3. The entry is credited to "NoVella McCracken, P.B. Ark. Dist. #2, 500 words FEC," and one of the citations in the bibliography is "Beaulah S. Hagg, Research Editor, Federal Writers' Project in Ark., Little Rock, Ark."

27. Ibid.

28. Broonzy and Bruynoghe, *Big Bill Blues*, 31.

29. Lomax, *Land Where the Blues Began*, 424–25.

30. Broonzy and Bruynoghe, *Big Bill Blues*, 31.

31. Ibid.

32. *The Big Bill Broonzy Story* (Verve CD 314 547 555-2), disc 2, track 6.

33. Broonzy and Bruynoghe, *Big Bill Blues*, 31–32; *The Big Bill Broonzy Story*, disc 2, track 6.

34. "My Name is William Lee Conley Broonzy," *An Evening with Big Bill Broonzy*, vol. 2 (Storyville STCD 8017), track 9.

35. *The Big Bill Broonzy Story*, disc 1, track 2.

36. Broonzy and Bruynoghe, *Big Bill Blues*, 55–56.

37. *The Big Bill Broonzy Story*, disc 1, track 2.

38. Ibid., disc 1, tracks 2 and 4.

Chapter Three

1. Broonzy and Bruynoghe, *Big Bill Blues*, 68.

2. Lomax, *Land Where the Blues Began*, 427. A biography of Grand Ole Opry star Roy Acuff, who was born the same year as Bill, contains a description of his experience with such an instrument, which was very likely based on Acuff's recollections: "During the summer the children would often make cornstalk fiddles. The pulp would be cleaned out with a length of stalk and the remaining stringly [*sic*] fibers were 'played' with a stick. It was impossible to get any real music out of one of these contraptions, of course, but everybody tried, including Roy." Elizabeth Schlappi, *Roy Acuff: The Smoky Mountain Boy* (Gretna, LA: Pelican, 1978), 8. A 1945 biography of scientist George Washington Carver includes a brief mention of the instrument in a description of Carver's childhood in the years following the end of the Civil War: "Little boys made cornstalk fiddles the same way little girls made rag dolls. 'Cornstalk fiddles and ransum bow makes the best old music you ever did know.' Young stalks had a better resonance than old, dried ones, and with a bow strung from the wisp of a horse's tail George could produce a sort of rhythm to jig to." Rackham Holt, *George Washington Carver: An American Biography* (New York: Doubleday, 1945), 18.

3. Lomax's handwritten notes from his interview with Bill only include the first verse of "Uncle Bud"; he added the second verse in his chapter on Bill in *Land Where the Blues Began*. Twelve-page set of handwritten notes on legal-size paper by Alan Lomax titled "Big Bill," on conversation/oral history with Big Bill Broonzy, c. 1947, Alan Lomax Collection, American Folklife Center, Library of Congress.

"Uncle Bud" was identified by numerous folk-song collectors in the 1920s and '30s, and a version was published in 1926 by Texas folklorist Gates Thomas: "South Texas Negro Work Songs: Collected and Uncollected," in *Publications of the Texas Folk-Lore Society*, no. 5, ed. Frank Dobie (Austin, 1926), 180.

Folklorist and author Zora Neale Hurston, who had collected a version of "Uncle Bud" in Florida while working for the Federal Writers' Project in the late 1930s, recorded her comments on the song and performed nearly a dozen verses for the Library of Congress in 1939. As she described it: "'Uncle Bud' is not a work song. It's a sort of social song for amusement, and it's so widely distributed, it's growing all the time by incremental repetition. And it is known all over the South. No matter where you go, you can find verses of 'Uncle Bud.'" When she was then asked, "Is it sung before the respectable ladies?" she replied emphatically, "Never! It's one of those jook songs. And the woman that they sing 'Uncle Bud' in front of is a jook woman." Readers who are interested are encouraged to listen to the full recording on the Library of Congress website, with the advance knowledge that the content is earthy. Zora Neale Hurston, Library of Congress recording, June 18, 1939, Florida Folklife from the WPA Collections, call number: AFS 3138A:1, digital ID: afcflwpa 3138a1, http://hdl.loc.gov/loc.afc/afcflwpa.3138a1, http://tinyurl.com/yztp989 (accessed on May 22, 2010).

4. Broonzy, nine-page handwritten manuscript to Lomax, Lomax Collection, 3.

5. Broonzy, "Baby, I Done Got Wise," *Jazz Record*, no. 42 (March 1946): 9.

6. Ibid. Thanks to one of my anonymous peer reviewers for the insight about the nickname. Ma Rainey had recorded a commercially successful version of "See See Rider" in 1924. Gates Thomas had also published a locally collected version of the song in his

1926 article for the Texas Folklore Society, which included a verse with the line "I'm a-gwain' to San 'Tonio, to see my soldier man." Thomas, "South Texas Negro Work Songs," 179. In the 1950s, Bill added "See See Rider" to his repertoire, along with comments both about the person named See See Rider and Ma Rainey's hit recording.

7. Broonzy, nine-page handwritten manuscript to Lomax, Lomax Collection, 4–7.

8. The 1900 Sears catalogue, in fact, presented two-page spreads on both fiddles and guitars. In each case, the write-ups highlighted the "liberal terms" for an instrument costing $7.85, which included "5 days trial free" if payment was sent in full. With six types of fiddles ranging from a "genuine Stradivarius model" for $2.50 to a top-of-the-line instrument for $9.60, and five guitar options priced nearly identically to those for the fiddles, there was an attractive set of choices for aspiring musicians. Thanks to Alan Balfour for providing this information.

9. Big Bill Broonzy Interviewed by Studs Terkel (Folkways F-3586), track 2.

10. Charles Edward Smith and Moses Asch, "Interviews with Big Bill Broonzy as Part of Recording Session for Big Bill Sings Country Blues," Smithsonian Folklife Reel RR-140, c. 1956, Collection of Smithsonian Folkways Records.

11. Chip Deffaa, "Ruth Brown: 'Nobody Knows You . . . ,'" in Blue Rhythms: Six Lives in Rhythm and Blues (New York: Da Capo, 2000), 39. Photographer and journalist Birney Imes has documented in words and images a roadside tavern in his native Mississippi called the Whispering Pines, where a version of this segregation endured even longer. Imes wrote of how in the mid-1970s he came "to stumble upon the place—the 'Eppie's Eats' sign out front, the rusting cars, the hedge in the parking lot dividing the White Side and the Black Side." Imes noted that blues guitarist Big Joe Williams, who was born in and often returned to nearby Crawford, referred to it in his song "Whistling Pines" (sic): "Think about the good times we had in Crawford, Mississippi, boys, runnin' round by Whistlin' Pines." Birney Imes, Whispering Pines (Oxford: University Press of Mississippi, 1994), 75.

12. Broonzy oral history, segment TD100R03, Lomax Collection.

13. Ibid.

14. Jim O'Neal and Amy van Singel, The Voice of the Blues: Classic Interviews from Living Blues Magazine (New York: Routledge, 2002), 51–52.

15. Ibid., 79, 81–82.

16. Paul Oliver, Conversation with the Blues (Cambridge: Cambridge University Press, 1965), 47.

17. David Evans, "Charley Patton: The Conscience of the Delta," in The Voice of the Delta: Charley Patton and the Mississippi Blues Traditions: Influences and Comparisons, ed. Robert Sacré (Liège: Presses Universitaires, 1987), 157.

18. W. C. Handy, Father of the Blues: An Autobiography (New York: Da Capo, 1991), 76–77.

19. Broonzy, interview by Asch and Smith, Smithsonian Folkways Collection.

20. The Big Bill Broonzy Story, disc 2, track 6.

21. Benjamin E. Mays, Born to Rebel: An Autobiography (New York: Charles Scribner's Sons, 1971), 11, quoted in Litwack, Trouble in Mind, 380.

22. Broonzy and Bruynoghe, Big Bill Blues, 35.

23. Broonzy oral history, segment TD100R03.

24. Lomax recording of Blues in the Mississippi Night materials, segment TD099R01, Lomax Collection. There were two well-known blues harmonica players who performed for several decades in the twentieth century using the name "Sonny Boy Williamson."

The one whom Alan Lomax recorded in this session, and who was a musical colleague and friend of Bill's, was John Lee Williamson (1914–1948). Over time he became variously identified by blues fans and historians as Sonny Boy No. 1, Sonny Boy No. One, or Sonny Boy Williamson I. This was done to distinguish him from Rice Miller (born Aleck Ford, c. 1912–1965), who appropriated the name of the successful recording artist. Rice Miller, who became prominent in the United States and Europe on the basis of his own considerable talents, came to be referred to as Sonny Boy No. 2. Throughout this book, all references to "Sonny Boy Williamson" describe John Lee Williamson. For an excellent introduction to the two men's careers, see the section on each musician by Chris Smith in Tony Russell and Chris Smith, with Neil Slaven, Ricky Russell, and Joe Faulkner, *The Penguin Guide to Blues Recordings* (London: Penguin, 2006).

25. "Conversation Continues," *Blues in the Mississippi Night* (Rounder CD 82161-1860-2), track 6.

26. John Cowley, "Shack Bullies and Levee Contractors—Black Protest Songs and Oral History, Part 1," *Juke Blues*, no. 3 (December 1985): 8; "Shack Bullies and Levee Contractors—Black Protest Songs and Oral History, Part 2," which contains the bibliography, appeared in *Juke Blues*, no. 4 (March 1986): 9–15.

27. H. N. Olds, *Report of Preliminary Sanitary Surveys of Labor Camps Maintained by Contractors Engaged in Mississippi Flood Control Operations, 1929–1930*, U.S. National Archives, record group 90, United States Public Health Service Files for 1924–1935, box 43, quoted in Cowley, "Shack Bullies, Part 1," 8.

28. Roy Wilkins, "Mississippi Slavery in 1933," *Crisis: A Record of the Darker Races* 40, no. 4 (April 1933): 81–82, quoted in Cowley, "Shack Bullies, Part 1," 9.

29. Alison Davis, Burleigh Gardner, and Mary R. Gardner, *Deep South* (Chicago: University of Chicago Press, 1941), 439–41, quoted in Cowley, "Shack Bullies, Part 1," 10.

30. Broonzy, nine-page 1946 handwritten manuscript to Alan Lomax, 8–9, Lomax Collection.

31. Broonzy oral history, segment TD101R02, Lomax Collection.

32. Combination of oral history and handwritten communication, Lomax Collection.

33. Broonzy oral history, segment TD101R02.

34. Ibid.

35. Guido van Rijn, *Roosevelt's Blues* (Jackson: University Press of Mississippi, 1997), 6.

36. Broonzy oral history, segment TD102R01.

37. Ibid.

38. Lomax twelve-page handwritten notes on oral history.

39. James Bradley World War I draft registration card, Arkansas History Commission, Little Rock, Arkansas.

40. Robert B. Edgerton, *Hidden Heroism: Black Soldiers in America's Wars* (Boulder, CO: Westview Press, 2001), 74.

41. Arthur E. Barbeau and Florette Henri, *The Unknown Soldiers: Black American Troops in World War One* (Philadelphia: Temple University Press, 1974), 194.

42. Library of Congress website, http://memory.loc.gov/ammem/aaohtml/exhibit/aopart7.html (accessed on November 2, 2007); Edgerton, *Hidden Heroism*, 76.

43. Broonzy oral history, segments TD102R01 and TD102R02.

44. Barbeau and Henri, *Unknown Soldiers*, 177–78.

45. Broonzy oral history, segment TD106R01.

46. "When Will I Get to be Called a Man" (Folkways FA 2326). Lyrics taken from *Big Bill Blues*, 70. Bill stated in *Big Bill Blues* that he wrote the song in 1928, but he first recorded the song in Great Britain in 1955 (Nixa EP 1005, recorded October 27, 1955).

47. Broonzy and Bruynoghe, *Big Bill Blues*, 71.

48. Editorial in *Hot Springs (Arkansas) Echo*, 1919 (no date), quoted in Robert T. Kerlin, *The Voice of the Negro, 1919* (New York: Dutton, 1920), 72–73.

49. "Negro Drowns While Working on Revetment," *Pine Bluff Commercial*, April 14, 1919, 4.

50. Death certificate for James Bradley, dated April 15, 1919, Arkansas Department of Health, Bureau of Vital Statistics.

51. "Negro Drowns While Working on Revetment," *Pine Bluff Commercial*.

52. "Fail to Find Body of Negro," *Pine Bluff Daily Graphic*, April 15, 1919.

53. "Body of Negro Who Drowned Thursday Recovered Today," *Pine Bluff Commercial*, April 15, 1919.

54. "Recover Body of Jim Bradley," *Pine Bluff Daily Graphic*, April 16, 1919.

Chapter Four

1. Marriage license and marriage certificate for Lee Bradley and Gertrude Emery in Jefferson County Marriage Records, Arkansas History Commission. Gertrude was counted as Gertrude Embrey on February 5, 1920, in Enumeration District 127, Plum Bayou Township, Jefferson County.

2. Broonzy and Bruynoghe, *Big Bill Blues*, 61, 62.

3. Ibid., 63.

4. The 1911 date from a one-page document with typewritten questions that Lomax had asked Bill, based on information Bill had provided to him, with Bill's handwritten responses, Alan Lomax Collection. The 1914 date and "I was a good Christian" quote from the twelve-page set of handwritten notes by Lomax, Alan Lomax Collection. Bill also wrote in 1955 to a researcher seeking information for a book on folk music that in 1916 he had married "Guitrue Embria" in Pine Bluff. Big Bill Broonzy file, Ray M. Lawless Collection, American Folklife Center, Library of Congress.

5. Broonzy and Bruynoghe, *Big Bill Blues*, 35.

6. Ibid.

7. Ibid., 35–36. According to the Consumer Price Index Inflation Calculator website, maintained by the U.S. Bureau of Labor Statistics, http://data.bls.gov/cgi-bin/cpicalc.pl (accessed on June 5, 2010), which adjusts prices for inflation based on historical data from the Consumer Price Index (CPI), the $50 gig in 1920 was worth $545.02 in 2010 dollars. Even before Bill and his buddy got their new instruments, they would have made the equivalent of more than $250 each for a four-day gig. If Bill's memory for the amount of the payment was at all accurate, it underscores the attraction of the secular choice to Gertrude and Bill.

8. Broonzy oral history, segment TD102R02.

9. Lomax, *Land Where Blues Began*, 436.

10. Broonzy oral history, segment TD103R01.

11. Entry on Stuart Pryce by Judith Kilpatrick, professor at the University of Arkansas Law School, on her website www.arkansasblacklawyers.net (accessed June 5, 2010). The data on the number of black lawyers in Arkansas appear in the notes on Carter Godwin Woodson, *The Negro Professional Man and the Community* (Washington,

D.C.: Association for the Study of Negro Life and History, 1934) that Professor Kilpatrick was kind enough to share with me.

12. *Gertrude Bradley, Plaintiff, vs. Lee Bradley, Defendant*, Complaint in Equity, Jefferson County Court Records, Pine Bluff, Arkansas.

13. Waiver in case of *Gertrude Bradley vs. Lee Bradley*, notarized on June 19, 1923.

14. Case no. 9874, *Gertrude Bradley vs. Lee Bradley*.

15. Case no. 9874, *Gertrude Bradley vs. Lee Bradley*, Jefferson County Court House Records.

16. Charles F. Robinson, "'Most Shamefully Common': Arkansas and Miscegenation," *Arkansas Historical Quarterly* 60, no. 3 (Autumn 2001): 276.

17. Broonzy oral history, segment TD102R02.

18. Ibid., segment TD102R01.

19. Litwack, *Trouble in Mind*, 429.

20. *Chicago Defender*, February 24, 1917, quoted in Douglas Bukowski, *Big Bill Thompson, Chicago, and the Politics of Image* (Urbana: University of Illinois Press, 1998), 93.

21. Liner notes to *Blues in the Mississippi Night* (Rounder CD 82116-1860-2), "Conversation Continues," track 17.

22. Richard Wright, *Black Boy (American Hunger)* (New York: Harper Perennial, 1993), 307–8.

23. Broonzy oral history, segment TD103R01.

24. St. Clair Drake and Horace Cayton, *Black Metropolis: A Study of Negro Life in a Northern City* (Chicago: University of Chicago Press, 1993), 221.

25. James R. Grossman, *Land of Hope: Chicago, Black Southerners, and the Great Migration* (Chicago: University of Chicago Press, 1989), 129.

26. Drake and Cayton, *Black Metropolis*, 228, 235.

27. Broonzy oral history, segment TD103R01.

28. Robert M. W. Dixon and John Godrich, "Recording the Blues," in *Yonder Come the Blues: The Evolution of a Genre*, by Paul Oliver, Tony Russell, Robert M. W. Dixon, John Godrich, and Howard Rye (Cambridge: Cambridge University Press, 2001), 251.

29. Chris Smith, liner notes to *Papa Charlie Jackson, Complete Recorded Works in Chronological Order, Vol. 1, 1924 to February 1926*, Document DOCD-5087.

30. Broonzy, "Baby, I Done Got Wise," 9.

31. Martin Bauml Duberman, *Paul Robeson* (New York: Knopf, 1988), 34.

32. Elliott S. Hurwitt, "Black Swan Records," in *Encyclopedia of the Blues*, vol. 1, ed. Edward Komara (New York: Routledge, 2006), 95.

33. Stephen Calt, "Anatomy of a 'Race' Label: Part 2," *78 Quarterly* 1, no. 4 (1989): 13.

34. Alex van der Tuuk, *Paramount's Rise and Fall* (Denver: Mainspring Press, 2003), 63–66; Calt, "Anatomy," 13–14.

35. Calt, "Anatomy," 24.

36. According to the book by Chicago political scientist Milton Rakove, who used it as the book's title, the phrase came from a story told by Abner Mikva. Mikva—who would go on to a distinguished career as a U.S. congressman, federal judge, and White House counsel in the Clinton administration—told of his unsuccessful attempt as an eager young law student to contribute his efforts to the Illinois Democratic Party in 1948. Hoping to work in support of a ticket that included Paul Douglas and Adlai Stevenson, both from the liberal wing of the party, Mikva went into the storefront office

of the Eighth Ward Regular Democratic Organization. When he said he wanted to help, there was "dead silence. 'Who sent you?' the committeeman said. I said, 'Nobody.' He said, 'We don't want nobody nobody sent.'" Milton Rakove, *We Don't Want Nobody Nobody Sent: An Oral History of the Daley Years* (Bloomington: Indiana University Press, 1979), 318.

37. Broonzy oral history, segment TD103R02.

38. Broonzy, "Baby, I Done Got Wise," 9.

39. Broonzy oral history, segment TD103R02.

40. Drake and Cayton, *Black Metropolis*, 184.

41. Quoted in O'Neal and Van Singel, *Voice of the Blues*, 23.

42. Paul Oliver, *Blues Fell This Morning: Meaning in the Blues* (Cambridge: Cambridge University Press, 1990), 150.

43. "Big Bill Blues," recorded c. February 1928 (Paramount 12656), lyrics from R. R. MacLeod, *Document Blues—2* (Edinburgh: PAT Publications, 1995), 14–15. Bill may have gotten the idea from the first two lines of Blind Lemon Jefferson's recording of his "Long Lonesome Blues," recorded c. May 1926 (Paramount 12354): "Tell me what's the matter, since I can't get no mail / Won't you tell me what's the matter, Papa Lemon can't get no mail." Bill's third line, though, bears his own stamp, as Blind Lemon sings, "Mama, dreamt last night, saw a black cat cross your trail." R. R. MacLeod, *Document Blues—1* (Edinburgh: PAT Publications, 1994), 154. The opening word "Mean" that Bill sings at the beginning of several lines is an abbreviated version of the phrase, "I mean."

44. Broonzy and Bruynoghe, *Big Bill Blues*, 46–47.

45. Ibid., 46–47.

46. Ibid, 46.

47. Broonzy, "Baby, I Done Got Wise," 9.

Chapter Five

1. "It's Tight Like That" (Vocalion 1216); lyrics from R. R. MacLeod, *Document Blues—2* (Edinburgh: PAT Publications, 1995), 321–22.

2. O'Neal and Van Singel, *Voice of the Blues*, 31.

3. Ibid. There were two men named Nix who were active in the black sacred music community at that time, and years later Dorsey was unable to be certain which one he had seen. When he was asked by an interviewer whether it was the Reverend A. W. Nix, who was an influential recording artist from 1927 to 1931, Dorsey replied that it was, "or, if it wasn't him, it was his brother. There was two Nix. One was a great singer, and then one was a preacher." Ibid., 31–32.

4. Mark Humphrey, *Tampa Red: The Bluebird Recordings 1934–1936* (RCA CD 078563-66721-2).

5. Michael W. Harris, *The Rise of Gospel Blues: The Music of Thomas Andrew Dorsey in the Urban Church* (New York: Oxford University Press, 1992), 139.

6. Ibid., 129.

7. Ibid., 148.

8. O'Neal and Van Singel, *Voice of the Blues*, 19–20.

9. *Chicago Defender*, November 24, 1928.

10. "Maltese Cat Blues," recorded c. August 1928 (Paramount 12712). As Luigi Monge and David Evans have documented, Jefferson also recorded an unissued song with the title "It's Tight Like That," most likely in July or August 1928. As they point out, Tampa Red and Georgia Tom's song is "musically and textually entirely different from

Jefferson's song." Monge and Evans, "New Songs of Blind Lemon Jefferson," *Journal of Texas Music History* 3, no. 2 (Fall 2003): 22. Louis Armstrong's spoken introduction to "Tight Like This," cited in Tom Fisher, "Tight Like That," in *Encyclopedia of the Blues*, vol. 2, ed. Edward Komara (New York: Routledge, 2006), 992. Blind Blake had also recorded a popular song titled "Too Tight" in 1926.

A measure of the success of Georgia Tom and Tampa Red's "It's Tight Like That" could be seen in the title of a record made two years later by the African American preacher Reverend J. M. Gates. By titling his sermon "These Hard Times Are Tight Like That," December 12, 1930 (OKeh 8850), Rev. Gates provided a fine illustration of the trend among black clergy making commercial recordings to make topical and often risqué references as a way to sell records. Alluding to a hit song was an effective way to connect with potential record buyers.

11. Harris, *Rise of Gospel Blues*, 148.

12. New release in January 29, 1929, Paramount dealers' list; first ad in *Chicago Defender* on January 12, 1929; cited by Max Vreede, *Paramount 12000/13000 Series* (London: Storyville, 1971).

13. "Down in the Basement," c. October 1928 (Paramount 12707); lyrics from R. R. MacLeod, *Yazoo 1–20* (Edinburgh: PAT Publications, 1992), 139; "Starvation Blues," c. October 1928 (Paramount 12707); lyrics from MacLeod, *Yazoo 21–83*, 2nd ed. (Edinburgh: PAT Publications, 2002), 105.

14. Lester Melrose, "My Life in Recording," *American Folk Music Occasional*, no. 2 (1970): 59.

15. Howard Reich and William Gaines, *Jelly's Blues: The Life, Music, and Redemption of Jelly Roll Morton* (New York: Da Capo, 2003), 76.

16. Melrose, "My Life in Recording," 59.

17. Melrose had some talent for storytelling himself. He described Morton's visit to the store this way: "One day a man wearing a Western-style hat with a red bandanna around his neck walked into our store and announced that he was Jelly Roll Morton, the greatest stomp and blues piano player this side of New Orleans. Cassius Clay had nothing on Jelly Roll!" Melrose, "My Life in Recording," 59–60.

18. Ibid., 60.

19. In his authoritative discography *Hit the Right Lick: The Recordings of Big Bill Broonzy* (Bromham, UK: Blues & Rhythm Magazine, 1996), Chris Smith presents a thorough discussion on page 16 of the recordings to which Bill may have been referring.

20. Contract dated October 15, 1929, Bill Randle Collection.

21. Stephen Calt and Gayle Dean Wardlow, "Paramount's Decline and Fall: Part 5," *78 Quarterly* 1, no. 7 (1992): 16.

22. Dixon and Godrich, "Recording the Blues," 295–301.

23. Melrose, "My Life in Recording," 60.

24. It likely also included Melrose's brother, jazz pianist Frank Melrose, who recorded several sides on piano during the week in New York.

25. Mention of Ford in undated notes by John Steiner on conversation with Thomas A. Dorsey, Collection of Chicago Jazz Archive, University of Chicago Library.

26. A "Frank Braswell" was listed in the 1928 Chicago city directory as renting an apartment at 235 East 51st Street. In a 1930 contract with Lester Melrose, his typed name appeared as "Frank Braswell," and his signature reads "James F. Braswell." In addition, Chris Smith has identified a James Braswell in Chicago in the 1930 census living at 4726 State Street. He was thirty years old and came from North Carolina, a fact that

Smith suggests may shed some light on Braswell's guitar skills, as that region was noted for producing excellent guitarists who played in a ragtime style. Personal communication with Chris Smith.

27. Comments contained in DVD of *The Guitar of Big Bill Broonzy*, by Woody Mann, Guitar Workshop 802.

28. Ibid.

29. "Eagle Riding Papa," April 9, 1930 (Banner 0712); lyrics from MacLeod, *Yazoo 1–20*, 104–5.

30. "Grandma's Farm," April 9, 1930 (Perfect 187); lyrics from MacLeod, *Yazoo 21–83*, 143.

31. The full listing is as follows: Brasswell: "Western Blues," "Mountain Girl Blues," and interestingly, one of the hot instrumentals, "Black Cat Rag." Broonzy: "Guitar Rag," "Pig Meat Strut," "Bowleg Blues," "Tad Pole Blues," "Grandmas [*sic*] Farm," "I Cant [*sic*] Be Satisfied," and "Skoodle Do Do." Contract in Bill Randle Collection.

32. In the 1930 census for Cook County in Chicago, Andrew and Mary Bradley were counted in Enumeration District 11-146, while Mattie and Ben Burford were counted in Enumeration District 16-86.

33. Rick Kennedy, introduction to *Jelly Roll, Bix, and Hoagy: Gennett Studios and the Birth of Recorded Jazz* (Bloomington: Indiana University Press, 1994).

34. Ibid., 145–46.

35. "Pussy Cat, Pussy Cat," September 15, 1930 (Banner 32138); lyrics from MacLeod, *Yazoo 21–83*, 144.

36. "What You Call That," September 15, 1930 (Banner 32138), on *Big Bill Broonzy: Volume 2, 1930* (Masters of Jazz MJCD 56).

37. Robert M. W. Dixon, John Godrich, and Howard Rye, in *Blues and Gospel Records, 1890–1943*, 4th ed. (Oxford: Oxford University Press, 1997), 3–6—the primary discographical reference volume for blues research—cite quotes from both Dorsey and Bill to support the judgment that the singer who had recorded as "Hannah May" in these sessions was a singer named Mozelle Alderson. Dixon, Godrich, and Rye also note that Alderson was likely the singer who recorded as Jane Lucas and Kansas City Kitty in sessions that included Bill in November 1930 and c. January 1931.

38. "Terrible Operation Blues," September 17, 1930 (Perfect 169); lyrics from MacLeod, *Yazoo 21–83*, 139–40.

39. Stephen Calt and Woody Mann, *Big Bill Broonzy: Do That Guitar Rag, 1928–1935* (Yazoo L-1035).

40. "Police Station Blues," September 16, 1930 (Perfect 199); lyrics from MacLeod, *Document Blues—2*, 16; "They Can't Do That," September 16, 1930 (Perfect 199); lyrics from ibid., 16–17. Bill may have listened to Clarence "Pine Top" Smith's recording "Big Boy They Can't Do That," recorded the year before. In the song, which has its origins in a hobo's recitation, the singer describes numerous instances of unjust treatment by judges, jailers, and fellow prisoners, all dismissed with the ironic comment, "Big boy, they can't do that." "Big Boy, They Can't Do That," January 15, 1929 (Vocalion 1256); lyrics from R. R. MacLeod, *Document Blues—3* (Edinburgh: PAT Publications, 1995), 196–97.

41. André Vasset, liner notes to *Big Bill Broonzy*, vol. 3 (Masters of Jazz MJCD 66).

42. Broonzy oral history, segment TD104R02, Lomax Collection. Bill may have incorporated into his recollections a memory of listening to Blind Blake's 1927 recording of "Sea Board Stomp." During the course of the three-minute song, Blake, playing only

his guitar, announced each section as a re-creation of performances by musicians play-ing, in succession, a piano, a cornet, a trombone, and a saxophone.

43. Samuel B. Charters, *The Country Blues* (New York: Rinehart, 1959), 171.

Chapter Six

1. Dixon, Godrich, and Rye, *Blues and Gospel Records*, xxiii.

2. Alex van der Tuuk, *Paramount's Rise and Fall* (Denver: Mainspring Press, 2003), 170.

3. Dixon, Godrich, and Rye, *Blues and Gospel Records*, identify the singer performing as "Jane Lucas" as being Mozelle Alderson. See note 37 in chapter 5.

4. "Station Blues" is likely a version of "Police Station Blues," although this is dif-ficult to confirm because no copy of the recording (Paramount 13084) has ever been found.

5. Bill's handwritten responses to typed form sent by Alan Lomax, Lomax Collec-tion.

6. Drake and Cayton, table 8, "Manual Labor Jobs with Highest Proportion of Ne-gro Men," in *Black Metropolis*, 222.

7. Ibid., table 24, "Percentage Distribution of Family Income in Chicago, 1935–36," 513. Also, table 8 shows that for laborers in steel mills, the "relatively good pay" was one of the "desirable aspects of [the] job."

8. Allan H. Spear, *Black Chicago: The Making of a Negro Ghetto, 1890–1920* (Chicago: University of Chicago Press, 1967), 157.

9. Royalty statement reproduced in notes to *Georgia Tom & Friends* (Riverside LP 8803). The biggest sellers were "Somebody's Been Using That Thing"/"My Texas Blues" (Champion 15794) at 1,221 copies, and "Broke Man's Blues"/"All Alone Blues" (Cham-pion 15903) at 1,169 copies. Dorsey received a total of 2 cents (1 cent per side) for "My Texas Blues"/"Eagle Ridin' Papa" (Gennett 6919), which sold one copy. However, the version of "Eagle Ridin' Papa"/"Broke Man's Blues" (Champion 15834) sold 863 copies, likely because it was issued on the cheaper label.

10. Royalty statement from Starr Piano Company to Thomas Dorsey & Co., 448 E. 40th St., Chicago, Ill., John Steiner Collection, Chicago Jazz Archive, University of Chicago Library. This time no record sold more than 1,000 copies, with "Maybe It's the Blues"/"Second Hand Love" (Champion 15994), recorded at the February 5, 1930, ses-sion in Richmond, Indiana—where Dorsey got the $50 advance—leading the way with sales of 908 copies.

11. According to the 1930 census, Smith was unusual among early (and many later) blues recording artists in that he owned his home at 3702 South Ellis Avenue in Chicago, which was valued at $10,000. He gave his occupation as "Musician, orchestra" and was born Steele J. Smith in North Carolina in about 1893. He had previously lived in Kansas and was married with six children ranging in ages from three to eighteen. Thanks to Bob Eagle for sharing his research on this.

12. Calt and Mann, liner notes to *Do That Guitar Rag* (Yazoo L-1035).

13. Mann's comments from phone interview by author July 12, 2006, instructional DVD *The Guitar of Big Bill Broonzy*, Guitar Workshop 802, and *Six Black Blues Guitarists* (New York: Oak Publications, 1973), 40.

14. Rukus (pronounced ROO-kis) juice was an alcoholic drink produced by ferment-ing a variety of crops commonly grown on farms for sale or for feed. Bill recorded an

ode to it, "Rukus Juice Blues," the following day, in which he declared, "Rukus juice I cry, rukus juice I crave," and added, "I wants the whole round world to know Big Bill's a rukus juice man." Years later Bill told Studs Terkel how it was made: "And back in those times they had those silos built that they put the sorghum, corn, and different stuff in, silo for the food for the different animals they had for winter. And I know that they used to take what they call a brace and bit, and they would bore a hole in the bottom of that thing, that silo. And that juice that would run down from that corn and that sorghum, and they would get it out of the bottom of that silo. And that's where the word rukus juice come from. Cause practically everything was in this silo, and the juice from the different things, they would draw that out and drink it." *The Big Bill Broonzy Story*, spoken introduction to "Crawdad Song," disc 3, track 9.

15. Marshall Wyatt, liner notes to *Folks, He Sure Do Pull Some Bow* (Old Hat CD-1003).

16. Dixon and Godrich, "Recording the Blues," 295–309.

17. Melrose, "My Life," 60.

18. Tony Russell, *The Blues from Robert Johnson to Robert Cray* (New York: Shirmer Books, 1997), 52.

19. Peter Guralnick, *The Listener's Guide to the Blues* (New York: Facts on File, 1982), 62.

20. Broonzy, "Baby, I Done Got Wise," 10.

21. *The Big Bill Broonzy Story*, disc 2, track 17.

22. April 11, 1930, ARC session in New York City: "Tadpole Blues" and "Bow Leg Baby," released as Sammy Sampson (Dorsey is listed by Dixon, Godrich, and Rye, *Blues and Gospel Records, 1890–1943*, 4th ed., and Smith, *Hit the Right Lick*, as probable, and by Vasset, *Black Brother*, as definite); September 17, 1930, ARC session in New York, "State Street Woman," "Meanest Kind of Blues," and "I Got the Blues for My Baby," released as Sammy Sampson. Bill backed Dorsey on a November 20, 1930, Gennett session in Richmond, Indiana: "Don't Leave Me Blues" and "Been Mistreated Blues."

23. Quoted in O'Neal and Van Singel, *Voice of the Blues*, 26. Dorsey goes on to note that this was not an exclusive arrangement with Bill: "Not only Bill, anybody, Frankie Jaxon or any of 'em."

24. Dixon, Godrich, and Rye, *Blues and Gospel Records*, and Smith, *Hit the Right Lick*, identify James (Jimmie) Gordon, who recorded for Bluebird later the same day, as the accompanist. André Vasset, who compiled a Broonzy discography as part of his memoir of Bill titled *Black Brother: La vie & l'oeuvre de Big Bill Broonzy* (Gerzat, France: Decombat, 1996), believes the session is the first collaboration between Bill and a pianist known as Black Bob, with whom Bill and others recorded frequently in the 1930s.

25. Paul Oliver, *The Story of the Blues* (Boston: Northeastern University Press, 1997), 112.

26. "Hungry Man Blues," March 23, 1934 (Bluebird B5706); lyrics from MacLeod, *Document Blues—2*, 28.

27. "Bull Cow Blues—Part 2," March 23, 1934 (Bluebird B5476); lyrics from ibid., 29.

28. "Starvation Blues," March 23, 1934 (Bluebird B5706); lyrics from ibid., 30–31.

29. "Serve It to Me Right," March 23, 1934 (Bluebird B5674); lyrics from ibid., 29–30.

30. "Milk Cow Blues," March 23, 1934 (Bluebird B5476); lyrics from ibid., 27–28.

31. "Mississippi River Blues," March 23, 1934 (Bluebird B5535); lyrics from MacLeod, *Yazoo 1–20*, 110.

32. Form SS-5 for Robert Brown, issued June 28, 1937. The Social Security number for Robert Brown that I used when I requested a copy of his SS-5 form from the Social Security Administration was the one I found in the RCA files at the Country Music Hall of Fame and Museum in Nashville, Tennessee. The session logs from two different RCA Washboard Sam recording sessions in the fall of 1947 list the same Social Security number and Chicago street address for Robert Brown, whose instrument is listed as "Vocal & Washboard" in each case.

This birth data about Washboard Sam differs from previously available information. The liner notes to the 2-CD set *Washboard Sam: Swinging the Blues, 1935–1947* (Frémeaux & Associés FA 263) identify a birth date for Robert Brown of July 15, 1910, in Walnut Ridge, Arkansas, and list his father as unknown and his mother at age sixteen with no occupation. The source cited is a birth certificate that was located by a researcher named Bill Benson, and the notes themselves are credited as "adapted by Frank Robinson from the French by Gérard Herzhaft."

It is reasonable to conclude that the 1937 SS-5 form contains the information about the Robert Brown who performed as Washboard Sam. The Social Security number is clearly the one that Washboard Sam had ten years later. In addition, while there may have been an incentive for him to make himself appear older than he was in order to get Social Security benefits, it seems unlikely that in the second year after its introduction he would have been trying to game the system for benefits he wouldn't receive for another three decades.

Also, the reason a blues researcher would have been looking for a birth certificate for Robert Brown in Walnut Ridge, Arkansas, was that Bill had mentioned that town by name in his tale about Sam being his father's illegitimate son. But Yannick Bruynoghe, in his "Additional Biographical Notes" to a U.S. edition of *Big Bill Blues* (New York: Oak Publications, 1964), expressed his view that Bill's story about "his half-brotherhood" with Sam was "inspired by imagination or pure fantasy" (150). Bill often used specific but inaccurate information about dates and locations to add verisimilitude to his tales, with the best example being the date and location of his own birth. Yannick Bruynoghe, along with his wife, Margo, probably spent more time with Bill than any other non-family member in the 1950s, and I am inclined to give significant weight to his assessment of Bill's tale.

33. *Washboard Sam: Swinging the Blues.*

34. Gillum's Illinois death certificate (with a date of death of March 29, 1966) listed September 11, 1904, as his birth date, with the information provided by his daughter, Rose M. Williams. It was also the date Gillum gave to Raeburn "Ray" Flerlage and his wife, Iola Swan Flerlage, in the September 3, 1961, interview that is the most comprehensive source of information about his life. Much of the interview was published in the liner notes to *Blues by Jazz Gillum* (Folkways FS 3826). It should be noted that Gillum's SS-5 form, dated June 30, 1937, listed his birth date as September 15, 1902, born in Indianola, Mississippi, to Irvin [sic] Gillum and Celia Buchanan. It also listed his present employer as "W.P.A. Project No. 122" in Chicago.

35. The biographical information for Jazz Gillum's early years comes from the liner notes to *Blues by Jazz Gillum*. To Ray Flerlage's chagrin, the typewritten paragraphs he submitted to Folkways were published in garbled order. Flerlage observed in the liner notes that although Gillum said that he "never quite knew why" he got the nickname "Jazz," he offered the sharp dressing style as his best guess. Flerlage speculated that it might have had more to do with the "jazzy" way he played.

36. *It Sure Had a Kick: The Essential Recordings of Jazz Gillum* (Indigo CD IGOCD 2132 Z-UK).

37. The contract dated April 14, 1930, was signed by Lester Melrose, "Willie Lee Broonzy," and "James F. Braswell." The list of Bill's songs included three instrumentals and the five songs issued by ARC under the Sammy Sampson name. The full listing is as follows: Brasswell: "Western Blues," "Mountain Girl Blues," and, interestingly, one of the hot instrumentals, "Black Cat Rag"; Broonzy: "Guitar Rag," "Pig Meat Strut," "Bowleg Blues," "Tad Pole Blues," "Grandmas [*sic*] Farm," "I Cant [*sic*] Be Satisfied," and "Skoodle Do Do."

The contract dated March 13, 1934, was executed ten days before Bill's first recording session for Bluebird. It was signed by "Willie Broonzy" and Melrose, who was still using the original Melrose Brothers form but this time had crossed out most of the title and had written in his first name so that the letterhead read simply "Lester Melrose." The songs listed were "I'll Be Home Again," "Bull Cow Blues," "Milk Cow Blues," "Serve It To Me Right," "Friendless Blues," "Starvation Blues," and "Mississippi Blues [*sic*]." Both contracts in Bill Randle Collection.

38. According to the U.S. Bureau of Labor Statistics CPI calculator website (http://data.bls.gov/cgi-bin/cpicalc.pl, accessed September 6, 2010), a payment of $26.25 in 1944 would be worth $325.16 in 2010 dollars.

39. Bob Koester, "Lester Melrose: An Appreciation," *American Folk Music Occasional* 2 (1970): 58.

40. Bob Koester, interview with author, December 18, 2002.

41. Willie Dixon with Don Snowden, *I Am the Blues: The Willie Dixon Story* (New York: Da Capo, 1989), 60. Dixon's assessment is borne out by the language in some of Bill's contracts. The one-year contract he signed with the Brunswick Record Corporation (which at that time was part of ARC) on January 21, 1938, stated specifically that "it is understood and agreed that LESTER MELROSE will be the manager of the party of the second part [Bill] for phonograph recordings during the term of this contract and that the said LESTER MELROSE will direct all recordings of the party of the second part." Contract in Bill Randle Collection.

Chapter Seven

1. Mike Rowe, *Chicago Blues: The City and the Music* (New York: Da Capo Press, 1975), 17.

2. Blind John Davis, interview by Jim O'Neal, December 2, 1974. Additional Blind John Davis information from Bob Rusch, "Blind John Davis: Interview," *Cadence* 4, no. 4 (June 1978): 18–22.

3. Broonzy and Bruynoghe, *Big Bill Blues*, 145.

4. Melrose, "My Life," 60–61.

5. Broonzy and Bruynoghe, *Big Bill Blues*, 141–42. Lester Melrose confirmed that he did run into problems in his trips down South in search of artists to record. "I used to travel all through the southern states in search of talent, and sometimes I had very good luck. As a rule, I had considerable trouble with plantation owners, as they were afraid that I would be the cause of their help refusing to return. This did happen on several occasions." Melrose, "My Life in Recording," 60–61.

6. Tony Russell, liner notes to *Blues Collection #27: Big Bill Broonzy*.

7. Erik Townley, *Tell Your Story: A Dictionary of Jazz and Blues Recordings, 1917–1950* (Chigwell, Essex: Storyville, 1976), 225. There were a number of commercially recorded

versions of "The Midnight Special," by both white and black performers, done prior to Alan Lomax's recording at Angola, which was for the Library of Congress.

8. Nearly thirty years after that, a young white audience would embrace the song when it appeared on the Blues Brothers' *Briefcase Full of Blues* LP.

9. The roots of the melody and lyrics of "Mama Don't Allow No. 1" can be traced to a series of songs recorded by both black and white artists in the 1920s and '30s. Peter C. Muir, in *Long Lost Blues: Popular Blues in America, 1850–1920* (Urbana: University of Illinois Press, 2010), identifies three primary sources, including two recorded in 1929 by Tampa Red, both of which were titled "Mama Don't Allow No Easy Riders Here." Muir, in assessing the significance of musician and composer W. C. Handy, argues that Handy incorporated portions of the melody, drawn from what he calls "folk culture," in composing his breakthrough hit, "The Memphis Blues," which he published in 1912 (110).

10. Broonzy and Bruynoghe, *Big Bill Blues*, 149.

11. Smith, *Hit the Right Lick*, 5.

Chapter Eight

1. John Hammond with Irving Townsend, *John Hammond on Record* (New York: Summit, 1977), 202, 199.

2. Ibid., 202.

3. Ibid., 201.

4. Ibid., 202. In his biography of Hammond, *The Producer: John Hammond and the Soul of American Music* (New York: Farrar, Straus and Giroux, 2003), Dunstan Prial writes that Hammond "signed up" Bill in Arkansas. But in the absence of evidence to support this, it is more likely that Bill was working in Chicago when Hammond got in touch with him through his ARC contacts.

5. Although the Vanguard 3-CD set *From Spirituals to Swing* (Vanguard 169/71-2) contains recordings of many of the performances in both the 1938 and 1939 concerts, the order of appearance by the performers, as well as which year each selection was performed and recorded, is uncertain in many cases. Discographer Howard Rye's carefully researched article "From Spirituals to Swing," *Names & Numbers* 16 (January 2001): 7–20, is the best resource I have been able to identify in addressing this challenge. Thanks to Chris Smith for bringing the article to my attention.

6. Review by John Sebastian, *New Masses*, January 3, 1939, included in *From Spirituals to Swing* 3-CD set (Vanguard 169/71-2).

7. Bill recorded several versions of this song, including Vocalion 04706 (February 6, 1939); Vocalion 05259 (recorded September 14, 1939, and released as "Just a Dream No. 2"), and during the July 1957 recording session that was organized by Bill Randle and released as *The Big Bill Broonzy Story* (Verve 314 547 555-2). The recording of his December 23, 1938, performance at the "From Spirituals to Swing" concert is available on Vanguard 169/71-2. Lyrics quoted from *Big Bill Blues*, 97.

8. Sebastian review, in *From Spirituals to Swing*.

9. Hammond, *John Hammond*, 232.

10. According to at least one contemporary account, Bill also played "Just a Dream" at the 1939 concert. J. D. Smith, "From Spirituals to Swing," *Jazz Information* 1, no. 16 (December 29, 1939): 2, quoted in Rye, "From Spirituals to Swing."

11. Michael Denning, *The Cultural Front* (London: Verso, 2000), 315.

12. E. Simms Campbell, "Blues," in *Jazzmen: The Story of Hot Jazz Told in the Lives of*

the Men Who Created It, ed. Frederic Ramsey Jr. and Charles Edward Smith (New York: Limelight Editions, 1985), 105.

13. On January 21, 1938, Bill had signed a one-year contract with the Brunswick Record Corporation, in which he agreed that he would "not record for any other company, or be a party to recording for any purpose whatsoever" except for recordings for Brunswick. Brunswick was affiliated with the American Record Corporation (ARC), with whom Bill had signed recording contracts for the previous several years. Contract in Bill Randle Collection.

14. Broonzy, "Truth about the Blues," 19.

Chapter Nine

1. Initiation fee from records of Local 208, Blues Archive, Chicago Public Library. Adjusted dollar amount ($784.21) calculated at the U.S. Bureau of Labor Statistics CPI Inflation Calculator website, accessed on June 5, 2010.

2. Clark Halker, "A History of Local 208 and the Struggle for Racial Equality in the American Federation of Musicians," *Black Music Research Journal* 8, no. 2 (Autumn 1988): 207–11.

3. Tom Tsotsi, "Chicago Blues Trumpet, Part 16," *Joslin's Jazz Journal* (May 11, 1988): 4. The article quotes a letter from Bob Koester describing a conversation he had with former Local 208 president Harry Gray, in which Gray said that for a number of 1938 recording sessions, "Bill was allowed to sing, but he could not play guitar officially." From the little information available on this subject, it seems there were very few exceptions to the standard that was being enforced at this time regarding union membership and that the only musicians who could record without being union members were non-playing vocalists.

4. Joshua Altheimer file, records of Local 208, in Collection of Blues Archive, Chicago Public Library. Adjusted dollar amount ($1,576.67) calculated at the U.S. Bureau of Labor Statistics CPI Inflation Calculator website, accessed on June 5, 2010.

5. Bill's handwritten response to typed questions from Alan Lomax, Lomax Collection.

6. Guido van Rijn, *Roosevelt's Blues*, 80.

7. Broonzy and Bruynoghe, *Big Bill Blues*, 94.

8. Ibid.

9. Ibid.

10. Beneficiary information from Broonzy file, records of Local 208, in collection of Blues Archive, Chicago Public Library. His beneficiary was changed to "Rosie Broonzy," listed as "Wife," on February 17, 1958.

11. Bill commented in a 1947 magazine profile that "while working a compress in a southern shop his second wife failed to show up with his lunch one day." While it is not impossible that he married someone down South between his 1923 divorce and his 1941 marriage in Houston, and therefore was legally married in 1940, that was the only reference he ever made to such a union. George Hoefer Jr., "The Hot Box," *Down Beat*, November 5, 1947.

12. Broonzy, "Truth about the Blues," 20.

13. Marriage license dated June 7, 1941, from Harris County, Texas, in Collection of the Clayton Library Center for Genealogical Research, Houston, Texas.

14. Broonzy, "Baby, I Done Got Wise," 11.

15. Broonzy, "Truth about the Blues."

16. Broonzy, "Baby, I Done Got Wise," 11.

17. Robert Pruter, "Lil Green: 'In the Dark' Mama. Pt. 1," *Juke Blues*, no. 53 (Spring/ Summer 2003): 24. On her Social Security application (SS-5) dated May 7, 1940, she listed her age as twenty-nine, with a birth date of December 22, 1910, and stated that she had been born in Port Gibson, Mississippi. Recent census research by Bob Eagle and Jim O'Neal indicates that she may have been several years older than that. Personal communication with Bob Eagle and Jim O'Neal.

18. Anthony Heilbut, *The Gospel Sound: Good News and Bad Times* (New York: Limelight, 1997), 81.

19. Leonard Feather, liner notes to LP, *Lil Green: Romance in the Dark* (RCA LPV 574).

20. Pruter, "Lil Green: 'In the Dark' Mama. Pt. 1," 26.

21. Bill's session was held in Chicago on March 1, while Washboard Sam and Jazz Gillum recorded at the Leland Hotel in Aurora, Illinois, on March 14. Barnes went on to a successful career as a jazz guitarist, both as a featured artist and backing performers such as Frank Sinatra and Dinah Washington. He later spoke with pride of his early work with Bill and his colleagues, noting that "I started recording with the top black blues artists of that time." "Jazz Guitar Wouldn't Be the Same without George Barnes," *Guitar Player* (February 1975): 15.

22. By the time Muddy Waters met him in the mid-1940s, Bill was playing electric guitar on his club dates. Muddy recalled that Bill "was the first one I looked at with my eyes playing electric [guitar]." Muddy Waters interview, in *Voice of the Blues*, ed. O'Neal and Van Singel, 172.

23. Broonzy and Bruynoghe, *Big Bill Blues*, 137.

24. Ibid.

25. Death record in collection of Rosie Tolbert.

26. Broonzy oral history, segments TD107R01, TD105R02, Lomax Collection.

27. U.S. census data from a 1941 report on the black communities in Little Rock and North Little Rock showed that the black population of the two cities had increased by 7,000, or nearly 40 percent, from 1910 to 1930. The authors noted that "of the 19,698 Negroes in Little Rock in 1930, 5,571 came from points outside of the State and nearly an equal number from rural sections and small towns in Arkansas. Many of them had once been field laborers or sharecroppers and had been attracted to the metropolis by hope of better living conditions or greater security." *Survey of Negroes in Little Rock and North Little Rock*, compiled by the Writers' Program of the Work Projects Administration in the State of Arkansas, sponsored by the Urban League of Greater Little Rock, Arkansas, 1941, 7–9.

28. In the 1930 census, the Wesleys were counted in an unincorporated section of North Little Rock called Rose City.

29. While there was no listing for Bill's mother, Mittie Bradley, in the 1939 city directory for North Little Rock, the 1940 city directory showed that she was now living at 303 West 22nd Street. Listed as the widow of Frank, Mittie was sharing the residence with Frank Jr. and her daughter Gustavia Dozier.

Among the family records in Rosie Tolbert's collection is a quitclaim deed for the property at 303 West 22nd Street, dated September 5, 1941. The deed identified Mittie and Frank Bradley as the buyers of two lots from Manie and Florence Shuman, for $1. There was no mention of Bill, and no other documents survive that might have been associated with the transfer of property, other than an acknowledgment by Florence that she approved of the deal (which was probably necessary because Manie was the legal owner), and a certificate that the deed was filed with the Pulaski County Clerk's office. By using a quitclaim deed, the seller told the buyer that he or she made no promises about the validity of the title to the property—in other words, while the buyer can take possession of the title, the seller does not swear that it is valid. It was not uncommon for a quitclaim deed to be used for real estate transactions in Arkansas in the early and middle part of the twentieth century by people who may not have been able to afford much in the way of legal representation or documentation. Thanks to Judith Kilpatrick and Ned Snow of the University of Arkansas School of Law for their help.

30. 1940 U.S. Census data.

31. Rosie Tolbert, interview by author, May 13, 2005.

32. Hermese White, interview by author, November 11, 2004.

33. Rosie Tolbert interview.

34. Broonzy oral history, segment TD105R02, Lomax Collection.

35. All royalty statements cited in this chapter from the Bill Randle Collection.

36. Broonzy oral history, segment TD105R02, Lomax Collection.

37. Information from royalty statements that Lester Melrose prepared and sent to Bill, from Bill Randle Collection.

38. Bill's written responses to a one-page typewritten sheet of questions from Alan Lomax, Lomax Collection.

39. According to Melrose's calculations, although Bill was due royalties of $230.40, Melrose had given Bill advances totaling $374.07, leaving Bill with a debt of over $140. Melrose itemized advances to Bill that amounted to $174.07 in May, June, and July, and then in December he gave Bill $50 on the fifth and another $100 on the fifteenth. Even without Melrose's mistake in adding up the advances—his $50 error in calculation meant that he inflated the total he advanced to Bill, and thus Bill's indebtedness—Bill would still have owed nearly $100 to Melrose at the end of the period. It is worth noting that Melrose's math errors worked both ways. On the statement dated September 29, 1941, he made two separate minor calculations that worked against him, so that the net total came out in Bill's favor by about $12.

40. Big Bill Broonzy, "Who Got the Money?" *Living Blues*, no. 55 (Winter/Spring 1982): 21.

41. Broonzy, "Baby, I Done Got Wise," 12.

42. Richard M. Dorson, *Negro Tales from Pine Bluff, Arkansas, and Calvin, Michigan* (Bloomington: University of Indiana Press, 1958), 3. Dorson, who directed the Folklore Institute at Indiana University for several decades, described Reverend Altheimer as "a fine informant," and in his later book *American Negro Folktales* (Greenwich, CT: Fawcett, 1968), 40, Dorson called him "a star narrator."

In confirming that Silas Altheimer was his father, nine-year-old Joshua is listed as a child in Silas's household in the 1920 census for Jefferson County, and Silas is identified as his father on Joshua's death certificate. Silas is identified in the census as being of mixed race, as is his wife (counted on February 20, 1920, Enumeration District 132, Vaugine Township, Jefferson County, Arkansas).

43. "Midnight Steppers," June 10, 1940 (OKeh 05758).

44. Jacques Demêtre, "Joshua Était Le Meilleur!" *Soul Bag* 161 (Winter 2001): 22.

45. Hugues Panassié and Madeleine Gautier, *Guide to Jazz* (Boston: Houghton Mifflin, 1956), 4.

46. Oliver, *Conversation with the Blues*, 153.

47. John Gatewood information from Nathan Thompson, *Kings: The True Story of Chicago's Policy Kings and Numbers Racketeers* (Chicago: Bronzeville Press, 2006), 205–6.

48. Christopher Thale, "Underground Economy," in *Encyclopedia of Chicago*, ed. James R. Grossman, Ann Durkin Keating, and Janice L. Rieff (Chicago: University of Chicago Press, 2004), 838.

49. Broonzy, "Baby, I Done Got Wise," 12; Broonzy and Bruynoghe, *Big Bill Blues*, 135.

50. Chris Smith, "Memphis Slim, U.S.A," *Juke Blues*, no. 49 (Spring 2001): 53.

51. Memphis Slim, interview by Jim O'Neal, December 30, 1975. On Memphis Slim's Social Security application (SS-5) dated April 23, 1937, he listed his name as John Len Chatman, born September 3, 1915, in Memphis, Tennessee, the son of Peter Chatman and Ella Garrett.

52. Francis Hofstein, "Memphis Slim: L'Interview," *Soul Bag*, no. 108 (Winter 1986): 6–12. Thanks to Chris Smith for the suggestion and the translation.

53. Bill had a residency for most of May at the 1410 Club, located at 1410 West Roosevelt Road, in a show advertised as "'Big Bill' and his Swing Troup," for which he would almost certainly have needed a piano player. *Chicago Defender* ads, May 3, 10, and 17, 1941. Cozy Corner dates in *Chicago Defender* ads, June 28, July 12, and August 2, 1941. December gig at the Triangle Club, 1403 Blue Island Avenue. *Chicago Defender* ad, December 6, 1941.

54. Eddie Boyd interview, in *Voice of the Blues*, ed. O'Neal and Van Singel, 239.

55. Contract from the collection of Jim O'Neal.

56. Quote in Smith, "Memphis Slim U.S.A.," 54.

57. Dempsey J. Travis, *An Autobiography of Black Jazz* (Chicago: Urban Research Press, 1983), 163–66.

58. Indiana Theater contracts from the collection of Jim O'Neal.

59. Broonzy and Bruynoghe, *Big Bill Blues*, 126–35.

60. Memphis Slim, "In My Opinion," *Jazz Journal* 14, no. 10 (October 1961): 5.

Chapter Ten

1. "Good Liquor Gonna Carry Me Down," October 31, 1935 (Bluebird 6230), MacLeod, *Yazoo 1–20*, 106–7; "Whiskey and Good Time Blues," February 6, 1939, unissued, on *Broonzy Complete Recorded Works*, vol. 8 (Document DOCD-5130). MacLeod, *Document Blues—4*, 67. The source for all lyrics in this chapter, except where otherwise noted, is MacLeod, *Document Blues—4*.

2. "Baby I Done Got Wise," February 6, 1939 (Vocalion 04706), MacLeod, 68.

3. "Looking Up at Down," June 10, 1940 (OKeh 05698), MacLeod, 92.

4. Studs Terkel, *Talking to Myself: A Memoir of My Times* (New York: Pantheon, 1977), 299.

5. "Down in the Alley," March 10, 1937 (Vocalion 03517), MacLeod, 32–33.

6. "The Mill Man Blues," April 5, 1938 (Vocalion 04280), MacLeod, 53–54.

7. "Nancy Jane," June 11, 1936 (Vocalion 03265), MacLeod, 17–18.

8. "Truckin' Little Woman," March 30, 1938 (Vocalion 04205), MacLeod, 50.

9. "Rockin' Chair Blues," December 17, 1940 (OKeh 06116), MacLeod, 100.

10. "Low Down Woman Blues," February 12, 1936 (ARC 6-06-56), MacLeod, 11.

11. "Looking for My Baby," January 26, 1940 (Vocalion 05452), MacLeod, 87–88.

12. "Oh Yes," September 14, 1939 (Vocalion 05205), MacLeod, 82.

13. "Somebody's Got to Go," October 21, 1937 (Vocalion 03400), MacLeod, 46–47.

14. "Evil Hearted Me," August 19, 1937 (ARC 7-10-66), MacLeod, 41.

15. "Made a Date with an Angel (Got No Walking Shoes)," October 13, 1937 (Conqueror 8999), MacLeod, 45.

16. "Lonesome Road Blues," December 17, 1940 (OKeh 06031), MacLeod, 97.

17. "Preachin' the Blues," February 6, 1939 (Vocalion 05096), MacLeod, 68–69.

18. "Mean Old World," January 31, 1937 (ARC 7-07-64), MacLeod, 31.

19. "When I Had Money," April 17, 1940 (Vocalion 05563), MacLeod, 89–90.

20. "Sad Letter Blues," April 5, 1938, Vocalion unissued, on *Broonzy Complete Recorded Works*, vol. 7 (Document DOCD-5129), MacLeod, 53.

21. *The Big Bill Broonzy Story*, disc 1, track 4.

22. Unedited recordings from three-day recording session organized by Bill Randle, July 12–14, 1957, from which material used in the 5-LP set *The Big Bill Broonzy Story* was taken. Recordings from Bill Randle Collection, tape 1, minutes 15–17.

23. "Lone Wolf Blues," June 10, 1940 (OKeh 05698), MacLeod, 93.

24. "I'm Just a Bum," July 27, 1935 (Bluebird 6111), MacLeod, 3–4.

25. "Dreamy Eyed Baby," September 14, 1939 (Vocalion 05360), MacLeod, 79.

26. Pianist and singer Billie Pierce told Paul Oliver, "Charlie Segar came from my home town in Pensacola, Florida." Oliver, *Conversation with the Blues*, 88.

27. In a twelve-bar blues, the first line is sung or played twice, with the third line completing the thought and the verse (the form in poetry is often described AAB). In an eight-bar blues, there is a total of two rather than three lines (in poetic terms, AB).

28. Gillum's claim of authorship: Flerlage interview, September 3, 1961, in liner notes to *Blues by Jazz Gillum* (Folkways FS3826). Bob Koester, "Taking Care of Relations: Jazz Gillum and the 'Key to the Highway,'" in *Rhythm & News*, no. 705 (2006 Chicago Blues Festival issue): 9.

29. "Key to the Highway," *Big Bill Broonzy Interviewed by Studs Terkel* (Folkways F-3586), track 5.

30. "Key to the Highway," May 2, 1941 (OKeh 06242), MacLeod, 103.

31. As Melrose presented the calculation on a royalty statement dated February 18, 1948, Bill received one-third of 1 percent of the 1,527 sides sold, or $5.04. Royalty statement in Bill Randle Collection.

32. Tony Glover, Scott Dirks, and Ward Gaines, *Blues with a Feeling: The Little Walter Story* (New York: Routledge, 2002), 185–86.

33. Eric Clapton, interview by author, November 23, 2007.

34. "That's All Right, Baby," May 11, 1939 (Vocalion 05043), MacLeod, 76–77. Rev. Tindley's hymn was titled "I'll Overcome Someday" and was published in 1901. Bernice Johnson Reagon, "Searching for Tindley," in *We'll Understand By and By: Pioneering African American Gospel Composers*, ed. Bernice Johnson Reagon (Washington, DC: Smithsonian Institution Press, 1992), 37–38.

Chapter Eleven

1. Quoted in Ronald Cohen, *Rainbow Quest: The Folk Music Revival and American Society, 1940–1970* (Amherst: University of Massachusetts Press, 2002), 42.

2. Robbie Lieberman, *My Song Is My Weapon: People's Songs, American Communism, and the Politics of Culture, 1930–50* (Urbana: University of Illinois Press, 1989), 116.

3. Ibid., 111.

4. "Folk Songs Concert Here," *Chicago Defender*, October 5, 1946. Flerlage's commitment to racial integration was not limited to his work. After World War II, he lived

for most of his life in predominately black neighborhoods. He was married a number of times, and at least two of his wives were African American, including his last wife, Luise, to whom he was married for the last thirty-six years of his life. In his own words, he "crossed over." Raeburn Flerlage, interview by Ronald D. Cohen, July 15, 1992.

5. Virgil Thomson, "Differentiated Counterpoint," *New York Herald Tribune*, November 11, 1946; unsigned review, "Blues Are Featured at Midnight Concert," *New York Times*, November 11, 1946.

6. The "Blues at Midnight" show was actually the second time Bill had performed that year at Town Hall. On New Year's Day of 1946, he had been one of many artists who had appeared at a benefit concert for Yugoslav relief that was organized by the Greenwich Village American Committee, "of which," according to the *New York Times* review, "Mrs. Eleanor Roosevelt is honorary national chairman." Orson Welles served as narrator, and other participants included Bunk Johnson's New Orleans Band and Josh White, as well as bands led by Clarence Williams and Red Allen. Unsigned review, "Program of Jazz Traces Its History," *New York Times*, January 2, 1946.

7. Unsigned review, "Midnight Blues at Town Hall," *American Jazz Review*, December 1946.

8. Thomson, "Differentiated Counterpoint."

9. "Midnight Blues at Town Hall."

10. Lomax, *Land Where the Blues Began*, 459–60.

11. "Conversation Continues," *Blues in the Mississippi Night* (Rounder CD 82161-1860-2), track 6.

12. "Levee Camp and Prison Songs/Conversation Continues," ibid., track 7.

13. "Conversation Continues," ibid., track 16.

14. Ibid.

15. "Conversation Continues," ibid., track 17.

16. William Beyer, "Langston Hughes and Common Ground in the 1940s," *American Studies in Scandinavia* 23 (1991): 31. In *The Land Where the Blues Began*, Lomax mentions that "this innovative dramatic interview was first presented in a lecture to the New York Folklore Society in 1947" (504n).

17. Alan Lomax to Big Bill Broonzy, April 8, 1947, Lomax Collection.

18. Alan Dundes, ed., *Mother Wit from the Laughing Barrel* (Jackson: University Press of Mississippi, 1981), 471.

19. Script for BBC Radio, Third Programme, "The Art of the Negro," No. 3: "Blues in the Mississippi Night," presented by Alan Lomax, broadcast on November 28 and 30, 1951, Alan Lomax Collection, American Folklife Center, Library of Congress.

20. Alan Lomax, liner notes to LP release of *Blues in the Mississippi Night* (Pye Nixa NJL 8).

21. *Melody Maker*, August 10, 1957 (tied for thirteenth for week of August 3); *Melody Maker*, August 17, 1957 (tied for tenth for week of August 10); *Melody Maker*, August 24, 1957 (tied for twelfth for week of August 17); *Melody Maker*, August 31, 1957 (tied for fifteenth for week of August 24).

22. LP release of *Blues in the Mississippi Night* (United Artists UAL 4027).

23. The real names of the three musicians did not appear on a commercial release of *Blues in the Mississippi Night* until the 1990 Rykodisc CD (RCD 90155). The last of the trio, Memphis Slim, had died in 1988, which freed Lomax from his commitment to preserve their anonymity.

24. Greil Marcus, *Mystery Train: Images of America in Rock 'n' Roll Music*, 4th rev. ed. (New York: Plume, 1997), 194.

25. Johnny Cash with Patrick Carr, *Johnny Cash: The Autobiography* (New York: HarperCollins, 1997), 95.

26. Unreleased portion of March 2, 1947, session, from recordings in Lomax Collection.

27. Ibid.

28. In the liner notes to the 1990 Rykodisc CD of *Blues in the Mississippi Night*, Lomax tells of meeting Charlie Houlin in 1960. Locating him with information he said that Bill had given him, Lomax writes of Houlin "leaning over the great mahogany bar in the saloon he ran in the Arkansas bottoms. Guns of every sort hung along the wall. . . . [Houlin had] the steely blue eyes of the western gunfighter. They said that no police car ever even slowed down while passing his place."

29. *People's Songs Bulletin*, November 1946, 9.

30. Quoted in Marshall Rosenthal, "The Six Decades of Win Stracke: Singing Out for the Joy of It," *Chicago Daily News*, September 25–26, 1971, 4.

31. Stracke told Chicago folksinger Mark Dvorak in one of two 1990 interviews, "I had worked for the Wobbly movement. Flat Wheel Harry out in Wyoming. We were coal miners." Win Stracke, interview by Mark Dvorak, July 26, 1990.

32. Quoted in Rosenthal, "The Six Decades of Win Stracke," 4.

33. All quotes from Rosenthal, "Six Decades of Win Stracke." Stracke cited the weekly performance of one song by one *Barn Dance* performer as particularly noteworthy: "Every Saturday night, for instance, Bradley Kincaid would sing 'Barbara Allen,' which indicated to me that this was music that had a deep hold on the American people."

34. Quoted in Richard Christiansen, *A Theater of Our Own: A History and Memoir of 1,001 Nights in Chicago* (Evanston: Northwestern University Press, 2004), 79.

35. Ibid., 81.

36. *Chicago Daily News* review from June 4, 1935, in Chicago Repertory Group Collection, Special Collections, University of Chicago Library.

37. Studs Terkel with Sydney Lewis. *Touch and Go: A Memoir* (New York: New Press, 2007), 95.

38. Jane Stracke Bradbury interview by author, August 31, 2005.

39. In *Touch and Go*, Terkel recalls that the specific prompt for his nickname was his appearance in the Rep Group's production of *Waiting for Lefty*, in which "two other guys in the cast were named Louis, which made for some confusion" (104).

40. Nathan and Metta Davis, interview by author, October 11, 2005.

41. Mary Gleason, "'Studs' Terkel, Former Disc Jockey, to Appear Tonight in Mandel Hall," *Chicago Maroon*, November 7, 1947, 1.

42. "Studs Terkel: Recollections," *Come for to Sing: Folk Music in Chicago and the Midwest* 6, no. 2 (Spring 1980): 9.

43. Studs Terkel, interview by author, July 18, 2002. The precise origins of the format are unclear. Terkel recalled in the "Studs Terkel: Recollections" interview: "I was doing the Wax Museum and a woman named June Myers came up to me one day and said, 'How about doing a program with Win Stracke and Larry Lane and Big Bill?'" Win Stracke remembered in a 1990 interview with Chicago folksinger Mark Dvorak that the program "was the idea of a girl named Lange—L-a-n-g-e—who was an undergraduate at the University of Chicago." Stracke went to on say, "That was her concept," but he was not specific as to what he meant by "that," as Dvorak had asked whether the "I Come

for to Sing" group had been Terkel's idea. Stracke, interview by Mark Dvorak, June 14, 1990. The *Chicago Maroon* article describes Myers as "music director of the student committee of the Renaissance Society," who "has been engaged in extensive research on the history of the ballad." "'Studs' Terkel . . . to Appear," 1.

44. Lieberman, *My Song Is My Weapon*, 122.

45. The *Maroon* described the program in advance in terms that could have come from a graduate seminar in ethnomusicology: "Three singers will present songs from three completely isolated cultures, with Terkel's narration stressing organic rather than historical continuity in the selections." From "Studs Terkel Here Nov. 7," *Chicago Maroon*, October 28, 1947, 1.

46. "Studs Terkel: Recollections," 9.

47. Stracke, interview by Dvorak, June 14, 1990.

Chapter Twelve

1. Arnold Shaw, *Honkers and Shouters: The Golden Years of Rhythm & Blues* (New York: Macmillan, 1978), xv.

2. Quoted in O'Neal and Van Singel, *The Voice of the Blues*, 172.

3. Ibid., 166.

4. Tony Standish, "Muddy Waters in London, Part II, Conclusion," *Jazz Journal* 12, no. 2 (February 1959): 3.

5. Oliver, *Conversation with the Blues*, 155. The spelling of the name of the proprietor of Silvio's has appeared in different forms in different places. In the interview with Muddy in *Conversation with the Blues*, the proprietor's first name was spelled "Sylvio." In Scott Dirks's 2002 article in *Blues & Rhythm* magazine on the Local 208 union records, he used the spelling "Silvio Corroza." "Union City Blues," *Blues & Rhythm* 167 (March 2002): 10. Recent research by Jim O'Neal suggests that another possibility may be "Silvio Corraza." Thanks to one of my anonymous readers for raising this question, and to Jim O'Neal for sharing his findings.

6. Margaret McKee and Fred Chisenhall, *Beale Street Black & Blue: Life and Music on Black America's Main Street* (Baton Rouge: Louisiana State University Press, 1981), 237.

7. Jimmy Rogers, interview by John Anthony Brisbin, in *Rollin' and Tumblin': The Postwar Blues Guitarists*, ed. Jas Obrecht (San Francisco: Miller Freeman, 2000), 127.

8. Jimmy Rogers, interview by Paul Trynka, quoted in Gordon, *Can't Be Satisfied*, 315.

9. Larry Hoffman, "Interview with Robert Lockwood, Jr.", in *Rollin' and Tumblin'*, ed. Obrecht, 170–72.

10. Quoted in Smith, *Hit the Right Lick*, 7.

11. Eddie Boyd interview by O'Neal and Van Singel, *Voice of the Blues*, 244.

12. For the period 1934–42, Bill played as a sideman on about 430 sessions, for an average of just under 50 a year, or once a week (the uncertainty as to the precise number of sessions reflects the absence of written documentation for his presence in all cases). By comparison, from 1945–50, he played as a sideman on a *total* of 50 sessions, and nearly two-thirds of them (32) were in one year, 1947.

13. Rowe, *Chicago Blues*, 45.

14. "Big Maceo Sings for Long Tour," *Chicago Defender*, January 5, 1946; "Well! Lookee Here!! Big Maceo Is Back at the Flame—Just Returned from a 6 Months Tour of the United States with Some New Blues and All of His Old Favorites," ad for the Flame Club at 3020 Indiana Avenue in *Chicago Defender*, May 18, 1946; "Apologies to

all our friends who were disappointed because "Big" Maceo was unable to be with us as advertised. He suffered a stroke and is now recuperating at home. But by good fortune we have managed to obtain for your enjoyment 'Tampa Red,'" ad for the Flame Club in *Chicago Defender*, May 25, 1946.

15. Broonzy and Bruynoghe, *Big Bill Blues*, 115. Unless otherwise indicated, all quotes in section on Big Maceo Merriweather are from *Big Bill Blues*, 112–16.

16. The two performed together in a two-week engagement during that summer of 1945 at the Flame Club on the South Side, at 3020 Indiana Avenue. The ad in the *Defender* announced that "Both of these Blues Singers are Nationally Known Artists; Don't fail to hear these great blues singers." It listed Bill as "Singing 'Oh Baby' and 'Rock Me Baby' Blues" and Big Maceo "Singing 'Worried Life' and 'Texas' Blues." For once, it wasn't Bill who had his name misspelled, as the pianist was listed both weeks as "Big Maco." *Chicago Defender*, July 28 and August 4, 1945.

17. Bill mentioned in a letter to the Dutch broadcaster Michiel de Ruyter after Big Maceo's death that the pianist "lived in apt 4 and I lived in apt 3." Letter from Bill to Michiel de Ruyter, no date but likely around March 15, 1953, collection of Guido van Rijn.

18. Hudson Shower (Little Hudson), interview by author, December 1, 2004.

19. Colin Escott and David Evans, liner notes to *Sonny Boy Williamson: Bluebird Blues* (BMG CD 82876 56156 2).

20. Rowe, *Chicago Blues*, 21.

21. Broonzy and Bruynoghe, *Big Bill Blues*, 121.

22. Hudson Shower interview, December 1, 2004.

23. Shaw, *Honkers and Shouters*, 419.

24. Quoted in ibid., 420.

25. Ad in *Amsterdam News*, June 2, 1945, 10, in *Jazz Advertised, 1910–1967*, ed. Franz Hoffmann (Berlin: F. Hoffmann, 1989), 676. Bill mentioned his connection with Glaser in the "Baby, I Done Got Wise" article in the March 1946 issue of the *Jazz Record* cited earlier, when he commented about his 1941 marriage in Houston to Rose Allen: "We had lived in Chicago ever since until this year, when I got connected to Joe Glaser and he brought me to New York" (11). The article, which despite being in the first-person and credited to Bill as the author, was almost certainly ghostwritten and based on an interview Bill had given, as there are relevant interview notes in the Art Hodes file in the Institute of Jazz Studies at the Rutgers University Library. Hodes was the publication's editor, and even if he did not conduct the interview, he would have been aware of it. The interview probably took place sometime in 1945, given the date of the Apollo appearance.

26. Big Bill Broonzy to Alan Lomax, December 15, 1948, Lomax Collection.

27. Ibid. While Bill may have been able to get reassurance from John Hammond before deciding to record for Mercury in January 1949, he succeeded in reaching Hammond directly two months later to ask about his publishing rights to the songs he recorded. On February 25, 1949, Beth Kramer at Mercury wrote to Bill on behalf of Mitch Miller, asking him to sign contracts with Wing Music Company, Mercury's publishing entity, for seven of the songs he had recorded in January and February. Three days later, on February 28, John Hammond replied to the letter Bill had evidently written him in response, reassuring Bill that he would be "perfectly safe in signing the contracts," as "your rights and copyright will be protected." Although Hammond expressed his interest in having "another session in the very near future," it would be nearly three years before Bill recorded again for Mercury. Both letters from Bill Randle Collection.

Chapter Thirteen

1. Nathan and Metta Davis, interview by author, October 11, 2005. Another member of the group of friends at the University of Illinois was Thomas Friedman from Texas, whose son, Richard, was later successful as a musician and author of detective novels under the name of Kinky Friedman.

2. Leonard Feinberg, "Big Bill Broonzy's Life in Iowa," in *Outside In: African American History in Iowa, 1838–2000*, ed. Bill Silag with Susan Koch-Bridgford and Hal Chase (Des Moines: State Historical Society of Iowa, 2001), 546.

3. Ibid.

4. "Then Big Bill introduced me to Sylvio and I played at Sylvio's along with Sonny Boy Williamson and old Tampa Red and Doctor Clayton and all those fellers." Muddy Waters interview in Oliver, *Conversation with the Blues*, 155.

5. While it is difficult to document the urgency of the threat to Bill's health, there is reason to accept it as legitimate. According to his 1958 death certificate, he had been treated for over a year for lung cancer, which was identified as the cause of death. He was a smoker, and the taverns and clubs in which he appeared for decades were hardly smoke-free environments. Although it is possible to speculate that he needed to remove himself from Chicago because of other problems, no evidence has survived to support this.

6. Bill described settling into his new environment when he wrote to Win Stracke shortly after arriving. "I got here Tuesday and went to work today but I did not get the job. Worse for me. But this one is all right. I don't have to get drunk to do it <smile>. You was right about it, [it] was Iowa State College. They have not my place ready so the one the[y] is fixing for me only cos[t] 35 dollars a month. That ain't bad, is it? I am staying with Mr. Fengburg till Saturday." He included Feinberg's address, added his Quonset hut address, and told Win that "either place I will get it. Tell Stut [Studs] and [Larry] Lane to write but don't give it to no one else please." Big Bill Broonzy to Win Stracke, c. August 1950, from Stracke Collection.

7. While the authors of the meticulously researched *Outside In* state that "Iowa State perceives him to be its first African American faculty member" (140–41), there seems to be a reasonable amount of evidence that he was, in fact, the first African American faculty member. Carver's name appears in a list of faculty in an 1895 yearbook, along with two other people then in a status similar to him as "Assistants in Biology." *The Bomb*, published by the Ishkoodahs, the Class of Ninety-six of the Iowa State College of Agriculture and Mechanical Arts, Ames Iowa, 1895. He was also described as "Professor Carver" in an 1897 biennial report to the governor of Iowa from the college. "Seventeenth Biennial Report of the Iowa State College of Agriculture and Mechanic Arts. Made to the Governor of the State for the years 1896 and 1897, Des Moines, 1897. His biographer Linda O. McMurry states that he "was appointed to the college faculty as an assistant in botany." *George Washington Carver: Scientist and Symbol* (Oxford: Oxford University Press, 1982), 39. Thanks to Tanya Zanish-Belcher, Associate Professor and Head, Special Collections, and Becky S. Jordan, Reference Specialist in Special Collections, Iowa State University, for their valuable help.

8. Except where otherwise noted, all quotes from Jav Walker, interview by author, May 12, 2006.

9. Jav Walker, telephone interview by author, September 9, 2004.

10. Silag, *Outside In*, 204.

11. Leonard Feinberg, telephone interview by author, August 12, 2004.

12. Ibid.

13. "Foreign Students Address Parent-Teachers Association," *Ames Daily Tribune,* January 19, 1951.

14. "Local Entertainers to Star on WOI-FM," *Iowa State Daily,* January 31, 1951; "Large Crowd Attends Lions 'Ladies Night,'" *Ames Daily Tribune,* February 24, 1951.

15. Fred Tunks, "Blues Singer Shelves Guitar to 'Just Relax' at Iowa State," *Iowa State Daily,* January 16, 1951.

16. Both Feinberg and Walker also recalled that Bill had encountered some difficulties with the Des Moines musicians' union for performing without joining the union and paying dues. However, according to Daniel B. Stevenson, an official of the American Federation of Musicians' Local 75 of Des Moines, there is no mention of Bill in the union minutes from the early 1950s. E-mail correspondence with Daniel B. Stevenson, March 29, 2009.

17. Norman Cleary, telephone interview by author, October 10, 2004.

18. "Piddles in Puddle: Little Ronnie Lost," *Iowa State Daily,* June 6, 1951.

19. Feinberg interview, August 12, 2004.

20. Tunks, "Blues Singer Shelves Guitar."

21. Cleary interview, October 10, 2004.

22. Source for 1951 Broonzy divorce records is file for Case 51s 6478. Superior Court of Cook County, William M. Broonzy vs. Rosia Broonzy, Archives of the Clerk of the Cook County Circuit Court, Chicago, IL.

23. Win Stracke to Yannick Bruynoghe, July 10, 1959, from Bruynoghe Collection.

24. Stracke to Ray Lawless, November 13, 1958, Win Stracke file, Ray M. Lawless Collection, American Folklife Center, Library of Congress.

25. Feinberg interview, August 12, 2004.

26. "Paris-Bound Big Bill," *Ames Daily Tribune,* June 28, 1951, 1.

27. Ibid.

Chapter Fourteen

1. John Chilton, *Sidney Bechet: The Wizard of Jazz* (New York: Oxford University Press, 1987), 39–40. Chilton notes that Ansermet's article was particularly significant because it was "the first occasion on which a jazz performance was seriously and skillfully reviewed in print."

2. Hugues Panassié, *The Real Jazz,* rev. and enl. ed. (New York: Barnes, 1960), 10.

3. Jeffrey H. Jackson, *Making Jazz French: Music and Modern Life in Interwar Paris* (Durham, NC: Duke University Press, 2003), 163.

4. Ibid., 168–69.

5. Michael Dregni, *Django: The Life and Music of a Gypsy Legend* (New York: Oxford University Press, 2004), 239.

6. Hugues Panassié, "Big Bill Broonzy: Un grand chanteur de Blues," *La Revue du Jazz* (August 1949): 218.

7. "Stop Press," *Melody Maker,* July 7, 1951.

8. Hugues Panassié, *Monsieur Jazz* (Paris: Stock, 1975), 307.

9. Vasset, *Black Brother,* 27.

10. Ibid., 27–28.

11. Essay by Ron Sweetman dated July 12, 2002, and sent to author; personal communication from Klaus Albrechtsen dated May 9, 2005, conveyed to author by Allan Stephensen.

12. Graeme Bell, *Graeme Bell, Australian Jazzman: His Autobiography* (Frenchs Forest, NSW: Childs & Associates, 1988), 168.

13. Elijah Wald, liner notes to CD, *When I Take My Vacation in Harlem: Blues Legends Sing Pop* (no catalogue number; purchased from author's website, www.elijahwald.com). British trumpeter and bandleader Humphrey Lyttelton had observed Bill's facility as a jazz guitarist when he and his wife had seen him perform the month before in France. Lyttelton was familiar with saxophonist Guy Lafitte, and when he saw Bill playing guitar behind Lafitte, his interpretation was that "on the night we were there, Guy Lafitte's guitar player didn't show." Lyttelton recalled that "Bill helped out, and he sat in with him and he played pretty good rhythm guitar, just [sitting] in with a jazz band." Humphrey Lyttelton, telephone interview by author, February 19, 2004.

14. Graeme Bell, "They Like Non-Commercial Jazz," *New Musical Express*, October 12, 1951.

15. Entry for Sunday, September 16, 1951, from diary kept by Norman "Bud" Baker of the Graeme Bell Band, collection of Mike Sutcliffe.

16. Broonzy and Bruynoghe, *Big Bill Blues*, 83–84.

17. Long John Baldry, telephone interview by author, March 1, 2005. The record was Vogue 2074, "Blues in 1890"/"John Henry."

18. Roberta Freund Schwartz, *How Britain Got the Blues: The Transmission and Reception of American Blues Style in the United Kingdom* (Aldershot, UK: Ashgate, 2007), 39. A similar arrangement had been made the year before for Josh White.

19. Paul Oliver, "Just a Dream: Big Bill Broonzy," in *Blues Off the Record* (New York: Da Capo, 1984), 111.

20. James Asman, "Frankly, I Am Disgusted!" *Musical Express*, September 28, 1951.

21. Ernest Borneman, "Big Bill Talkin'," *Melody Maker*, September 29, 1951.

22. Stanley Dance, "Lightly and Politely: About Big Bill Broonzy," in *Jazz Journal* 4, no. 11 (November 1951): 2.

23. Oliver, "Just a Dream," 111.

24. Borneman, "Big Bill Talkin'."

25. Ibid.

26. Ibid.

27. Ibid.

28. "William Johnson" harkened back to "Big Bill Johnson," the pseudonym under which several of his recordings for Champion had been released nearly twenty years before. Thanks to Chris Smith for making this connection. Melodisc contract from Bill Randle Collection.

Chapter Fifteen

1. Smith, *Hit the Right Lick*, identifies the pianist as probably being Memphis Slim, while André Vasset, in his discography in *Black Brother*, believes it is Bob Call.

2. "Enjoys Folk Music Concert," *Chicago Maroon*, December 7, 1951, 13.

3. Billy Boy Arnold, quoted in Glover, Dirks, and Gaines, *Blues with a Feeling*, 88.

4. Adjusted dollar amount ($3,702.04/month × 12 months = $44,424.48) calculated on U.S. Bureau of Labor Statistics CPI Inflation Calculator website, accessed on June 5, 2010.

5. Broonzy, "Truth about the Blues," 20. ". . . when I came North and could not read or write and I got a job at the Iowa State College as janitor, every night it would be three or four of them [white female students] to come and teach me, because I told them I wanted to read and write and they would sit and show me."

6. Big Bill Broonzy to Win Stracke, January 2, 1952, Stracke Collection.

7. Big Bill Broonzy to Win Stracke, March 2, 1952 (envelope postmarked March 1), Stracke Collection.

8. Ibid.

9. Tyler Stovall, *Paris Noir: African Americans in the City of Light* (Boston: Houghton Mifflin, 1996), 171.

10. Henry Kahn, "They Don't Appreciate Real Blues in France," *Melody Maker*, February 2, 1952, 9.

11. Frank J. Gillis and John W. Miner, *Oh, Didn't He Ramble: The Life Story of Lee Collins, as Told to Mary Collins* (Urbana: University of Illinois Press, 1989), 94–95.

12. Mezzrow's comments come at the end of the preceding song. "Nobody Knows the Trouble I've Seen," *The Complete Vogue Recordings* (Vogue 82876643512), disc 2, track 13.

13. Later that year Bill declined a request in Great Britain for "How Long, How Long Blues" by onstage interviewer Derrick Stewart-Baxter on the basis that "you're supposed to be accompanied with that number. And it don't sound so good because there's too many open spaces in it, you know." "Presentation of Portrait," *Big Bill Broonzy: On Tour in Britain, 1952,* (Jasmine CD 3011/12), disc 2, track 17.

14. "Folk Singer Struck a Bad Patch," *Evening Dispatch* (Edinburgh), February 25, 1952, 3.

15. "Scottish District News: American Jazz Concert," *Scotsman*, February 25, 1952.

16. The recording can be found as disc 1 of *Big Bill Broonzy: On Tour in Britain, 1952.* The information about the pre-concert visit to the bar, the backstage drinking, and the terms of the bequest for Usher Hall come from a letter from Sandy Currie to Paul Pelletier, October 13, 2000, used courtesy of Paul Pelletier. Quotes from the *Evening Dispatch* are from "Folk Singer Struck a Bad Patch."

17. Steve Race, "The Other Side of the Picture," *Jazz Journal* 5, no. 4 (April 1952): 2.

18. Derrick Stewart-Baxter, "Preachin' the Blues," *Jazz Journal* 5, no. 4 (April 1952): 6–7.

19. Program for "From Spirituals to Swing" concert, December 23, 1938, reproduced in *From Spirituals to Swing* box set (Vanguard 169/71-2).

20. Big Bill Broonzy to Win Stracke, April 15, 1952, Stracke Collection.

21. Alan Lomax to Woody Guthrie, December 5, 1952, quoted in Andrew L. Kaye and Matthew Barton, introduction, "The 1950's: World Music," in *Alan Lomax: Selected Writings, 1934–1997,* ed. Ronald D. Cohen (New York: Routledge, 2003), 101.

22. Recording made by Alan Lomax of performance and conversation with Big Bill Broonzy in Paris, France, c. May 1952, Alan Lomax Collection, American Folklife Center, Library of Congress.

23. Ibid. for all quotes in the description and ensuing discussion of this recording.

24. Flyer in Bruynoghe Collection.

25. "Studs Terkel: Recollections," 9.

26. Ibid., 8.

27. Comments from recording of "I Come for to Sing" performance, August 11, 1952, private recording from Holzfeind family collection.

28. "Monday Night a Birthday, Too," *Blue Note News* 2, no. 9 (July 3, 1953), from Chicago History Museum Collection.

29. Duke Ellington, "Adventures of Duke on a Busman's Holiday," *Blue Note News* 1, no. 7 (August 29, 1952), from Chicago History Museum Collection.

30. "Meet Our 'Fifteen-Timer' Club," *Blue Note News* 2, no. 10 (July 31, 1953).

31. Terkel, *Talking to Myself*, 300–301.

32. "Mahalia—Greatest of Gospellers: Henry Kahn Reviews the First Mahalia Jackson Concert in Paris," *Melody Maker*, November 1, 1952, 3.

33. "No 'Sinful' Songs from Big Bill, Pleads Mahalia," *Melody Maker*, November 1, 1952, 1.

34. Ibid., 12.

35. "London Scares Mahalia," in *Melody Maker*, November 8, 1952, 8.

36. *The Big Bill Broonzy Story*, disc 1, track 8.

37. Derrick Stewart-Baxter, "Preachin' the Blues," *Jazz Journal* 6, no. 1 (January 1953): 3.

38. Humphrey Lyttelton, *I Play as I Please: The Memoirs of an Old Etonian Trumpeter* (London: Macgibbon & Kee, 1954), 180. Club listings in *Melody Maker*, November 8, 1952, 10 and December 6, 1952, 10.

39. Script for BBC Radio, Third Programme, *Song of the Iron Road*, with Big Bill Broonzy, Ewan MacColl, Isla Cameron, and Humphrey Lyttelton and His Band, recorded on November 28, 1952, Alan Lomax Collection, American Folklife Center, Library of Congress. A photo of Bill with producer Dennis Mitchell, Lyttelton, MacColl, Isla Cameron, and singer Neva Raphaello appeared with the headline "Jazzmen on the Iron Road" in the December 6, 1952, edition of the *Melody Maker*, 6–7.

40. "Bill Broonzy's Leaving Blues," *Melody Maker*, December 13, 1952.

41. It was one of the first photos of a performer taken by Belgian photographer Raymond Saublains, who later photographed many jazz artists performing in Belgium and elsewhere. Photograph in Raymond Saublains Collection.

Chapter Sixteen

1. Margo Bruynoghe, interview by author, February 25, 2004.

2. Bill's quotes are taken from his letter to Win Stracke, January 24, 1953, Collection of Old Town School of Folk Music, Chicago, Illinois. All Herbert Wilcox quotes from telephone interview by author, February 19, 2004.

3. Big Bill Broonzy to Yannick Bruynoghe, December 31, 1952, Bruynoghe Collection.

4. The Paris nightclub exemption likely reflected Bill's preexisting relationships with the concert bookers there, as well as the absence of any need for travel and hotel arrangements.

5. Contract between William Lee "Big Bill" Broonzy and Yannick Bruynoghe, dated January 8, 1953, Bruynoghe Collection.

6. Margo Bruynoghe interview.

7. Ibid.

8. Big Bill Broonzy to Yannick Bruynoghe, December 31, 1952, Bruynoghe Collection.

9. Ibid.

10. Margo Bruynoghe interview.

11. Ibid.

12. Stovall, *Paris Noir*, 160.

13. Margo Bruynoghe interview.

14. This draws on material in chapters 13 and 14 of Elijah Wald, *Josh White: Society Blues* (Amherst: University of Massachusetts Press, 2000).

15. Big Bill Broonzy to Win Stracke, January 20, 1953, Stracke Collection.

16. Michel Lavite, "Enthousiasme a L'Empire: L'âme du Jazz avec Big Bill Broonzy et Mezz Mezzrow," no specific date but c. January 1953, unknown Oran (Algeria) newspaper. The Olympic reference was presumably an allusion to African American track-and-field star Jesse Owens, whose victories in the 1936 Summer Olympics in Berlin brought him international recognition. From Bill Randle Collection.

17. Big Bill Broonzy to Win Stracke, January 20, 1953, Stracke Collection.

18. Michiel de Ruyter to Big Bill Broonzy, March 14, 1953, Collection of Nederlands Jazz Archief, Amsterdam, Holland.

19. Ibid.

20. Guido van Rijn, liner notes to *Big Bill Broonzy: Amsterdam Live Concerts, 1953* (Munich: MRCD 275), 28.

21. Introduction to February 28, 1953, performance of "Backwater Blues," track 3 on *Big Bill Broonzy: Amsterdam Live Concerts, 1953*.

22. "Groot Jazz Consert in K. en W.," *Het Binnenhof*, March 2, 1953; quoted in Leo Bruin, "Big Bill Broonzy in Nederland," *Block* no. 76 (1990): 26.

23. Big Bill Broonzy to Michiel de Ruyter, n.d. but likely c. March 10 and 15, 1953, Collection of Nederlands Jazz Archief.

24. Broonzy to De Ruyter, c. March 15, 1953.

25. Big Bill Broonzy to André Vasset, February 1953, collection of André Vasset.

26. Letter from Lore Boas (Günter Boas's wife) to author, June 23, 2005.

27. The overview of Günter Boas's life draws on three sources: an interview by author with Lore Boas, October 12, 2004; Walter Liniger, "Wind Chimes: A Sketch of the Boas Collection," published as Bulletin No. 1 by the International Jazz & Blues Archive Eisenach, Eisenach, Germany, 2003; and Scott Barretta, "The International Jazz Archive, Eisenach, Germany," *Living Blues*, no. 173 (July/August 2004): 84–85.

28. Big Bill Broonzy to Günter Boas, sent from Paris in February or early March 1953, Collection of the International Jazz & Blues Archive, Eisenach, Germany.

29. Ibid.

30. Lore Boas to author, June 23, 2005.

31. Lore Boas, telephone interview by author, October 12, 2004.

32. Bill performed at the Teatro Caspa in Barcelona on May 11, 1953. The concert was arranged by Alfredo Papo, a founding member of the Hot Club of Barcelona, at the suggestion of Hugues Panassié. The notes on the concert flyer, most likely by Papo, note a connection between Bill's music and the Spanish musical tradition of "cante jondo," a point that Studs Terkel also made in his commentaries on Bill. Alfredo Papo, "Big Bill en Barcelona," *Solo Blues* 1, no. 2 (Fall 1985).

33. Nadine Cohodas, *Spinning Blues into Gold: The Chess Brothers and the Legendary Chess Records* (New York: St. Martin's Press, 2000), 85.

34. Ibid., 85.

35. John Brisbin, "A Tribute to Sunnyland Slim," *Living Blues*, no. 121 (May/June 1995): 54.

36. "Romance without Finance," *Big Bill Broonzy and Washboard Sam* (Chess MCA CHD-9251).

37. "Jacqueline," *Big Bill Broonzy and Washboard Sam* (Chess MCA CHD-9251).

38. Big Bill Broonzy to André Vasset, February 1953 (date uncertain), Vasset Collection.

39. Big Bill Broonzy postcard to André Vasset, February 19, 1953, Vasset Collection.

40. Big Bill Broonzy to Yannick Bruynoghe, June or July 1953, Bruynoghe Collection.

41. Big Bill Broonzy to André Vasset, November 19, 1953, Vasset Collection.

42. Big Bill Broonzy to Yannick Bruynoghe, undated, likely late 1953 or early 1954, Bruynoghe Collection.

43. Big Bill Broonzy to Yannick Bruynoghe, April 14, 1954, Bruynoghe Collection.

44. Big Bill Broonzy to André Vasset, December 27, 1954, Vasset Collection.

45. Big Bill Broonzy to André Vasset, March 17, 1955, Vasset Collection.

46. E-mail from André Vasset to author, May 30, 2006.

47. Margo Bruynoghe interview.

48. Contract dated June 11, 1953, from Bill Randle Collection.

49. Advertisement in Valparaiso (IN) *Vidette-Messenger*, Friday, August 1, 1952, 10.

50. Ray Nordstrand, "Aural History: WFMT Began as One Couple's Vision," *City Talk*, published by WFMT/Network Chicago, September 12–27, 2001, 27. Also Terkel, *Touch and Go*, 154–55.

51. Big Bill Broonzy, interview by Studs Terkel on WFMT, July 22, 1953. Recording in collection Chicago History Museum.

52. Nordstrand, "Aural History."

53. Information on early days of the *Midnight Special* from Dave Hoekstra, "Isn't That 'Special'!" *Chicago Sun-Times*, December 30, 2003, 38.

54. Big Bill Broonzy to Yannick Bruynoghe, October 7, 1953, Bruynoghe Collection.

55. Milton Rakove, *Don't Make No Waves . . . Don't Back No Losers: An Insider's Analysis of the Daley Machine* (Bloomington: Indiana University Press, 1975), 259.

56. Oliver, *Conversation with the Blues*, 159; information on "Mama Talk to Your Daughter" from Gene Tomko, "J. B. Lenoir," *Encyclopedia of the Blues*, vol. 2, ed. Komara, 594–95.

57. Billy Boy Arnold, interview by author, October 30, 2002.

Chapter Seventeen

1. Jo Ann Jackson and Rosie Tolbert interview by Scott Barretta and author, April 21, 2009.

2. Jo Ann Jackson and Rosie Tolbert interview by author, January 22, 2004.

3. Big Bill Broonzy to Yannick Bruynoghe, April 15, 1954, Bruynoghe Collection.

4. Ibid.

5. Frank Wesley, telephone interview by author, October 6, 2004.

6. *Radio Programme Number 4: Studs Terkel's Weekly Almanac on Folk Music Blues on WFMT with Big Bill Broonzy and Pete Seeger*, recorded April 4, 1954 (Folkways FA 3864).

7. Preface of booklet titled *Sixty Years of Memories: Circle Pines Center: 1938–1998*, published for the sixtieth anniversary of Circle Pines Center, Delton, Michigan, 1998.

8. Vera King, interviewed by author with her husband, Leo King, August 3, 2001.

9. *Pine Needles: News Organ of Circle Pines Center* 15, no. 6 (June 1955).

10. Hanne Sonquist, telephone interview by author, July 28, 2005. Vera King recalled the experience of the cook, Clara Schultz: "Bill drove her crazy. She loved him and adored him like we all did, but he was supposed to help set up breakfast, and he had been up all night singing with the kids and he never could get up in time for breakfast. And I remember her, in her gentle way, cussing him out for that." Vera and Leo King interview.

11. Big Bill Broonzy to André Vasset, 1955, Vasset Collection.

12. Margo Bruynoghe interview.

13. Ibid.

14. Big Bill Broonzy to Yannick Bruynoghe, July 14, 1953, Bruynoghe Collection.

15. Margo Bruynoghe interview.

16. Ibid.

17. Broonzy and Bruynoghe, *Big Bill Blues*, 29.

18. Ibid., 30–31.

19. Ibid., 38–39. A nearly identical folktale is included in Richard M. Dorson's *American Negro Folk Tales* (Greenwich, CT: Fawcett, 1968), 184–85. In that version, with the title "The Hog and the Colored Man," the black manager of a restaurant that featured barbeque decides to kill a pig because he has run out of meat for his patrons. After running one over with his car, he places the animal in the backseat, covering everything but the head with a blanket. Just as in Bill's version, the police officer who stops him is about to let him go before he decides to examine his passenger, whom the driver has identified as his brother, more carefully. His comment is similar as well: "Go ahead, but tell your brother he is the blackest and ugliest bastard I ever saw." Thanks to one of my anonymous readers for pointing out this connection.

20. Ibid., 40–41. Bill had previously described Mr. White to Alan Lomax in the *Blues in the Mississippi Night* sessions (see chap. 11).

21. Ibid., 85.

22. Ibid., 45.

23. Ibid., 123.

24. Ibid., 121.

25. Ibid., 138.

26. Advertisement in *Chicago Defender*, November 5, 1949. An indication of the extent to which the blues scene was peripheral to the entertainment coverage in the *Defender* could be found in the same issue in the "What the Cats Do While the Squares Sleep" column. The columnist, who kept the *Defender*'s readers abreast of current doings in the Chicago music world, noted that "Memphis Minnie and her son supply the music at 708 Club on 47th st." Although Ernest Lawlers performed under the name "Little Son Joe," he was, in fact, Memphis Minnie's husband. In addition, Jimmy Rogers's last name was incorrectly spelled as "Rodgers."

27. Big Bill Broonzy, interview by Studs Terkel on WFMT, September 13, 1955. Recording in collection Chicago History Museum.

28. Paul Oliver, liner notes to "Southern Saga: Big Bill Broonzy Sings and Plays" 45 rpm EP (Nixa NJE 1047).

29. Max Jones and Sinclair Traill, "Don't Miss These Books," *Melody Maker*, November 12, 1955, 6.

30. In his memoir, jazz singer and cultural commentator George Melly describes how members of "some of the smaller groups, unable to afford proper instruments over and above the leader's guitar, began to use washboards and kazoos and especially teachest basses with broomstick handles." George Melly, *Owning Up: The Trilogy* (London: Penguin, 2000), 522.

31. The skiffle interval dated back to when Ken Colyer was a member of the group: "While Ken Colyer was still in the band they decided to introduce skiffle into the set." Harry Shapiro, *Alexis Korner: The Biography* (London: Bloomsbury, 1997), 49.

32. Chris Barber interview, "Blues History," *fROOTS Magazine*, nos. 266/267 (Au-

gust/September 2005); posted on http://www.chrisbarber.net/archives/froots/froots .htm (accessed June 5, 2010).

33. Ibid.

34. Chris Barber, interview by author, February 18, 2004.

35. Chas McDevitt, e-mail correspondence with author, March 5, 2005.

36. Max Jones and Sinclair Traill, "Rosy View of Skiffle," *Melody Maker*, April 6, 1957.

37. Bobbie Korner, telephone interview by author, June 7, 2005.

38. Ibid.

39. Chris Barber interview, February 18, 2004.

40. Shapiro, *Alexis Korner*, 60.

41. Ibid.

42. "Jim Crow, Says Bill; No, Says Notts Hotel," *Melody Maker*, November 12, 1955, 8.

43. Ibid.

44. Peter Fryer, *Staying Power: The History of Black People in Britain* (London: Pluto Press, 1991), 376–78.

45. Jack Hutton, "Big Bill Took a Back Seat," *Melody Maker*, November 12, 1955, 3.

46. "Famous Blues Singers Unite," photo with caption, *Melody Maker*, November 12, 1955, 1.

47. Charles Govey, "Are Singers Visual Entertainment?" *New Musical Express*, November 18, 1955.

48. Louis van Gasteren, "How Did I Come to Make These Recordings?" essay in liner notes to *Big Bill Broonzy: Amsterdam Live Recordings, 1953*, 38. Van Gasteren quotes Pim as telling him that she met Bill at the second concert at the Doelenzaal, which was held on Monday, November 28, 1955. Although the flyer Pim kept in her scrapbook is dated Sunday, November 27, 1955, which was the first night Bill played there, suggesting that she might have attended that performance, it seems reasonable that Pim would have recalled which night she attended and that van Gasteren would be an accurate reporter of his conversation with her.

49. Paul Breman, *Blues* (Den Haag: Servire, 1961).

50. Tape of party at home of Michiel de Ruyter, Amsterdam, Holland, November 29, 1955, collection of Guido van Rijn.

51. Ibid. for all quotes in the description and ensuing discussion of this recording.

52. Jeroen is pronounced "yuh-ROON."

53. Margo Bruynoghe interview.

54. Ibid.

55. According to Margo Bruynoghe, the exterior shots were filmed at a different location from the interior ones. Even on a limited budget, Delire liked the look of the stairs so much that he filmed Bill walking there, while shooting the rest of the film at a club located elsewhere in Brussels. Margo Bruynoghe interview.

56. Eric Clapton, interview by author, November 23, 2007.

57. Ray Davies, interview by author, April 3, 2006.

58. Keith Richards, interview by Jas Obrecht, September 17, 1992, http://www.geo cities.com/abexile/keithintgpl.htm (accessed September 10, 2009).

59. Vasset, *Black Brother*, 21.

60. Pim van Isveldt, interview by author, Guido van Rijn, and Erik Mossel, April 29, 2003.

61. The session also led to a falling-out between Bill and De Ruyter. Soon after he made the recordings, Bill wrote De Ruyter asking for his help in persuading the person who had run the session to send Yannick Bruynoghe a copy of the contract he had signed and the set list he had played. Bill acknowledged that he bore some responsibility for not having insisted on this at the time because he had "got drunk" during the session, but he also emphasized that he had taken "that man's word because you told me that he was OK." Letter from Bill Broonzy to Michiel de Ruyter, February 1956, from Collection of Nederlands Jazz Archief. De Ruyter apparently contacted Yannick directly with the relevant information, because when Bill wrote him again on March 1, he was livid. The letter is the most legible Bill ever wrote, because he printed every letter in capitals. "WHY, MR. MIKE, YOU DID NOT WRITE TO ME? WHY DID YOU WRITE TO YANNICK? BECAUSE HE IS WHITE AND I AM A NEGRO? OR BECAUSE I WROTE YOU A LETTER AND SAID KISS YOUR WIFE FOR ME? OR YOU JUST DON'T LIKE ME? OR BECAUSE I SAID SHE WAS A WONDERFUL WOMAN?" Bill threatened to tell "EVERY NEWSPAPER AND MAGAZINE" in Holland that "MIKE RUYTER FED WHISKEY TO BIG BILL BROONZY, A MISSISSIPPI BLUES SINGER, UNTIL HE GOT DRUNK." He would accuse de Ruyter of deceiving him by telling him, "THEY WASN'T RECORDING, BUT THEY WAS," and he wanted "EVERY BLUES SINGER TO KNOW MR. MIKE RUYTER AND WHAT HE DONE TO BIG BILL BROONZY." Big Bill Broonzy to Michiel de Ruyter, March 1, 1956, Collection of Nederlands Jazz Archief.

The next surviving letter from Bill to De Ruyter is dated April 26, and while Bill's anger had receded, there were still signs that the blow-up had affected the relationship between the two men. Bill's primary goal in writing was to ask De Ruyter to send a demo recording from the Baarn session to Yannick, so that he and Bill could listen to it and then reassure Philips that the quality was good enough for commercial release. Although it is unclear from the letter whether Philips had paid Bill anything up to that point, his clear implication is that he would not get paid until the quality of the recording was confirmed. When Bill instructed De Ruyter to send the demo to Yannick, he underscored his awareness of the racial differences that set Yannick and the Dutch broadcaster apart from himself by writing, "Yannick is a white man and he knows more about the blues than I do." Near the end of the letter, Bill praised De Ruyter's wife and parents "because we don't find people in the world that know how to treat Negroes, but your wife does, and your father does. We are just people." Philips did release the record, so evidently some agreement was reached. In the absence of additional correspondence or other information, it is hard to know the extent to which the two were able to repair the bond between them. What is known is that De Ruyter, through liner notes and articles, continued to be the most visible and vocal champion of Bill's work in Holland until and then after his death.

62. "Big Bill Talks," *An Evening with Big Bill Broonzy*, vol. 1, *Recorded in Club Montmartre, Copenhagen, 1956* (Storyville STCD 8016), track 7.

63. "Goodnight Irene," *An Evening with Big Bill Broonzy*, vol. 1 (Storyville STCD 8016), track 18.

64. Edoardo Fassio, "Big Bill Broonzy," *Il Blues*, no. 53 (1995): 18–20.

65. Silvio Botto, "Blues Memories: I Primi Concert Di Blues in Italia: Il Soggiorno Italiano di Big Bill Broonzy," *Feelin' Good*, no. 11 (1987): 23.

66. After the murderers had shot and killed Emmett Till, they used the wire to tie his body to a heavy piece of machinery, which they then threw in a nearby river.

Chapter Eighteen

1. Marriage date from marriage certificate, Office of Cook County (Illinois) Clerk, Vital Records. Her date and place of birth comes from her SS-5, dated December 29, 1936, in which she gave her full name as Rose Walker Lawson.

2. WFMT Program Guide, September 1956, Collection of Ronald D. Cohen.

3. Quoted in Cohen, *Rainbow Quest*, 114.

4. Sy Stern, "Commerce Club's Folk Song Concert Applauded by 125 Northwesterners." *Northwestern News*, March 20, 1950, 2.

5. John von Rhein, "Highlights from a Half-Century on the Air," *Chicago Tribune*, December 16, 2001, sec. 7, p. 5.

6. "This Train Is Bound for Glory," *Big Bill Broonzy and Pete Seeger in Concert: Recorded by WFMT Chicago*, Verve/Folkways LP FW 9008. Also on *Big Bill Broonzy: Trouble in Mind*, Smithsonian Folkways, SFW CD 40131, track 21: "This Train—Spoken Introduction."

7. It was not the first time Bill had used the phrase, as a 1953 recording in Amsterdam preserves a similar comment: "And to me, I think that all songs in the world that you sing is folk songs because horses don't sing songs that I've been around." "Big Bill Talks—on Folk Songs," *Big Bill Broonzy: Amsterdam Live Concerts 1953*, disc 1, track 1. Versions of this quote also appeared in two magazines with national visibility in the United States in the late 1950s and early 1960s. In February 1958, *Down Beat* ran a profile of Bill during his final illness written by Don Gold, in which Bill commented, "You know, you hear people talking about folk songs. You hear people talking about the blues, like it's something else. It's all folk songs. You never hear horses sing 'em." *Down Beat* 25, no. 3, 16. In November 1962, *Time's* lead story focused on "the prevalence and proliferation of folk singing in the land" and featured Joan Baez on the cover. Written by John McPhee, the article noted that Bill "had short patience with all the folk curators who insist that a true folk song has to be of unknown authorship and come down through the oral tradition. 'I guess all songs is folk songs,' he said. 'I never heard no horse sing 'em.'" *Time*, November 23, 1962, 60.

8. "This Train," *Big Bill Broonzy Interviewed by Studs Terkel*, recorded at WFMT on November 14, 1956, Folkways F-3586.

9. Max Jones, "Not Enough of Big Bill," *Melody Maker*, February 23, 1957, 14.

10. Tony Brown, "The Amazing Success Story of Chris Barber," *Melody Maker*, January 5, 1957, 3.

11. Shapiro, *Alexis Korner*, 56.

12. Bobbie Korner, telephone interview with author, June 7, 2005.

13. Ibid.

14. Martin Carthy, telephone interview with author, April 5, 2005.

15. Eric Clapton, interview with author, November 23, 2007.

16. John Pilgrim, interview with author, March 29, 2002. Other background from John Pilgrim from "Davy Graham: Virtuoso Guitarist at the Heart of the British Folk Revival Whose Playing Influenced a Generation," *Independent* (UK), December 17, 2008.

17. Martin Carthy interview.

18. Ibid.

19. Bert Jansch, interview with author, February 17, 2004.

20. John Pilgrim interview.

21. John Renbourn, interview with author, April 23, 2004.

22. "Jack Good," *BFI Screen Online*, http://www.screenonline.org.uk/people/id/574 989/index.html (accessed October 1, 2009).

23. Script for March 9, 1957, broadcast of *Six-Five Special*, collection of Brian Towers.

24. Undated card from Big Bill Broonzy to Pim van Isveldt, Pim van Isveldt Collection.

25. Ibid.

26. "Broonzy and Sellers Welcomed by Barber," *Melody Maker*, February 23, 1957, 14.

27. In a 2003 interview, Pim stated, "That's what I didn't understand. Because he married, I find out, two times, Rose, but not the same." Pim van Isveldt interview with Guido van Rijn, Erik Mossel, and author, April 29, 2003.

28. "Talk on Spirituals," *The Blues, with Studs Terkel Interviewing Big Bill Broonzy, Sonny Terry, Brownie McGhee* (Folkways FS 3817), track 10. The track is listed in the liner notes as "Side II, Band 3."

29. Tape of Big Bill Broonzy and Pete Seeger performing at Circle Pines Center, July 6, 1957, from Collection of American Folklife Center, Library of Congress, Washington, DC.

30. Mary Katherine Aldin, notes to *A Musical Journey: The Films of Pete, Toshi, and Dan Seeger*, Vestapol VHS 13042.

31. Pete Seeger, interview with author, August 18, 2002.

32. "Music: Top Jock," *Time*, February 14, 1955.

33. Randle's introduction of Presley is described in Peter Guralnick, *Last Train to Memphis: The Rise of Elvis Presley* (Boston: Little, Brown, 1994), 244–45.

34. Bill Randle, "Big Bill Broonzy: Last Session," *ABC TV Hootenanny* magazine, vol. 1, no. 2 (April 1964): 68.

35. Bill Randle interview with author, April 13, 2004.

36. Robert Pruter, *Doowop: The Chicago Scene* (Urbana: University of Illinois Press, 1996), 16.

37. Unedited recording of Randle sessions, July 12–14, 1957, reels 1 and 2, track 1, Bill Randle Collection.

38. Ibid., reel 17.

39. *The Big Bill Broonzy Story*, disc 2, track 17.

40. Ibid., disc 3, track 3.

41. Ibid.

42. Unedited recording of Randle sessions, July 12–14, 1957, reels 1 and 2.

43. *The Big Bill Broonzy Story*, disc 1, track 8.

44. This exchange was not included in the commercially released set. Remarks about Elvis Presley from disc 1, track 8.

45. Quoted in Peter Guralnick, "Elvis Presley," in *Rolling Stone Illustrated History of Rock & Roll*, ed. Anthony DeCurtis and James Henske with Holly George-Warren, original editor Jim Miller (New York: Random House, 1980), 24.

46. Unedited recording of Big Bill Broonzy sessions, July 12–14, 1957, reels 5 and 6. Yannick Bruynoghe, in an essay written after Bill's death for a British collection of articles on jazz, recalled Bill singing the same song: "And by the way, Bill, you, too, sometimes sang *Dirty Mother for You* on that same tune, and what lyrics you had to sing it!" Yannick Bruynoghe, "Big Bill," in *This Is Jazz*, ed. Ken Williamson (London: Newnes, 1960), 94.

47. Randle sessions, reels 11 and 12.

48. On March 16, 1953, Michiel de Ruyter wrote to Bill that "you told me last

Wednesday that you were going to Algiers and Senegal once again." Letter from Collection of Nederlands Jazz Archief. Bill did travel to Algeria in January 1953, as he mailed a postcard to Win Stracke from Oran, and his performance with Mezz Mezzrow had been written up in an Algerian newspaper. If he traveled to Senegal, it would almost certainly have been part of the January trip to North Africa.

49. Randle sessions, reel 17.

50. Ibid.

51. Randle, "Big Bill Broonzy: Last Session," 24.

52. John S. Wilson, "Document of a Blues Singer," *New York Times*, July 19, 1961.

53. Bruynoghe, "Big Bill," 89. In this article, Bruynoghe recalls that the surgery took place in August 1957. It seems likely that the surgery took place closer to the session, given that Yannick referred in a 1958 article to the operation taking place the day after the final Randle session in "Chicago, Home of the Blues," in *Just Jazz 2*, ed. Sinclair Traill and Gerald Lescalles (London: Peter Davis, 1958). In a 1964 article, Bill Randle also noted that the surgery took place "a few days after the sessions were completed." Randle, "Big Bill Broonzy: Last Session," 24.

54. Bruynoghe, "Big Bill," 89.

55. Don Gold, "Big Bill Broonzy Benefit Concert," *Down Beat* 25, no. 1 (January 9, 1958): 37.

56. Ibid.

57. Hoke Norris, "A Singing Man Sits Silent at His Rousing Benefit," *Chicago Sun-Times*, November 29, 1957, 57.

58. Ibid.

59. Ibid.

60. Cohen, *Rainbow Quest*, 114.

61. Gold, "Broonzy Benefit Concert," 37–38.

62. Norris, "Singing Man Sits Silent."

63. Gold, "Broonzy Benefit Concert," 37.

64. Win Stracke interview by Mark Dvorak, June 14, 1990.

65. Win Stracke, "Biography of a Hunch," in *Biography of a Hunch: The History of Chicago's Legendary Old Town School of Folk Music*, ed. Lisa Grayson (Chicago: Old Town School of Folk Music, 1992), 1.

66. Stracke interview by Mark Dvorak, June 14, 1990.

67. Stracke, "Biography of a Hunch," in *Biography of a Hunch*, 1–2.

68. Dawn Greening had been involved from before the beginning—as Hamilton noted, "Dawn and [her husband] Nate Greening officially started the School by having my classes in their living room"—and later succeeded Soltker as administrator. E-mail from Frank Hamilton to author, November 8, 2002.

69. Win Stracke, essay in pamphlet, "The Old Town School of Folk Music: Its First Ten Years, or The Biography of a Hunch," 1967, 2. From Collection of Old Town School of Folk Music.

70. Ibid., 2–3.

71. Frank Hamilton, "Old Town School of Folkmusic [sic] and Other News from Chicago," undated newsletter, likely January–February 1958. Collection of Ronald D. Cohen.

72. Margo Bruynoghe interview.

73. Yannick Bruynoghe, "In Chicago with Big Bill and Friends," *Living Blues*, no. 55 (Winter 1982/83): 7.

74. Margo Bruynoghe interview.

75. Yannick Bruynoghe, "In Chicago with Big Bill and Friends," 13, 11.

76. Bruynoghe, "Chicago, Home of the Blues," 67–76.

77. "Big Bill Broonzy May Never Sing Again," *Melody Maker*, January 11, 1958, 1.

78. "Skiffle and Jazz to Help Broonzy," *Melody Maker*, January 18, 1958, 1.

79. Humphrey Lyttelton, "Humph Says . . . Big Bill Broonzy Is in Trouble—You Can Help," *Melody Maker*, February 1, 1958, 2.

80. Pat Brand, "Silent Broonzy," from "On the Beat with Pat Brand," *Melody Maker*, February 22, 1958, 10.

81. Bernie Asbell, "The Whisper of Big Bill Broonzy," *Melody Maker*, February 8, 1958, 13.

82. Tony Brown, "Well Done! Broonzy Benefit," *Melody Maker*, March 15, 1958, 3.

83. Bob Dawbarn, "Reunion at Broonzy Concert," *Melody Maker*, March 22, 1958, 6.

84. Circle Pines Center newsletter, *Pine Needles* 18, no. 3 (April–May 1958).

85. Max Jones, "Big Bill: 'Thanks,'" in "This World of Jazz," *Melody Maker*, April 5, 1958, 10.

86. Ibid.

87. Chris Smith—in his essay "An Overview of the Recordings," in his discography *That's the Stuff: The Recordings of Brownie McGhee, Sonny Terry, Stick McGhee and J. C. Burris* (Shetland: The Housay Press, 1999), xiv—notes that "Brownie, for one, was adamant on his arrival in London that he was only making the trip as a favour to Bill."

88. Recording dated spring 1958, made by Sonny Terry and Brownie McGhee in Germany, with the assistance of Günter Boas. Collection of Lore Boas.

89. Win Stracke to Yannick Bruynoghe, August 12, 1958, from Bruynoghe Collection.

90. Win Stracke to Yannick Bruynoghe, August 30, 1958, Bruynoghe Collection.

91. Telegrams from collection of the Stracke family.

92. Rosie Tolbert, Lannie Wesley's granddaughter, interview with author, May 13, 2005.

93. Jo Ann Jackson and Rosie Tolbert, interview with Scott Barretta and author, Scott, Mississippi, April 21, 2009.

94. Don Gold, "Tangents: Big Bill Broonzy," *Down Beat* 25, no. 20 (October 2, 1958): 42.

95. Ibid.

96. "Best of the Blues," *Time*, September 1, 1958, 39.

97. "Weep No More," *Ebony*, November 1958, 154–55.

98. Whitney Balliett, "The Best Medicine," in *Collected Works: A Journal of Jazz, 1954–2000* (London: Granta Books, 2000), 71, 72. The original article appeared in the October 25, 1958, issue of the *New Yorker*.

99. Alexis Korner to Win Stracke, August 18, 1958, from Stracke family collection.

Epilogue

1. Borneman, "Big Bill Talkin'."

2. Nat Hentoff, "A Life in the Blues," *HiFi Stereo Review* 7, no. 2 (August 1961): 72; Ralph J. Gleason, "Big Bill Reminiscences through a Life in the Blues," in "The Rhythm Section" of "This World" section, *San Francisco Sunday Chronicle*, March 26, 1961, 23.

3. Charters, *The Country Blues*, 172–73.

4. Charles Keil, *Urban Blues* (Chicago: University of Chicago Press, 1966), 100–101, 224. Studs Terkel, in his August 1966 book review of *Urban Blues* for the *Chicago Tribune*, described the book as containing "dazzling insights and equally dazzling errors," and highlighted the reference to Bill as "pseudo-country" as "an unforgiveably [*sic*] whopping howler." Terkel commented, "The crowning irony is the author's tribute to Muddy Waters while dismissing Broonzy," and he added that if Keil had attended Bill's funeral, "He'd have heard Muddy, a pallbearer, speak of the dead man as 'my great influence.'" Studs Terkel, "Making a Case for a Plural Culture," *Chicago Tribune*, August 7, 1966, "Books Today" section, 5.

5. Charlie Gillett, "Getting to Know Snooks Eaglin," *Freedom Anarchist Weekly*, August 31, 1968, reprinted in *Backwoods Blues* (Bexhill-on-Sea, Sussex: Blues Unlimited, 1968), 36–37.

6. Willie Dixon, in his autobiography *I Am the Blues*, commented that "Big Bill Broonzy had been going over to Europe and telling people that he was the last of the blues artists in America" (126).

7. Eric Clapton interviewed on *All Things Considered*, National Public Radio, October 17, 2007.

8. Eric Clapton, interview by author, November 23, 2007.

9. Ibid.

10. "Eric Clapton Interviewed," *Guitarist*, no. 233 (February 2003): 116.

11. Ibid.

12. Pete Townshend, e-mail interview by author, May 26, 2005.

13. Will Hodgkinson, "Home Entertainment," *Guardian*, May 17, 2002.

14. *Ray Davies: The Storyteller* (KOC-CD-9995), track 28.

15. Hodgkinson, "Home Entertainment."

16. Ray Davies, interview by author, April 3, 2006.

17. Ibid.

18. Email correspondence with Michael van Isveldt, October 23, 2003.

19. McKee and Chisenhall, *Beale Street Black & Blue*, 237.

20. Henry Miller to Yannick Bruynoghe, October 7, 1956, reprinted in *Living Blues*, no. 55 (Winter 1982/83): 23.

21. After Yannick Bruynoghe died of cancer in 1984, Margo Bruynoghe worked with Ludd, a French publisher, to produce a new French-language edition in 1987 of *Big Bill Blues*. It included several previously unpublished photos from their collection and a new preface by Margo. William Lee Conley Broonzy and Yannick Bruynoghe, *Big Bill Blues* (Paris: Ludd, 1987).

22. Studs Terkel, "Big Bill's Last Session," in *Jazz: a Quarterly of American Music*, October 1958, 13. Terkel also honored the memory of Win Stracke in the years after Stracke's death in 1991. The obituary he wrote in *Sing Out!* magazine began, "Win Stracke was my oldest friend." "Win Stracke—Bard of Chicago," *Sing Out!* 36, no. 3 (November/December 1991/January 1992).

23. Willie Dixon, liner notes to *Remembering Big Bill: Soul Blues Sung by Big Bill Broonzy* (Mercury SR 60905).

24. Pim van Isveldt interview.

25. "Big Bill Broonzy Sings the Songs of His People," *Haagsche Courant*, November 8, 1952; reprinted in *Block*, no. 76 (1990): 27.

26. Gerry Miga, "Big Bill Broonzy Memories," *Haagse Jazz Club* 3, no. 7 (April 8, 1953), from Nederlands Jazz Archives, Amsterdam.

27. Introduction to "Black, Brown, and White," February 26, 1953, *Amsterdam Live Concerts, 1953.*

28. Big Bill Broonzy file, Ray M. Lawless Collection, American Folklife Center, Library of Congress. Professor Lawless was compiling information for his book *Folksingers and Folksongs of America* (New York: Duell, Sloan and Pearce, 1960). Quote to Terkel from Randle sessions, reel 17, track 1.

29. Billy Boy Arnold, interview by author, October 30, 2002. It is possible that Hattie Harrell may be the "Harriet" who Bill identified for the Dutch audiences as his daughter. In a letter to Yannick shortly after Bill's death, Win Stracke mentioned an outstanding "loan of about [$]230.00" against Bill's $500 life insurance policy from the Local 208 musicians' union. Win identified the reason for the loan as "legal expenses when Bill shot Hattie's husband in Mrs. Moore's tavern." Win Stracke to Yannick Bruynoghe, August 30, 1958, Bruynoghe Collection. No documentation for this was found in Bill's file in the Local 208 records in the Blues Archive of the Chicago Public Library. Hattie Harrell's death certificate, for which her mother, Rose Lawson Broonzy, provided the information, stated that she was never married.

Jav Walker described visiting Bill's apartment with her husband while attending a Modern Language Association conference in Chicago in the 1950s. She recalled meeting a daughter of Bill's (whom she believed might have been Hattie, based on looking at photos of Hattie taken at the funeral) and her husband. Mrs. Walker noted that the daughter's husband "really disliked us being there," and added, "Bill said afterwards that he was really a mean person." She remembered hearing later that "after Bill had been doing well in Chicago and got his own night club, the son-in-law came in and started a fight inside, and Bill said, 'OK, we're going to take this out in the street.' And he got a gun from behind the bar and went out and shot the son-in-law. And everybody said it was in self-defense, because the son-in-law had been really mean, evil-acting, and he had a knife, also a gun." She recalled that she had this information because Bill "wrote about that to the Feinbergs." Jav Walker, interview by author, May 12, 2006. No documentation has been found to date to support this account, as there is no surviving correspondence from the Feinbergs, and there is no mention of Bill in the Criminal Felony Index of the Cook County Court Records from September 1949 through August 1958.

30. Frank Wesley, interview by author, October 17, 2004.

31. Death notice for Rose Lawson Broonzy, *Arkansas Democrat-Gazette*, July 24, 1997.

32. Transcribed from footage of "President Obama 2009 Inaugural Ceremony," found in the C-Span online video archive at http://www.c-spanvideo.org/program/283479-1 (accessed June 4, 2010).

33. Chris Smith, "Words, Words, Words," *Blues & Rhythm: The Gospel Truth*, no. 239 (May 2009): 24. Smith identifies several sources, including a 1942 Zora Neale Hurston article in the *American Mercury*, with phrasing very close to the language Bill used in "Black, Brown, and White Blues."

INDEX

bebop, 157–58, 172

Bechet, Sidney: in "Blues at Midnight," 126; in Chicago, 45–46; in "From Spirituals to Swing" concert (Carnegie Hall, 1938), 92; in "From Spirituals to Swing" concert (Carnegie Hall, 1939), 95; in "Honky Tonk Blues at Midnight," 128; honorary membership in The Hague Jazz Club, 194; marriage of, 160; performance in London (1919), 156; at the Vieux-Colombier (Juan-les-Pins, French Riviera), 160; at the Vieux-Colombier (Paris), 169–70

Beiderbecke, Bix, 65

Belchaire, Jerry, 19, 266n3

Belcher, Jerry, 19–20, 23–24, 40, 56, 113, 121, 235

Belcher, Mittie. *See* Bradley, Mittie

Bell, Graeme, 160–62

Bell Band (Graeme Bell Australian Jazz Band), 160–62, 164

Bernay, Eric, 95

Berry, Chuck, 249

Bertrand, Jimmy, 73

Big Bill and His Rhythm Band, 127

Big Bill and Moore's Lounge (Chicago), 202–3, 253, 306n29

"Big Bill Blues," 48, 51–52, 58, 69, 274n43

Big Bill Blues (W. Broonzy): anecdotes/tales in, 210, 212; and *The Big Bill Broonzy Story*, 235; on Big Maceo Merriweather, 143; on "Black, Brown, and White Blues," 162–63, 210; the Bruynoghes' work on, 152, 201, 207–8, 211, 251, 305n21; on contest with Memphis Minnie, 211–12; editing of, 4, 209; errata to, 211; French-language edition of, 213, 305n21; on Green, 104; on "Mr. White," 210; on musicians' vices, 210–11; organization of, 208; on parents, 7–8; on poverty of/hardships suffered by family, 12–13; promotion of, 213; publication of, 208–9; serialized by *Melody Maker*, 213; on Sonny Boy Williamson, 144; on Washboard Sam, 78; white audience for, 209; writing skill in, ix, 209

Big Bill Broonzy & His Fat Four, 127

Big Bill Broonzy and Pete Seeger in Concert, 226

Big Bill Broonzy Story, The, 234–38, 247, 281n7

"Big Bill's Last Session," 252

"Big Rock Candy Mountain, The," 133

Billboard, 130, 139

Bishop, Wally, 159

"Black, Brown, and White Blues," 126–27, 132–33, 162–63, 170, 210, 232, 248, 254–55, 261, 306n33

Black Bob, 79, 87, 89, 278n24

"Black Cat Rag," 62

blacks. *See* African Americans

Black Swan Records, 47

Blackwell, Scrapper, 75–76, 83

Blake, Blind, 46, 49, 68, 87, 275n10, 276–77n42

Blitzstein, Marc, 134

Bluebird label, 74, 78, 80, 82, 101–2, 121

Bluebirds, 215

Blue Note (Chicago), 180–82

blues: acoustic, 248; American Folk Blues Festivals, 161, 197, 252; beginnings of, 46; Bill on, 223, 236; Bill on urban vs. rural, 164; British blues scene, 228–29; Bruynoghes' photographs of Chicago musicians, 241–42, 251; Chicago venues for in 1920s and 30s, 51; contest between Bill and Memphis Minnie, 211–12; coverage in *Chicago Defender*, 102; eight-bar, 121, 286n27; first tribute album, 250–51; growth of, 83–84; guitar-piano pairings in, 66, 75–76, 83–84, 109–12; at house rent parties, 49–51; and jazz, 89–90, 95–96, 158, 164; and New Orleans jazz, 89–90; overseas tours by musicians, 247; popularity among white audiences, 247–48; and rock music in 1960s, 248–49; sources of, 164–65, 232 (*see also* reels; spirituals); twelve-bar, 121, 164, 286n27. *See also individual musicians and groups*

"Blues at Midnight" (Town Hall, NYC, 1946), 126–28, 287n6

"Blues Before Sunrise," 75

Blues for Monday (radio program), 197

Blues in the Mississippi Night, 14, 30–31, 128–32, 232, 261, 287n21, 288n26

Boas, Günter, 196–97, 244

Boas, Lore, 197

Boigelot, Jacques, 220

bottleneck guitar, 56–57

"Bourgeois Blues," 239

Bowden, Bernice, 16

Boyd, Eddie, 112, 142, 223, 242

Bradbury, Jane Stracke, 135

Bradley, Andrew (brother), 7, 45, 64–65, 276n32

Bradley, Anna Lou (*née* Sparks), 6, 265n2 (ch. 2)
Bradley, Bertha (sister-in-law), 204
Bradley, Frank (father): on Bill's marriage to Gertrude, 39; birth/background of, 6, 265–66n2; children of (*see* Bradley, Andrew; Bradley, Frank, Jr.; Bradley, James; Bradley, Rachel; Broonzy, Big Bill; Burford, Mattie; Dove, Mary; Dozier, Gustavia; Taffie, Sallie; Wesley, Lannie); death of, 104; finances of/property owned by, 10, 12–13; in Jefferson County, 10; marriage to Anna, 6, 265n2 (ch. 2); marriage to Mittie, 6–7, 265n2 (ch. 2), 266n3 (*see also* Bradley, Mittie); as a porter/salesman, 15–16; religious life of, 28; as a sharecropper, 9
Bradley, Frank, Jr. (brother): birth of, 266n3; finances of, 204–5; house shared with his mother, 105, 283n29; in North Little Rock, 204
Bradley, Gustavia. *See* Dozier, Gustavia
Bradley, Heaster, 266–67n4
Bradley, James (brother), 7, 33, 37–38, 266n3
Bradley, Lannie. *See* Wesley, Lannie
Bradley, Lee. *See* Broonzy, Big Bill
Bradley, Mary (sister). *See* Dove, Mary
Bradley, Mary (sister-in-law), 64–65, 276n32
Bradley, Mattie. *See* Burford, Mattie
Bradley, Mittie (*née* Belcher; mother): attends Bill's performance, 120; birth/background of, 6, 266n2, 267n3; children of (*see* Bradley, Frank, Jr.; Bradley, James; Broonzy, Big Bill; Burford, Mattie; Dove, Mary; Dozier, Gustavia; Taffie, Sallie; Wesley, Lannie); as dark-skinned, 18; death of, 267n3, 268n18; finances of, 204–5; in Jefferson County, 10; marriage to Frank, 6–7, 265n2 (ch. 2), 266n3; in North Little Rock, 104, 120, 204, 283–84n29; religious life of, 28, 119–20
Bradley, Rachel (sister), 7, 266–67n3–4
Bradley, Sallie. *See* Taffie, Sallie
Bradley family: Bill's account of history of, 7–8, 11–12 (see also *Big Bill Blues*); crop failure's impact on, 204–5; in Jefferson County, 8–10, 15; records/documents concerning, 6, 10
Brasswell, Frank (or Braswell), 61–65, 260, 275–76n26
Breman, Paul, 217–19, 268n21
British Musicians' Union, 163

Broonzy, Big Bill (Lee Conley Bradley), 236–37; in Algeria, 302n48; in Ames, 147–54, 291n6; arrival in Chicago, 44–45; auditions with Mayo Williams, 47–49; autobiography of (see *Big Bill Blues*); Big Bill and Moore's Lounge owned by, 202–3; birth of, 7, 10, 12; on blues, 223, 236; brothel story by, 39–40; and the Bruynoghes (*See* Bruynoghe, Margo; Bruynoghe, Yannick); Carr praised by, 75–76; Chicago benefit concert for (1957), 238–40; children, at ease with, 152; at Circle Pines Center, 206–7, 232–33, 297n10; collaboration with Memphis Slim, 111–13, 128; criticism of, 141, 248, 305n6; death of, 1, 122, 223, 244, 291n5; in Denmark, 18, 223; departure from Ames, 154–55; departure from Arkansas, 10–11; and de Ruyter, 194–95, 217–18, 222, 299–300n61, 302n48; diddley bow played by, 205; divorce from Gertrude, 41–43; divorce from Rose Allen Broonzy, 153–54, 231; Dutch grandchildren of, 252–53; eating preferences of, 191; education of, 16, 168, 268n24, 293n5; extended family of, 18–19; fame/popularity of, 1, 247, 251; family history according to, 7–8; in the Famous Hokum Boys, 61–64, 66; farming learned by, 14–15; and the Feinbergs, 147–50, 152, 154, 291n6; as a fiddler, 21–23, 26, 54, 73, 86–87; finances of, 71, 106–8, 148, 174, 179, 182, 238–40; flat-picking (guitar) by, 68, 72; as a folk-oriented musician, 137–38, 200, 225–26; on folk songs, 226, 301n7; as a foundry worker, 71; funeral of, 1–4, 144, 245, 253–54, 265n8; in Germany, 160–62, 164, 166, 196–97, 223; grave site of, 4, 244, 254; as Green's guitarist, 103–4; as a grocery boy, 71; as a guitarist, 21, 23, 26, 45–47, 62, 68, 70, 73, 90, 161, 173, 250, 293n13; guitar thumb-stroke of, 73, 230, 232–33; and Günter Boas, 196–97, 244; and Hammond, 91–92, 97, 146, 281n4, 290n27; health of, 147–48, 291n5; as a historian of blues, 164–65; in Holland, 193–95, 217, 222, 230–31; honorary membership in The Hague Jazz Club, 194; in Iceland, 193; influence on musicians, ix, 3–4, 140, 163, 229–30, 236, 244, 248–50, 304n4; influences on, 68–69, 76, 87–88; interviewed by Terkel on WFMT, 200–201, 205–6, 213, 227, 232;

Broonzy, Big Bill (continued)
at Iowa State College (University), 16, 148, 150–51, 268n24, 291n6; in Italy, 223–24; Lester Melrose criticized by, 146; and Lester Melrose's success, Bill's contributions to, 84–86; letters to friends/acquaintances, 168–69; in Local 208 union, 98–99, 251, 282n1, 282n3, 306n29; London benefit concert for (Dominion Theater, 1958), 242–43; London benefit concert for (London Coliseum, 1958), 242–43; in *Low Light and Blue Smoke*, 220–22, 230, 233–34, 263–64, 299n55; lung cancer/surgeries of, 2, 234–35, 238, 242–44, 291n5; marriage to Gertrude (*see* Embrey, Gertrude); marriage to Rose Allen (*see* Broonzy, Rose ("Texas Rose"; *née* Allen; wife)); marriage to Rose Lawson, 225, 231–32, 253–54, 300n1, 306; Martin guitar of, 251; as a mentor, ix, 15, 53, 111, 113–14, 140–42, 178–79; musical career, choice of, 41, 272n7; musical origins/training of, 21–25, 27–28, 46–47, 87, 173–74, 235; musicians endorsed by, 165; Papa Charlie Jackson's mentoring of, 46–49; persona crafted by, 164–65; personality/worldview of, 131, 165, 178–79; photos on EP and LP covers, 174, 222–23; plays at opening night of Old Town School of Folk Music, 241; politics of, 192–93; praised by other musicians, 140–42; as a preacher, 28–29, 40–41; provides descriptions of his children, 252–53, 306n29 (*see also* van Isveldt, Michael); as a Pullman porter, 44–45; Quaye's portrait of, 184; on racial equality, 218–20; on racial prejudice, 175–76; reading/writing learned by, 16, 168, 268n24, 293n5; relationship with Jacqueline, 175, 185, 196, 199–200; relationship with Lannie (*see* Wesley, Lannie); relationship with mother, 104, 119–20; relationship with Pim (*see* van Isveldt, Pim); relationship with Washboard Sam, 78–79, 279n32; religious life of, 28–29; royalties for, 52–53, 61, 71, 80–81, 106–9, 169, 280n37, 284n39, 286n30; on self-respect/dignity, 177–79; in Senegal, 237, 302n48; siblings of (*see* Bradley, Andrew; Bradley, Frank, Jr.; Bradley, James; Bradley, Rachel; Burford, Mattie; Dove, Mary; Dozier, Gustavia; Taffie, Sallie; Wesley, Lannie); singing style/voice of,

28, 73; and skiffle, 214; as a smoker, 234; songwriting skills of, 80, 103, 115–16; on southern violence against blacks, 128–32 (see also *Blues in the Mississippi Night*); in Spain, 197, 296n32; speculates on his African roots, 237; on spirituals, 245; stature of, 4–5, 142, 165, 232, 247, 252; stories written down by, 152; as a storyteller, 5, 7–8, 13–14; and Vasset, 195–96, 199, 207; versatility/adaptability of, 27, 54, 96, 103, 161; visits to North Little Rock, 13, 104–6, 204–5; voice lost following surgery, 238, 303n53; and the Walkers, 149–53, 292n16, 306n29; works at Merchandise Mart, 99–100, 108; WPA work by, 99–100
—EUROPEAN TOURS: first (1951), 1, 4, 157, 159–64; second (1951–52), 168–75, 179; third (1952–53), 182–85, 193–97; fourth (1955), 212–17, 220–22; fifth (1956), 222–24; sixth (1957), 227–32
—NAMES AND PSEUDONYMS: Big Bill Broonzy, 11, 18–19, 53–54; Big Bill Johnson, 66, 72, 293n28; Chicago Bill, 165–66; Lee Bradley, 10, 18, 267n14, 268n17; Sammy Sampson, 64, 278n22, 280n37; Slim Hunter, 72; William Johnson, 165–66, 293n28
—PERFORMANCES: in Ames, 150–51; at the Apollo Theater, 145; artistry/presentation in, 173–74, 215, 246; in Barcelona, 197, 296n32; at the Barrelhouse and Blues Club, 228–29; at the Blue Note, 181–82; "Blues at Midnight"/"Midnight Special," 126–28, 287n6; at Cambridge Theatre (London), 172–73; at the Club Montmartre, 223; at the Cozy Corner, 112; at dances/picnics, 25, 40–41; at the de Ruyters's, 217–18; at the Dew Drop Inn, 151; at the Doelenzaal, 217; with Dorsey, 76, 278nn22–23; on *Downbeat*, 216; with electric guitar, 283n22; final, 243; first *Chicago Defender* ad for, 110; at folk music school, 1; at the 1410 Club, 285n53; friends' arrangement of, 4; "From Spirituals to Swing" concert (Carnegie Hall, 1938), 92–97, 126; "From Spirituals to Swing" concert (Carnegie Hall, 1939), 94–95, 97, 126, 232; at the Gate of Horn, 226; at the German Jazz Festival, 196–97; Glaser's bookings for, 145; with the Graeme Bell Australian Jazz Band, 160–62, 164; at Hollywood

Rendezvous, 127, 168; on the *Ile de France* (ocean liner), 168; on *Jazz Sociëteit*, 217; at Kingsway Hall (London), 163–64, 214–15; with Mahalia Jackson, 183–84, 239; on the "Midnight Ramble," 112–13; *Midnight Special* (radio program), 201, 225–26; at Northwestern University, 226; at 100 Oxford Street, 184, 216; at opening night of Old Town School of Folk Music, 1, 241; in People's Songs events, 125–26, 132–33; repertoire in string band as young man, 26–27; at Roosevelt University, 227; at the Royal Festival Hall, 216, 228; at Ruby's Tavern, 110–12, 127; at the Salle Pleyel (Paris), 170–71; at Silvio's, 179–80, 222; on *Six-Five Special*, 230; at the Stoll Theatre, 230–31; at Temple Sinai, 151; at the University of Chicago, 205, 212–13, 243; at Usher Hall (Edinburgh), 171–72, 294n13; at the Vieux-Colombier (Juan-les-Pins, French Riviera), 160; at the Vieux-Colombier (Paris), 169–70; Yugoslav relief, benefit for, 287n6; at the Zanzibar, 151
Broonzy, Rose ("Texas Rose"; *née* Allen; wife), 101, 153–54, 225, 231, 290n25
Broonzy, Rose (*née* Lawson; wife), 1, 225, 231–32, 238, 244, 253–54, 282n10, 300n1, 306n31
Broonzy family. *See* Bradley family
Brown, Charles, 139
Brown, Fleming, 201, 212–13, 226, 239
Brown, Henry and Mary, 78
Brown, Les, 226
Brown, Robert. *See* Washboard Sam
Brown, Ruth, 25
Brown, Sterling, 94
Brown, Willie, 60
"Brown Skin Girls," 88
"Brown Skin Shuffle," 72
Brunswick Record Corporation, 96–97, 280n41, 282n13 (ch. 8)
Bruynoghe, Guy, 186
Bruynoghe, Margo (*née* Vanbesien): background of, 187; Bill's relationship with, 4, 185, 190–91; Bill's writing/storytelling encouraged by, 190; courtship with/ marriage to Yannick, 187–88, 207; and Jacqueline, 200; on *Low Light and Blue Smoke*, 221, 299n55; visits Bill in Chicago, 104, 241–42; work on Bill's autobiography, 152, 207–8, 251, 305n21 (see also *Big Bill Blues*)

Bruynoghe, Yannick: in the army, 186; with Bill in Brussels, 159, 187; Bill's bookings/travel arrangements handled by, 188–90, 193, 295n4; on Bill's claim of Washboard Sam as his half-brother, 279n32; and Bill's conflict with de Ruyter, 299–300n61; Bill's letters to, 199, 205, 251; Bill's relationship with, 4, 185; on Bill's surgery, 303n53; Bill's writing/ storytelling encouraged by, 190; birth/ background of, 186; courtship with/marriage to Margo, 187–88, 207; death of, 305n21; Hines recording session organized by, 242; jazz program of, 186–87; *Low Light and Blue Smoke*, role in producing, 220–21, 241; *Midnight Movie Club* hosted by, 207; in New York City, 186; and Panassié, 186–87; photography by, 186, 241–42, 251; records bought by, 242; on "Truckin' Little Woman," 302n46; visits Bill in Chicago, 104, 241–42; work on Bill's autobiography, 152, 201, 207–8, 211, 251 (see also *Big Bill Blues*)
"Bull Cow Blues," 73, 77, 116
Bumble Bee Slim (Amos Easton), 85, 88
Burford, Ben (brother-in-law), 65, 101, 276n32
Burford, Mattie (*née* Bradley; sister), 7, 65, 101, 276n32
Burton, James, 249
Buter, Hans, 231
Butterbeans and Susie, 46
Byas, Don, 145

Cabat, Léon, 162
Calhoun, Cora (*pseud.* Lovie Austin), 48
Call, Bob, 167, 291n1
Cambridge Theatre (London), 172–73
Camp Robinson (*formerly* Camp Pike, near Little Rock), 31–34
"C and A Blues, 89
Capone, Al, 111
Carmichael, Hoagy, 65
Carr, Leroy, 4, 75–76, 83, 88
Carter, A. P., 236–37
Carter, Louis, 40
Carter Family, 89
Carthy, Eliza, 229
Carthy, Martin, 229–30
Carver, George Washington, 148–49, 269n2, 291n7
Cash, Johnny, ix, 40, 131
Casimir, Bill, 167

Gillum, Jazz (continued)
collaboration with, 78, 85–87; birth/
background of, 79, 279n34; death of,
279n34; decline of, 142; harmonica play-
ing by, 144; "Jazz" nickname acquired
by, 80, 279n35; "Key to the Highway"
recorded by, 121–22; musical origins/
training of, 79–80; popularity of, 78;
recordings with Bluebird, 80; style of,
80
"Give Your Mama One More Smile," 103
Glaser, Joe, 145, 290n25
Gleason, Ralph J., 247
"Glory of Love, The," 237
"Going to Memphis," 131
Golden Gate Quartet, 94
Good, Jack, 230
Goodman, Benny, 90, 94, 102, 181
"Good Morning, School Girl," 143–44
"Goodnight Irene," 223
Gordon, James ("Jimmie"), 278n24
gospel music, 56–57, 274n3
Graeme Bell Australian Jazz Band (Bell
Band), 160–62, 164
Graham, Davy, 229–30
"Grandma's Farm," 63
Grand Ole Opry (Nashville), 134
Grand Theatre (Chicago), 46
Granz, Norman, 238, 247
Great Depression, 51, 95
Green, Lil, 85; Bill as guitarist for, 103–4;
birth/background of, 101, 283n17; death
of, 104; decline of, 142; launch of musi-
cal career, 101; media coverage of, 102,
104; Lester Melrose's recordings of,
101–2; popularity/success of, 101–2;
in prison, 101; "Romance in the Dark,"
101–2; on tour, 90, 101–4, 107, 120;
"Why Don't You Do Right?" recorded
by, 102
Greening, Dawn, 240, 303n68
"Greensleeves," 137
Grossman, Albert, 226
Grossman, Stefan, 233
guitar, bottleneck, 56–57
"Guitar Rag," 62
Guthrie, Woody, 125, 175, 206

Hadjo, Georges, 159–60
Hague Jazz Club, The, 194
Hall, Vera, 175
Ham Gravy. See Washboard Sam
Hamilton, Frank, 239–41, 303n68

Hammond, John: Bill seeks advice from,
146, 290n27; Bill signs with, 91–92, 97,
281n4; on Bill's origins, 173; "From Spiri-
tuals to Swing" concert (Carnegie Hall,
1938) organized by, 92–93, 96; "From
Spirituals to Swing" concert (Carnegie
Hall, 1939) organized by, 94–95; at
Mercury, 146; and recording session for
Sellers, 227–28; on the Scottsboro Boys'
trials, 95
Handy, W. C., 26, 281n9 (ch. 7)
Hanlon, Walter, 174
Hard Day's Night, A, 216
"Hard Headed Woman," 115
"Hard Hearted Woman," 108
Harlem Hamfats, 89–90
harmonicas, 80, 144
Harrell, Hattie (stepdaughter), 253–54,
306n29
Harris, R. H., 101
Harris, Wynonie, 139
Hawes, Bess Lomax, 240
Haynes, Leroy, 191–92
Haynes restaurant (Paris), 191–92
Hegamin, Lucille, 46
"Hellfighters" Band, 156
Hellmuth, Joseph K., 153
Help!, 216
Henderson, Fletcher, 65
Henry, Simeon, 101, 103–4
Hentoff, Nat, 247
"Hey, Hey," 167, 204, 221–22, 249
High Fidelity (magazine), 201
Hill Top Inn Orchestra, 65
Hines, Earl, 242
"Hip Shakin' Strut," 68
Hitler, Adolf, 161–62
"Hit the Right Lick," 107
Hogg, Smokey, 223
hokum (music style), 55, 61, 67–68
"Hokum Stomp," 68
Hollywood Rendezvous (Chicago), 127, 168
Holzfeind, Frank, 180–81
"Honky Tonk Blues at Midnight" (Town
Hall, NYC, 1947), 128
Hooker, John Lee, 122, 223
hootenannies, 4, 125, 127, 132–33, 135, 232
Hopkins, Lightnin', 223
Hot Club of Barcelona, 197, 296n32
Hot Club of Düsseldorf, 161
Hot Club of France (HCF), 154, 156–58, 179,
190, 192–93
Hot Club of Frankfurt, 197

Jefferson, Blind Lemon, 46, 49, 58, 68–69, 86, 274–75n10, 274n43
Jefferson County (Arkansas), 8–10, 16–17, 267n9
Jenkins, Ella, 212–13, 239
Jim Crow, 29, 43, 133, 176. *See also* racial prejudice
"Jimmy Rodgers Blue Yodel," 49
"Joe Turner Blues," 23–24, 132
"John Henry," 137, 160–61, 163–64, 167, 172, 184, 214
Johnson, Big Bill. *See* Broonzy, Big Bill
Johnson, Bunk, 209, 287n6
Johnson, James P., 94, 128
Johnson, Lonnie, 110
Johnson, Merline ("The Yas Yas Girl"), 85, 132, 142
Johnson, Pete, 92, 126
Johnson, Robert, 75, 91, 141, 247–48
Johnson, William. *See* Broonzy, Big Bill
Jones, Caroline, 266n3
Jones, Curtis, 111–12
Jones, Max, 142, 214–15, 228, 242–43
Jones, Richard, 212, 236
Jones, Wizz, 230
Jordan, Louis, 139, 158, 228
"Juke," 168
jukeboxes, 74, 106–7, 236
juke joints, 21, 40, 50, 106, 111, 140
"Just a Closer Walk with Thee," 239
"Just a Dream," 92–93, 96–97, 106–7, 145, 236–37, 281n7 (ch. 8), 281n10 (ch. 8)

Kansas City Kitty (Mozelle Alderson). *See* Alderson, Mozelle
Keil, Charles, 248, 304–5n4
Kenton, Stan, 181
"Key to the Highway," 68, 78, 121–23, 137, 164, 232, 249–50
King, B.B., 248
King, Martin Luther, Jr., 3
King Oliver's Creole Jazz Band, 59
Kingsway Hall (London), 163–64, 214–15
Kinks, 249–50
Knowling, Ransom, 3, 101–4, 121, 167, 265nn8–9
Knudsen, Karl-Emil, 223
Koester, Bob, 81–82, 121, 282n3
Korner, Alexis: admiration for Bill, 215, 246; Barrelhouse and Blues Club started by, 228; Bill as houseguest of, 214–15, 222; as a guitarist, 215; influenced by Colyer, 173; introduction to blues and jazz, 215;

1958 London benefit concert organized by, 4, 242
Korner, Roberta (Bobbie), 214–15, 222, 228–29, 246

Ladnier, Tommy, 95
Lafitte, Guy, 159, 293n13
Land Where the Blues Began, The, 21–22, 251–52, 267n6, 269n3, 287n14
Lane, James A. *See* Rogers, Jimmy
Lane, Larry, 136–37, 181, 239
Lardner, Ring, 212
Lasky, Louis, 88–89
Lawlers, Ernest (Little Son Joe), 212, 298n26
Lawson, Rose. *See* Broonzy, Rose
Layla and Other Assorted Love Songs, 123
Lead Belly (Huddie Ledbetter): Alan Lomax's recordings of, 96; "Bourgeois Blues" sung by, 239; death of, 158; at Folkways, 206; influence of, 249; "Midnight Special" sung by, 87, 201; in Paris, 158; and People's Songs, 125; and "Rock Island Line," 213–14
lead sheets, 81
"Leap Year Blues," 107
"Leavin' Day," 167
Ledbetter, Huddie. *See* Lead Belly
Lee, Peggy, 90, 102
Leloir, Jean-Pierre, 174, 222–23
Lenoir, J. B., 15, 203, 238–39
Lester, Richard, 216
"Let's Have a Little Fun," 115
levees, levee camps, and levee contractors, 8, 29–31, 35, 37–38, 128–29
Lewis, Jerry Lee, 40
Lewis, Meade Lux, 92
Leydi, Roberto, 224
Library of Congress, 81, 96, 140
Life, 95
Lincoln Gardens (*formerly* Royal Gardens; Chicago), 45–46, 59
Lippmann, Horst, 161, 196–97
Little Rock, school integration in (Arkansas), 3
Little Son Joe (Ernest Lawlers), 212, 298n26
Little Walter. *See* Jacobs, Little Walter
Living Blues, 251
Local 10 (Chicago white musicians' union), 98–99
Local 208 (Chicago black musicians' union), 98–99, 251, 282n1, 282n3, 306n29
Lockwood, Robert Junior, 141
Lofton, Cripple Clarence: "I Don't Know," 88

recording industry: decline in early 1930s, 70; exploitation of musicians, 53; 45 rpm records, 174; growth in 1920s, 46; growth of urban blues in (*see also* blues); growth of urban blues in mid-1930s, 83–84; musicians' strikes, 107–8, 142, 145; royalties, 48, 72, 80–82, 85, 107–8, 169; 78 rpm records, 46, 174; stock market crash's effects on, 60–61; success of black female singers in 1920s, 46; in transition following World War II, 139. *See also individual musicians and recording companies*

Red Channels, 192–93

reels, 19, 26–27, 164–65. *See also* blues

Reese, Dock, 125, 175

Regal Theater (Chicago), 103, 113, 225

Reinhardt, Django, 188

Renbourn, John, 229–30

Rep Group. *See* Chicago Repertory Group

Rich, Buddy, 181

Richards, Keith, 222

Richigan Company, 71

Rider, See See, 22–23

Ride This Train, 131

Riley, Judge, 167

Robert Johnson: King of the Delta Blues Singers, 247–48

Robeson, Paul, 47

Roble, Chet, 3, 180–82, 265n8

"Rockin' Chair Blues," 116

"Rock Island Line," 213–14

Rogers, Jimmy (James A. Lane), 15, 140–41, 212, 242, 298n26

"Romance in the Dark," 101–2

"Romance without Finance," 198

Roosevelt, Eleanor, 158–59, 287n6

Roosevelt, Franklin, 99

Roosevelt University (Chicago), 227

"Root Hog or Die," 90

Roundhouse pub (London), 228–29

Rowe, Mike, 84, 142, 144

Royal Festival Hall, 216, 228

Royal Gardens (*later named* Lincoln Gardens; Chicago), 45–46, 59

Ruby's Tavern (Chicago), 110–12, 127

rukus juice, 277–78n14

"Rukus Juice Shuffle," 73–74

"Rumblin' and Ramblin' Boa Constrictor Blues," 49

Rush, Otis, 242

Russell, Tony, 75, 86–87

Sabath, Joseph, 153

"Sad Letter Blues," 119

Salle Pleyel (Paris), 170–71

"Sally Goodin," 26–27

"Salty Dog Blues," 46

Sampson, Sammy. *See* Broonzy, Big Bill

Saroyan, William, 129–30

"Saturday Evening Blues," 132

"Saturday Night Rub," 62, 66

Saublains, Raymond, 295n38

Schilletter, Julian ("Shorty"), 148, 154

schottisches, 27

Scotsman (Edinburgh), 171

Scottsboro Boys' trials, 95

Sears and Roebuck, 23–24, 270n8

Second City, 202

Seeger, Pete: in the Almanac Singers, 124; at Bill's 1957 Chicago benefit concert, 238–39; Bill's performances with, 205–6, 212, 226; blacklisting of, 226; at Circle Pines Center, 232–33; college concerts/hootenannies with Bill, 4; in "Midnight Special" concerts, 128; musicians filmed by, 233–34; in People's Songs, 124–25; politics of, 192

"See See Rider" (song), 23, 86, 269–70n6

Segar, Charlie, 121–22, 286n26

segregation: in entertainment venues, 25–26, 270n11; in housing, 50, 137; in labor unions, 98–99; in schools, 3, 16, 150; in the U.S. after World War II, 124; in the U.S. Army in World War I, 32–33

Sellers, Brother John, 2–3, 227–28, 230–31, 242, 244

"Selling That Stuff," 61

Senegal, 237, 302n48

708 Club (Chicago), 212

"Shake That Thing," 57–58

sharecropping, 9–10, 13, 15, 43, 129, 283n27

"She Caught the Train," 86–87

"Shelby County Blues," 73

Shindig (U.S. TV program), 230

Shower, Hudson (Little Hudson), 144

Silvio's Tavern (Chicago), 140, 148, 179–80, 197, 222, 289n5

Simon, Paul, 229

Simone, Nina, 102

"Sittin' on Top of the World," 70

Six-Five Special (British TV program), 230

"Sixteen Tons," 223

skiffle, 213–14, 228–31, 242–43, 249, 298nn30–31

Vocalion Records, 57, 74–75, 91, 109, 121
Vogue Records, 159, 162–63, 169, 174, 229

Waiting for Lefty, 134–35, 288n37
Wald, Elijah, 161
Walker, Albert, 149, 152, 209
Walker, Jauvanta ("Jav"), 149–53, 292n16, 306n29
Warfield, Louis, 49
washboards, 79, 198
Washboard Sam (Robert Brown): Barnes records with, 103, 283n21; Bill's collaboration with, 78, 85, 121, 128, 132, 198; Bill's songs used by, 85; birth/background of, 78–79, 279n32; and Black Bob, 87; at Chess Records, 198; decline of, 142; piano accompanists to, 79; popularity of, 78; relationship with Bill, 78–79, 279n32; singing style of, 79
Washington, Booker T., 149
Washington, Dinah, 102, 122, 283n21
Waters, Muddy (McKinley Morganfield): arrival in Chicago, 140; at Big Bill and Moore's Lounge, 203; Bill's endorsements of in Europe, 165, 223; at Bill's funeral, 2–4, 304n4; Bill's influence on, ix, 3–4, 140, 250, 304n4; Bill's mentoring of, 15, 140–41, 291n4; on Bill's playing electric guitar, 283n22; birth/background of, 140; at Chess Records, 141, 198, 250–51; and the Chris Barber Band, 228; funeral of, 144; influences on, 75; judges contest between Bill and Memphis Minnie, 212; Lomax's recordings of, 140; meets Bill's son Michael, 250; Mississippi origins of, 3; *Muddy Waters Sings Big Bill Broonzy*, 250–51; musical origins/training of, 140; popularity among white audiences in 1960s, 247–48; stature in Chicago blues community, 3–4
Waterson, Norma, 229
Wax Museum, The (Terkel's radio program), 135–36, 201
Weavers, 137, 182, 192, 226, 243
Webb, George, 172
"Weed Smoker's Dream," 90
Weldon, Casey Bill, 85, 87
Wells, Dickie, 188
"We Shall Overcome," 163
Wesley, Frank (nephew), 13, 205, 253–54
Wesley, Lannie (*née* Bradley; sister), 267n6; as a beautician, 204; at Bill's death/fu-

neral, 245, 253; Bill's relationship with, x, 13, 205; birth of, 7, 12; education of, 16; marriage to Mack, 105, 204–5; in North Little Rock, 105, 204, 283n28
Wesley, Mack (brother-in-law), 105, 204–5, 283n28
"Western Blues, The," 62–63
WFMT, 200–202, 205–6, 213, 225–27, 232, 238, 244
"What's That I Smell," 68
"What You Call That," 66
"When Did You Leave Heaven?," 164, 218, 222
"When I Get to Thinkin'," 250–51
"When I Had Money," 119
"When the Saints Go Marching In," 49, 161, 239
"When the Sun Goes Down," 154, 235–36. *See also* "In the Evening (When the Sun Goes Down)"
"When Will I Get to Be Called a Man," 36, 272n46
Whiskey, Nancy, 213
White, Hermese, 105–6
White, Josh: and Bill, 216; criticism of, 248; in Europe, 158–59, 216; House Committee on Un-American Activities investigation of, 192–93; in New York, 158; and Odetta, 239; at Orchestra Hall (Chicago), 181; and People's Songs, 125; politics of, 192–93; recordings with Vogue, 159; White House performance by, 158; in Yugoslav relief benefit concert, 287n6
Whiting, Richard, 218
Whittaker, Hudson. *See* Tampa Red
"Who's Sorry Now?," 161
"Why Don't You Do Right?," 90, 102
Wilcox, Herbert ("Bert"), 163, 183, 188–89
Wilkins, Roy, 30
Williams, Bill, 72
Williams, J. Mayo ("Ink"), 47–49, 56–57, 81–84, 89
Williams, Tennessee, 232
Williamson, Lacey Belle, 144, 211
Williamson, Sonny Boy (John Lee), 29, 111–12, 270–71n24; Bill's guitar backup for, 132, 143, 203; Bill's relationship with, 144; death of, 144; "Good Morning, School Girl," 143–44; harmonica brought to forefront by, 144; in "Honky Tonk Blues at Midnight," 128; on levee camps, 30–31; marriage to Lacey Belle, 144, 211; popularity of, 143; on southern violence